PRIVATE VOICES, PUBLIC LIVES
WOMEN SPEAK ON THE LITERARY LIFE

PRIVATE VOICES, PUBLIC LIVES
WOMEN SPEAK ON THE LITERARY LIFE

EDITED BY

NANCY OWEN NELSON

FOREWORD BY JANE TOMPKINS

UNIVERSITY OF NORTH TEXAS PRESS
DENTON, TEXAS
1995

First edition 1995

10 9 8 7 6 5 4 3 2 1

Rights to individual essays retained by their authors.
Requests for permission to reproduce material from this work should be
sent to:

Permissions
University of North Texas Press
PO Box 13856
Denton TX 76203

The paper used in this book meets the minimum requirements of the
American National Standard for Permanence of Paper for Printed
Library Materials Z39.48.1984. Binding materials have been chosen for
durability.

Library of Congress Cataloging-in-Publication Data

Private voices, public lives : essays on text and the private self /
edited by Nancy Owen Nelson
p.   cm.
Includes bibliographical references and index.
ISBN 0-929398-88-2
1. American literature—Women authors—History and criticism.
2. Literature—Women authors—History and criticism—Theory, etc. 3.
Feminism and literature—United States. 4. Women and literature—
United States. 5. Authorship—Sex differences. 6. Self in literature. I.
Nelson, Nancy Owen, 1946–
PS147.P75   1995   94-48327
110.9′9287—dc20   CIP

To the memory of
Lorne N. "Larry" Colter
1930–1995
Who showed me his deep
and burning passion
for life

CONTENTS

III
TEACHING AND WRITING THE SELF

ACKNOWLEDGMENTS

This book would not have happened were it not for the support and encouragement of my friends and family. Ann Putnam, whose original idea grew into the realities of *Private Voices, Public Lives,* has been a constant companion to the project, cheerleading on a regular basis from Washington across the Midwest plains to Michigan. Certainly my institution, Henry Ford Community College, deserves much credit for granting me a sabbatical in the fall of 1993 to begin the real "muscle work" of the project; colleagues and friends at the College and friends on the outside, too many to name, have supported my efforts and praised my energy when I was uncertain as to how long either would last. And, of course, my son and my mother always knew I could "do it." Last but certainly not least are the women whose work is present in this volume: women who took the risk of opening the doors to their *inner lives* to make public the connection to their *outer*; and my editor and Western Literature Association colleague, Charlotte Wright, whose encouragement never wavered from the inception to the end of this project. I also owe thanks to the following publishers who have allowed the reprinting of these fine essays:

a/b: Auto/Biography Studies: "Growing Up with Doctor Spock: An Auto/ Biography," by Lynn Z. Bloom.
Iris: A Journal About Women: "Love, Work, and Willa Cather," (originally entitled "Love, Work and the Zuni Runners"), by Ann Fisher-Wirth.

FOREWORD

When I was taking Shakespeare in college, of all the parts in the plays we read the one I wanted to play was Emilia, in *Othello*. It's Emilia, at the end, who finally exposes Iago. When she speaks, it's a moment of almost unbearable relief. Acting, for me, was the road not taken, the what-I-would-have-done if I hadn't become a college professor, so I never played the part. Still, it always thrills me to hear someone giving voice to a truth no one else has dared to speak. The sound of Emilia's voice breaking the silence is one I am always unconsciously listening for.

I hear that sound in this volume, over and over. And I'm amazed, as I am always amazed when Emilia speaks at the end of *Othello*, at the courage it takes. Iago kills her, and she knows that that will probably happen. She speaks anyway. The writers who speak here aren't risking death, but they're risking something: embarrassment, shame, possible ridicule or humiliation, the charges of narcissism and self-indulgence, even the hazard of self-discovery. The truths that academic women speak are often less easily named than Emilia's, more diffuse, more deeply buried. Often the problem is that we don't even know we're holding something back until someone else says it, and bingo!

I lived for years with the shame, disappointment and underlying despair of infertility, yet it never occurred to me to find a parallel, much less solace, in literature mourning the loss of children, until I read Melody Graulich's essay, "Speaking Across Boundaries." Over and over as I read the articles in this collection, a piece of my past would come up, reminding me of unfinished business, and I saw how I could have dealt with it in and through my work, though I never did, not knowing how, or that such a thing was possible.

These essays, as they move back and forth from autobiographical fact to literary text, give us permission to make ourselves whole through our work. It becomes clear not only that it's unnecessary to hide who we are in the course of doing literary criticism, but also that *making* the connection between our lives and the literature we write about illuminates our own predicaments at the same time that it charges literary works with immediacy and point. It's startling and liberating to watch these authors use what is at hand—a novel they're teaching by Willa Cather, a seventeenth-century captivity narrative—to interpret and heal present pain.

In their arresting juxtaposition of lived experience and literary creation these essays embody the creative impulse that gives literature birth in the first place. What we have here is the beginning of a new genre, a criticism that opens the door to a richer variety of subject matter, and a proliferation of new forms. It binds disparate experiences together, blends differently timbred voices, allows the dead and the living, the fictional and the real, to occupy the same field of contemplation. For each author the relationship between text and life is unique; no two combinations are alike.

This element of surprise makes the criticism practiced here a pleasure to read. With the introduction of real live material, all bets are off. You can't predict the end of an essay from its beginning, or even the second paragraph from the first. The author's voice, speaking in the first person about what happened to her, pulls you in and makes you want to know how things turned out. My favorite opener is Grace Stewart's in "Diversity and the American Dream": "When I was about nine, I casually mentioned to my mother while we were doing dishes together that I would like to marry a Chinese man." Who could resist reading on?

What makes this kind of criticism so refreshing—and so important—is that it acknowledges the reality of emotional life. So much of our daily activity as human beings consists of putting a lid on what we feel in order to get by. We teach the class, write the article, attend the meeting, do the grocery shopping, cook the dinner, and put our feelings on the back burner. Absorbed by the narratives we interpret as our business, we ignore the narratives that are unfolding in our lives. When I started out, I used to write articles analyzing what was going on in the minds of Henry James's characters; I pored over the complex forms of consciousness expressed in James's elegant, convoluted style. But for my own heart I had little time and less understanding. Now, these authors are saying, it's all right to look at yourself as well as at the text you're analyzing. It's OK to be an I-witness.

These writers show generosity in sharing their lives with strangers. They are open-hearted in their willingness to give themselves away. And yet that is not how they see it. Near the beginning of an unspeakably moving essay, Beverly Conner writes:

> I have never written before about my daughter's death. Pain has silenced me, pain and some sense of propriety that I ought not to be so uncivil as to inflict her murder on the reader (on the student, the colleague, the friend), who might flinch from its violence.

Yet reading her essay is like receiving a precious treasure. It is the distillation of infinite pain, offered with care and courtesy, steeped in wisdom, made lustrous by time. It is hard not to feel honored by such a gift. And so it goes from one essay to the next, as the authors bring up from the depths of their lives the gold of their experience.

As I read, I kept thinking how good it would be for students to see this writing. How much it would help them to understand what literature can be for, how it would help them to look at their own experience, how it would validate their inner lives to see professors paying attention to these matters. The model of self-revelation is powerful in the classroom. One of the best classes I ever had followed on my telling my students that a book we were reading made me remember a scandalous and painful affair I'd had, an episode of my life which for several years I'd managed to "forget."

Establishing real connections between ourselves and our students requires personal risk, a willingness to show our own vulnerability so that they can take what is for them the much greater risk of showing who they are. *Private Voices, Public Lives* sets a standard for critical writing that I hope will affect classroom practice, too.

The standard it sets is one of honesty, courage, and joy in experimentation. It's energizing to see people trying something new, inspiring to witness their bravery, and comforting to come into real contact with their lives. Finally, the gift of personal writing is that of breaking down the barriers that divide people, keeping them lonely, and frozen, and scared. It's liberating to find out that you're not so different as you thought, not alone in your trouble. If everyone wrote like this, our profession would be less competitive and intimidating. People might stop tearing each other's work apart. Who knows what could happen? I'm grateful to the authors in this collection for what they've done. I hope that many others will be inspired to do the same.

Jane Tompkins
March 1995

INTRODUCTION

Honesty, excitement, poignancy, frustration, and exuberance pervade the essays in this collection. *Private Voices, Public Lives* is the direct result of our desire, after years of academic training, to break out of the masculinist mode of communication, and in breaking free, to explore the deepest parts of ourselves as we relate to the texts which have shaped our lives.

It all began in the spring of 1991, when I received an excited phone call from my friend Ann Putnam; Ann was proposing that I participate in a revolutionary panel for the fall meeting of the Western Literature Association. Although feminist themes and topics had been a frequent part of the program in years past, Ann's panel, "Loving Work and Working Love," was to be different. Four participants, Ann, Charlotte McClure, Ann Fisher-Wirth, and myself, presented essays in a *personal voice*, an approach foreign to most traditional academic conferences. That day each presenter exposed a raw nerve: in a familiar tone and voice, we each risked talking about how the study of text had helped us to reconcile the conflict between our private worlds and our public lives.

When the meeting was over, a silence reigned in the small room. After some polite questions, the session ended. Only then did one or two people come forward to express their appreciation for the honesty of the papers. One man in particular stated: "I don't believe I've ever heard anything quite like this session before."

The approach to the discussion of literature which we used that day is clearly articulated in Olivia Frey's article, "Beyond Literary Darwinism: Women's Voices and Critical Discourse." Frey analyzes the masculine, "adversary" mode of literary criticism, pointing out that it not only encourages an argumentative, combative interaction with others but also limits the critical writer's ability to relate to the literature personally. In her discussion, Frey cites Daniel Calhoun's social constructionist concept of knowledge in his book *The Intelligence of the People*: ". . . both women and men require healthy communities of discourse, or one might say discourse relationships" (Frey's words 517). In addition, in putting aside the adversary method, the writer is freed from traditional constraints of argumentation and "imagines who she is writing for and how they might respond. The motivation is intensely personal—to connect with someone else in a meaningful way. A nurturing relationship is important" (517). Frey concludes that the "masculine" or "adversary" method does not promote collegiality in academic life:

> [T]he adversary method in our pedagogy and classroom structures, in our faculty meetings, in the formats of our conferences, in informal encounters in the hall, in every corner of our public lives. . . . stresses competition and individualistic achievement at the expense of connectedness to others. (522)

My awareness of the effects of the personal voice was heightened after our meeting; I noticed at the next year's conference that there were other women who wrote in a nonadversarial, *personal voice*; they talked about text and how it had shaped their visions of themselves— their professional *and* personal lives. I began to see a correspondence between this approach and the "particularly female dilemma," as Ann Putnam puts it in her essay, of balancing the distractions and demands of daily life with the desire for focused scholarly pursuits. After an impromptu session, sprawled on our hotel beds, Ann, Charlotte McClure, and I, along with Michele Potter, an inductee into the project, began to explore the possibility of a collection of essays making use of this feminist mode of communication. The essayists would write in the *first person*, using the analytical voice only on occasion. Thus began the evolution of *Private Voices, Public Lives*.

Others have come before me. Three books in particular which provide rich materials using the feminist mode are *Changing Subjects: The Making of Feminist Literary Criticism, The Intimate Critique:Autobiographical Literary Criticism*, and *Between Women: Biographers, Novelists, Critics, Teachers and Artists Write about Their Work on Women*. Co-editor of *Changing Subjects*, Gayle Greene, says that the essays in her collection "tell the story of second-wave feminism, a story you can read in history books, but narrated here in the first person" (2). She goes on to stress the balance contained in the essays between "self-reflection and critical practice in the rebuilding of connections—between personal and political, between academic and non-academic, between writers and readers . . . " (22). Likewise, in *The Intimate Critique*, co-editor Frances Murphy Zauhar acknowledges the validity of the personal response to literature: "Our reading and a variety of other experiences in our lives do connect to make us very capable, dynamic respondents to the worlds around us and within us—and effective, learned readers of the texts we study" (105). Further, "allowing a text to matter and considering what matter it makes in one's life affords a reader a legitimate and good reading of a text" (109). Zauhar cites also three books which "engage . . . readers by presenting a reading of the presenter, as well as of the text" (108).[1] Additionally, in the "Foreword: Ten Years Later" of *Between Women*, Carolyn Heilbrun cites the importance of women's ongoing search for personal power: "Their right to own their own thoughts, their own opinions, their own interpretations, their own work" (viii). The "Introduction" to the book also affirms the new form of criticism as "alternative forms of cooperation" that will replace the old ways, work that is "less compulsive, aggressive, lonely, competitive; more communal, caring, and integrated with love and politics" (xxii). Thus the door is wide open to such as book a *Private Voices, Public Lives*.

In interacting with the authors in this text, I have discovered a community of like minds. In truth, as I read through the volume, I feel that I *know these women*, even the ones whom I have never officially met. I know them because their voices are pure and uncluttered. They are honest writers; many write of situations which brought considerable personal pain, while others explore how their relationships with certain texts have helped them to understand and define themselves in a deep and meaningful way.

Without exception, all of the women included here have written with enthusiasm and honesty. That does not mean, however, that the shift from argumentation to personal voice has been easy. The questions and comments from contributors have ranged from "How psychoanalytical would you like me to be?" to "It was really more difficult than I imagined to bare my inner self in the process of discussing my materials." One contributor stated, "This is the most difficult article I have ever written." The struggle has been great for many of us because we were breaking a long-ingrained habit of strictly masculinist argumentation, a mode in which, on some level, we were *safe*. In using our personal voices, we take risks: we do not hide the pain, angst, sorrow or fear. We confront it, indeed, make it work for us. As one essayist stated, "We are writing our mythic identity," and another, "I am growing in understanding of how this 'mode' works, and that alone is valuable." Yet another contributor thanked me for the opportunity to write the paper, which helped her to break out of a long term writer's block.

All contributors, without exception, have been supportive and enthusiastic about the project and its possibilities. And once each writer passed the barrier from objective to personal territory, she blossomed, each in her own way, into a new and fresh voice. As one essayist commented, this book represents the coming together of power and richness.

The original parameters of the book—the personal response to literature—have broadened somewhat: the essays now include how the public and private selves have been brought together by the study of, teaching of, or writing of text in its broadest senses: traditional literature, essays, criticism, biography, journals, and letters.

Part One, called "The Work/Love Paradigm," focuses on each writer's exploration of the relationship between her *love* of text and how it helps her define the *work* of both her public and her private life. Ann Putnam in "Tangled Together Like Badly Cast Fishing Line" uses Katherine Anne Porter's "Pale Horse, Pale Rider" to delineate the entanglements and distractions of her daily life as teacher, mother, wife, daughter. Putnam finds that the "attachments" of life, "even as they diminish [her] capacity for work . . . have enriched that work in strange and wondrous and continually surprising ways."

Ann Fisher-Wirth, in her study, "Love, Work, and Willa Cather," traces how a deep loss in her young adulthood led her to discover that working with literature can help override grief. She states, "I learned that work can be fulfillment in itself, that literature did not fail me, and that my staunchest ally was my mind." For Fisher-Wirth, the fusion of private and public lies in her life's work: "Reading, writing, and teaching must be forms of telling the truth. . . ."

Ann Romines in "The Voices from the Little House" discusses the "addictive satisfaction" of rereading good literature. Her adolescent love of Laura Ingalls Wilder's Little House series, as well as a childhood meeting with the author, helped Romines to find an ultimate connection between her academic, public identity and her private life in the domestic arena. For Romines, the Little House books "embody a complicated narrative of female survival" which affirms both the power of writing and the role of women in the ordering of life through domestic ritual.

Finally in this section, Susan Rosowski's "Rewriting the Love Plot Our Way: Women and Work" traces how her study of literature from early childhood to her adult academic life allowed her to evolve, to articulate her identity as a woman at work, to "write truthfully of the emotional life of working" (a challenge for all women). The study of Willa Cather, a fellow Nebraskan, "offers a forum for exploring growing up defined by gender expectations, of protecting a personal voice and desiring to engage in a public discourse, of loving work and also family, of negotiating private lives and public voices"—certainly a key theme for our collection.

Part Two, "The Text as Mirror," explores the impact of literature on the personal lives of the writers, especially as it serves as "mirror" to the self.

Carol S. Chadwick in "Nancy Drew—The Perfect Solution" traces her evolution from an abused childhood to a balanced, defined adulthood through her reading of female detective novels. From her earliest years, books provided an escape from the oppressive surroundings of a dysfunctional family, and more recently, from the rigors of graduate study: from Nancy Drew, a role model of self-reliance, to Agatha Christie, an escape into genteel English society; from Dorothy Sayers's Harriet Vane, a well-defined individual capable of a "co-equal bond" with a man, to numerous other British authors and, later, American mystery writers. All in all, female detectives "serve" the author in her own exploration of self.

In "Wrestling with the Mother and the Father: 'His' and 'Her' in Adrienne Rich," Betty S. Flowers discusses her struggle with the polarization of gender in academic life; while observing subtle sexism, Flowers states that "in our profession, the mothers serve the fathers in us all." The study and teaching of the poetry of Adrienne Rich helped Flowers to refute the "mirror image" of women to men; the resolution lies in a dialogue of the two poles, a telling of stories "while searching for common threads" of understanding.

The search to balance the polarization of gender continues in my own "In Search of the Androgynous Self," a call for the end of polarization of the sexes and a blending of "the male and female into a healthy totality." Here I narrate my early struggles with sexism in college and graduate school and the subsequent discovery of the androgynous potential in myself through the study of Western American literature.

Likewise, Jo C. Searles in "From Robot to Roarer" traces her early rebellion against sexism in graduate studies. Moving from the robotic, traditional female role to the robust "roarer" of feminist truths, Searles attributes much of her awakening to the study of feminist literature and criticism. In exploring images of the goddess, Searles finds her own voice, one which accepts women's life changes and expresses the wisdom of aging.

Catherine Lamb explores the poignancy and pain of divorce in the retrospective "A White Bird Flying Straight Down." In both her childhood and marriage, her parents and husband "betray[ed] a primary relationship" with Lamb, justifying their actions as "God's will." While the study of Mary Rowlandson's captivity narrative (1682) illustrates a world governed by outside authority (God), Emily Dickinson's poetry reveals the triumph of a mature "voice" which becomes its own authority and provides a model for Lamb's healing and self-definition.

In "Being an I-Witness: My Life as a Lesbian Teacher," Barbara DiBernard traces her process of "coming out" to her students. Using journal and essay responses, DiBernard illustrates the difficulty, yet the freedom and relief which come from honest communication with her students. For her, "writing this essay was a crucial part of . . . finally being able to be fully out in the classroom—a tribute to the power of writing and visibility."

Bonnie Braendlin's "Mother/Daughter Dialog(ic)s in, around and about Amy Tan's *The Joy Luck Club*" illustrates, with the relationship with her own daughter as a backdrop, the constantly changing landscape of relationships and the attempt at resolution of the conflicts. Braendlin finds that between mothers and daughters, there is "no end to the dialogue; it continues in our social and literary lives."

To find her voice and place in travel at sea, Nancy Pagh in "Offshore Women: A Personal Log" explores sea logs written about and by women. Searching early memories of her family at sea, Pagh moves away from the search for a role model to recognize her admiration for "offshore women [in] their ability to love and master sea travel while they maintain relationships and guard tender connections to the land."

Olga Klekner's "Metamorphosis" explores how, through literary study, the author made a transition from socialist Hungary to capitalist America. Aided by the poetic writings of Frederick Manfred and Maya Angelou, Klekner shows a growing love and appreciation for the American language and the American people, a love generated by the poetry of the language: "The poet's heart inherits bursting words and generations of fertile soil."

Similarly, Lois Hassan's transition into midlife is aided by the reading and study of Anne Morrow Lindbergh's *Gift from the Sea*. Hassan shows how the writings of a woman four decades ago can address the conflicts of a woman in the '90s, in the "hectic world of work, marriage, and motherhood." In Lindbergh's book, Hassan finds an identifiable voice helping her to break out of a "closing shell" and experience "the beauty of [her] life."

Melody Graulich confronts yet another challenge of womanhood in "Speaking Across Boundaries and Sharing the Loss of a Child." For Graulich, reading writers such as Harriet Beecher Stowe, Toni Morrison, Edith Summers Kelley, and numerous others, aided her in identifying other women's pain at the loss of a child. Graulich traces her own struggle to have a child, the birth of her "miracle baby," and her eminent adoption of a Korean orphan. Throughout her struggle to have a child, she has been aided by women's literature in the articulation of her grief, pain, and joy, and in connecting with other women "across boundaries" of difference.

For two writers in this section, place and its representation in literature have played a major role in the identity process. Susan Naramore Maher in "Trailing West" learns to adjust her eastern consciousness to the Nebraska landscape through the study and teaching of women writers of the region. The "adaptability, suppleness, bending to the conditions of Nebraska life" of many of the women of the plains served as model concepts for Maher, as she became a "trailing spouse" to her husband's academic pursuits. In asking the central question "How does uprooting, the experience of displacement, alter a woman's psyche?" Maher has found an answer in the readings—"part of our intersubjective realities, part of our created community of voices, part of our journeys."

Unlike Maher, Michele Potter is a displaced westerner living in the East who finds self through Kathleen Norris's *Dakota: A Spiritual Geography*. In examining the tensions between the "inner and outer" geography of place, Potter uses Norris's work as a guidebook for her own spiritual discovery of her identity, a return home to Dakota.

Part Three, "Teaching and Writing the Self," includes essays which discuss how the acts of teaching and writing have aided the writers in defining their public and private identities.

Lynn Z. Bloom, in "Growing Up with Dr. Spock," narrates her coming of age through the writing of biography. Alienated from her family by their rejection of her husband, Bloom illustrates that writing the book and studying the life of Benjamin Spock allowed her to "write [her] own independence" from approval of family and the academic community. For Bloom, biography has a "human heart," and research, if inventive, has a "heart and soul."

Charlotte S. McClure in "Impersonators to Persons: Breaking Patterns, Finding Voices" identifies three "literary grandmothers" who struggled to break from the public, "impersonated self" into a private voice. Gertrude Atherton, Mary Austin, and Kate Chopin all faced social forces contrary to their desire to write: "the real-life protective title of lady, a denial of bonding with women and their concerns and achievements, and the pressure to accept the values of their patriarchal mainstream of business and competition." While writing her doctoral dissertation on the American Eve, McClure found that these women's struggles cast light on her own search for a voice.

Four contributors find consolation and enlightenment through teaching. In an extremely poignant account of her daughter's disappearance and the subsequent discovery of her remains, Beverly Conner in "Search and Rescue" illustrates that "the only way through tragedy is straight ahead." It was a temporary teaching position during her period of uncertainty about her daughter's fate which helped her to survive the awful reality of her murder. In dealing with Anne Tyler's

The Accidental Tourist in the classroom, Conner found Tyler's description of grief brought comfort and helped her to articulate her own pain.

Grace Stewart, having questioned the issues of diversity of sex, race, and class in American culture, illustrates in "Diversity and the American Dream" how the teaching of Lorraine Hansberry's *A Raisin in the Sun* helped to answer some complex questions about diversity. Through examination of her own developing views on culture, Stewart shows how student interaction helped her to remember that even versions of the American dream are diversified: "One rears children with love and by example, and allows them to fly toward their dream in their own way . . ."

Likewise, Julie Houston explores the effects on students of the teaching of women's literature. In "Women's Literature as Individuation for College Students," she finds the course a "means of self-awareness and self-expression for both women and men." While women students are freed to write by reading women writers, men students develop a new pride in their female ancestors and a new awareness of the woman's experience.

Sandra Parker probes political correctness and the curriculum of Gender Studies in "Finding My Voice: Caught between a Woolf and A Crane." In making the unusual comparison of Hart Crane to Virginia Woolf, Parker shows how both writers immortalized place, dealt with gender struggles, and faced literary prejudice because of their sexual orientations. Parker's purpose, to broaden the inclusions in Gender Studies, illustrates how Hart Crane's frequent and improper exclusion from the literary canon was the result of his lifestyle, not his work: "Gender Studies courses must not yield to narrow, provincial protocol but struggle to incorporate multicultural readings that include sensitive topics like androgyny and homosexuality."

The final piece in the volume, Elsie Mayer's "Literary Criticism with a Human Face: Virginia Woolf and *The Common Reader*," is an appropriate capstone for *Private Voices, Public Lives*. Mayer's essay attempts a reconciliation between masculinist criticism and feminist epistemology; such a division of critical approaches, contends Mayer, encourages the "binary distinctions" between men and women which result in unnecessary conflict. In working with new feminist approaches to writing about literature, Mayer believes that a balance of both argumentation and personal response, illustrated so well in Woolf's *The Common Reader*, is the answer to the conflict, the result being "to liberate literary criticism from the inertia of masculinist criticism and move it closer to a position that acknowledges equality and difference."

It is with great pleasure that I bring to readers this volume of essays by women whose honest voices can give us all a new, fresh approach to the study of text.

---

[1] Rachel M. Brownstein, *Becoming a Heroine: Reading about Women in Novels*; Blanche Gelfant, *Women Writing in America*; Judith Fetterley, *Provisions: A Reader from Nineteenth-Century American Women*.

Works Cited

Ascher, Carol, Louise DeSalvo, and Sara Ruddick, eds. *Between Women: Biographers, Novelists, Critics, Teachers and Artists Write about Their Work on Women*. New York and London: Routledge, 1993.

Brownstein, Rachel. *Becoming a Heroine: Reading about Women in Novels*. New York: Viking, 1982.

Calhoun, Daniel. *The Intelligence of a People*. Princeton: Princeton UP, 1973.

Fetterley, Judith. *Provisions: A Reader from Nineteenth-Century American Women*. Bloomington: Indiana UP, 1985.

Freedman, Diane P., Olivia Frey, and Frances Murphy Zauhar, eds. *The Intimate Critique: Autobiographical Literary Criticism*. Durham: Duke UP, 1993.

Frey, Olivia. "Beyond Literary Darwinism: Women's Voices and Critical Discourse." *College English* 52.5 (September 1990): 507–26.

Gelfant, Blanche. *Women Writing in America: Voices in Collage*. Hanover, N. H.: Dartmouth College and the University Press of New England, 1984.

Greene, Gayle and Coppélia Kahn, eds. *Changing Subjects: The Making of Feminist Literary Criticism*. London: Routledge, 1993.

I

THE WORK/LOVE PARADIGM

"Tangled Together Like Badly Cast Fishing Line"
The Reader and the Text in Katherine Anne Porter's "Pale Horse, Pale Rider"

Ann L. Putnam

I tried all summer to write this paper. But there was "too much of everything" last summer and I couldn't do it. Part of the text of the paper has become my growing understanding of why this was so. My topic was Katherine Anne Porter's "Pale Horse, Pale Rider" (hereafter "PHPR"), a work I have always loved, taught often, but never written about, or so I thought. I was trying to explain the power the work has always held for me in terms of the relationship between reader and text. But what I found was that the conflict between autonomy and connectedness in "PHPR," a central theme in all works by Porter, was being played out in my attempts to write the paper itself, as I struggled to balance the claims of connectedness and a sense of my own work in the world. What I became interested in was the way my approach to the paper changed as it became clearer to me to what degree the textual issue was also a personal one. As I continued to try and then fail to write the paper, it became increasingly apparent to me how important it was to understand the sense of dividedness I have always felt in trying to be wife, mother, and daughter on the one hand, and to do what I have always considered to be my work in the world on the other.

There was no time last summer for any sustained period of writing, no time for anything but notes in the margins, off-hand thoughts in off-hand moments. But finally, after summer school grades were turned in, after the race across the state to visit my ailing father-in-law, after the two-week visit from the California relatives, after sending my son off to college on the East Coast, I did get a title for the paper from the opening dream sequence of "PHPR." Miranda is dreaming of riding away before everyone else in the house is awake and asking, *"where are you going, what are you doing, what are you thinking, how do you feel, why do you say such things, what do you mean?"*—riding away before "we are all awake and tangled together like badly cast fishing lines."[1] Well, that was exactly the sense I was trying to write about even as that very "tangling" was keeping me from doing so. It is a dream of foreboding, for death appears in the figure of a "lank greenish stranger [who was] always hanging about," that old pale rider who had "been welcomed by my grandfather, my great-aunt, . . . my decrepit hound . . . my silver kitten" (269–70). Later on in the story, as Miranda lies dying from influenza, she has a vision of paradise where it is always morning, where moving towards her "through the shimmering air" come "all of the living she had [ever] known." Each is "transfigured," each one is *alone but not solitary*" and Miranda moves among them "as a wave among waves" (311). It is this sense of human relationships that Miranda seeks but never finds, for what she always experiences is a series of tanglings— relationships which are complicating, shifting, ambiguous, which are always asking for more than she can give, and thus are always seen as threatening to the autonomy of the self. Anyone who knows the Miranda stories of *Old Mortality* and *The Old Order* has seen the destructive limitations put upon the female spirit by the patriarchy of the Old South from which Miranda is always running. I could see that this paper would be about entanglements too, both human and literary, because I'd become immersed in the entanglements of *reading*, that unruly tug and pull which goes on between reader and text that had set me wondering about my own entanglements.

One of the things I wanted to think about was how the inevitable conflict between human attachments and autonomy, this tension between love and work that had kept me from my paper, is a particularly female dilemma. In the story "Holiday," which can be read as a sort of sequel to "PHPR," Miranda travels deep into Texas farmland to stay with a German family for a month's holiday to recover from some recent and unnamed disaster. She requires privacy, yet does not exactly want to be alone. The family speaks little English and Miranda speaks no German. It becomes the ideal way for her to be "alone but not solitary."

"It was good not to have to understand what they were saying. I loved that silence which means freedom from the constant pressure of other minds and other opinions and other feelings, that freedom to fold up in quiet and go back to my own center."[2] She watches the family closely and gets the distinct "impression that they were all, even the sons-in-law, one human being divided into several separate appearances. [Ottilie] the crippled servant girl brought in more food and . . . and went away in her limping run, and she seemed to me the only individual in the house. Even I felt divided into many fragments, having left or lost a part of myself in every place I had travelled, in every life mine had touched, above all, in every death of someone near to me that had carried into the grave some part of my living cells." Miranda envies Ottilie, who is in a world of her own. "But the servant, she was whole, and belonged nowhere" ("Holiday," 417).

Yet Miranda is pulled against her will toward an identification with this servant girl whom, at the story's close, she takes for a carriage ride the day Ottilie's mother is to be buried. "I caught hold of her stout belt with my free hand, and my fingers slipped between her clothes and bare flesh. . . . My sense of her realness, her humanity, this shattered being that was a *woman*, was so shocking to me that a howl as doglike and despairing as her own rose in me unuttered and died again, to be a perpetual ghost" (434). When Miranda touches her, she recognizes their shared identity as *women*, and recognizes too, the tug of the heart she cannot deny—a recognition of her own capacity for compassion, however that entangles her in the misfortunes of others. Whether by training or nature, it is her female legacy: "She was beyond my reach as well as any other human reach, and yet, had I not come nearer to her than I had to anyone else in my attempt to deny . . . the distance between us?" (434). Thus Miranda becomes immersed once again in the great human entanglement and so finds her place once more in the magnetic chain of humanity.

An interviewer once asked Porter, "But haven't you found that being a woman presented to you, as an artist, certain special problems? It seems to me that a great deal of the upbringing of women encourages the dispersion of the self in many small bits, and that the practice of any kind of art demands a coralling and concentrating of that self and its always insufficient energies."[3] To which Porter answers: "You're brought up with the notion of feminine chastity and inaccessibility, yet with the curious idea of feminine availability in all spiritual ways, and in giving service to anyone who demands it. And I suppose that's why it has taken me twenty years to write this novel" (*Paris Interviews*, 65). Such were the constraints even Porter felt, who remained unmarried for most of her life, who had no children, who was an expatriate everywhere she lived. Porter must have known from the beginning that such fierce privacy of spirit was what her art would require, must have known from the start she would have to travel light.

In an essay on Willa Cather, Porter quotes Cather, who is writing about Katherine Mansfield, but the description holds true for all three women: "Yet every individual in that household (even the children) is clinging passionately to his individual soul, is in terror of losing it in the general family flavor. . . . Always in his mind, each member is escaping, running away, trying to break the net which circumstances and his own affections have woven about him. One realizes that human

---

relationships are the tragic necessity of human life . . . that every ego is half the time greedily seeking them, and half the time pulling away from them." "This is autobiography enough for me," says Porter of Cather, and of course by implication of Porter herself.[4]

Knowing the potential sorrow and complexity of all attachments, my strategy has often been, not so much to run from attachments, as to make another attachment, which may explain, in part, why I have one husband, three children, two birds, three dogs, and forty-seven plants, not to mention eighty-five students and thirty-one advisees. Then the issue becomes how to preserve the integrity of my soul when I am tied inextricably to the joys and sorrows of the people I love, when my own sense of my work in the world has not diminished but only grown, and who must for good or ill, do that work in the same context that holds the pain and triumph of all those I most love. In practical terms, it's a question of how to get the work done.

I know now that it is not just a matter of time and space—though there is rarely enough of either—but it is also a matter of detachment—one's ability to go away, to lock the door, to say *no* and mean it, to claim the privacy of one's soul, the primacy of one's inner terrain, to find one's unassailable center. It's what Porter was always writing about, what she was always meaning in story after story of female protagonists struggling between autonomy and connectedness.

In the same interview Porter was asked to describe her preferred method of working. "But I [like] to get up very early in the morning and work," she said. "I don't want to speak to anybody or see anybody. Perfect silence. I work until the vein is out. There's something about the way you feel, you know, when the well is dry, that you'll have to wait until tomorrow and it'll be full again." The interviewer then asks, "The important thing, then, is to avoid any breaks or distractions while you're writing?" (67).

"Yes," said Porter. "To keep at a boiling point. So that I can get up in the morning with my mind still working where it was yesterday" (67).

I had worked all summer in the margins—ideas written on cereal boxes while cooking dinner, on receipts, restaurant napkins, junk mail, once on my car registration form because I got an idea sitting at a stoplight and couldn't find anything else to write it on. I had been infinitely interruptible all summer, such that the *expectation* of interruption had become a habit of mind. But if I could manage to get a whole, complete day, say from nine to five, or even nine to three, to bring my thoughts to the "boiling point," I would be on my way. If I could have just a

ANN L. PUTNAM

single day completely *alone* to get the pot onto the stove and crank up the heat.

Then, finally, everybody went back to school. I'd run all the errands, bought the school clothes, school supplies, filled out all the school forms, taken the kids for the school physicals, to the dentist and the orthodontist, helped get the boxes packed and shipped off to college; I'd even managed to get the dogs in for their shots. My classes wouldn't start until the next day, so there was no homework, not even a class list to copy into my gradebook.

Then at last I was alone. Truth to tell, I was lonely. Absolutely dazed by the silence. I have become so connected to the rhythms of my children, I have lost my edge. Unaccustomed as I am to the quiet and the solitude, I fear my affections will take some weaning, for such habits of mind and heart are not easily broken. I must learn all over again how to be *alone but not solitary*. I know instantly that I will need days to recover, to discover the rhythms of my psyche, the edges of my soul, days I will not have, not in time. And I know right away that there are ghosts in the house. I hear voices that do not speak. Footsteps and no one's there. Unaccustomed as I am to this, it is what I have wanted all summer.

But I finally settle down and the ideas begin to roll. I'd earned this day, I'd done my homework, gathered ideas, taken notes, made outlines, done all the reading, all the things you can do in bits and snatches, and now I was going to bring it all to the "boiling point." What I needed was the opening line, a first line with the rhetorical distances just right, one which would tangle the reader in my own entanglings.

I had decided ahead of time that I was *not* going to answer the phone. "Do you have any reusable clothing to donate, carpets to clean, furniture to shampoo, chimneys to sweep, cemetery plots, life insurance, home insurance, auto insurance, will you buy a ticket to send a child to the circus, march in the cancer crusade, the heart campaign, keep kids off drugs, out of gangs, off the streets?" So when the phone rings an hour later, of course I answer it. How I have hated and loved that phone, that tangled line which connects me even now in this empty house to lives I care for more than my own. Nope. I'd never be able to stop myself from answering the phone, just like I'd never be able to kill the "angel of the house," though I have surely tried.

It's my little girl. She's lost her field trip permission slip to spend the day with her class on a marine biology ship. She'll have to spend

---

the whole day in the library, could I please bring it over? It would take me almost an hour and a half to drive over and back. If I went to school it would cost me the morning and I was getting panicky about the way this paper wasn't getting written. But could I really work, trying not to think of her sitting there in the library all day? No, they wouldn't take my permission over the phone, they had to have the note, the note that had started out tucked in her book bag but had somehow gotten lost along the way. But for once I would say *no*! If she lost the note, well, it would be a learning experience. I would try to claim, for once, the boundaries of my own autonomy. I would *not* get caught in those tangled, entangling lines, phone or otherwise. I did not have to answer to their every pull and tug.

But it wasn't as easy as that. If my day felt long, wouldn't hers feel longer? How would I switch off that inevitable and automatic response to her, such that I too would sit in the hot September library eating my sack lunch all alone? Other than death, I do believe that having a child is probably the most life-altering experience a person can have. Certain ways of feeling, thinking, reacting, reading, writing, my very episte-mology, the way I know things, are changed forever. I would go to school.

But then it's after lunch and I'm comfortably settled back at the computer with what's left of the day. At least I'd have the afternoon. By now the computer was downright warm to the touch, but only be-cause it had been sitting there humming to itself all morning. The sun coming through the window is almost too warm, but I'd be glad enough of this come the rainy light of November. I crack open a window. The air floats cool over my skin. I can do this, I am thinking.

The dog, with whom I can be "alone but not solitary," has settled down beneath the computer table, by my feet. She follows me every-where, makes no demands I cannot meet, my eighty-five pound, black and white shadow friend. She's lying under the computer table chew-ing on an old sock. Time flies. Or maybe it stops. Anyway, the screen begins to fill with green letters that turn into words, into sentences, into actual *paragraphs*. I'd written the introduction, laid claim to my thesis, had just written about the tug I have always felt in trying to be a wife, mother, and daughter on the one hand, and to do what I have always considered to be my work in the world on the other. But then I'm interrupted by a funny sound coming from under the table. The dog is getting up, and she bumps my leg as she crawls out from under the table. She's making a funny noise, sort of like choking or gagging.

"Alex, what are you *doing*?" I say. But she's watching the rug in front her, waiting for something to happen. I start to rush her outside, but whatever was going to come up must have gone back down, because now she's sitting there, looking up at me, wagging her tail. Then I notice that the sock is gone.

The trip to the vet, even when taking into account my accelerated speed, the half-hour wait in the office—during which time the dog made a dozen arm-wrenching lunges for the door—the examination, x-rays and diagnosis, pretty well took care of the rest of the afternoon.

"It certainly was lucky you were home, today," the vet said. "It could have been life threatening." Ah, there it is, I'm thinking, proving once again the shifty presence of that old pale rider and the necessity of my constant vigilance. But I get weary, keeping track of everything. I know where the room I need is, and it's the one inside my head, in the country of my imagination. But always I am drawn back by those lines whose tugs and pulls are the center of my heart.

Now where was my unassailable center, my still, quiet center of concentration? I'd never begun to reach the "boiling point."

We would watch to see if the sock reappeared, which I am happy to report it did, quite unceremoniously, the next day. Well, you can't live real life with pets and kids without a dog swallowing a sock now and then, or, say, a kid putting a bean up his nose, though all of this makes me feel sometimes that there really is "too much of everything."

I began the paper with Porter's "Pale Horse, Pale Rider," and I've ended up with the dog swallowing a sock. This tangling between reader and text has gotten out of control. The desire to seek wholeness, instead of a wrenching division of affections, has entangled me hopelessly in affective fallacies. I thought that I had never written anything about "PHPR." What I have found was how all that time when I didn't know I was paying attention, I was gathering the sense of the pale rider into my own stories. That is one discovery of this paper. I'd looked over some of my fiction and there was my pale rider, all right—a ghostly old woman in periwinkle blue who pursued my protagonist down a long hospital corridor one rainy January night; a man in a baseball cap pulled down over his eyes my protagonist sees one night from her kitchen window; a little old man who sits benignly in the lobby of a nursing home, whose eyes seem to glow red when you aren't exactly looking. And there are at least three other stories about that pale rider who is always at my window, whose presence I keep at bay with secret pacts, tokens, charms, cruciferous vegetables, vitamins, seat belts, long distance phone calls, mittens and scarves—incantations all, against certain unspoken things. When I read Porter, when I read "my grandfather, my great-aunt, .. my decrepit hound and my silver kitten," it is always *my* tall quiet grandfather I see, *my* beloved aunt, *my* black and white puppy, an accumulation of sorrows such as any life knows.

I do not know what the answer is to this conflict between one's attachments and one's work in the world, because I have never learned how to be in two places at once. And I do not know how to love either any less. What I do know is this: that even as they diminish my capacity for work, the attachments of my life, the tugs and pulls of those I most love, have enriched that work in strange and wondrous and continually surprising ways.

---

[1] Katherine Anne Porter, "Pale Horse, Pale Rider," in *The Collected Stories of Katherine Anne Porter* (New York: Harcourt Brace Jovanovich, 1972), p. 269. All references to Porter's fiction are taken from this volume and will be noted parenthetically in the text.

[2] Porter, "Holiday," in *The Collected Stories*, p. 413.

[3] Porter in *The* Paris Review *Interviews: Women Writers at Work*, ed. George Plimpton (New York: Viking Penguin, 1989), p. 65.

[4] Porter, *The Collected Essays and Occasional Writings of Katherine Anne Porter* (Boston: Houghton Mifflin, 1970), pp. 31–32.

WORKS CONSULTED

DeMouy, Jane Krause. *Katherine Anne Porter's Women: The Eye of Her Fiction*. Austin: U of Texas P, 1983.

Flanders, Jane. "Katherine Anne Porter and the Ordeal of Southern Womanhood." *The Southern Literary Journal* 9 (Fall 1976): 47–60.

Flynn, Elizabeth A. and Patrocinio P. Schweickart, eds. *Gender and Reading: Essays on Readers, Texts, and Contexts*. Baltimore & London: Johns Hopkins UP, 1986.

Frey, Olivia. "Beyond Literary Darwinism: Women's Voices and Critical Discourse." *College English* 52 (September 1990): 507–26.

Givner, Joan. *Katherine Anne Porter: A Life*. New York: Simon and Schuster, 1982.

Lopez Enrique Hank. *Katherine Anne Porter: Refugee from Indian Creek*. Boston: Little, Brown and Company, 1981.

Nance, William L. *Katherine Anne Porter and the Art of Rejection*. Chapel Hill: U of North Carolina P, 1964.

Olsen, Tillie. *Silences*. New York: Dell Publishing, 1978.

Plimpton, George, ed. *The* Paris Review *Interviews: Women Writers at Work*. New York: Viking Penguin, 1989.

Porter, Katherine Anne. *The Collected Stories of Katherine Anne Porter*. New York: Harcourt Brace Jovanovich, 1972.

_____. *The Collected Essays and Occasional Writings of Katherine Anne Porter*. Boston: Houghton Mifflin, 1970.

_____. *Letters of Katherine Anne Porter*. Edited by Isabel Bayley. New York: Atlantic Monthly Press, 1990.

Spender, Dale. *The Writing or the Sex?* New York: Pergamon Press, 1989.

Stout, Janis P. "Miranda's Guarded Speech: Porter and the Problem of Truth-Telling." *Philological Quarterly* 66 (Spring 1987): 259–78.

Sternburg, Janet, ed. *The Writer on Her Work*. New York: Norton, 1980.

Tompkins, Jane. "Fighting Words: Unlearning to Write the Critical Essay." *Georgia Review* 42 (1988): 585–90.

ANN L. PUTNAM

LOVE, WORK, AND WILLA CATHER

ANN FISHER-WIRTH

Oxford, Mississippi. The barely discernible season between late summer and early autumn. It is late at night; sheet lightning breaks off through the trees, and the throb of cicadas encircles the house. Inside, I sit on the bed, clammy with the cool wet air stirred up by the ceiling fan, which has whirred and churned all summer. Everyone else is asleep. This has always been my favorite time, when the claims of life grow still and thought comes forth to roam about its treasures. I have a slew of papers on the bed and books on the floor beside me while I try to climb inside language and find a way to talk about love and work, my life, and Willa Cather.

Two moments recur to my mind—have been recurring, these past few weeks—when I try to arrive at the ways in which love and work have braided themselves together in my experience. In the first, I am fifteen, and I am sitting on my double bed at sunset, looking out my window above the hills of Berkeley, California. Over the quiet waters of San Francisco Bay, the clouds burn copper and gold, and as I watch they shift and flow like the words I have been reading. My mother has given me this book to read, Virginia Woolf's *To the Lighthouse*, and though I can't make sense of the words, though at fifteen they are all a swirl to me with neither plot nor termination, because this is my mother's favorite novel I sit blissfully with it for twenty minutes a day, reading a paragraph or two, then drifting off into the sunset, until her call for dinner breaks the silence. When I remember those years, I always remember the silence: a big house with few people, full of patience and grief, myself sitting high in my bedroom like the captain of a ship, wishing I could sail us to the other side of silence, those first years after my father slowly died.

The second moment, very similar to the first, occurred three years later, a few months after I gave birth to my first child, a stillborn daughter. People sometimes told me I was lucky she was dead, for I had no way to keep her and could not bear to give her up; this way, in a sense, I got my life back. But I loved her very much and when she was born dead, with no apparent cause, I felt an overwhelming sense of grief and failure. In 1965, besides, it was socially grim to be an unwed mother. People were tactful when I got back to college, but I suffered from the atmosphere of conformity. Not only had I become a statistic, whispered about on campus; worse, I was expected to resume my life as a happy coed, playing bridge and painting my nails and gossiping about boyfriends. I had no one to talk to about what had really happened, how the world had opened up during the months I spent at a home for unwed mothers, how—against all expectations—my life became vital and splendid during those months when I was pregnant, how having visibly transgressed freed me from the burden of social expectations and permitted me to treasure my experience. I had been such a sheltered girl, so well-behaved outwardly, though my true sense of the world was very different. Pregnant, I fell through the safety net, and learned how much of the world remained outside. I would take the dog that belonged to the home for long walks every day. Striding through Golden Gate Park, with my baby tucked inside me and Flossie the gray poodle straining at her leash, I felt like the freest creature in the world.

I learned to work when I learned to love. I learned to love when I learned what death is, what it is to grieve. For me, death is the third term, love and work and death, inextricably connected. One night, shortly after my return to college, I took dexedrine pills, sat by my dormitory window, and read *Waiting for Godot* until dawn. That was the night I learned to work. I burned myself out translating from French to English and back to French, reading every page in both languages, taking loving and careful notes on the slightest discrepancy in translation, working slowly and yet more slowly until the train whistle blew at dawn down by the Santa Fe station and the rainbird sprinklers went on outside my window. I could not bear to think of anything else, not her death, not my loneliness. I worked as the world grew silent, and my concentration steadied and burned like my single light. The sparse, hypnotic language of *Waiting for Godot* became the raft that carried me over the waters. And what at first had been merely a desperate maneuver, burning myself out on dexedrine because I could not sleep, reading all night because I could not bear to think, became in the end a source of strength and comfort. I learned that work could be fulfillment in itself, that literature did not fail me, and that my staunchest ally was my mind.

Willa Cather suffered a passage from love through loss to work rather like mine. At the University of Nebraska, she fell in love with Louise Pound, "a brilliant student, talented musician, outstanding athlete, and campus leader" who came from a prominent Lincoln family

(O'Brien, 129). Cather's relationship with her began because they shared an interest in the arts, lasted from 1892 to 1894, and ended abruptly and with bitterness; the actual cause of the breakup remains obscure. Cather moved to Pittsburgh in 1896, but her letters to a confidante, Mariel Gere, reveal how much, and for how long, her past feelings and behavior continued to disturb her.[1]

Cather's biographers disagree as to the importance of her relationship with Pound. James Woodress, for example, writes of it as a "short-lived freshman's 'crush' on a senior," and adds, "To call this a lesbian relationship, as some critics have done, is to give it undue importance" (85). I agree instead, however, with Sharon O'Brien, who describes Cather's feelings as love, a "turbulent, passionate attachment" (131), and argues that, though Cather and Pound were not physically lovers and though Cather never uses the word "lesbian" in existing letters to describe her feelings, Cather herself considered them to be unnatural, deviant. Cather's response to this issue was complex: on the one hand, in a letter to Pound, she challenges the linking of same-sex friendships with deviance by calling it "unfair," while on the other, she agrees, however reluctantly, with the accuracy of the linking (O'Brien, 132). What interests me here is the way in which this ambivalence colors the letters to Mariel Gere. While in the midst of her love relationship, Cather's letters to Mariel reveal her ability to speak of it candidly and freely, even though, as O'Brien maintains, she may also already judge it to be unnatural. She can joke with Mariel that Louise doesn't like her first name yet refuses to call her by her adopted middle name, "Love," at least not in public (1 June 1893). In another letter, she can wistfully allude to bruises she received while driving Louise around the country on her visit to Red Cloud, driving sometimes with one hand and sometimes with none at all. Louise, she says, didn't mind her method of driving—and as for her, now that Louise has gone, she drives with one hand all night in her dreams (1 August 1893). Enthusiasm, it seems, blinds Cather here to the conventionality of her correspondent. After the breakup, though, once ardor gives way to grief and reflection, the letters to Mariel change. Candor gives way to embarrassment, pride to humiliation. The rebel desires to be good. Loss activates the censor, which defensively begins to denigrate the old mistakes (25 April 1897), the past, and the self that experienced passion.

Cather is known among those who study her for her privacy. Not only is lesbianism almost entirely occluded in her fiction, but she burned many of her letters during the later years of her life. In those that do survive she keeps a certain distance: She is forthright, friendly, charming, but rarely self-expressive and never confiding about her intimate life. This reticence, however, does *not* characterize the early letters to Mariel, in which Cather seems to take pleasure in being mildly ribald and shyly, boastfully self-revealing. The poignant thing about the breakup with Pound, as revealed in the letters to Gere, is Cather's subsequent self-distancing from the anarchy of her feelings. She encounters the problem I also encountered after the birth of my baby. How does one grieve for a love which is socially condemned, once one begins to accept the condemnation?

A letter soon after the breakup speaks eloquently of Cather's pain and of her gratitude to Mariel for listening patiently over the years as Cather raved over the grace and beauty of Louise, and her beautiful piano playing and dancing (16 June 1894). But even in this passage, where Cather's grief is fresh, there are hints of incipient self-loathing, present in the verb "raved," and the underlining of certain key words such as "grace" and "beauty," as if to scorn love's enthusiasms. Self-condemnation intensified once Cather moved to Pittsburgh, developed a new social circle, and, as editor of the *Home Monthly*, a ladies' magazine, became the purveyor of virtue. "Gad: how we like to be liked," she quotes Charles Lamb at one point (25 April 1897). In the letters to Gere from Pittsburgh, "Bohemia" becomes Cather's word for what she now wishes to repress, the path of passionate unconventionality she had been on in Nebraska. Praising Mariel's steadfastness in 1896, she refers to the Pound affair and to herself as a shaved-headed student who affected the Bohemian (2 May 1896). Some months later she writes that she never for a moment considered becoming a citizen of Bohemia, the desert country by the sea. Even though, during a difficult time, her parents and the Lord himself deserted her, she had more regard for her family than to embark upon a program of "Bohemia" (4 August 1896). By 1897 she goes further, reminding Mariel that Mariel always said that Cather never was and never could be a "Bohemian" (September 1897). And finally, in January of 1898, she writes once again of when Mariel had comforted her, years earlier, and comments that she looks back on those years with wonder, doubting if that past self were really she (10 January 1898).

Coleridge remarks that to disparage one's former self is the beginning of all hard-heartedness.[2] Yet such disparagement has been common among women, especially those who have suffered shame for sexual transgression. One sees this in Cather's letters to Mariel Gere; she splits off the aberrant, passional self, the self which has lost what it had been living for and in (16 June 1894), and begins to doubt if it were really she. I did this too for years; this is the first time, for instance, that I have ever alluded in print to my experience twenty-six years ago of being an unwed mother, giving birth to a stillborn child. I took part in a process Julia Kristeva describes as women's refusal to speak of the "unconscious, drive-related" scene whose eruptions determine both speech and interpersonal relations. I projected a self based on "a series of inhibitions and prohibitions," rather than "the underlying causality that shapes it, which I repress in order that I may enter the socio-symbolic order, and which is capable of blowing up the whole construct" (*The Kristeva Reader* 153). And Cather, of course, was far more public and less self-revealing than I.

It is not that Cather never loved again. The deepest love of her life began soon after the events I am describing, when she met Isabelle McClung, the daughter of a Pittsburgh judge who offered residence in her father's house to Cather in 1901. But in her surviving letters, Cather lost much of the naive, candid exuberance of the early Nebraska letters to Mariel Gere. And in her fiction, she learned to speak in code; it takes a long time to find her in her novels. Denying her own Bohemianism, for instance, she backed away from her youthful aberration; and yet, a decade later, after quitting her job as an editor at *McClure's* magazine, while spending some months with Isabelle on vacation at Cherry Valley, she wrote "The Bohemian Girl," the vibrant Nebraska story in which she found her voice. This experience opened a rich vein of camouflaged self-rescue and retrieval. Clara Vavrika of this story, Marie Tovesky of *O Pioneers!*, Ántonia Shimerda of *My Ántonia*: all are Bohemian girls not only literally but symbolically. The first two are adulteresses, the third, an unwed mother, yet each finds the reckless courage to affirm her own desire. Behind them, disguising her desire, one catches a poignant glimpse of the youthful, shaved-headed Cather.

As it did me, work rescued Willa Cather. She writes to Mariel Gere, in the letter in which she eschews the desert country of Bohemia, that there is only one God and Art is his revealer; that's her creed and she'll follow it anywhere, to more of a hell than Pittsburgh if need be (4 August 1896). Writing became her life, not a *pis-aller* but a passion, and so love and work conjoined. Many years later, in 1933, she wrote to Dorothy Canfield Fisher how sick she was of the legend of her as life's pale creature martyred to art. Refreshingly, she insisted that she never in her life had made a sacrifice to art; writing, instead, was a joy, and gave her a life of self-indulgence (January or February 1933).

For me, too, love and work are inextricably commingled. My work began as a way to preserve and affirm my love against the conventional dicta of a repressive social order. In an age increasingly poisoned by conformity and lies, reading, writing, teaching must be forms of telling the truth, itself an illicit passion. My life is more scattered than

Cather's, but I wanted it that way. Some lines of a poem by Sharon Olds express the sense of plenitude I feel now that I have a family—a husband and five children—and work that I believe in; the poem is for a boyfriend who was killed in 1960, but it reminds me of myself and my firstborn daughter. "I went ahead and had the children," Olds writes,

> the life of ease and faithfulness, the
> palm and the breast, every millimeter of delight in the body,
> I took the road we stood on at the start together, I
> took it all without you as if
> in taking it after all I could most
> honor you
> ("Cambridge Elegy," *The Gold Cell*, 53–54).

Coda. It has been two years since I first worked on this essay. Short as it is, it has come to mark a turning point in my life, in that it both helped me to clarify the center of the book I am writing about Willa Cather, and led me to begin writing poetry again. The essay is about camouflage, but also about loss—the one loss in a person's life that seems to constitute loss itself and that becomes the groundswell, as it were, for everything that takes place thereafter. This loss need not remain simply a cause for lamentation. Affirmed, transformed, by love and work, it can become a source of power, a bittersweet source of consolation. Here, art enters in. My book, called "Parables of Loss: Woman's Body and Desire in the Novels of Willa Cather," begins with an expanded version of the events and losses I have presented in this essay, and goes on to explore Cather's representations of *le féminin* and woman's desire through the fictive transformations—both the camouflages *and* the recuperations—of her major novels.

As for myself, there is no way—and I hope no need—to end this essay neatly, knotting all its threads. So I'll end by not ending, with a poem I wrote a few days ago for my first daughter.

After

You are more gone
than the last wisp of dream
I chase, waking.

And therefore you become the slow
shift of sand
at the bottom of all waters.

The widening space
when leaf lets go
of branch, the balm

my bones breathe out.
I have only the names of tenderness
for you now.
Little chuck. Falling star.

---

[1] Willa Cather's will forbids direct quotation from any of her letters. I have para-
phrased throughout; some flavor of the original is inevitably lost.

Mariel Gere was Cather's classmate at the University of Nebraska; Cather was a close
friend of the whole Gere family for years. Charles Gere, Mariel's father, had come to Lincoln
in 1867; he established the *Nebraska State Journal* and served as editor-in-chief until his death
in 1904. He was Cather's employer during the last three years of her residence in Lincoln. In a
1912 letter to Mariel, Cather told her that Mariel's mother had been the one to convince
Cather, while in Lincoln, to grow out her hair and adopt more feminine dress. Mariel herself
went on to become a science teacher at Lincoln High School; she traveled widely at different
times in her life, was a member of the American Chemical Society and the Episcopal Church,
and was included in *Who's Who in Nebraska*. By 1916, relations between Cather and Mariel
had reached the point where Cather would write ruefully to her close friend and fellow
novelist Dorothy Canfield Fisher that Mariel found Cather's fiction rotten and immoral, with
a flavor she just couldn't understand, all the more insidious for not being *very* vulgar.

I am grateful to Susan Rosowski of the University of Nebraska English Department
and Lynn B. Porn of the University of Nebraska library archives for information about Mariel
Gere's adult life. I am also grateful to the librarians of the Willa Cather Center, Red Cloud,
Nebraska, the location of the early letters from Cather to Gere, for their helpfulness and
kindness.

[2] Samuel Taylor Coleridge, *The Friend*, in *The Complete Works*, ed. W. G. T. Shedd, 7 vols.
(New York, 1884), II; General Introduction, Essay V, p. 46. Quoted in Robert Langbaum, *The
Modern Spirit* (New York: Oxford, 1970), p. 34, as follows:

If men laugh at the falsehoods that were imposed on themselves during their
childhood, it is because they are not good and wise enough to contemplate the past in the
present, and so to produce by a virtuous and thoughtful sensibility that continuity in their
self-consciousness, which nature has made the law of their animal life. Ingratitude, sensuality,
and hardness of heart, all flow from this source. Men are ungrateful to others only when they
have ceased to look back on their former selves with joy and tenderness. They exist in
fragments.

WORKS CITED

Cather, Willa. Letter to Louise Pound, 15 June 1892, Pound Collection, Duke University Library,
    Durham, North Carolina. Referred to in O'Brien. To examine the Pound letters at Duke

---

University Library, scholars must obtain special permission from the university and the library.

_____. Letters to Mariel Gere, Willa Cather Center, Red Cloud, Nebraska; and Bernice Slote Collection, University of Nebraska Library, Lincoln, Nebraska. Cather's will forbids quotation from any of her letters.

Coleridge, Samuel Taylor. *The Friend. The Complete Works*, Ed. W. G. T. Shedd. 7 volumes. New York, 1884.

Kristeva, Julia. *About Chinese Women. The Kristeva Reader*. Ed. Toril Moi. New York: Columbia UP, 1986.

O'Brien, Sharon. *Willa Cather: The Emerging Voice*. New York and Oxford: Oxford University Press, 1987.

Olds, Sharon. *The Gold Cell*. New York: Alfred A. Knopf, 1991.

Woodress, James. *Willa Cather: A Literary Life*. Lincoln and London: U of Nebraska P, 1987.

THE VOICES FROM THE LITTLE HOUSE

ANN ROMINES

I discovered them—the first thick, square volumes—on the low
shelves of the children's library. They became a passion, potent as a
drug. The Little House books, by Laura Ingalls Wilder. A whole
row of them, a series, to be traded back and forth with other girls, and
then to be endlessly discussed, debated, enacted and (more blissfully
with each return) reread.

That was my introduction, at the age of seven or eight, to a staple
of twentieth-century U.S. children's literature. Wilder's seven novels
of her Anglo-American girlhood on the nineteenth-century frontier,
written in the 1930s and '40s when she was in her sixties and seventies,
were an immediate success with children (particularly girls) and their
parents and teachers, even in a Depression market. By the time I found
the Little House books, around 1950, they had been around for almost
twenty years and had acquired the cachet of "classics"; in 1953 all the
volumes were reissued in a uniform edition (still in print) with illustrations by Garth Williams, one of this century's most prestigious
illustrators of children's books. In my small, under-funded Ozark public library, the new edition came none too soon; the original books, sturdy
as they were, had been worn to tatters, their paper limp and frayed as
old linen, by the second and third grade girls who, year after year, discovered them on the shelves.

For me, those fictional little houses that the Ingalls family built on
the nineteenth-century prairie were inescapably compelling. They epito-
mized all the intensity, durability and transience that I (too) knew, living
at home in the 1950s. At the heart of them all was that entrancing protagonist—the brown-haired second daughter, Laura Ingalls. Her fresh,
steady vision, printed out in a library book, seemed to legitimize my
own vision, my sometimes-furtive life as a child. When my best friend
Jimmilee won the part of Laura in the Book Pageant and I (too tall) was
cast as the gawky narrator in my Girl Scout uniform, I was bereft. For that
was the role *I* had dreamed of—as Laura, living in a Little House book.

Part of the allure of these books was the fact that they were multiple. When you had finished all seven (skipping *Farmer Boy*, the less

satisfactory book about the boy Laura married), you could go back and begin again with the first House, *Little House in the Big Woods*—and on, again. That serial ritual of repetition was the deepest, most addictive satisfaction. The same houses, the same things, the same family, again and again. My adult life as an English professor began there, when I got hooked on rereading. (Even today, I annually look forward to rereading and reteaching *My Ántonia*, *The Portrait of a Lady*, *Huckleberry Finn*.) And perhaps my interest in reading women's culture, an interest that fuels everything I write, began there too, inside the Little Houses that were books.

I did my childhood reading in rural Missouri, during the postwar 1950s. Fifty miles from my town, in a white farmhouse visible from the main highway, lived the famous author, Laura Ingalls Wilder. When we drove by with our parents, my best friend and I begged them to slow the car to a near-standstill, so we could look and look, scanning the porch and lawn for Mrs. Wilder. But once, when Jimmilee's mother took pity on us and offered to drive us to the door so we could knock and say hello (as many children did, and were kindly welcomed), we were shocked. Unthinkable that we should knock at a Little House and speak to an Author!

Then came what promised to be the greatest day of my life. For my tenth birthday present, my grandmother drove me to Springfield, the nearest city, where Mrs. Wilder was scheduled to autograph books at Brown Bookstore. (Such occasions were rare for her; at eighty-five, this was to be her last.) Through the hundred-mile drive, I chattered in high excitement to Grandmother, who always did me the honor of taking me seriously. When we arrived at the bookstore, with its towering dark shelves, Grandmother bought me the last book in the series, the only one I hadn't read yet: *These Happy Golden Years*.[1] (On the last page was printed, "The End of the Little House Books.") We joined a line of girls I didn't know, city girls as intimidating to me as Laura's nemesis, Nellie Olsen.

Then I saw her, sitting at a table. Mrs. Wilder! She was as tiny as I and my stout grandmother were not. Her hair was pure white and naturally curly (mine was not). Her dress was a rich dark red with a matching velvet hat (Grandmother and I wore navy blue). Grandmother nudged me forward and said, in her sociable voice, "Marjorie Ann loves your books, Mrs. Wilder." The Author smiled and opened my new book. On a blank page, she wrote, in a squarish capable hand like Grandmother's. She wrote her name, "Laura Ingalls Wilder."

What did I say? Nothing. Like the young Laura Ingalls at moments charged with emotion and import, I "could not say a word" (*Big*

Woods 76), although I was ten and tall, above Grandmother's shoulder. Speechless, I took my book from its author's hand. Grandmother was probably embarrassed by her stony charge, mute among the charming, chattering little girls who filled the store. In the car on the long drive home, I stayed quiet. I was reading, voraciously—lost in my last new Little House book.

In the forty years since that birthday, I have not stopped reading. My autographed copy of *These Happy Golden Years* is spineless and worn, spotted with mold from a leak in my first apartment. Every few years I have returned to reread the Little House books, sometimes with a child as accomplice; most often alone.

But not alone. For the Little House books are longtime bestsellers. Since they began to appear in 1932, they have never been out of print. Although the final volume was published in 1943, the series has become a snowballing cultural phenomenon, spinning off more books by other authors (including Wilder's daughter and her daughter's adopted grandson), pageants, restorations and reconstructions, products ranging from dolls to bumper stickers, and—in the 1970s—a longrunning television series that is still popular in reruns. After Mrs. Wilder's death in 1957, her white farmhouse near Mansfield, Missouri, became a museum whose parking lot is regularly crowded with vans and station wagons from all over the United States. When I go there now (no longer too shy to approach the door), I find that the most avid of my fellow visitors are women my age. Intent, we crowd as close to the glass cases as we can, calling to our children and companions, "Look! Mary's nine patch quilt! Pa's fiddle! Laura's bread plate!"

Such things, the ordinary keepsakes and accoutrements of a hardpressed household, are mute in their cases. But for Wilder's readers, especially the white, middle-class women who—like me—came of age in the 1960s and '70s, these familiar objects reiterate the Little House story. It is a story in which American women have made heavy, sometimes fatal investments. Now the books and the things seem inseparable. Relentlessly material, stubbornly domestic, they confirm each other and embody a complicated narrative of female survival. Wilder and her sisters and daughter are all dead now, leaving no descendants. Yet here these things still are, freighted with stories.

The survival of such objects is doubly important because the Little Houses Wilder wrote about did not survive. The Little House, like the books, is serial. One by one, these dwellings are built, furnished, inhabited, abandoned and left behind. These transient shelters derived their enduring meaning from the repeated rituals of furnishing, maintenance and housekeeping that were supervised by Laura's fictional mother, Ma, and crowned with her signifier of domestic approval, a fragile, cherished china shepherdess which only Ma could touch and which she withheld from any dwelling below her standard. Such things as the shepherdess take on amazing weight and stability; they appear and reappear, recycled, refurbished, and reread, in consecutive chapters and volumes. When an occasional object must be left behind (such as the glass windows, abandoned in the Kansas house of *Little House on the Prairie*), Ma preserves it in memories that her daughter, Laura Ingalls Wilder, will eventually inscribe. For me and many of my fellow readers, finding these very things corporeally present in the Mansfield museum seems to confirm the triumphant durability of the Little House myth. The house, the unchanging family, the undying things—all are preserved by women who, however transient their emigrant lives may have been, understood the powers of housekeeping. And the powers of writing.

Much of Laura Ingalls' story involves a girl's discovery of a voice, in which she may speak and, eventually, write. Yet, as I've said, at moments of great stress the fictional Laura finds herself speechless. Why can't she speak? And why do I share her silence? In the world of these books, the Little House is the defining term; it *must* signify. As Wilder's series makes abundantly clear, if a Little House is to signify, there must be a woman inside. (Until she marries, Laura Ingalls never enters a house kept by a man; as far as she knows, such houses do not exist.)

Throughout the series, in winter, months of fictional time pass without a single depiction of Ma's leaving the house, although Pa is out every day, by choice and necessity. Ma's confinement, shared by her daughters, is most severe in the fifth Little House book, *The Long Winter*, a narrative of blizzard-enforced indoor seclusion and near-starvation.[2] As Laura learns, the great peril of such seclusion, exacerbated by hunger, inactivity and cold, is stupor and silence. If there are to be houses, the Little House series always implies, there must be housekeeping women. But if there are to be articulate women (such as Laura herself, in her triumphs of speaking and writing at school), those women must find a way outside the silencing, sheltering walls of the Little House.

Laura Ingalls, the fictional character, was a girl as ambivalent and headstrong as I was, as a reading child. That's what drew me to her. Had Laura and I met and recognized each other at Brown Bookstore, we could have spoken to each other. But Laura Ingalls Wilder, the author in the regal wine-colored dress, seemed to me a silencing figure. Calm, controlling and assured, she handed me a commodity about which she seemed to have no doubts. A book, a name, a myth. She looked like a powerful woman—powerful because she had learned to speak, to write and to sell her writing. What she sold was the Little House story, the series that held me quivering in its thrall. In the warm car with my sympathetic grandmother, hurtling toward the end of the Little House Books, I could find no words to tell her how this story seduced me and frightened me. She was in the story. I was in it. What could we say?

———————

Forty years later, my career as a writing scholar is still a continuing effort to discover what I can say. Repeatedly, in my Ph.D. dissertation and then in essays, papers and a book, I've returned to issues of house-keeping, the very issues that my mother and grandmother impressed on me as crucially important for girls and women. Although *things* were more profuse in the relative abundance of my postwar childhood than they had been on Wilder's nineteenth-century frontier, I too learned the iconic force of a treasured ornament like Ma's china shepherdess (with us, was it Grandmother's porcelain chocolate set?). And I never questioned the importance of a Christmas dinner menu or the plotting of a furniture arrangement or a domestic work routine—all issues about which Laura Ingalls, too, had collaborated with her mother and sisters. In our household of daughters, as in the Ingalls' Little Houses, such priorities were seldom *spoken*, let alone written. Instead, they were as-sumed and then reinforced by the rituals of repetition.

When, as a graduate student in the 1960s and '70s, I began to try to write about women's literature and culture, there was no available lit-erary vocabulary that allowed me to take seriously the domestic values I'd learned as a child, those values that had been reinforced (and subtly questioned) by the Little House books. As a scholar, I came of age in an extraordinary, exhilarating flowering of feminist scholarship. That schol-arship has been the foundation of my own work, as a teacher and writer. Writing about women's domestic texts and the evolution of domestic culture in the nineteenth and twentieth century U.S., I hope I've had some success in showing that the worlds women have created inside houses are required reading for anyone with a serious interest in U.S. culture. But my writing has been largely in the language of the acad-emy, where I work as an associate professor of English. It is not executed in the private, silent codes of housekeeping, a language in which I still conduct some of the most deeply satisfying and deeply conflicted acts of my life. As I write this essay, hurrying to meet an editor's deadline, I'm concurrently preparing the traditional foods for my family Thanks-giving dinner, a project I care about as much as I care about the essay—or more. (Will we be able to find good turnips this year? Should I serve two kinds of pie or three? Will I successfully reproduce Grandmother's turkey dressing?)

More than any writing I've done before, this current project—a book on Laura Ingalls Wilder and the myth of the Little House—pushes me to think about the inadequacies of everything I've written up to now. My enduring sense of how much Thanksgiving dinner matters is one reason why the Little House books have been persistently important to me. Wilder's great achievement is that she was able to *write* that importance—and then to show how it warred with a girl's access to spoken and written language. Like me—child and adult—young Laura Ingalls wanted both vocabularies. As a mature woman, older than I am now, Laura Ingalls Wilder triumphantly inscribed her series, a great public success, by putting the silent world inside the Little Houses into words.

Thus, perhaps the most liberating moment of my life as a scholar occurred when I realized that I could use my professional skills to write a book about my favorite childhood writer. To my own amazement, I sat at my desk in an almost trancelike state and typed, on the annual report form by which George Washington University requires me to chart (or invent) my professional goals, that my next major project would be a book-length feminist study of the Little House series by Laura Ingalls Wilder.

In the following months, as I graded papers, taught classes, attended committee meetings and read proofs, I fantasized about the book that lay ahead, like a mirage of perfect bliss. In the years of intermittent reading, rereading, research, travel, talking, writing and rewriting that my new project would require, I would be doing what I'd dreamed of as a girl: living inside the world and the language of the Little House books.

Years have passed, articles are published, the book is half complete. And, as this essay has already suggested, perfect bliss has turned out to be more complicated than I'd imagined. Rereading the Little House books in the 1990s, I want (and need) to access my own rapt involvement with these texts as a child in the 1950s. My current interest in Wilder's series as a gendered cultural document is rooted in those early feelings. But it's hard to reach such feelings in my accustomed scholarly language. Up to now, my readers have been mostly scholars in my own and related fields. Through those readers, I have acquired jobs, credentials, space in print. In return, I have paid obeisance to their language, the feminist/post-structuralist argot that I've picked up during the past dozen years and have found, for the most part, useful and enabling. But in this new book, which I hope will be my strongest work yet, I must go back further than a dozen years, to access the continuity of my life as a U.S. female reader and writer, a dweller in and keeper of houses.

So now I need language that helps me to draw more fully on my resources as a thinking, feeling, reading, writing, loving, cooking woman. Thinking about the Little House books, I find that I'm also thinking about the simultaneous pressures in my life to *write* and to *suppress* much of the story of my female experience. Reading Wilder's autobiographical narrative of Laura Ingalls' coming of age, I find a parallel tale of a silent girl, drawn to the confirming outlet of the written word. Despite its demands and complications, this new book I'm writing does still hold out a promise of bliss, because it is pushing me deeper into the project of acknowledging unspoken territories of my life, on the page.

My maternal grandmother, who took me to see Laura Ingalls Wilder, was widowed before I was born. In all the years I knew her, she lived alone (as I do now) in a nourishing surround of domestic ritual, palpable as milk. But she also worked as a beloved, effective high school English teacher until she was seventy, never earning as much as $5000 a year. She taught me and my sister grammar, cooking and poems (my first introduction to Emily Dickinson and the Book of Psalms came from her, before I was three). And, at sixty-six, she was willing to drive two hundred miles in November, on a winding blacktop road, to buy me a book and a glimpse of a woman writer. Now, for the first time, it occurs to me to wonder how *Grandmother* felt about Laura Ingalls Wilder. At sixty-six, she was herself the age Mrs. Wilder had been when she wrote the series, and she had just received an M.A. the previous year. With children, Grandmother was a gifted storyteller; her long series of "Really Truly Stories" had made her nineteenth-century Missouri farm girlhood as vivid to me as the Little Houses were. In 1952, did Grandmother view Laura Ingalls Wilder as a model for her own life as a housekeeper, storyteller, and possibly a writer? Or did she see her as an ally? As a rival? On that memorable day in Brown Bookstore, such questions would not have entered my mind. Only now, middle-aged myself, am I beginning to realize that many of the values of my grandmother's life—housekeeping, storytelling, solitude, teaching, books—are the deepest source of my own, 1990s feminist scholarship.

Researching Wilder's papers, I'm learning how her writing career was also intergenerational. Her series presents the Little House ideology as an inheritance Laura received from both her parents. But the actual writing of the books seems to have been a complicated collaboration between Wilder and her daughter, Rose Wilder Lane, who had a thriving career as a novelist and journalist long before the first Little House book appeared. When the series is read in the context of the mother/daughter correspondence between Wilder and Lane, Lane's voluminous diaries, and the multiple drafts of revisions on which both women labored, it looks like an ongoing (and sometimes acrimonious) debate about how to tell a female story. And the name of the author, *Laura Ingalls Wilder*, begins to seem a construct, invented to facilitate this multigenerational collaboration. Having grown up in a culture where women routinely collaborated on cooking, housework, sewing, and such large, ambitious projects as quilts, Wilder was probably more accustomed to the idea of collaborative authorship (and collective, "authorless" texts) than was her New Woman daughter, Rose Wilder Lane. As a young woman, Lane had set out to make a name for herself by writing and publishing.[3] As a young scholar with a new Ph.D., I was enjoined to do about the same thing. Only now am I recognizing the communal, collaborative, inherited elements in my own writing, as I try to discover and acknowledge my grandmother's large part in my work on Laura Ingalls Wilder.

At this point, I feel that this essay has slipped out of all the controlling nets I know how to employ. (And by now I'm a practiced writer and teacher of writing.) It seems too late and I'm in too deep to go back, recast, make an outline. . . . For a conference paper or a classroom lecture, I can shape a mean argument. But this essay seems like a clouded, viscous gel, in which hang suspended, partially and tantalizingly visible, some of the most intimate and pressing concerns of my past and present life as an American woman.

Now I long for models of the kind of writing I wish this essay were, from women academics like me, writers who are trying to merge their "scholarship" with "personal writing," in order to do fuller justice to subjects as large and self-implicating as (for me) the Little House books. I think about the urgency and passion with which (in private) I've heard many of the women scholars I most admire talk about their work. (In fact, this very essay was engendered by such a conversation, squeezed between sessions at an academic conference.) Certain exemplary careers suggest ongoing experiments with the possibilities of personal writing: I've been inspired by Nancy K. Miller, Jane Tompkins, Rachel Blau DuPlessis, bell hooks. But it's far more usual to find "personal" materials and voice employed as a charming, ingratiating anecdote in an introduction or epilogue to a work of standard scholarship, a ploy (and one I've used myself) that reduces the personal to trivial window dressing. Recent scholarship reminds us again and again of how *situated* is our every act of reading and writing. But the authoritarian mode of much published scholarship seems little changed. At conferences, I'm often most interested by the informal prefatory remarks that precede written texts, dutifully read. In those remarks, scholars may tell how they became engaged with a particular subject or problem. I listen avidly for the clues that will make the story of an intellectual project more complete—human—*personal*? Right now, in my life as a reading, writing woman/scholar, I'm especially hungry for these seldom-written narratives of work, narratives that eschew reductive, hierarchal distinctions between the "professional" and the "personal." Written or spoken, such narratives are as important to me as the Little House books once were; they make it more possible to go on with the book I am laboring to write, the life I am trying to live.

I'm writing about Laura Ingalls Wilder because she seems to raise the questions that are now at the center of my life and work. I chose my profession because I was a child who read passionately. Yet most of my professional experience has enjoined me to forget that child and to keep quiet about what she learned at home, from women, even though those lessons—learned through combat and collaboration with my female forebears—still control much of my deepest experience. The language of this essay may seem cloudy and mixed and inchoate; I can't keep myself from apologizing (I just did) for such language. But slowly, truly, I am beginning to draw from more of the multiple vocabularies that articulate my life. As I never have before in print, I feel scared, uncomfortable, exposed—with the stinging mixture of shame and excitement that the prospect of exposure elicits. I think of my mother, my colleagues, my godchild, my dean, my sister, my oldest friends, and of the pain of their scorn, condescension, or incomprehension—all of which my present writing might well evoke. But I also think of this new possibility of perfect bliss: writing from my whole self. And I keep on working.

---

[1] This 1943 novel, Wilder's last, chronicles Laura Ingalls's brief teaching career and her courtship with Almanzo Wilder; it ends with her marriage.

[2] For an extended discussion of female confinement in this book, see my earlier essay, "The Long Winter: An Introduction to Western Womanhood," *Great Plains Quarterly* 10 (Winter 1990): 36–47.

[3] William Holtz's recent biography of Rose Wilder Lane is an authoritative account of her rich and significant career. However, I see the writing of the Little House books as a collaboration of mother and daughter, not—as Holtz argues—as a case of Lane's "ghost writing" for Wilder.

Holtz, William. *The Ghost in the Little House: A Life of Rose Wilder Lane*. Columbia: U of Missouri P, 1993.

Romines, Ann. *"The Long Winter*: An Introduction to Western Womanhood." *Great Plains Quarterly* 10 (Winter 1990): 36–47.

Wilder, Laura Ingalls. *Little House in the Big Woods, Farmer Boy, Little House on the Prairie, On the Banks of Plum Creek, By the Shores of Silver Lake, The Long Winter, Little Town on the Prairie, These Happy Golden Years*. 1932, 1933, 1937, 1939, 1940, 1941, 1943. New York: Harper, 1953.

REWRITING THE LOVE PLOT OUR WAY
WOMEN AND WORK

SUSAN J. ROSOWSKI

I n my office at the university a shelf of books represents two decades of women working, or more accurately but more difficult to find, of working women. *Women and Success: The Anatomy of Achievement* (1974), *Working It Out* (1977), *Women Working* (1979), *Between Women: Biographers, Novelists, Critics, Teachers and Artists Write about Their Work on Women* (1984); *The Confidence Woman* (1991); and *The Writer on Her Work* (I, 1980; II, 1991). Now, I am struck by how the paradigm has changed. That is, we've moved from a model of success defined by hierarchy to one of love, and the move suggests that we're at last comfortable with our own (*i.e.*, individual) ways of dressing (*Dress for Success* would be comical today), and that we're comfortable also in talking about how we juggle the parts of our days. Our challenge now is to write truthfully of the emotional life of working.

In doing so here, I am speaking not for working women generally but for myself, and I acknowledge that I am doing so with a personal vocabulary that reflects the privilege of choice and discrimination: I teach, do research, edit, meet committee responsibilities, do community service, and carry out administrative responsibilities. I also work, a verb I reserve for that which matters most to me and as something I do because I choose to do so. When I'm working, I am not conscious of an audience, or a reader, or of students or colleagues, or of my self.

A vocabulary for work did not come easily to me, for it meant articulating distinctions by which I wished to shape my life but that I believed might not be possible. Loving to read was altogether different, something I assumed as naturally and indiscriminately as I assumed breathing. It was simply what I did—on school nights with a flashlight under the cover, telling myself I'd finish "just one more chapter" and not stopping until Nancy Drew and her chums solved whatever mystery they had put themselves to; on vacations risking car sickness by reading in the back seat and, when the book was especially good (one of the Black Stallion series, for example), considering the Sights of the Trip a distraction. "Susan, just *look* at the Grand Canyon," my mother would say, drawing me back to other wonders.

Books remained a private part of my life through undergraduate school, where I majored in Social Work (a good field for a woman, I was advised). Now I recall almost nothing of social work, but I remember shading the lamp so I'd not keep roommates awake while I read *Middlemarch* and skipping dinner to remain with *Grapes of Wrath*. For my electives each semester, I "took" literature classes, which basically meant that we convened at appointed times to hear our teachers lecture to us, rather as one "took" a dose of medicine. But there was one exception. For a class on contemporary literature, Paul Zall sat on the edge of the stage (we were meeting in an auditorium) and conducted a conversation—not with us (the class was too large for that, he explained in apology), but *with the texts*. Literary study as carrying on an open conversation in a personal voice—it was a revelation, and five of us who wanted more of the same formed a reading group that met for the next two years, talking about books. What I remember from those days are voices mingling, sometimes joined by critics we dragged in for assistance (Stuart Gilbert's explication of *Ulysses* formed a counterpoint to Joyce's novel), but mostly Jo talking about Nabokov, and Nate, whose passion for Isak Dineson revealed him as much as it illuminated *Out of Africa*.

Until this point my love of books was the most personal of pleasures taking place in the private spaces of my life: under the covers, in the back seat, or after hours with friends I trusted. I entered graduate school because I exited a B.A. program (my electives in English had resulted in a second major) and couldn't imagine stopping there; doing so meant finding myself embarked upon a formal pursuit of literary study. "So, you've signed up for the PhD program rather than the M.A.," the graduate advisor commented upon looking at my file during my admissions interview. Long silence. "That's *very* ambitious, don't you think?" His tone wasn't so much censorious of me as (more damning still) embarrassed *for* me; I was startled that he judged my potential without knowing my work but even more so that he linked ambition to literary study.

In the mid-sixties, graduate study in the University of Arizona's English department meant being educated in a hierarchy of academic ambition as well as in the canon (we would never have called it such, of course; it was simply "literature" in those days). British literature was at the top of the ladder; American literature was uneasily positioned somewhere in its middle, uncertain whether its fate was to move upward or sink down; and as if a would-be field, folklore precariously held to the bottom rung. Composition was off the ladder, not even a field but rather an accumulation of courses designed to meet the crassest of student needs.

The faculty existed in a similarly clear pecking order. The scholars at the top, distinguishable because others' voices would lower a notch when mentioning their names, worked on Chaucer and Shakespeare. The "American lit people" (that is, the American lit *men*) were clumped in the middle, their names joined in one long hyphenation. The two women on the faculty were in folklore and Victorian studies (the one in Victorian studies was, however, writing a composition textbook). Finally, off the hierarchal ladder, a "pool" of nameless women taught composition.

As for the literature we studied, for that I return to notes that survived from a graduate seminar on seventeenth-century English literature (I prided myself, I remember upon seeing those pages from 1965, upon my clear hand and logical note-taking ability):

Overview: will stress Donne and Milton.
There is an uncrowned literary dictator for every period
T. S. Eliot was such a dictator between WWI and II;
Ben Jonson was such a dictator in the 17th C.
A friend of Marlowe, Shakespeare, and Donne
"the Sons of Ben" produced most cavalier poets.

Searching through that notebook for the women, I find "On My First Daughter," "Queen and Huntress, Chaste and Fair," and "A Fair and Happy Milkmaid." We must have read women writers in some of our classes, but I haven't notes to return to, and I now recall only Elizabeth Gaskell's *Mary Barton*, presented as a social document of political issues.

I remember those years at Arizona as a time of joy, for it was the most concentrated period of discovery in my life. But I remember it also by a fear of failure—whatever that meant. Even at the time, I wasn't quite sure—other than that it had nothing to do with grades (mine were excellent) but rather with what one professor told his class, of which I was a member, "It's better to say nothing than to say something stupid." The lesson that remaining silent is preferable to admitting ignorance possibly perceived as stupidity was, I recognized even then, ironic, for I knew that a love of learning comes from acknowledging that one is inevitably and inescapably ignorant in the face of all there is to know. Today I would define failure as not speaking out against such a comment as that professor made, but even while doing so I acknowledge that speaking out remains one thing for a graduate student and another for faculty with rank and tenure. Certainly, that was the case in the sixties, when lessons about power and gatekeeping were articulated so explicitly.

After my husband moved to Nebraska and a faculty appointment in Botany, I remained in Tucson to take my comprehensives, then joined him. In Lincoln, I set about writing a dissertation on Laurence Sterne and sentimentalism. Whatever that meant. I was endlessly researching trivial points, spinning notes but going nowhere, filling time. Outside of our marriage and aside from the compassion of relatives inherited from my mother's side of the family, I was very much on my own; after two years, my loneliness and depression were such that it was an act of courage to apply for a temporary position in the English department at the University of Nebraska, and upon being told there was no possibility of such a job, to return again—and again.

The one-year appointment I finally landed resulted not from my qualifications so much as from my returning "to check on the status of my application" (the phrase I carried with me into the chair's office) on the very day that an instructor had resigned to take a "real" job (*i.e.*, on a tenure line; the job market was as dismal in 1971 as today). On that temporary appointment I became part of a department that seemed an expanded version of my undergraduate reading group, with faculty and students who would talk (really talk) with one another, and look each other in the face (*really* look) as they passed in the halls. Speaking up was not only encouraged, but expected, and I felt as if I'd died and gone to heaven. That year I began to explore issues and ideas that I'd not been able to face alone: with women mainly (but not only), I discovered Woolf and Lessing, Millet and Gilman, and I finished *The Feminine Mystique*. Finally. As my parents' generation describes where they were upon hearing that Pearl Harbor was attacked and my generation where we were upon hearing that President Kennedy was assassinated, so women from the sixties describe first reading Betty Friedan's book. Over Thanksgiving break in 1963 I was riding the bus from Whittier College to Phoenix, and when I reached its final chapter, "The Independent Woman," I was unable to continue—not only closing the book but actually hiding it in my suitcase, out of sight.

Also in 1971 on that term appointment at the University of Nebraska, I began reading Willa Cather. Never having heard her name mentioned in any of my classes—undergraduate or graduate, I came to *A Lost Lady* fresh, and I was hooked. That's what I say, but what I mean is that I began what has been one of the most important relationships of my life. Cather's novel is about Marian Forrester, the lost lady of the title, as seen by a boy who expected her "to immolate herself" to the memory of her husband, then as interpreted by critics (male) who condemned her as a Madame Bovary of the plains. So it was assumed at the time. Though I didn't put it in these terms, I knew this was a book about silencing and gender, and because I wanted to say so, I wrote about Cather's novel while completing my dissertation on Sterne. The result was "*A Lost Lady* and the Paradox of Change"—my first publication on Cather, and the first in which I wrote personally (albeit in an objective voice) of what it meant to read as a woman.

There are some writers who invite an exchange (what the psychologists call "mutuality") of intimate friendship in their art by creating a sense of privacy through restraint, establishing a sense of form akin to manners in society, within which they offer themselves generously and openly. Samuel Johnson, John Keats, and Virginia Woolf are such writers, and so is Willa Cather. Here's my story, her narrator Jim Burden says in the original preface to *My Ántonia*, "Now, what about yours?": it is an offer and invitation basic to Cather's writing more generally.[1]

For those of us reading Cather in Nebraska, this exchange involves a common landscape and, at the University, even a common English department, for she was once a student here. But more broadly, discovering her offers a forum for exploring growing up defined by gender expectations, of protecting a personal voice and desiring to engage in a public discourse, of loving work and also family, of negotiating private lives and public voices. Alexandra Bergson, Thea Kronborg, Ántonia Shimerda Cuzak and Lena Lingard, Marian Forrester, Myra Henshawe, Vickie and Victoria Templeton, Lucy Gayheart, Sapphira Dodderidge— each offers her own story; together, they offer a forum for considering issues on a very broad scale.

Titles on an academic's curriculum vitae represent her ongoing intellectual life much as photographs in an album document the ongoing life of a family, I've come to recognize in others' files, and to admit in my own. Completing my schooling and envisioning an adult life, I wrote on the female *Bildungsroman*; coinciding with a move from an appointment in the Romantics to one in Cather studies, my work was on Cather's romanticism; when our children became teenagers, I turned to explorations of adolescence and the family. In recent years I've been working on issues of creativity, and I've begun to assemble materials on aging. In each case, pleasure has come from turning to different writers as I explore a particular subject—Smedley, Chopin, and Eliot, for example, in thinking about the female *Bildungsroman* as a novel of awakening, Atwood for female adolescent development, and Fuller, Stafford, and Robinson for women who aspired to create from the West a national identity. I've not wanted to stick with any of them, however, as I have with Cather. Certain writers offer companionship for a lifetime.

While Cather offers an invitation to make a personal voice public, in my case it was a personal voice formed at home. I learned to argue with my father (one of the truest intellectuals I know, in seeking to understand how things are and to imagine how they might be), and to make things work with my mother (a fierce realist who knows that life is hard and accepts the challenge to make it good). From both of them, I learned to respect straight talk and getting on with things. "Such parents are providential," a friend from India commented when I spoke of them. She had defied her family in refusing at thirteen an arranged marriage to a seventeen-year-old boy. My own defiances were the less dramatic ones familiar to many women in academia in this country today: conceiving of a future in the field, though no member of the faculty in my graduate program spoke of that possibility to me; refusing to accept that the chances for an academic appointment were "nil" (as the head of a department told me); applying for a position in a research department after being counseled to be content where I was ("remember, you have children, and you now can take summers off").

Though "the system" was consistently indifferent and often hostile to women during those years, my husband was as consistently involved and supportive. At eighteen and twenty-one, our sons are now precisely the ages we were when we met; realizing this means realizing how young we were. But we agreed on most things, including assuming that we'd both have a life within as well as outside the home, and we were willing to accommodate each other as we grew up: Jim taught in the California public schools and completed an M.S. while I completed an undergraduate degree at Whittier; we selected a graduate school that offered solid programs in both Botany and English; one summer I traveled to a marine biology station with Jim, and one fall he traveled to research libraries with me. Because he finished before I did, Jim was the first on the job market, and we moved to Nebraska when he was appointed to a faculty there; once there, we set ourselves to making two careers possible. Throughout these years, I protected a private space for doing what I wanted, though I couldn't bring myself to call it work. That is, I turned to subjects that I chose and wrote about them because I wanted to figure something out.

In "The Way We Live Now," Jane Tompkins writes of walking through the halls outside her university office, "looking for someone to talk to. But with only one exception, there [were] no professors" about, and she returned to her office, deflated:

A momentary disappointment but the roots go deep. For some time now I've been restless and dissatisfied with my life in the university, hungry for some emotional or spiritual fulfillment that it doesn't seem to afford. I crave a sense of belonging, the feeling that I'm part of an enterprise larger than myself, part of a group that shares some common purpose. (13)

This essay struck a responsive chord among women faculty in my department. We convened over lunch, named ourselves a caucus, and with echoes of the consciousness raising groups of the sixties, we told our stories. That is, each spoke of her life in the department, the university, and the profession, and together we reviewed who was on what committee, what percentage of women were in various ranks, and where were the women in administration? We, the heirs of the most recent women's movement, have claimed for ourselves the *Bildungsroman*; that is, we expect to take our place in the world, and we're comfortable with language borrowed from business and politics. "Agenda," "power," "strategy," "caucus," "negotiate" and "the job market" come as easily from our lips as recipes did from our mothers'. What we didn't speak of was our own work. Perhaps in a university where research and writing are so often identified with competition, we avoid speaking openly about them in our desire to form a community; perhaps our writing is so central to who we are that we reserve speaking of it for not merely personal, but intimate conversation.

Cancer released me from the fearfulness of graduate school. When I was thirty-two, trying to complete a dissertation while teaching part time and thinking I needed a correction in my glasses, I visited the doctor and learned that melanoma in my left eye was affecting my vision. The only procedure was to remove the eye; until that was done, we could not know if the tumor was contained. "If the cancer has spread beyond the eye, will it be terminal?" I asked. "Yes," I was told. The diagnosis was liberating in the sense that upon hearing it I knew exactly what was important to me: I would grieve that our son, barely two then, would not remember me, and I could scarcely bear to contemplate not being a part of his growing up, not seeing who he would become. And, I would regret not knowing whether I could complete a dissertation or make work that I loved an ongoing part of my life. The prognosis was a gift: if I wasn't afraid of dying (and I wasn't), I surely wasn't afraid of saying something stupid.

Now—at fifty-two, I see the world through one eye and three pair of glasses: outside glasses with a single prescription tinted a reddish hue; inside bifocals for conversation and reading; and working bifocals for reading at a desk and on a computer screen. For the past fifteen years, I have had three rooms of my own. First, an office at the university, where I deal with mail, talk with students or colleagues, and see to committee business. Aside from the standard furniture, the room contains a clutter that I find comfortable: on a shelf, remembrances of students—a blue cloth rocking horse made for me by the mother of one of my students after he completed his doctorate, a crystal paperweight from another student following her first conference paper, and on the shelves as well as the walls, pictures of people and places. The room is my version of a scrapbook.

Then there is my study at home, where I prepare for class and, when facing a deadline, sometimes do my own writing. Inherited when our son moved to the basement, it contains a guest bed on which are piled boxes of pictures that we intend—sometime—to get into scrapbooks, presents to be wrapped and family debris to be discarded. Books and papers are piled on the floor, spilling off the shelves. I have written this essay here; my husband, our sons, and the cat have wandered in and out again, and the phone rings several times an hour. This is catchall space in which I am keenly conscious of jostling commitments.

My third room is in the library. It is accessible only by two keys, one (a standard university-style key) activating the elevator to the fourth floor, and the second (an antique gold key inscribed in scrollwork about its edge) opening its door. It is a narrow, long, and high ceilinged space, like the utility closet it was before it was assigned to me. Three windows let in light but no view (they look onto the library's roof). The door opens onto a table on which are piled drafts from the past decade, not litter that I want to sort and discard, but physical confirmation that phrases turn into sentences and sentences take shape as paragraphs. At the far end of the room is an oak linoleum-topped library table, adjacent to the desk on which my computer sits. Other than purchasing a second-hand reading light (cheap) and a typewriter, a computer, and a printer (expensive), I've never felt the slightest impulse to attend to this room. It has no public face, and it suits me perfectly exactly as it is. It is my diary translated into physical space; I recognize it in Suzannne Juhasz's description, "traditionally, a diary belongs to and stays in the private world. It is personal and thus secret: it comes with a lock and a little gold key."

"Traditionally, too, women and their lives have belonged to and stayed in that same private world" (224), Suzanne Juhasz continues, and it is here that we (she and I, but also, I believe, other academic women and I) part ways. For loving work/working love means moving back and forth, and such movement (I believe) means reclaiming love and family plots, not as they have been scripted for us in the past but as we have written them for ourselves, to include our work.

Poets and fiction writers speak automatically of their writing in terms of love, passion, and friendship: Annie Dillard approaches "fiction, and the world . . . as a reader, and a writer, and a lover" (14); Joan Didion describes herself as "a person whose most absorbed and passionate hours are spent arranging words on pieces of paper" (20), and Patricia Goedicke identifies her best friend as one who "loved poetry almost as much as I did" (83–4). Scholars and critics, too, employ a language of love when they speak *not as academics* about their departments or the profession, but of their relations to their subjects with which/ whom they work. Louise DeSalvo describes Virginia Woolf as the "woman of my dreams" (41); Janet Sternburg writes of finding herself "increasingly engaged" in Isak Dinesen's writing, feeling herself "drawn to this woman," and finally entering "into a changing relationship with her" (216); Gloria T. Hull of being "locked in uneasy sisterhood" with Alice Dunbar-Nelson (110); and Lynda Koolish describes how "photographing women I love, whose work nurtures and inspires my life, feeds the vision that makes me passionate about writers and ideas in the classroom" (120).

I return to the definitions with which I began, for reclaiming a love plot and rewriting it to encompass the emotional life of working results in distinctions. For me (as for many other women, I believe), gratitude at being part of an academic community that I (we) respect takes the form of the reply, "of course, I'd be happy to serve on that committee, give that talk, read that paper, write that letter, and meet with the visiting speaker. Thank you for thinking of me." It's not merely habit speaking; I *am* happy to do these things; I *do* appreciate being thought of, and I *do* enjoy doing my part. But unless I am irresponsible and get myself so tied up in them that I never get to my room in the library, such activities have nothing to do with loving work.

---

[1] This is an idea I have explored in "Willa Cather and the Intimacy of Art, or: In Defense of Privacy."

Cather, Willa. *My Ántonia*. Boston: Houghton Mifflin, 1918.

DeSalvo, Louise. "A Portrait of the *Puttana* as a Middle-Aged Woolf Scholar." *Between Women: Biographers, Novelists, Critics, Teachers and Artists Write about Their Work on Women*. Ed. Carol Ascher, Louise DeSalvo, Sara Ruddick. Boston: Beacon P, 1984. 35–53.

Didion, Joan. "Why I Write." *The Writer on Her Work*. I. Ed. Janet Sternburg. New York: W. W. Norton, 1981. 17–25.

Dillard, Annie. *Living By Fiction*. New York: Harper and Row, 1982.

Goedicke, Patricia. "Entering the Garden." *The Confidence Woman: 26 Women Writers at Work*. Ed. Eve Shelnutt. Atlanta, Georgia: Longstreet Press, 1991. 75–97.

Hoffman, Nancy and Florence Howe, eds. *Women Working: An Anthology of Stories and Poems*. Old Westbury, New York: The Feminist P, 1979.

Hull, Gloria T. "Alice Dunbar-Nelson: A Personal and Literary Perspective." *Between Women: Biographers, Novelists, Critics, Teachers and Artists Write about Their Work on Women*. Ed. Carol Ascher, Louise DeSalvo, Sara Ruddick. Boston: Beacon P, 1984. 105–11.

Juhasz, Suzanne. "Towards a Theory of Form in Feminist Autobiography: Kate Millett's *Flying* and *Sita*; Maxine Hong Kingston's *The Woman Warrior*." *Women's Autobiography: Essays in Criticism*. Ed. Estelle C. Jelinek. Bloomington: Indiana UP, 1980. 221–37.

Koolish, Lynda. "This is Who She is to Me: On Photographing Women." *Between Women: Biographers, Novelists, Critics, Teachers and Artists Writer about Their Work on Women*. Ed. Carol Ascher, Louise DeSalvo, Sara Ruddick. Boston: Beacon P, 1984. 113–35.

Kundsin, Ruth B., ed. *Women and Success: The Anatomy of Achievement*. New York: William Morrow, 1974.

Rosowski, Susan J. "Willa Cather and the Intimacy of Art, Or: In Defense of Privacy." *Willa Cather Pioneer Memorial Newsletter* 36 (Winter 1992–93): 47–53.

Ruddick, Sara and Pamela Daniels, eds. *Working It Out: 23 Women Writers, Artists, Scientists, and Scholars Write About Their Lives and Work*. New York: Pantheon Books, 1977.

Shelnutt, Eve, ed. *The Confidence Woman: 26 Women Writers at Work*. Atlanta, Georgia: Longstreet Press, 1991.

Sternburg, Janet. "Farewell to the Farm." *Between Women: Biographers, Novelists, Critics, Teachers and Artists Write about Their Work on Women*. Ed. Carol Ascher, Louise DeSalvo, Sara Ruddick. Boston: Beacon Press, 1984. 213–18.

Stimpson, Catherine R. "Feminist Criticism." *Redrawing the Boundaries: The Transformation of English and American Literary Studies*. Ed. Stephen Greenblatt and Giles Gunn. New York: MLA, 1992. 251–70.

Tompkins, Jane. "The Way We Live Now." *Change*. November/ December, 1992: 13–19.

II

THE TEXT AS MIRROR

Nancy Drew—The Perfect Solution

Carol S. Chadwick

T oday I started reading Elizabeth George's latest detective story *Missing Joseph*. In it an English woman confesses to a vicar she meets in the National Gallery her feelings about being unable to bear a child. At first glance, this seems a far cry from anything I would care about, a middle-aged, single, childless, American, college professor. But there is something which draws me to the characters in mysteries like this; they are my friends and have been since I was a child. I feel a kinship both with the characters and the authors. I share the prospective from which the story is told as keenly as I can identify with the characters.

Soon I will take the thick hard-bound volume to bed with me, read for a while before sleeping. This is a practice I have maintained with spotty, albeit dogged regularity, roughly the last four decades of my life. Over the years, I have read many different kinds of things in bed for various purposes, yet I always end up reading detective novels which are, for me, the ultimate literary reward at the completion of a project.

The characters, situations, and concerns which are set forth in the books I read today are much more subtle and sophisticated than those of my youth. Over the years their increasing complexity has kept pace with this reader. As I have grown, my taste has become more discriminating and analytical, so that today I spend more time reading, writing and thinking about mystery books than reading them first hand.

Reading mysteries started with Nancy Drew novels when I was in the fifth or sixth grade. A school chum named Peggy Cole showed me one of her Nancy Drew books and confided her delight in reading them. I became hooked immediately. I still can see the vivid illustrations of the book covers, *The Secret of the Old Clock* (1930), *The Hidden Staircase* (1930), *The Password to Larkspur Lane* (1933), *The Message in the Hollow Oak* (1935), *The Mystery of the Moss Covered Mansion* (1941), *The Clue in the Crumbling Wall* (1941). By trading these books and discussing them with me, Peggy became my first intellectual partner. I bought my copies with baby-sitting money, since my local branch librarian refused to order them because they were not considered "literature." In high school Peggy and I drifted off into different crowds and we never saw each other again after graduation. She probably never realized that she had given me a life-long gift.

At the time I read the Nancy Drew books in the late forties or fifties, they were already somewhat dated, most of them having been written before I was born. Unknown to me, the stage was being set in America for the social changes which occurred in the sixties. The days of mansions, like those in the Nancy Drew novels, big enough to have hidden passages, girls whose widowed fathers could provide live-in housekeepers, or country estates with secret gardens were passing quickly away. Situations like this were more fantasy than fact for most Americans anyway. What was new was the possibility that for the first time, poor working class girls like me could believe that, through education and/or marriage, there was a chance to climb up a social rung or two. My hopes were fueled by the fact that I had some distant relatives who might accept me into an environment much like that which I perceived to be the world of Nancy Drew.

The fictional settings and social situations of the Nancy Drew novels paralleled my real life experiences and memories of my wealthy Great Aunt Mattie and Uncle Boyd who lived just far enough away in Cleveland, Ohio, not to be a real part of my life. Aunt Mattie and Uncle Boyd lived opulently in an impressive house in Shaker Heights with a staff of servants, a sleek car and driver, manicured gardens. My Uncle Boyd was suave, sending me off when I left for home with boxes of French bon-bons. My Aunt Mattie wore floating chiffon dressing gowns with ostrich feathers and called people "darling." To me they were characters from books or movies, come to life. My mother and I were often invited there for visits and the contrast between their lives and mine at home was staggering.

Born in 1940, I was an only child. In the blue-collar Detroit neighborhood where we lived, fathers worked hard and were worn out at the end of the day. There was no such thing as "quality time." Both my parents were remote and unreachable. My father drank and my mother, after doing "her housework," encapsulated herself in a world of radio stories and cigarette smoke. She never wanted me to "bother her" and frequently went into sudden violent rages over unstated offenses.

It didn't take me long to figure out that the best way to stay out of trouble was to become silent and invisible. Books were my instruments for disappearance. They were also my companions. Ignored by my parents, I was the loneliest child in the world. My mother was unable to bear more children, so there was no hope that I would ever have a brother or sister. By day I wandered around the neighborhood, drifting through people's gardens, little backyard beds of roses, zinnias, asters and the like. At dusk I peered into people's windows as they sat around their dinner tables *en famille*. When it became cold and dark I went back home and lost myself in the lives and situations of fictional characters. People thought I was a good child because I was "seen and not heard."

Our visits to Cleveland were like walks onto a Nick and Nora Charles movie set. My mother hated every moment, complaining that life there "made her nervous." Eventually she stopped going, and I was permitted to travel alone, but only on the condition that I behaved myself and never let anyone know certain "family secrets." These secrets consisted of things no small children should ever know about. Perhaps one reason detective stories have always appealed to me rests with the fact that so much of my life was influenced by the keeping of secrets. Una Rae Hark points out that in mysteries like Agatha Christie's and others, "the efforts of the detective and the unfolding of the narrative produce gradual revelations of previously concealed information about the characters" (36). The things I knew about as a kindergartner eventually came to light over the next twenty years but I had to live with them throughout my childhood. I had first hand knowledge of cruel child abuse, lying, theft and cheating amongst family members, and the stealing and hiding of my illegitimate cousin from her natural mother, who knew of the girl's existence but was not able to find her. Yet, before I entered kindergarten, I knew all about the secrets and my parents were aware of this.

My parents warned me that if my great-aunt and uncle ever found out about these things, I would never be permitted to see them again. I believed this. So for year after year I went on my summer visits with sealed lips, secretly hoping, longing and praying that my great-aunt and uncle would somehow decide that they wanted me to come and live with them. Each time I went to see them I coveted their world because it was so beautiful and carefree, but I never dared tell them about the realities of mine.

My parents had me convinced that people didn't take seriously what little girls said and that talking to anyone about "family business" was the worst form of ingratitude. They had shown me very forcefully what happens to an "ungrateful child." I feared that if I told my great-aunt and uncle the "secrets," they wouldn't believe me, that they would think I was "telling stories," or they would be disgusted and not like me any more. Who would ever want an ungrateful child, I questioned. Occasionally I had tried running away but I was a little girl and not very articulate. I suppose it was because I showed no outward signs of abuse that the police or the people on whose front porches

I deposited myself simply took me home. Later, I ran away by reading. Today, as an adult, I wonder at how forcefully I was trapped by my parent's power to intimidate, imprisoned by the "silence" that Mary Field Belenky and her associates describe in *Women's Ways of Knowing*. Many years were to pass before I would find a voice.

So I waited. As if there were some magic in time, I thought that my aunt and uncle would eventually send for me or I would go away to college. During these years, thanks to the beautiful Book Lady from the local public library, I became a dedicated reader. As I hoped and dreamed that someday I would grow up and have a life of my own, I passed the time with books. I planned to model my life after what I found from looking in windows, inveigling myself into other family situations, movies, but most of all, from books.

This was when Peggy introduced me to Nancy Drew. For the first time, I found a fictional "friend" and role model, someone with whom I could identify. Nancy was high-spirited, intelligent, inquisitive and independent. These attributes were beginning to manifest themselves in me and Nancy's characterization offered a finished picture of a person who both possessed and used them in a positive way. In *Rascals at Large; or, The Clue in the Old Nostalgia*, Arthur Prager reports that Nancy is a character that little girls can plausibly "pretend to be." She "inhabits the fantasy world in which pre-pubescent girls live in day-dreams." Russel B. Nye adds that Nancy is "a poised, capable, self-sufficient girl in control of her life; one who can take care of herself and who needs neither guidance nor exhortation" (both qtd. in Shepherd 262).

Since I was basically on my own, in spite of my parents, friends, and neighborhood, Nancy's image was very important. Lois Marchino observes that people read detective stories because they "can simultaneously and safely identify with the victim, the wrong-doer, and the detective, most consciously with the admirable qualities of the detective" (98). Even more than this, however, Nancy Drew and her fictional world gave me inspiration. In them I found lessons in deportment for when I would enter the middle class, even upper-middle class, worlds which, up until the time I started reading, I had known only through movies, books and my trips to Cleveland.

During this period of the late forties and early fifties, many young girls like myself were beginning to get a taste of a better life through mass media. Opportunities were opening up, primarily through public education, for girls to develop their brains and talents and find use for them in a broader world than that of their mothers. At this time of incipient social ferment and upward mobility, I was more than ready to leave my childhood behind. While my classmates, neighbors and parents were content with the limited social interactions amongst their own parents, siblings, and a few close neighbors, I put myself in ever new situations. I explored unfamiliar neighborhoods on my bike, rode the bus "downtown" to wander around the stores and office buildings, just looking around. No one seemed to share my curiosity, so I did this wandering alone, too lacking in social skills or confidence to interact with the strangers I observed.

By reading Nancy Drew novels I was able to enter Aunt Mattie and Uncle Boyd's world, only I didn't have to worry about making mistakes. I could dwell there whenever I opened the book. Additionally, these novels provided me with the illusion of desired family and possessions. Nancy Drew's father, a lawyer, was a man a girl could be proud of and emulate. There was no mother to complicate things. Also, Nancy had girl "chums" and an enviable boyfriend named Ned. She also had the poise, charm and confidence in social situations that would paralyze me with fear. In addition to her personal characteristics, Nancy had desirable possessions. She wore "smart" clothes and drove her own car, a snappy little roadster. I longed for Nancy's ease and grace and I believed that if I read enough books in the series I would somehow learn all that I needed to know. From observing her in various situations I thought I would learn how to act so that when the time came to start living the life I dreamed about, I would be prepared.

Most important, I identified with Nancy because, like me, she operated independently. For example, *The Hidden Staircase* (1930) begins as Nancy, alone in the house, confronts an angry visitor who has forced his way in.

> Nancy knew that she must act quickly, for she saw the man was beside himself with rage. Unless she handed over the papers he demanded she did not doubt but that he would attempt to do her bodily injury. She must depend upon her own wits to save her, for there was no one within calling distance. If only she could reach the telephone! (8)

Even though she had friends and associates, it was Nancy's unique curiosity that got her involved in the mysteries and her keen intelligence that enabled them to solve them. She saw things that others didn't and even when others become confused or misled, Nancy kept to her own council. In *The Haunted Bridge* (1937), Nancy's ball gets lost in the rough and her caddy is reluctant to help her look for it because he and the others believe they have seen a ghost there. Nancy's girlfriend, George, is content to forget about the ball and continue: but not the young detective. "Nancy's thoughts were upon the remark made by her caddy. She meant to learn more from him about the haunted bridge. She would question the lad as soon as the round should be over" (6). It's hard to tell today if I became like Nancy or if I was attracted to her as a character because she was like me. For the first time in my young life, the character and life of Nancy Drew gave me something on which to focus.

Although Nancy seemed like a good role model for me, some critics have pointed out her inadequacies (Caprio 2). Nancy Drew never has to deal with some of the hard facts of life. She never seems to want for money, is never bored or affected by personal tragedy. Since she has no mother, she does not have to deal with that complex relationship. Her father has little involvement in the stories and she has no brothers or sisters. Like me, she is on her own. Nor is there much said, at least in the earlier books, about her relationship with Ned, other than that he is somewhat remotely there to introduce her to people and situations and occasionally help in her sleuthing.

Like Peter Pan, she is eternally young and carefree. At the time I was reading these books I wasn't confronting reality either; I was escaping it. I didn't have the opportunities or wherewithal to deal straightforwardly and confidently with life until I was much older. Carol Billman asserts that Nancy is "so far removed from the little qualms and the big frustrations and decisions facing real girls and women that she cannot be considered a helpful fictional model of successful womanhood" (Shepherd 262). For these very reasons, however, she was helpful to me. Most of my childhood, it seems, was a time of waiting, patiently sitting it out until adulthood, when I would have acquired the education, money, contacts and social graces to live the way I thought Nancy lived.

As I progressed through high school, I drifted away from the Nancy Drew series. Learning wasn't easy; I was a bright but sloppy, disorganized and careless student, wanting to do well but not knowing how. A college-prep curriculum was mandatory for the education which I had been planning on all my life, although I had no concrete idea of what I expected to get from college. Like many girls of my generation, I hoped to meet a man like Nancy's Ned, who was studying for one of the professions, and marry him, thereby entering into a middle-class land of dreams.

I lost sight of Nancy Drew when my tenth grade English teacher scared me into reading the Canon. He haughtily announced that no one could truly be considered "educated" without having read the entire Hutchinson list of Great Books. In my mind, becoming "educated" was the only way out of the slums, into college and, ultimately, down the aisle. Therefore, reading the classics took precedence over mysteries and all other extracurricular reading. Years passed before I, then quite "educated" but unhappily still single, ran across Agatha Christie in an airport bookstore. *The Murder of Henry Ackroyd* vaulted me out of the real world of my studies and job and into the land of my former dreams. Over the next several years, I escaped into many Agatha Christie mysteries. They depicted a world in complete contrast to the one in which I lived as a single, urban-dwelling high school teacher. The plots moved along, the settings were distant and the characters were different from the people with whom I came in daily contact. Reading Agatha Christie was like having a cup of tea with an old friend after a long day. I liked the quiet English country villages where genteel people handled delicate issues discretely, even those involved with murder. Christie's formulaic plots were soothing because of the basic underlying tenant of all standard murder mysteries: the reader always knows the mystery is going to be solved and good will triumph over evil. Unlike the tumult of the sixties, things in the world of the mystery are always orderly. The reader knows that all the riddles put forth in the beginning of an Agatha Christie mystery will be solved without ambiguity.

I no longer looked at Christie's detectives as role models, as I had with Nancy Drew, although I admired and envied their powers of deduction. Instead, I began to view them as alter-egos. They were characters with whom I shared important values. Though Christie presents a wide, and sometimes conflicting, range of female characters, Vipond maintains that, "the independent, self-sufficient, capable and courageous woman who is respected for those qualities and treated as an equal partner in adventure and in life coexisted with the silly, emotional woman who has no identity except through her husband and her children" (122). A similar duality existed in me as I tried to work out that conflict between autonomy and interdependence which confronts many professional women.

Also, in spite of their sometimes comic quirks and peculiarities, Miss Marple and Hercule Poirot wanted to help and protect decent people. Their endeavors were always concerned with getting at the root of evil, exposing it, and getting rid of it. In the end, evil was taken away by the constable. Like many others at the time, I was developing a social consciousness. My emergent sense of social responsibility was reinforced by these characters all the while they were helping me run away from alarming issues in the real world. Television, a supreme avenue of mind flight, brought me right into the jungles of Vietnam and into the midst of peace marches, sit-ins and other demonstrations to confront the realities of intolerance, brutality and death. Then, as now, I sometimes need to find respite in the controlled atmosphere of a book which does not raise new questions but which provides predictable and comforting answers to old ones.

Someone suggested that if I liked reading Agatha Christie I ought to try reading Dorothy Sayers, whose characters were more intellectually sophisticated than Christies' were. In Harriet Vane of *Gaudy Night* I again found a woman I wanted to emulate. I was reading these books at a time in my life when I was trying to work out just what kind of woman I wanted to be.

In college I had been engrossed in discovering new worlds of ideas, yet learning was so difficult and time-consuming that I had no time for dating or a social life. Consequently, I completely forgot that I had gone there, in the first place, to get an M.R.S. degree. By my late twenties, when I started thinking about marriage, I knew the conventional home and family I had instantiated into Nancy Drew's future was not to be for me. In college I had discovered that ideas were things to actively pursue and exchange and, more importantly, I found people with whom to share these ideas. However, I feared that marriage and a family would force me to give up my career and encroach on my intellectual life, as it probably would have then. Also, I was reluctant to lose the financial security which a teaching contract then offered and/or to become dependent on a man. Recollections of my childhood family trapped in its misery because of my father's failures and my mother's dependence ever haunted me.

Sayers' romance between Harriet Vane and Lord Peter Wimsey provided hope of a relationship different from that of my parents. Like other classic detectives, Sir Peter and Harriet were benign people. They did good deeds and had real class. Sir Peter loved Harriet because she was intelligent and independent. True, their marriage in *Busman's Honeymoon* was pure fantasy. There was little likelihood that I would meet, much less marry, a titled nobleman with a valet or that we would rent a house in the English countryside and, unfettered by jobs, solve mysteries. Clearly, I was still dreaming.

Nonetheless, Harriet Vane struck sympathetic chords in me even though she was unlike any woman I knew. Similar to many English women, both real and fictional, she was private, independent and intellectual. Gayle F. Wald points out that Harriet is "neither beautiful nor virginal," "a woman who haunts apartments peopled with feminists, intellectuals, androgynes, and Bolsheviks" (101–102). Thus she was, in certain ways, a prototype for the woman I was then becoming. In a departure from traditional detective fiction, Sayers depicts the relationship between the two detectives in an innovative way. In *Gaudy Night*, Peter is seen entirely through Harriet's eyes and thus is shown as "an object of female vision . . . a male sex object" (Heilbrun 306). Sayers herself says in an essay entitled "Gaudy Night" that she intentionally violated the rules of detective story writing by having the characters fall in love. Peter, who is on the surface a "comedian," is drawn to Harriet by her intellectual integrity. "Harriet, with her lively and inquisitive mind and her soul grounded upon reality, is his [Peter's] complement" (219). Their love affair, which defies the traditions of classical detective fiction, inspired my own incipient desire to form a lasting co-equal bond with a man who could both fascinate and save me, but as my partner, not my controller.

In the years that followed I read widely and diversely. I left high school teaching, ran a private research foundation, obtained a Master's degree, and became a member of a college faculty. As my professional and intellectual life grew, I developed a wide circle of friends and associates. Like Nancy, in my twenties I had girl friends and beaux. With one or two exceptions, these female friends were "chums," but because we were competitive for male attention these relationships were predictably shallow; we were unaware then that we needed each other.

Later, in my thirties, I found another social strata. I lived in a neighborhood not unlike a village and, like Miss Marple, I had a place in it. I became one of the community leaders and made some genuine friends. I fell in love with a man, a little like Ned and Peter Whimsey, who helped from the sidelines when asked but did not try to run my life. We had some happy years together and then he died, still a young man in his forties. Suddenly and unexpectedly I was alone again. After that, the self-sufficiency I admired in all these fictional women detectives ceased to be merely an admirable quality and became an attribute I needed for my own security.

I started reading and being influenced by classic feminist authors like Gloria Steinem, Phyllis Chessler, Kate Millet, Simone de Beauvoir. My personal relationships with women deepened and became more intimate. I began to see that my response to the detectives I had enjoyed reading about, especially but not exclusively the female ones, was changing. With the passage of time, they had gradually and imperceptibly ceased to be my idols and had become, in many important ways, my equals.

When I had finished reading all the Dorothy Sayers mysteries, I moved on to P. D. James, Martha Grimes, Margery Allingham, Catherine Aird, Antonia Fraser, Ruth Rendell, Ngaio Marsh and others. I still needed to get away to the English countryside and spend weekends in stately mansions. Without being conscious of any prejudice, I almost always selected books by women authors.

For the most part, the detectives or protagonists of many of these authors are women unencumbered by marriage or family. It has been pointed out by critics that even when the detectives are male, as in the case of Sayers's Lord Peter Wimsey, Christie's Hercule Poirot, James's Adam Dalgliesh, or Grimes's Superintendent Richard Jury or Braun's Qwilleran, they are not traditionally masculine. Compared to such types as Ellery Queen or Mickey Spillane, they are definitely soft-boiled. Wimsey could be described as prissy, Poirot wears a hair net to bed, Dalgliesh is a respected poet who relies on his intellect instead of force (Irons 128), Jury falls in love with a woman who is murdered, and Qwilleran has fled his job as a crime writer to live alone in a remote Michigan town with two Siamese cats. All of these men but Wimsey and Jury distance themselves from marriage and eschew physical intimacy. Like these characters, I was unencumbered by marriage. On the other hand, I still enjoyed sexual relationships with men and believed that someday one of these relationships would culminate in marriage.

During this time I was starting to become a little dissatisfied with the asexuality of the protagonists of many of these novels.[1] I empathized with the sleuths' competence in solving crimes, but wished they were a little more like me in desiring a home and family. As far back as Nancy Drew and even before, sex seems to be antithetical to sleuthing.[2] In fact, it was against the rules of traditional detective fiction (Van Dine 169). The suggestion lurks that an active sex life might diminish the detective's powers, like the athlete warned by the football coach to maintain sexual abstinence before the game or the troops advised to do so by the commander on the eve of battle. The absence of entanglements is, of course, a plot device which allows the detective to proceed toward the crime's solution unhampered by the unexpected events which occur during the course of a normal intimate relationship. Also, it is easier for an author to control a character whose primary artistic purpose is to solve a crime, when that character is alone.

Eventually, I found my way back to finishing my doctorate and was compelled to read through stacks of difficult tomes to prepare for my exams and dissertation. There was little time for recreational reading or for anything else. Still I found that reading mysteries gave me the balance and escape I needed. This time, however, I started reading American writers. I felt I had pretty much read through the canon of British mysteries and felt I needed a change. Now I believe it was because I, myself, had changed.

The light-as-air cat mysteries, for instance, by Lillian Jackson Braun, counter-balanced the writings of such people as Roman Imgarden, Wolfgang Iser, Roland Barthes, Fredric Jameson, or Noam Chomsky, and a host of empirical researchers who published in such journals as

CAROL S. CHADWICK

Reading Research Quarterly or *Journal of Experimental Psychology*. The importance of the work of these outstanding and deserving scholars is well-known and acknowledged, but they tend to weigh heavily even on those gluttons for punishment like me who view thinking alone as a form of entertainment. So I escaped into mysteries.

During the week, I rose before dawn, read the academic material, and then went to work with a paperback mystery in my briefcase to read during free moments. The paperbacks kept me from thinking and worrying about my studies at times when I couldn't work on them. Evenings I read or wrote until nightfall. On weekends I either read or wrote during the day and went to the movies when my brain gave out. Around midnight each night I retreated to my bed and read my mystery novels. Since I tend to dream about what I've been reading, the mystery novels kept me from having nightmares about my dissertation. Once someone, a male, asked why I was always reading books by and about women when I wasn't studying. A good question, I thought. It made me realize that I had made the books, the authors, and the detectives my guardian angels, talismans which protected me from harshness of my academic and professional worlds. They allowed me to disappear into the mysteries and hide, just as I did when I was a child. Old habits die hard. Deep into the writing of my dissertation I started to find great pleasure and satisfaction in the mysteries by American writers like Amanda Cross (Carolyn Heilbrun), Sara Paretsky, Sue Grafton, Susan Kenny and Elizabeth George. Marele Day, an Australian feminist private-eye novelist, says she modeled her feminist private investigator after those of the American school, "because it allowed a greater questioning of traditional roles, both in terms of the real world and the conventions of the genre" (Littler 121).

In many ways the lives of these more recent fictional detectives were similar to mine. Apparently, I no longer felt compelled to flee to the English countryside, since these novels' protagonists live in urban settings, as do I. Furthermore, Cross's Kay Fanzler and Kenny's Rosamund Howard are academics like Cross and Kenny themselves. Both writers' women are shrewd and cerebral, two qualities I recognize and admire in myself. Kay Fanzler seems to like men and is happily married without letting her relationship get in the way of her professional life or her sleuthing which, of course, are interconnected. I can buy that too. Growing up as I did, always the maverick, made me weed-tough, so I can also find a source of identification in the gumshoes of Paretsky and Grafton. That all of these female detectives express an active interest in heterosexual relationships, albeit with varying degrees of depth and intensity, parallels my own life.

By this time there existed around me an extensive network of friends, both men and women, some of whom I had known since college, who had become the surrogate family I sought as a child. There were older women, friends and mentors, to whom I turned for advice, other women who were like older sisters, and eventually there were women who looked up to me. I was drawn to the fictional women of these American authors because I had become like them. Glenwood Irons points out that, unlike hard-boiled male detectives, female detectives "exhibit emotional and intellectual concern for many of the characters," that their "strength comes from [their] emotions," and they accept help from other women (130).

The characters of all these novels have more depth and humanity than those of traditional classic detective stories. The creators of Nancy Drew gave a superficial picture of a stereotyped middle-class female—adventurous, intelligent and independent—who is at the same time shallow, sexless, and lacking a real life or future. It is even questionable that she was an appropriate model for young girls, like me, in the fifties. For a girl today the Nancy Drew of the thirties must have little credibility. As time went by I chose characters like Miss Marple, Harriet Vane and others who were progressively more subtle and complex. The prissy male detectives blended with the ever stronger female sleuths to merge into characters as androgynous as V. I. Warshawski, who, while being a woman, takes her licks like a man, or BBC's hard-boiled Jane Tennison, who has never existed in literature at all but has become one of the most popular androgynous mystery icons to date.

Tonight I return to my Elizabeth George mystery. Even though her novels are set in England and the main detective is male, unmarried, and a peer, they are not traditional British Novels of Manners. The consummated heterosexuality of Scotland Yard Detective Lord Lynly is unambiguous, even though he, like me, still hasn't quite worked out all the details of settling into a relationship and getting married. Lynly proceeds with his investigation and the murder will eventually be solved, but in the course of the story the various characters will work on their personal and social problems. Tomorrow night I will watch the final installment of *Prime Suspect: Three* to see if Scotland Yard CID, Vice Division, Jane Tennison will be able to find a seamy murderer. Still in keeping with feminist detectives, she is surrounded with violence but she does not partake in it herself, not yet. I will also find out how the no longer young, never married detective will deal with the pregnancy that has resulted from an affair with a married man she does not love. The ancillary problems and issues presented in these modern works are or have been the concerns of my friends and myself.

One of the ways literature enhances the lives of readers is by providing characters with which readers can identify and situations which they can experience vicariously. In light of observations from political literary criticism, it is no surprise to me that detectives and their cadre of surrounding characters enact solutions to these thorny problems of life, while they go about their usual job of entertaining through detection. They are on the cutting edge and, as they always have, they serve me.

---

[1] This is in marked contrast to the more sexually active protagonists of very recent detective fiction by such authors as Linda Barnes or Sue Grafton.

[2] We must note that even though I read most of these British Novels of Manners during the late seventies and eighties, many of them were written in an earlier time when readers were not privy to the sex lives of the characters.

BIBLIOGRAPHY

Belenky, Mary Field, Blythe McVicker Clinchy, Nancy Rule Goldberger, and Jill Mattuck Tarule. *Women's Ways of Knowing*. New York: Basic Books, 1986.

Caprio, Betsy. *The Mystery of Nancy Drew: Girl Sleuth on the Couch*. Trabuco Canyon, California: Source Books, 1992.

Cawelti, John G. *Adventure, Mystery and Romance: Formula Stories as Art and Popular Culture*. Chicago: U of Chicago P, 1976.

George, Elizabeth. *Missing Joseph*. New York: Bantam, 1993.

Hark, Ina Rae. "Twelve Angry People: Conflicting Revelatory Strategies in *Murder on the Orient Express*." *Literature/Film Quarterly* 51 (1987): 36–42.

Heilbrun, Carolyn G. *Hamlet's Mother and Other Women*. New York: Ballantine Books, 1990.

Irons, Glenwood, ed. *Gender, Language and Myth: Essays on Popular Narrative*. Toronto: University of Toronto P, 1992.

Littler, Alison. "Marele Day's 'Cold Hard Bitch': The Masculine Imperatives of the Private-Eye Genre." *Journal of Narrative Technique* 21 (Winter 1991): 121–55.

Marchino, Lois A. "The Female Sleuth in Academe." *Journal of Popular Culture* 3 (Winter 1989): 89–100.

Sayers, Dorothy L. "Gaudy Night." *The Art of the Mystery Story*. Ed. Howard Haycraft. New York: Carroll & Graf Publishers, Inc., 1992. 208–21.

Shepherd, Kenneth R. "Carolyn Keene [Collective Pseudonym]." *Contemporary Authors*. New Revision Series. 42 Vol. to date. Ed. Hal May, James G. Lesniak. Vol. 27. 259–263. Detroit: Gale, 1989–.

Van Dine, S. S. "Twenty Rules for Writing Detective Stories." *The Art of the Mystery Story*. Ed. Howard Haycraft. New York: Carroll & Graf Publishers, Inc., 1992. 189–93.

Vipond, M. "Agatha Christie's Women." *The International Fiction Review* 8 (Summer 1981): 119–23.

Wald, Gayle F. "*Strong Poison*: Love and the Novelistic in Dorothy Sayers." *The Cunning Craft: Original Essays on Detective Fiction and Contemporary Literary Theory*. Ed. Ronald G.Walker, June S. Frazer. Macomb, Illinois: Yeast Printing, Inc., 1990.

WRESTLING WITH THE MOTHER AND THE FATHER
"HIS" AND "HER" IN ADRIENNE RICH

BETTY S. FLOWERS

O n a summer Texas day twenty years ago, a footnote to a poem shifted the geography of my mind. I have been wrestling with the issues this footnote raised ever since. The poem was Adrienne Rich's lyric "Afterward":

> Now that your hopes are shamed, you stand
> At last believing and resigned,
> And none of us who touch your hand
> Know how to give you back in kind
> The words you flung when hopes were proud:
> *Being born to happiness*
> *Above the asking of the crowd,*
> *You would not take a finger less.*
> We who know limits now give room
> To one who grows to fit her doom. (2)

The footnote simply said that "her doom" was originally "his doom." Rich explained this change in a note to "The Tourist and the Town":

> The pronouns in the third part of the poem were origi-
> nally masculine. But the tourist was a woman, myself, and I
> never saw her as anything else. In 1953, when the poem was
> written, some notion of "universality" prevailed which made
> the feminine pronoun suspect, "personal." In this poem, and
> in "Afterward" in *A Change of World*, I have altered the pro-
> nouns not simply as a matter of fact but because they alter, for
> me, the dimensions of the poem. (247)

What Rich was saying to me is that she took a poem that was originally universal ("his") and simply by changing one pronoun ("his" to
"her") made it "merely" subjective, personal, and political. When the

pronoun is masculine, "We who know limits" is all humankind; when the pronoun is feminine, "We who know limits" are the other women now giving room "To one who grows to fit her doom." With "his" now "her," would the poem last beyond the feminist politics of the times within which it was written? Had Rich limited the long-term impact of the poem—its life?—by packing it in the fiery passion of the political moment rather than the salt and ice of the universal human condition?

More to the point: would I, in my role as teacher and literary critic, ever make such a "his" to "her" move, knowing how it would limit the impact of my voice? It seemed unthinkable, for I had worked most of my life to move out of the circumscribed realm of the mother, with its swamps of subjectivity and endless round of chores and dependencies upon the male, into the rock-like realm of the father, with its clear, cool, dispassionate atmosphere (so I imagined) and its world of books rather than babies. What hard labor it had cost to fly out of "her" nest and up into "his" tower. And once in the tower, what dangers of falling were all around.

I remember during my first semester as an assistant professor, one of my colleagues asking me how I felt knowing that I had taken a job that might otherwise have gone to a man who had to support a family. I remember considering submitting articles under non-gendered initials—except that I had the misfortune of having "B. S." as those initials. I remember . . . but these sorts of things happened to many of us who lived through this time.

Some dangers were more subtle. My first semester, a number of female graduate students asked me to help found a consciousness-raising group. In the heady early days of feminism, these CR groups formed the living cells of what became a new body of thought leading to action. Small and without media scrutiny, intimate and honest, these groups did just what they were called—they raised consciousness. We discovered that our most private fears were shared, that, for example, we all felt we had gotten into graduate school by some kind of fluke and that we would sooner or later be unmasked as the charlatans that we were. But I was not in graduate school any more, I was the one professor in a group of students who might take a course from me. Feminist solidarity?—or conduct unbecoming a professional? What would it mean for my academic reputation that my female students were hearing my most intimate fears as a woman? Soon I observed that my male colleagues were "Dr. Smith" and "Professor Jones," and I was "Betty Sue."

Other dangers were more subtle yet. As a five-year-old, sitting in the front row of the Methodist Church in Abilene, Texas, I whiled away the sermons of Dallas Denver Denison (some names are worse than "Betty Sue") by looking at the stained glass windows. My favorite was the one of Mary and Martha. Mary, the attentive student, was sitting at the feet of the Lord, and Martha was standing in the doorway holding a tray. I could almost hear her complaint because it echoed what my mother would say to my father: "Why don't you tell her to come help me in the kitchen?" And then the words of the Lord: "Martha, Martha, thou art careful and troubled about many things: But one thing is needful: and Mary hath chosen that good part, which shall not be taken away from her."

I was determined to choose the "good part," not the serving tray—the world of teachers and students, which I identified with the master in the living room (fathers) and not the mothers in the kitchen.

> Nervy, glowering, your daughter
> wipes the teaspoons, grows another way.
> (from Rich, "Snapshots of a Daughter-in-Law" 12)

But in my first year as an assistant professor, I was appointed to seventeen committees as the "token woman." And I spent countless hours counseling female students, including three who were suffering sexual harassment (as we later learned to call it) from senior professors in my college—what to do? I quickly realized that the job of female literature professor involved so much counseling that I needed to know more about psychology and so began a formal study of the subject. And then one day the associate dean of my college said, "Every minute you spend with a student is a minute you're not spending doing your research." And I was told that seventeen committees was fifteen more than my assistant professor colleagues had been asked to serve on. I was not so different from my mother after all, "careful and troubled about many things." And what was "that good part" that would not be taken away from me? My research leading to tenure? Should I turn away all the young women who were trying to find their voice so that I could write feminist literary criticism? So I could find my own voice of authority? So I could forget "her" problems and enter "his" universal world? What was my work in the world?

And what was the world in which I was working? I was in the same department as my male colleagues—but we seemed to be in utterly different worlds.

Which was the "real world" of a literature professor in a large, research university? What did it mean to teach human beings, especially women, and not just texts? What was the function of criticism:

Knowledge for its own sake? To lead readers to a greater appreciation of a poem? To make students better readers and writers and so more effective as workers and citizens and leaders? To increase the capacity for joy through art? To serve my university by enhancing my reputation as a critic, thereby adding to the reputation of the university? Was the best thing I could do as a professor to close my door and read and write? After all, that is what had drawn me to the profession in the first place.

> There must be ways, and we will be finding out more and more about them, in which the energy of creation and the energy of relation can be united. But in those earlier years I always felt the conflict as a failure of love in myself. (Rich, "When We Dead Awaken" 2)

Now, here, in the middle of this article, I also am wrestling with the mother and the father. The energy of relation moves me in the direction of service—I want what I am saying to be of some use to you. I'm afraid I haven't said enough about Adrienne Rich's poetry, to share my admiration for her work and her life. I feel I should go to the kitchen and make some literary criticism and come back with a tray of it for you. In our profession, the mothers serve the fathers in us all.

But the voice that speaks with this desire is not the voice of the professional critic. The professional critic was not invited to this party. Instead, as the editor of this book says, "each woman is concerned with telling how the pursuit of literary study has, in a real sense, shaped her perceptions of her self and her work."

So what happened when I pursued the poetry of Adrienne Rich, the poet who changed "his" to "her"? First I went "Diving Into the Wreck":

I am she: I am he

whose drowned face sleeps with open eyes
whose breasts still bear the stress
whose silver, copper, vermeil cargo lies
obscurely inside barrels
half-wedged and left to rot
we are the half-destroyed instruments
that once held to a course

---

the water-eaten log
the fouled compass

We are, I am, you are
by cowardice or courage
the one who find our way back to this scene
carrying a knife, a camera
a book of myths
in which
our names do not appear. (67–68)

Yes, that was what I was up to—plotting a new course, asserting my identity apart from the old myths, uniting the male and female within:

if I come into a room out of the sharp misty light
and hear them talking a dead language
if they ask me my identity
what can I say but
I am the androgyne
I am the living mind you fail to describe
in your dead language.
(from Rich, "The Stranger" 65)

The image of the androgyne was compelling, for it seemed to offer a way beyond the polarized dualities of creation and relation that so plagued my work. True there was no androgynous pronoun to take the place of the polarized "his" and "her"; true there was no history or literature of androgyny to speak of and so nothing to ground it in. The androgyne was the vision of a future, not a clue to what had shaped us. No wonder female writers like Virginia Woolf and Adrienne Rich were drawn to it.

But then Rich moved more fully into "her," repudiating the androgyne in both her poetry and her prose:

There are words I cannot choose again:
humanism   androgyny

Such words have no shame in them, no diffidence
before the raging stoic grandmothers:
their glint is too shallow, like a dye
that does not permeate

---

the fibres of actual life
as we live it, now . . .
(from Rich, "Natural Resources" 62)

As Rich put it, "The very structure of the word replicates the sexual dichotomy and the priority of *andros* (male) over *gyne* (female)" ("The Kingdom of the Fathers" fn. 30).

I could see Rich's point about androgyny, but I only half agreed with her about the raging grandmothers. I could not join with enthusiasm the more separatist feminists who were trying to find a new female voice, because the voice I knew when I honored the grandmothers was a voice of relation. At that point I began a long journey, a dialogue between the world of the past and the world of the future, mediated by whatever fullness of consciousness I could gather in the present. I could see my profession through that dialogue, knowing that whatever it would be in the future could not be a mere continuation of the past. Certain freedoms began to emerge.

One had to do with polarization, the tendency of the mind to turn difference into opposites. I began to emerge from the world of duality when I read a simple story in Irene de Castillejo's *Knowing Woman* about a woman who dreamed of her soul as a young girl. De Castillejo, a Jungian analyst, was familiar with Jung's dictum: "If, therefore, we speak of the *anima* of a man we must logically speak of the *animus* of a woman, if we are to give the soul of woman its right name" (de Castillejo 170). But what de Castillejo saw was that the female psyche was not set up as the mirror image of the male psyche—that difference was not opposition in spite of what our child minds might have concluded. I once was talking with a six-year-old nephew about a boxer we had seen on TV. He said, "Boys are strong, aren't they?" I said, "Yes." And then he added, "Girls are weak, aren't they?" I could see his thought process at work, its primitive logic: if boys are opposite from girls, and boys are strong, it follows that girls are weak.

We see this oppositional "logic" in much of literature: if men are logical, women are emotional; if men are logos, women are love. The left brain that writes is fascinated by the mystery of the Other. "Until we can understand the assumptions in which we are drenched," says Rich, "we cannot know ourselves" ("When We Dead Awaken" 90).

Understanding "the assumptions in which we are drenched"— that has come to be the passion that motivates my life as a literary critic. I say it a slightly different way—understanding the myths that have made us, the stories we tell about who we are. Like Rich, I have come to see this activity as a combination of poetry and politics. Deconstructing the stories we tell about who we are is political, for it involves wrestling with both the mother and the father of our culture. Seeing the new stories that might be emerging—or helping to give birth to them—falls into the realm of poetry, of mythos. Analysis is useful in the destruction of the old; but mythos holds the energies of vision that create the new.

At one point in the recent feminist re-visioning of early history, it was popular to speak of early matriarchal societies. The archeological evidence for such early cultures has been shown to be problematic—but one image from that conversation about "the matriarchy" has remained with me as a vivid and useful one. It was said that the reason we couldn't find unequivocal evidence of a period of matriarchy was that we were looking for cultures in which queens reigned instead of kings. But that's a polarized, patriarchal way of looking—it's not that a matriarchy would be the polar opposite of a patriarchy, with a queen on the throne instead of a king, but that it would be a different paradigm altogether, one of co-rulership.

With this complex image as a background, I asked the question: what would a methodology look like that was not simply a replacement of "his" by "her"? What if the move to replace the analytical, objective, and universal by the experiential, subjective, and personal is simply a move along the same continuum, like replacing "king" with "queen"? What would an entirely new methodology look like, one that lay outside this bipolar construct?

I have no immediate answer to this question—simply two responses. The first is represented by this article, which, like the other essays in this book, is written in an experiential, subjective, and personal mode. So little has been done from "her" end of the continuum that we have a limited idea of the possibilities or of what new ways of seeing might arise out of this more subjective practice. Even where the methodology has been "objective," as in much feminist criticism, the very act of looking at literature through feminist eyes has led us to put quotation marks around "objective" and "universal." Probably, were we to explore the subjective and personal in greater depth, we would be led to add quotation marks around those adjectives, also. For example, if we remained conscious that "the personal is political," we would be tempted to say "personal," adding the quotation marks to highlight our awareness of the always, already existing interconnectedness of the self with others.

In other words, a methodology that highlights "her" *within* the bipolar construct changes the nature of the poles. I came to appreciate the more separatist aspects of Rich's feminism through understanding this principle.

> . . . and we still have to reckon with Swift
> loathing the woman's flesh while praising her mind,
> Goethe's dread of the Mothers, Claudel vilifying Gide,
> and the ghosts—their hands clasped for centuries—
> of artists dying in childbirth, wise-women charred at the stake,
> centuries of books unwritten piled behind these shelves;
> and we still have to stare into the absence
> of men who would not, women who could not, speak
> to our life—this still unexcavated hole
> called civilization, this act of translation, this half-world.
> (from Rich, "Twenty-One Love Poems" V, 27.)

But my second response to the question of methodology is to suggest a different model, one that lies outside current bipolarizations but takes the tendency toward bipolarization into account. My name for it at the moment is "dialogue," and I mean by this, putting disparate elements into a "working community" with each other and seeing what happens. I'm still groping towards this, but my experiments on the edge of the discipline lead me to feel there is treasure in the area, even if I have not found it in a usable form.

Let me give an example. One of the major assumptions in which we are drenched, to use Rich's phrasing, is what might be called "the economic myth." Material reality is bottom-line reality, and we look at history and literature through the lenses of class and power. We have great difficulty, for example, reading religious literature from within its own assumptions. But what if we consciously created an economic myth—a story about the future of the world, say, which was held as a fiction but used in planning?

Two years ago I joined a team of twenty people, most of them economists, to write global scenarios—the future of the world for the next thirty years. The project was sponsored by a multinational corporation as part of its planning cycle. What made it interesting to a literary critic experimenting with methodological boundaries was the fact that we were to create two equally plausible fictions about the future. These fictions would then be disseminated to company managers worldwide as a way of holding the corporate culture together—but also as a way to think about the future in common without falling under the illusion that we could know what that future might be.

During the time I was writing these stories, the company also sponsored scenario-building for the future of South Africa. Participants in South Africa came to the table to work on "fictions" who had never worked on politics together, and the four stories they created led the participants to adopt a common vision for change. Meanwhile, back in London, three of our team members began talking about the changes that occurred in their thinking about reality from working with the stories. To put it too simply, but briefly: they began to see that while the scenarios we had created were equally plausible, enough people "believing" in one could push events toward that story's conclusions. The dialogue of economic fact and narrative fiction began to result in a view of reality that was much more pliable and that reflected more of the "subjective" mind that looked "out" upon it than the team members had originally thought possible.

"This book is about desire and daily life," says Rich in the preface to *What is Found There: Notebooks on Poetry and Politics*:

> I began it because I needed a way of thinking about poetry outside of writing poems; and about the society I was living and writing in, which smelled to me of timidity, docility, demoralization, acceptance of the unacceptable. In the general public disarray of thinking, of feeling, I saw an atrophy of our power to imagine other ways of navigating into our collective future. (xiii)

"To imagine other ways"—that to me is the power of literature, the essence of the dialogue between readers and poets. Even when literature seems to reflect our experience almost exactly, we are led to see that we are not alone in our sorrow or joy—and in seeing that community of experience, we are seeing "another way."

But I think there are other ways of imagining our roles as literary critics, also. What if our dialogue were not only *with* literature but *from* literature—looking through literature at culture? What if we taught our students and our culture to hold the stories we tell about who we are *as* stories rather than as beliefs? Perhaps we could learn how to listen to each other and how to welcome different stories while searching for common threads. And perhaps as we wrestle with the bipolar categories of mother and father, creation and relation, that have shaped our thinking, we can begin "to imagine other ways of navigating into our collective future."

de Castillejo, Irene Claremont. *Knowing Woman: A Feminine Psychology*. New York: Harper & Row, 1973.

Rich, Adrienne. *Adrienne Rich's Poetry*. Ed. Barbara Charlesworth Gelpi and Albert Gelpi. New York: Norton, 1975.

_____. "Afterward." *Poetry* 2.

_____. "Diving Into the Wreck." *Poetry* 65–68.

_____. "The Kingdom of the Fathers." *Partisan Review* 43 (1976):17–37.

_____. "Natural Resources." *Ms* (Dec. 1977): 62.

_____. *Poems Selected and New, 1950–1974*. New York: Norton, 1975.

_____. Preface. *What is Found There: Notebooks on Poetry and Politics*. By Rich. New York: Norton, 1993. xiii–xv.

_____. "Snapshots of a Daughter-In-Law." *Poetry* 12–16.

_____. "The Stranger." *Poetry* 65.

_____. "The Tourist and the Town." *Poetry* 247.

_____. "Twenty-One Love Poems. V." *The Dream of a Common Language*. New York: Norton, 1978. 27.

_____. "When We Dead Awaken: Writing as Re-Vision." *Poetry* 90–98.

In Search of the Androgynous Self

Nancy Owen Nelson

As I begin this essay, my son, Owen, has spent his day primarily in activities that anyone would expect of a pre-adolescent boy: playing soccer, swinging over a mud patch with two friends, and fencing in the backyard with broom handles and a plastic bat. Yet on another afternoon, he was intent on *discussing* a disagreement with a friend about backyard basketball. As I passed by them, I heard the friend ask, with exasperation: "Do you want to play or talk, Owen?"

Owen's propensity to *discuss* the argument, to talk over differences and feelings, to fear that disagreements may jeopardize a friendship—is counter to what we, as a society, have been led to associate with masculine behavior. Ironically, I was recently told by a female colleague that my classroom manner was "patriarchal"—that I control my classroom in a hierarchical manner. My own organizational approach and my "controlling" manner are apparently not characteristic of the "feminine" style. Carol Gilligan, in her psychological study of men and women, *In a Different Voice*, contends that men "individuate" by separating themselves from their mothers, and in the process see the world in terms of violence and aggression. Women, on the other hand, locate themselves *in relation* to others and see the world as a place to mediate, to respond to others' needs (8–9). In my search to understand the mysteries of relationships of all kinds, I believe both women and men have masculine and feminine traits buried deep in their primordial selves, and that our failure to acknowledge and cultivate these has entrapped us and limited our potential.

The seeds of my questioning about gender were planted in my college years, when I attended a Methodist liberal arts college in Birmingham, Alabama. While adjusting to the rigors of college work—responsibility, new study skills, the occasional stinging "C" grade (I was used to A's in high school), I went through a period of depression and self-doubt. My advisor at the time, a *male* music professor, encouraged me during a counseling session to read *The Feminine Mystique*, which was causing heated controversy. Betty Friedan's shocking exposé of women's subservience to masculine values fueled the feminist movement of the 1960s. Friedan's definition of the problem of what she called the "feminine mystique"—which says that "the highest value and the only commitment for women is the fulfillment of their own femininity"—opened my eyes to the source of my own self-doubt and insecurity. "The great mistake of Western culture," she claims, "has been the undervaluation of this femininity. . . . [T]he root of women's troubles in the past is that women envied men, women tried to be like men, instead of accepting their own nature, which can find fulfillment only in sexual passivity, male domination, and nurturing maternal love" (37).

As I read into the book, I recall being suddenly struck with how much I was expected to *please others* with the academic and personal directions I was taking. I had no *sense of self*, no "individuation" (e.g. Gilligan). I also wondered how much of my previous passivity could be attributed to inherent gender traits. Why was I beginning to feel the pull to speak out for myself and other women? Why was I ready to challenge traditional gender limitations? Why did I see certain traits emerging in myself which were considered "masculine"? Another counselor a year later advised me, despite my future plans to marry, that I be prepared under any circumstances to "take care of myself." (This gentleman, by the way, was an aging scholar, the "Southern gentleman" type, whom one would expect to advise me on the ways and manners of being a "proper lady").

These two incidents were revelations which started me on a difficult yet challenging path of self-discovery, one which continues today. On that journey, my central questions have remained the same: "Who am I, myself, alone?", "Who am I in relation to my gender?", "What limitations, if any, does my gender place on my life?"

The 1970s were spent in pursuit of my masters and doctorate degrees at Auburn University, with intermediate work in the public sector when I tired of the academic treadmill. During this decade I did much to support the raising of consciousness of males and females, attending NOW reading groups, throwing light on obvious sexual biases in my seminars, and having discussions with fellow workers and graduate students in social situations. I was often confronted with jealousy on the part of males who felt I should remember my "place" in society, which was definitely *not* in the professional arena. In the course of working in seminars with other students who were male, I was once confronted by an outright misogynist (he proudly acknowledged the label, though he was married and had two small children); pointing at my modified miniskirt, he challenged me with the following question:

"Nancy, if you don't want men to view you as a sex symbol, why do you wear such short skirts?" I remember being so horrified at the question that I was unable to answer. On another occasion, this same student proclaimed to the professor and other students in a Milton seminar that Adam's lament against Eve's sin was a justified view of *all women:*

> O why did God,
> Creator wise, that peopl'd highest Heav'n
> With Spirits Masculine, create at last
> This novelty on Earth, this fair defect
> Of Nature, and not fill the World at once
> With Men as Angels without Feminine,
> Or find some other way to generate
> Mankind? (427)

Thank God the feminist movement of the sixties had identified the chauvinism illustrated by the poet of *Paradise Lost!* And because I had been made aware of such gender attitudes by the kindly college advisors, I was able to recreate the war of the angels that day against the misogynist classmate.

As the decade of the 1970s came to a close, I completed my doctorate in English and took a job at Albion College in Michigan. I had married in the mid-70s, and the end of the decade represented a coming together of both my *personal* and my professional lives. In 1979, just prior to the birth of my son Owen, I became interested in Western American literature. This new academic direction was to have a profound influence on my *personal* exploration of the issue of female and male dynamics. It was as if I gave birth simultaneously to two very important aspects of myself: my nurturing female self, and my questing, energized male critic.

As the 1980s opened, I focused my research on the writings of a Minnesota author, Frederick Manfred. Manfred, the author of over thirty books, including fiction of the midwestern plains states and the American West, provided me with a new literary approach to the female and male question. As critic and author John R. Milton states, much of serious western literature is decidedly Jungian in nature, dominated by characters who are shaped by the land, by the unconscious archetypal and natural symbols, and by a mythical presence of both good and evil (57–60). I found this to be true with Manfred's fiction, in which he pays close attention to characters' relationships to the land, a kind of cosmic, spiritual relationship which is inherent also in Native American mystical belief.

Two novels in particular came under my scrutiny and helped influence my continuing exploration of androgyny. The first, Manfred's 1976 *Milk of Wolves*, is a story of sculptor Juhl Melander, whose life is portrayed in two distinct segments: city life—"Villain in the Cities"—and life in nature—"Hermit in the Woods." The first half of the novel portrays Juhl in a city life of moral degeneracy, in which he marries into society, sleeps with numerous women before and during his marriage, and in general fails to channel his own creative impulse. In this portion of the novel, Juhl is driven almost exclusively by primal masculine characteristics. The second half of the novel shows his discovery of his own connection to nature; he establishes a home on an island, marries an Indian maiden, Flur, and with her has a baby son. In the course of his "wilderness" life, Juhl rediscovers the other, more feminine part of himself in the physical and spiritual joining with Flur:

> Flur became his religion. . . . [I]n Flur Stoneboiler the Assiniboine maiden, a dark and lovely forest nymph, swollen and spiritual both, he discovered something that awoke in him a profound respect for the sacred. (224)

Consequently, when Flur is murdered by her jealous brother, Juhl is able to draw upon his own *feminine* side in order to save their infant son from starvation. Juhl cuts his left teat with his bowie knife, to give young Wulf a drink of his blood: "Juhl could feel himself leaching away into the boy. His son was taking on his own soul" (242). Several days later, Juhl discovers "a swelling under the nipple about the size of a crab apple. Milk." (242). Juhl has discovered the feminine in himself. This incident, I found out during a telephone interview, relates directly to Manfred's personal experience. In this conversation, Manfred related how in 1944, during his wife's labor with their first child, Freya, he developed a tingling sensation above his left breast. When asked to examine the breast, the doctor discovered a milk sac from which he was able to extract milk. The physician told Manfred that the condition was more common than one would think, *especially when the male was in full sympathy with the biological process of the female!* In reading this novel in the early 1980s, I was still aware of the maternal sensations experienced when I nursed my baby boy; though I found the incident almost incredible, it opened up possibilities for me to view my male friends in a different light.

A second novel by Frederick Manfred which influenced my exploration of the issue of androgyny is *The Manly-Hearted Woman*, a 1975 publication which tells a tale of the Yankton Dakota. In it, Manfred reveals his interest in seeing what would happen if a somewhat androgynous woman and a somewhat androgynous man crossed paths. The plot involves Manly Heart, a woman who takes on a man's role in the tribe, and Flat Warclub, a not-too-masculine brave who dreams of finding clams rather than doing brave and manly deeds.

After Flat Warclub's god-ordained "talking" (sexual intercourse) with many of the maidens in the tribe, Manly Heart has cause to question her own sexual nature. Although the gods have ordained her to be a husband, she laments her femaleness, the frustration of never achieving the "lightning" spoken of by other women: "Manly Heart cried to herself. 'Why wasn't I born a man? Why was I given these breasts? They are of as much use to me as empty cornhusks'" (109).

Flat Warclub's initiation into manhood parallels Manly Heart's initiation into womanhood. Having been with all of the women in the tribe but Manly Heart, he is slain in a battle to protect the tribe's buffalo jump. When the war party brings his body to camp, Manly Heart insists on burying him on the scaffold, allowing none of the mourning maidens with whom he "talked" to participate. Her reasons? That she was his host, that she made her tepee his "new home," that to "separate him from [her would] cut [her] in two" (181). As a result of the rediscovery of her female self, Manly Heart divorces Prettyhead, becomes a recluse, and returns to the separation hut for her monthly menstrual visit. The final image of her in the novel is not as Manly Heart the brave hunter and rider, but as "Silent Woman," with her body "bowed over, a hand to one side of her face as though to hide herself from the people" (185).

When I completed the novel for the first time, I thought Manfred was suggesting the failure of androgyny. Yet when asked about the ending, Manfred said that his interest in writing the novel was in seeing what the meeting of Manly Heart and Flat Warclub *could mean*, to say that, at the very least, it is alright for a man to have feminine qualities and for a woman to have masculine qualities. He felt that what happened between "two people who are catastrophically bound" would perhaps "jump out" at the reader (Interview).

What ultimately "jumped out" at me as I considered *The Manly-Hearted Woman* was not the disillusionment and bitterness which might be suggested in Silent Woman's ending. Rather, Manfred offered me a new way of seeing myself. By showing a woman and a man who have identified their androgynous selves, Manfred presents the possibility of a beautiful relationship, one in which such a female and male may co-exist harmoniously. Indeed, Manfred suggests that, had the gods allowed, the union of Manly Heart with Flat Warclub would have been a sacred, ideal relationship. Mick McAllister's analysis threw light on this issue: "Together the two spirit-touched warriors represent a truly androgynous, psychologically bisexual pair, potentially an ideal marriage couple. Their androgyny is a treasure, to be passed along and cherished, even at the expense of the carriers" (124).

These two novels by Frederick Manfred provide just a sampling of how the more primordial nature of western literature gave me an avenue to explore my own gender definition. In these and other novels, the Native American concept of humankind's closeness to the cosmic order has provided a vehicle for understanding the function of the male and female principles in all of us. Manfred's *Conquering Horse,* as well as works by Native Americans such as Scott Momaday and Frank Waters, reveal an awareness of the female principle, represented by the earth, and the male principle, represented by the sun. And as did *The Manly-Hearted Woman*, these novels showed me the necessity of an interdependence, a blending of both elements to achieve a world in balance. And ironically, I thought, I am seeing these concepts from novels by men, works which I had always considered to represent the bastion of masculinity. The barriers between men and women, it seemed to me, were disappearing.

It is only in recent years that I have found evidence to support the connection between the androgynous principle and Native American thought. Dr. A. C. Ross, of the Mdewakantonwan tribe of the Dakota Sioux, has illustrated the direct connection of the male/female dichotomy to the Native American belief system and to recent research about left and right brain activity. In his unusual book, *Mitakuye Oyasin: "We Are All Related,"* Ross confirms the parallels which exist between Native American ideas and the notion of androgyny. Ross cites Barbara Vitale's delineation of brain activity, which aligns the left brain with the "logical, linear, verbal, abstract, sequential, serial, and *masculine* thought" and the right brain with the "instinctive, wholistic, non-verbal, concrete, random, spatial, and *feminine* thought" (cited in Ross 45, my italics). While Ross concludes that "the right hemisphere [or feminine thought process] forms the doorway to the collective unconscious" (46), he traces a recent resurgence of respect for Native American philosophy and thought, resulting in more "respect for people's individuality" (49). And if, indeed, the male principle is associated with reason and the female with intuition, then Ross agrees with Jung that "one needs to maintain a balance between pairs of opposites, between feeling and thinking, between sensation and intuition" (24).

The possibilities of the androgynous character which I have discovered through both personal experience and formal study have recently led me to consider other approaches to gender. In Betty Friedan's *The Second Stage* (1981), she looks back on the impact of the Vietnam War and the feminist movement. The initial effect of *The Feminine Mystique* and other feminist treatises was to create a dichotomy of the sexes, an angry, back-lashing *separation*; the resulting female independence (131) helped to create a power struggle between men and women (20). Now, Friedan concludes, there is a second stage which involves working *with* men—not against them, "a restructuring of our institutions on a basis of real equality for women and men" (28, 41). Friedan's formula for a successful working out has the flavor of an androgynous balance: "If we can eliminate the false polarities and appreciate the limits and true potential of women's power, we will be able to join with men—follow or lead—in the new human politics that must emerge beyond reaction" (317).

Not only are there signals of a balance coming from the women, but also from the men. For instance, a cover story for the *USA Today Magazine* by Christopher Kimball explores the question of "What Do Men Want?" in the 1990s. Kimball's conclusion, in this more "popular" magazine, is that, while men have been sensitized by the feminist movement, their inner core of male identity has been threatened. Happily, however, the feminist movement has served to "strengthen [men's] inner resolve, sense of identity and sure-footedness"; as a result, the men of the nineties have the "ability to sustain a warm, nurturing relationship with friends and family members. . . . as better fathers and better husbands—but not as better men" (6).

Finally, I find hope in the "men's movement," which, though its force has diminished, has left a lasting impression on male consciousness. On a 1989 Bill Moyers program, "A Gathering of Men," poet Robert Bly, leader of the movement, recreates his pain, grief and ultimately his joy at the loss and rediscovery of his own father. Discussing it further in a recent article in *New Age Journal*, Bly traces the archetypal myths associated with the male rite of passage, claiming that the Industrial Revolution was the beginning of the end of a close father-son relationship in our society. Bly states that we have a "defective mythology" inherited from the Greeks, one which created a polarized world, in which feminine and masculine were torn asunder (44–45). In the wake of this separation, Bly rejects the notion of a dichotomy between the thinking (male) and feeling (female) sides of ourselves. According to Bly, in the "second act" of our understanding of ourselves, we must acknowledge that "men have a tremendous amount of feeling on their masculine side. They don't have to depend on women for feeling" (109).

Bly's viewpoint calls me to challenge the traditional notion that certain characteristics are specifically associated with males or females. It leads me to realize that I need not be afraid to find the opposite sexual character within myself, or to find both characters in those to whom I relate. I would hope that we could move beyond the anguish of separation of our two selves expressed in these lines from an early Bly poem, "A Man Writes to a Part of Himself," wherein the poet speaks to his *feminine side*:

> Which of us two then is the worse off?
> And how did this separation come
> about? (108)

Perhaps the next generation of women and men, now girls and boys, will be more able to put aside the barriers which have separated us and our forebears. As for me, I will strive to accept both parts of myself—the feminine and the "masculine." While I see my son Owen reenact the "traditional" masculine rituals, I also see him continue to explore and express feelings, tap into his own intuitive powers, and live at least comfortably in a world which understands the necessity to blend the male and the female into a healthy totality.

WORKS CITED

Bly, Robert. "The Secret Life of Men." Interview in *New Age Journal* (October 1990):40+.
_____. "A Gathering of Men." With Bill Moyers. National Public Television, 1989.
Friedan, Betty. *The Feminine Mystique*. New York: Dell, 1977.
_____. *The Second Stage*. New York: Summit Books, 1981.
Gilligan, Carol. *In a Different Voice*. Cambridge: Harvard UP, 1982.
Kimball, Christopher. "What Men Want." *USA Weekend* (24–26 August 1990):1+.
McAllister, Mick. Review of *The Manly-Hearted Woman* by Frederick Manfred. *Denver Quarterly* 12 (1977):124.
Manfred, Frederick. Personal interviews. May 8, 1981 and September 1990.
_____. *The Manly-Hearted Woman*. Lincoln: U of Nebraska P, 1975.
_____. *Milk of Wolves*. Boston: Avenue Victor Hugo, 1976.
Milton, John. *Paradise Lost*, Book X. In *Complete Poems and Major Prose*. Indianapolis: Odyssey Press, 1957.
Milton, John R. *The Novel of the American West*. Lincoln: U of Nebraska P, 1980.
Nelson (McCord), Nancy Owen. "Manfred's Developing Vision of the Sexes." Paper delivered at Western Literature Association Meeting, Boise Idaho, 1981.
Ross, A. C. *Mitakuye Oyasin: "We Are All Related."* Fort Yates, N. D.: Bear, 1990.

FROM ROBOT TO ROARER

Jo C. Searles

I t is a truism in the nineties for women to realize that they have been feminists all along, or even, as Carolyn Heilbrun declares, "I had been born a feminist and never wavered from that position" (16). Not I. Considering the power of social conditioning, I would call my previous self, instead, a robot. My girlhood in the thirties and forties consisted of patent-leather shoes at Easter; Sunday school, an earned Bible, confirmation; Brownies, Girl Scout camp, and National Honor Society; Saturday afternoon movies, tennis in the summer, skiing and bowling in the winter. Even a traditional first date, with parents checking him out by inviting him for Sunday chicken dinner before we went to a movie—not to mention going steady in high school, just as all my girlfriends did.

Eventually, I would encounter Anne Wilson Schaef's positive re-definition of "selfish" as a positive process of valuing our own needs, self-discovery, and creativity, of establishing a relationship with the self (115–16), the very thing I am doing this minute.

But not yet. Caught happily in wedded bliss and amateur use of available contraceptives, I had four children in six years, assisted by the then state-of-the-art process of natural childbirth (which had just arrived in southern California), by a co-op nursery and baby-bank, by the feeling of pure joy in raising and loving new lives, and by a husband as excited and challenged by the prospect of parenthood as I was.

There were moments—suffocation, when I ran from the house, returning hours later with no explanation; mental stagnation that led me to start reading groups for other young housewives equally bored with the quotidian and sharing a hunger for reading and discussion that was finding no outlet. Yet I was swept along to complete my mother's—and my culture's—agenda.

Through it all, college courses were my salvation, the one place that provided intellectual excitement. By the time that we had moved to Pennsylvania and the youngest child was in school for a full day, I was ready to dive into a patriarchal institution so rigid and humorless that when my flippant response to the English Department Head's question of why I wanted to get a doctorate was, "It's more fun than washing windows!" that irreverence almost got me kicked out of the graduate program. After several explanations and a character reference from a prof who knew my work, I squeaked in. In to a soft patriarchal cloud of study, floating along happily on Milton, Blake, Thoreau, Emerson, and eventually Roger Williams. No, as I often had to explain to outsiders, not the musician—but the founder of Rhode Island. A single phrase hooked me into the dissertation ditch: the opening line of a Williams poem in his *A Key into the Language of America*, a dictionary/ cultural study of the Narragansetts. That line?

"Truth is a native, naked beauty."

Charming—a sentence that clearly reflected a new world, one that imaged so strongly both his passionate ethics and his openness to a new culture. A latter-day parallel, I too was soaking adventurously in a new world, immersing unquestioningly in new works, new ideas, new challenges.

In the hindsight that gives us all wisdom, I find my innocence and dedication not nearly so attractive as Roger Williams's. I was blind then to signs along the way that I was *in*, but not *of*, The Group, such as when the professor who, since I was working on the same author he was, invited me to hear his lecture on William Golding at a prestigious luncheon. One problem: women were not allowed. So he graciously set a chair around the corner, out of sight, then came out to the corridor and surreptitiously motioned me to sit down and shhh! not let anyone catch me listening. I was grateful.

Then there were the occasional remarks from *fellow* (literally) graduate students to the effect that my academic progress was no problem; I could always drop out and live on my husband's salary. Or the grad-party relaxation night when, in the midst of wide-ranging and non-academic discussion, I made an anti-douche remark (later codified by others as "If God had meant women to use douches, he would have built them in") and was told, "You know, Jo, you're a regular Wife of Bath!" I had *enjoyed* that scandalous Chaucerian character, but the tone of friend Mike's comparison was far from complimentary. Oops—overstepping the bounds, being an assertive female.

What would it take to pry the scales from my eyes? Obviously, something academic. Of the two major paths by which women arrive at a sense of feminism and/or women's spirituality—through experience or through books, both profound activities—mine was the latter.

Somehow the name of Adrienne Rich had surfaced in my academic world. How, I remember not, but I decided to write a paper on her, and there were critics to consult before I could summarize the literary background. First came W. H. Auden, noting in the introduction to Rich's first book of poetry, *A Change of World* (1951), that the poems were "neatly and modestly dressed, speak quietly but do not mumble, respect their elders but are not cowed by them, and do not tell fibs" (Gelpi 127). The implicit patronizing was lost on me. Then Randall Jarrell, in a review of her second volume, *The Diamond Cutters* (1956), speaking of her "ordinary subjects," but forecasting the possibility that she is "one who can afford to be wild tomorrow." At the time, I paid no heed.

Finally, though, the proverbial straw: an evaluation of her work by William Pritchard, obviously a critic of note and one familiar with Rich's work, who found that she had moved from "accomplished verse, intelligently aware of its limits and careful not to overreach" to "a call over the megaphone . . . liberated into occasional plain or dirty talk." So far, so good. An eminent critic, he. Who was I to argue?—until brought to attention by his response to Rich's poetic declaration in *The Will to Change*. The lines that provoked his scorn:

> An Ashanti woman tilts the flattened basin on her head
> to let the water slide downward: I am that woman and
> that water. (20)

"One wants to say," Pritchard mocked, "no, no you are not that woman, surely; if the Ashanti could hear this, would she be grateful for the poet's solicitude?"

I had heard that tone before. Where? Suddenly a concatenation of voices swirled through the quiet air . . . my father disgustedly laying down the law, my viola teacher shrugging his shoulders at a few sour notes, my high school boyfriend insisting that his weekend plans were superior to mine, my obstetrician extolling the joys of birth and motherhood (experiences he obviously had never had)—in every case, the quiet purr of authority, a superiority gained through making its target look ridiculous.

I read Rich's line again: "I am that woman and that water." Those words, too, had a familiar ring.

> I am the hounded slave. . . . I wince at the bite of the dogs. . . .
> I do not ask the wounded person how he feels. . . . I myself
>   become the wounded person. . . .
> I am the mashed fireman with breastbone broken. . . . tumbling
>   walls buried me in their debris. . . . (Whitman, 62–63)

Of course. Walt Whitman! And would Mr. Pritchard have inquired ironically: "If the mashed fireman could hear this, would he be grateful for the poet's solicitude?" Even the notion was ridiculous.

The "click" had occurred; I felt free of such nonsense, and since then have collected many similar gems, including the evaluation by a pontifical professor friend several years later that Rich's early work was well done, "but lately she has been going too far, getting strident and political." My response was in Rich's own words:

The moment when a feeling enters the body
is political. This touch is political. (*The Will to Change* 24)

But struggle is never so simple. It moves on step by step—a few advancing, then lockstepping in place, then slipping back, as Maya Angelou recently said, "We stand on plateaus till—oh, oh—they become mirey and clayey, and then we have to move on." Times of freedom and freshness, then the dust and stale air lower again, breathing becomes difficult, even reading a drudgery. The dailiness is there, the deadening straitjacket of habit, the unremarking hours sludging by . . . text lists, syllabi, paper-grading, test-making.

1980. My teaching absorbed all energy, day and night. As for literary critics? My eye was jaundiced; my enthusiasm, dim. Yet they were a necessary evil for one expected not only to teach, but also to research and write. Partying one night in San Francisco with a group of lesbian friends, I was jolted out of that mind frame.

Oh, you're an English prof?

You teach literature?

All right! Tell us all about Natalie Barney!

Hmm. Natalie *who*?

The questioners were intensely interested in a literary flowering of women writers in Paris after the First World War. What could I tell them about Gertrude Stein? Colette? Here I was on safe ground. Vita Sackville-West? Friend of Virginia Woolf, etc. Natalie Barney? Barney? Never heard of her. Sorry.

Chagrined, I returned home to search for information. After all, what good was a Ph.D. that had left such a large black hole in my knowledge of literary worlds? Later I would learn about expatriate Barney's extravagant Friday salons for women and her book, *Pensées d'une Amazone*. Far more important was the search itself (as it generally is for all of us), for it led me to Louise Bernikow's *Among Women* and a whole new world.

Settling down one weekday afternoon, surrounded by stacks of books; unruly hills of paper, their corners sticking out at all angles; coffee mug, pencils, and warm, still, stale air; I picked up the Bernikow book, noted some index entries on Barney, then decided to case the book by first glancing at the author's introduction: "Two Women Alone in a Room." How apt, I thought, yawning and turning the page. The first words on that page: "I was sitting at a table on a cloudy day. The table was stacked with books."

Shock. I read more rapidly. . . .

"My mind was running along a certain track, thinking about the books, what was in them, and the life around me, what was in it, simultaneously."

A current of fresh air began to swirl around the stuffy room. The books and papers seemed to quiver with anticipation. This was no ordinary academic exercise. We were, Louise Bernikow and I, indeed, two women alone in a room. And she was talking with (not *to*, not *at*) me, providing me with my first taste of feminist criticism, a heady mixture, one on which I soon grew hooked.

Marge Piercy has said, "Anything that is not an energy source is an energy sink." William Pritchard and his clones had sapped my psychic energy; Bernikow restored it. In her Acknowledgments, she described helpful colleagues as providing "the intellectual and emotional support . . . so well articulated by Gertrude Stein when she described how, at some point in the work, someone says 'yes' to it." I, on the receiving end, voiced a heartfelt echo: Yes, yes, and yes. Three-dimensional criticism—heart, mind, and spirit.

In the decade that followed, the fresh air continued to blow. Marge Piercy, Mary Daly, Judith Fetterley, Alicia Ostriker. . . . Novels, too, and poetry. I was "filling up and spilling over," in singer Cris Williamson's exuberant phrase, spilling my reading experiences into the classroom, sharing my sense of joy and involvement with students, colleagues, and friends. Excitement entered my classroom—young women interviewing their grandmothers, aunts, or other older women and discovering their fascinating stories and lives; young women and men so immersed in Ntozake Shange's *Sassafrass, Cypress, and Indigo* that they spontaneously brought to class the music and food that filled that fine novel; many writing at semester's end that their Women's Studies course was the first they had ever encountered that touched their private lives and made a difference.

That joy was being echoed on every side by other professors who had caught the same vision. A heady and growing time, triggered by the work of—yes—critics! But a different breed. Bettina Aptheker's introductory remarks in *Tapestries of Life: Women's Work, Women's Consciousness, and the Meaning of Daily Experience* show that new spirit:

> This is . . . a book about healing, and beauty, and balance. It is about restoring these things to ourselves as women . . . about how to change women's consciousness of themselves, about how to help women heal from the racist and sexual violence that permeates our lives, about how to restore a sense of beauty in women whose aesthetic senses are continually assaulted, mocked, and degraded. . . .(7)

> We have begun to place women at the center of our work . . . . We have begun to write from the core of our own experiences as women without apologizing for it, with less fear of humiliation or annihilation. We are rebuilding a literary and artistic tradition [with] the potential for handing on a collective female vision, weaving corroborative threads. (35)

Yes, I say, and yes. And toward the end of the paragraph, a phrase catches me by the scalp: "with less or no regard for the male critic."

I pondered, while other selves were shadowing through the days. As Virginia Woolf hypothesizes in *Orlando*, "If there are (at a venture) seventy-six different times all ticking in the mind at once, how many different people are there not—Heaven help us—having lodgment at one time or another in the human spirit? . . . These selves of which we are built up, one on top of another, as plates are piled on a waiter's hand, have attachments elsewhere, sympathies, little constitutions and rights of their own, call them what you will" (200).

My own Second-Self sprang directly from two words uttered at an early eighties Women's Studies conference during a tea-and-cookies reception after a full day of papers and panels, as a motley group of teachers, staff, students, secretaries, and townsfolk were making the small talk demanded by courtesy before sneaking off to home and late dinner. Small circles around the fluorescent-lighted reception room. Six or seven of us in one of them, commenting haphazardly on this paper, that question, quick impressions. Eventually, one of those painful pauses, clear evidence that we were all talked out, when one squarejawed, nondescript woman from town commented softly, "But no one said anything about women's *spirituality*." Silence for a few seconds, then a disappearing act that looked as if Dorothy of Oz had thrown water on a group of wicked witches, who all simply melted away from the circle and misted into invisibility.

Intriguing. Evidently those two words were powerful; perhaps they were also neither socially nor academically acceptable?

Again, back to the books. New names: Charlene Spretnak, Barbara Walker, Christine Downing, Carol Christ. That last name, which kept popping up, was familiar, its short-i pronunciation already known, its appearance bringing an image of a tall blond woman who had given memorable multi-media programs at National Women's Studies conferences. Always ahead of the annual wave of feminist discoveries, she had one year brought us images of goddesses; the next, a powerful collage, "Genesis/Genocide: Women for Peace"; third, an unpopular insistence that women must establish communication with the masculine "hands that control the [atomic bomb] buttons."

So when Carol spoke at nearby Bucknell in '84, I was there. She spoke on peace, her announced topic, but more. As she concluded, her voice grew softer, her body leaned forward, her eyes moved beyond the auditorium walls, and she created for us a vision of another land— of a tiny island in the Northeast Aegean where Sappho had dwelt, a place of red poppies struggling through sun-baked earth, of dusty olive-tree terraces, of whitewashed chapels and herds of sheep, but the most striking image, one that hovered in the still air that evening, the caves at water's edge—flesh colored, rose-gold at sunset, their curved, ridged, inward-moving forms the very vulva and womb of Gaia. Birthplace of the world. . . .

June, '85. I was there. Well, in a way. Balanced precariously on a slimy rock, holding onto a sharp cliff face, gazing into clear Aegean waters suddenly teeming with spiny sea urchins not noticed earlier, I was questioning my sanity. How had I ever gotten into this mess? The day had started so well, with a happy bus trip across the island of Lesvos, a delightful lunch waterside with all seventeen women offering poems by Sappho, then a hike to the beach where we gazed breathless at the reality of those huge, convoluted caves, more spectacular even than Carol had pictured them, and dived ecstatically into the clear, azure water. Soon there were skyclad women on each rock outcrop, singing like legendary mermaids their siren songs. Lovely.

So why the panic as I scrutinized the twenty feet of narrow rock ledge leading along the caves' edges to the safety of the beach? Because my right arm, the one needed to hold to the cliff, had been severely sprained and was useless. I felt suddenly helpless, alone, and out of place. Someone waved; I smiled and waved gaily back. Best to put a good face on it, but I was frozen to one slimy rock. A few long seconds passed. Suddenly I realized that two women were moving slowly toward me: Frankie, a young athlete, and tall deliberate Deborah. One positioned herself behind me, the other in front. With scarcely a word, they became extensions of my body and gently moved me step by step from one rock to the next until—glory be to Goddess—I was able to jump happily onto the warm sand.

That International Women's Studies Institute trip introduced me to women's spirituality in many ways—through books, lectures, writing, workshops, discussions into the night, rituals, meetings with Greek women, and travel from Athens to Lesvos and up the west coast of Turkey—yet the most important lesson was spontaneous and kinesthetic: instant physical and spiritual support from two perceptive and loving women who saw a need and moved without hesitation to help. Sisterhood, a concept and practice of solidarity often couched in terms of Goddess, the Goddess in every woman.

School and home stretched their dimensions and began to glow with an infusion of energy. It seemed as if every publisher's catalog I skimmed, every book I picked up, every lecture I heard, glinted with references to Goddess lore. The symbols and iconography of women's spirituality—spirals, serpents, eggs, moons—whirled through familiar landscapes, turning them strange and fresh. The present gained new dimensions.

As did the past. Several years earlier, I had given a series of academic papers on domestic imagery in women's writing (perhaps compensation for deserting the kitchen in favor of the library those days). Now those homey images of food, cooking pots, utensils, and cleaning tools were gathering new reverberations, for they were also the traditional implements of early healers, midwives, widows, and solitaries. Hestia, ancient goddess of the hearth and home, was generally represented only as a flame, but Hecate and her cauldron stirred boldly in many prints and pictures. Stories of healing brews and midwives' tools being disguised as household paraphernalia to save witches and wise women from the persecution of the Inquisition made a horrible kind of sense, and feelings of empathy and sisterhood surfaced as slowly, reading by reading, the kitchen became a center of warmth, love, and—yes—power.

A woman's queendom, where connections were established, traditions passed on, decisions made. Marge Piercy's kitchen, refuge from male abstract talk, where she went "to talk cabbages and habits"(8); Maya Angelou as a child listening to her mother and friends creating their lives midst camaraderie and coffee cups; Brazilian Adélia Prado salvaging bits of good pineapple from the garbage while musing about what her search "had to do with holiness"; Adrienne Rich, home after loving and grocery shopping:

I let myself into the kitchen, unload my bundles,
make coffee, open the window, put on Nina Simone
singing Here comes the sun . . . I open the mail,
drinking delicious coffee, delicious music, my body still both
  light and
        heavy with you (Dream, 26)

Student papers, too, one young woman interviewing her grand-mother "in the kitchen, of course," another noting that she knew her parents were having a serious discussion "because all major decisions in my house are made at the kitchen table." Domestic no longer seems a proper word to describe what has become a re-sanctified and de-lightfully wild space: Hestia's hearth.

Patricia Monaghan gives a whiff of that sense in "Housemagic," her poem about a woman waking at night, sitting by her window, half asleep, half awake:

There, on the boundary of
boundlessness, you dream
and, dreaming, remember what
you have not utterly forgotten:
how your kitchen always has at least one
Witch's broomstick, how clove and garlic
are domesticated on your spicerack,
how everything has power. (72)

As my academic and spiritual selves continued their interior con-versations, Third-Self was progressing slowly and steadily, but largely unnoticed—odd, too, since she was the only exterior one of the three. Eventually, the traits already obvious to others crept into my conscious-ness. It started with questions, all of them variations on, "Jo, are you having your hair frosted?" A mirror-look at the back of my head showed me the streaks which I could truthfully explain, "Yes, by Mother Na-ture, and she doesn't charge a cent!"

In what seemed like only months, but was probably a couple of years, the proportions reversed, and my mane was no longer chestnut frosted, but gray streaked with brown. I was turning into a silver . . . senior. Senior? Me? Wrinkles were etching across my face like the cracks in dry Grecian earth. Eyelids drooped in a fashion that looked intriguingly like those of a Native American grandmother. A stranger appeared in the mirror, smiling back at me as she always had (why do we always smile at ourselves, but not always at others?), but she wasn't me! Imagine, then, the start, and again the sense of conversation *à deux*, when Ruth Fainlight looked up at me from a stray page and asked, "Friends, sisters, are you used to your face in the mirror?/ Can you accept or even recognize it?/ I can't. . ./ the face reflected back is always a shock"(76–77).

Other poems appeared, unbidden, thoughts that found me nodding, again in affirmation. First, Erica Jong's "Aging (balm for a 27th birthday)":

> it starts around the eyes. . .   but
> it's only the beginning   as ruin proceeds downward
> lingering for a while around the mouth   hardening the smile
> into prearranged patterns (irreversible!)   writing furrows
> from the wings of the nose. . . .
> & plotting lower to the corners of the mouth   drooping them
> a little   like the tragic mask. . . . (45–46)

and so on and on. At twenty-seven she felt this way? And the thought hadn't occurred to me until I reached my fifth decade!

The decades rolled through the women's poetry I was now reading, but, to my amazement, many were celebrations:

> *40*: At 40 I can drop the masks:
> Mrs. Good, Ms. Dependable, Mama Ever-So-Nice.
> Honestly, isn't Superwoman a drag? (Nancy Corson Carter)
> *50*: I've awaked to find
> that somehow I've slipped
> into the cloak of the fifth decade.
> And behold, it seems to fit! (Roberta Harper Roberts)
> *60*: As I approach sixty
> I turn my face toward the sea. . . .
> I shall go with the changes . . . (May Sarton)
> *70*: Go into seventy/ hoping and loving
> you will be women/ made beautiful
> by having lived/ well and long. (Ruth Harriet Jacobs)

Here was new territory, a landscape I had never seen. These were the voices of women actively discovering *terra incognita*, the third quarter-century of their lives. They had lived through the lives, loves, and lusts, the sloughs and mountain tops and plateaus, the plodding and dancing and raging and laughing—and look! they had come through! The ageism that disliked my hair and deplored my wrinkles began to slip away, leaving me free to explore a new world. Literature, my first and constant love, which had for years lifted me into the lives of others, was now leading me into the selves of my own life.

Fourth-Self has been with me since the last day of class one junior high school spring when I marched into our kitchen stunningly clad, I thought, in a thick six-foot snake. My mother's scream was daunting. Where was the love for animals that had led her to adopt two stray dogs? Where the delight in nature that had made her such a fine Girl Scout leader? My explanation, that the biology teacher had pleaded for someone to give it a happy summer home and no one else had responded, was scarcely acknowledged.

"Jo Ann!" A familiar tone and emphasis; I was in trouble again. "*Jo Ann*! Get that thing out of here immediately, right now. *Now!*" No matter that it was only a water snake. No matter that I whined full responsibility. The sentence: exile to a small box in the back yard. I sulked. The snake sulked. Eventually, through a hunger strike, it gained its freedom, but my fascination continued.

Snakes, serpents, scorpions. . . . I was, after all, like Jo in *Little Women*, a stubborn Scorpio. A paper toy here, a sculpture there, earrings and bracelets at a craft fair: gradually corners and shelves of my private space became occupied by snakes and slithery things. Teaching poetry, I used snake poems as examples. Making bread, I formed snake coils. In a class exercise where we all chose to become animals, I hissed—and empathized. I wrote poetry:

Life Rattle

Next time I want to be a snake.
I stretch luxuriously in this dark corner . . .
Wombed in close air that gives life to my blood.
I glide out to the rock-hard sun,
Warm and glow in its piercing touch,
Feel my skin taut as it dries into dust,
Digest lumpy days that lie deep in my entrails . . .

Beware my wild fury, Medusean madness

As, now disturbed, my pit turns to venom.
Already my poison sickens.
Next time I want to be a water snake.

That was 1976, early acknowledgment of the Dark Side, of Poe's "imp of the perverse," of the Harrowing of Hell, of Blake's sick rose, of—call it what you will—all of the supposedly creepy, shameful, hidden shadows that flee at daylight—the impulses that we all feel, but seldom acknowledge.

Student essays screen them out with abstract language. Acquaintances hide them behind smiles and noncommital conversation. Families ignore them by preserving the delicate balance of silence. Friends neglect them in favor of loving and categorical support. We all deny their existence. Only in literature—and in daily newspaper headlines—do they raise their ugly, unsettling heads.

Surely there must be a way to name them, to bring them into the sunlight and see their dimensions, even, perhaps, to become friends with them. Unwittingly I had given women's wildness an image in that early poem, one that surfaced again in May Sarton's "The Muse as Medusa":

I saw you once, Medusa; we were alone.
I looked you straight in the cold eye, cold.
I was not punished, was not turned to stone—
How to believe the legends I am told?

In the snake-hair of Medusa lay the process of re-membering my selves, of coming to terms with those inner impulses—grounding myself in Gaia earth and spirit, and accepting aging as saging. Finally, the significance of the snakes that surrounded me came clear: rebirth, regeneration, the constant sloughing off of the old and transformation into the new. Sarton's poem concludes,

I turn your face around! It is my face.
That frozen rage is what I must explore—
Oh secret, self-enclosed, and ravaged place!
This is the gift I thank Medusa for. (160)

A spiritual gift, truly, this recognition of the shadow-self. The visceral sense of sisterhood engendered that sunny day in Greece has since rippled outward to a world of women, especially to the crones who are, like me, adventuring through years scarcely charted. These are women who revere the strong, wild, wonderful Dark Mother in us all. I seek out the writings of Barbara Macdonald, Baba Copper, Florida Scott-Maxwell, Maggie Kuhn, and others.

And I cheer Marilyn Zuckerman's declaration, "There are places on this planet/ where women past the menopause/ put on the tribal robes/ smoke pipes of wisdom/ —fly" (405).

Fourth Self has moved beyond books, into a world of women, and spirituality infused for me with another crone: Queen of the Crossroads and the Underworld, Goddess of Death, Rebirth, and Transformation—Hecate herself. In classrooms and behind podiums, I have introduced her to others. In performance, I have taunted audiences into thoughts of death at Samhain, the night of her Witchery. I have invoked her, and she has come, especially one dark night when a hundred women, gathered in a Midwestern meadow, had danced the grace and joy of youth, had chanted the ripeness and creativity of maturity, then began to recognize and celebrate age. I raised my voice: "Hecate!" We shivered in the chilly night air—silent, hopeful. Gesturing to the circle, I drew them in, and a hundred voices roared, *"Hecate! Hecate!"* As the voices died away, we warmed to the power of her presence. Ribald, sexy, wise, darkly powerful—she was with us.

Her spirit continues to guide the frontier of my sixth decade. A new dimension of language becomes ever more intriguing: the power of silence and repetition to create a place beyond space and time . . . the compressions of poetry and the chants of ritual where, like the "black sound" of flamenco, power is created through the interplay of being and void. For me, as little robot behavior as possible. Rather, silver hair streaming and Hecate in my step, I meditate in silence and roar with delight as the adventures of each day unfold. And I am not alone on my path. With Sarah Lairo, in growing numbers, we aging, saging women say:

Old Woman, You give me the courage to live my life in
freedom. Though the vision of you is sometimes frightening,
the laughter in your eyes dares me to live boldly. . . .
You are the silence in the Way I walk. Wisdom comes
when I am calm enough to listen. In those moments when I am
Your echo, I understand.

Aptheker, Bettina. *Tapestries of Life: Women's Work, Women's Consciousness, and the Meaning of Daily Experience*. Amherst: U of Massachusetts P, 1989.

Bernikow, Louise. *Among Women*. New York: Harmony Books, 1980.

Carter, Nancy Corson. "Unmasking." *Broomstick* (Sept./Oct. 1985): 21.

Fainlight, Ruth. "It Must." *Sibyls and Others*. London: Hutchinson & Company, 1980. 76–77.

Gelpi, Barbara Charlesworth and Albert Gelpi. *Adrienne Rich's Poetry*. New York: Norton Critical Edition, 1975.

Heilbrun, Carolyn G. *Reinventing Womanhood*. New York: Norton, 1979.

Jacobs, Ruth Harriet. "Seventy." *Be an OUTRAGEOUS Older Woman—A R*A*S*P*. Manchester, CT: Knowledge, Ideas and Trends, 1991. 205.

Jarrell, Randall. "New Book in Review." *The Yale Review* 46:1 (Sept. 1956): 100–103.

Jong, Erica. *Fruits & Vegetables*. New York: Holt, Rinehart and Winston, 1968.

Lairo, Sarah. "Hag's Song." *Stardust Salamander* 2:1 (1987): 12.

Monaghan, Patricia. *Seasons of the Witch*. Oak Park, IL: Delphi Press, 1992. 8.

Piercy, Marge. "In the men(s) rooms." *To Be of Use*. Garden City, NY: Doubleday, 1973.

Pritchard, William. "Despairing of Styles." *Poetry* 127 (Fall, 1976): 292–302.

Rich, Adrienne. "Twenty-One Love Poems—IV." *The Dream of a Common Language*. New York: Norton, 1978.

_____ "The Blue Ghazals." *The Will to Change*. New York: Norton, 1971.

Roberts, Roberta Harper. "Happy birthday to those of us." *Broomstick* 4:6 (November/December, 1982): 13.

Sarton, May. "Gestalt at Sixty," "The Muse as Medusa." *Selected Poems of May Sarton*. New York: Norton, 1978.

Schaef, Anne Wilson. *Women's Reality*. San Francisco, CA: HarperCollins, 1981.

Shange, Ntozake. *Sassafrass, Cypress, and Indigo*. New York: St. Martin's, 1982.

Whitman, Walt. *Leaves of Grass. The First (1855) Edition*. New York: Penguin Books, 1946.

Williamson, Cris. "Waterfall." *The Changer and the Changed*. (LP Recording)Olivia, LF904, 1975.

Zuckerman, Marilyn. "After Sixty." In *Ourselves, Growing Older*. Ed. Paula Brown Doress et al. New York: Simon and Schuster, 1987.

A White Bird Flying Straight Down

Catherine E. Lamb

About halfway through a painful separation which eventually led to a divorce, I was driving in rural southwestern Michigan, through hills white with new snow deep enough to cover last year's stubble of corn stalks. A white bird, which I couldn't identify, separated itself from the flock of crows it was in and flew swiftly, cleanly, and apparently fearlessly, straight down towards the ground. Its flight seemed suicidal, sure to result in a collision with the earth. Yet of course, no such thing happened. It seems birds can always sense when to swoop up off the ground. In my own journey, I have felt there was no choice but to fly straight down, fast, embracing the reality of what has happened. At the same time I am separating myself from an intense, deep connection of twenty-three years, I am wondering whether I ever truly had a voice of my own, and where the authority will come from now for a new voice.

I am the daughter of a man and woman who spent forty years as Lutheran missionaries in what is now Papua New Guinea, an island north of Australia. Most of the time we lived in remote areas, making boarding school a necessity even for the primary grades. I left home with my older brother when I was six, to attend a missionary-run boarding school on the island. We would see our parents three times a year, twice for vacations and once when they would come to stay for two weeks with my younger siblings in a guest house at the school. Later, there was high school in Australia during which we went home once a year, and then college in the United States. All during my childhood and teenage years, I never cried when I left home and I have no clear memories of being homesick. But when my parents got on the train for California on their way back to New Guinea, leaving my brother and me to continue our college education, I sobbed uncontrollably at the station, sure that I would never see them or my other siblings again, wondering how anything could be more important than for parents to be with their children. For the next seven years, we could not afford any travel to see one another, except for a brief visit by my mother, paid for by her family, when my brother got married and I graduated from college. I did not see my father from the second semester of my freshman year in college until just before I turned twenty-five, one month before I got married.

My parents had chosen their calling as missionaries over their calling as parents and even as spouses. I grew up knowing by heart the verse from Matthew: "He who loves father or mother more than me is not worthy of me; and he who loves son or daughter more than me is not worthy of me; and he who does not take up the cross and follow me is not worthy of me." If my father struggled with his choice, I was never aware of it. When I taped an interview with him a few years before he died, he was clear about his priorities and made no apologies: "First there was my relationship to God, then to your mother, and then to you children." Even though I was then in my mid-thirties, I was only beginning the process of looking honestly at my childhood and acknowledging the costs of my upbringing. I never challenged my father in any way that might have helped us both to make our separate peace with ourselves. As for my mother, I knew that she cried when we children left home. She has since said that she would often cry herself to sleep at night when we were gone, a depth of pain she probably felt she could not share with anyone at the time. As far as I know, even with her feelings, she, along with my father, never seriously considered giving up mission work to be with their children.

The same day that I saw the white bird flying straight down, I made the connection between my parents and my husband. Both were willing to sacrifice me for something or someone else they wanted. Both were willing to betray a primary relationship. In a parallel that is still a cruel irony, my ex-husband also believes at least as firmly as my father believed in his vocation, that his affair with a girlfriend is a direct expression of God's will. With no choice but to leave, I had no say in the breakup of the marriage. As a child, I silenced myself: I could survive only by convincing myself that what was happening wasn't affecting me. As an adult, with much more awareness and many more resources, I believe I now have the chance *not* to repeat my childhood behavior.

My ex-husband has, and my father had, what we all want at least some of the time: reliance on an authority that above all represents strength and solidity, something we can trust unquestioningly. Richard Sennett, in his book-length study of authority, makes this point, noting as well that our desire for this sort of "autonomous" authority persists even if the need is unsatisfied. The issue, then, is how to respond to the desire. Sennett's answer is to emphasize the *way* authority is exercised—with care for others—in what might be called organic authority. A user of this authority recognizes she possesses nothing that can be exercised unilaterally. Her authority always exists only in a particular context. She creates a space for the other party's views, even at the expense of modifying her own. Authority expressed this way is egalitarian in another way: the participants see both the basis on which claims are made and the way in which they evolve. Sennett says we thus make authority "visible."

If one is fortunate, as I have been, one never goes on a journey like this alone. One set of companions was the literature I had already planned to teach the semester of my separation, much of which I can never again read in the old ways.

"Narrative of the Captivity of Mrs. Mary Rowlandson, 1682" is Rowlandson's account of being captured and held prisoner for eleven weeks in 1676 by some Wampanoag Indians in Lancaster, Massachusetts. She watches her house being burned. Her husband is away in Boston at the time of the attack and thus is spared, but one of her three children is wounded and dies shortly after being taken captive, and she is separated from the other two for most of her captivity. She is finally reunited with her family when the Wampanoags accept a ransom from her husband.

There are several layers to Rowlandson's telling of her story. Taken together, they raise questions of voice and authority. When is an experience so important that a Puritan woman—who, like a child, was expected to be seen and not heard—is justified in writing about it for publication? Some of Rowlandson's answers are predictable. Part of her story is an encounter with the Indians as Other, as what we most fear and what we perceive to be most unlike us, the antithesis of what we say we value. She sees herself being taken into "a vast and desolate Wilderness" (122), by savages who seize any opportunity to mistreat her and to kill others less fortunate. Early in her journey, she is put on a horse with her six-year-old daughter, who is wounded. Riding without a saddle, they both slide over the horse's head when they are descending a steep hill, "at which they [the Indians], like inhumane creatures, laught, and rejoyced to see it, though I thought we should there have ended our dayes, as overcome with so many difficulties" (123). A few days later, the daughter dies, alone with Rowlandson in a wigwam to which they have been sent; Rowlandson is forced to leave her to be buried later by the Indians. In what may be the narrative's most gruesome scene, another of the women taken captive, who is about to give birth and is also carrying a two-year-old, keeps begging the Indians to free her. Finally, the Indians strip her naked and burn her and her child, threatening to do the same of the children watching if they attempt to escape.

A relatively small amount of the story is taken up with accounts such as these, however. Rowlandson is much more interested in seeing her experience within her world view as a Puritan, in which she is an instrument of God's will and everything that happens can somehow be seen as an expression of God's will. She is a modern-day Job, or the psalmist crying out in his afflictions, who only happens to be a woman. She accepts unquestioningly as her own the voice of the Father, as in the full title of Rowlandson's story:

> The Soveraignty and Goodness of GOD, together with the Faithfulness of His Promises Displayed; Being a Narrative Of the Captivity and Restauration of Mrs. Mary Rowlandson. Commended by her, to all that desires to know the Lord's doings to, and dealings with Her. Especially to her dear Children and Relations. Written by Her own Hand for Her private Use, and now made Publick at the earnest Desire of some Friends, and for the benefit of the Afflicted. Deut. 32.39. See now that I, even I am he, and there is no god with me; I kill and make alive, I wound and I heal, neither is there any can deliver out of my hand. (112)

A student of mine once counted the number of Bible verses Rowlandson cites—sixty-one of them, one for virtually every occasion of trial *and* of thanksgiving. If there isn't a Bible verse, there is at least Rowlandson's theological interpretation of the event. At the end of the scene in which she and her daughter fall off the horse, she comments, "But the Lord renewed my strength still, and carried me along, that I might see more of his Power; yea, so much that I could never have thought of, had I not experienced it" (123). Several days later, the captives and the Indians are pursued by the English army; had the English been able to cross a river, Rowlandson would have been free. She responds, "God did not give them courage or activity to go over after us; we were not ready for so great a mercy as victory and deliverance" (131).

The captivity experience—her separation from her husband and other children, the complete uncertainty about her future and theirs, the physical conditions under which she lived—becomes an occasion for Rowlandson to re-examine her entire life. Early on, she acknowledges "how many sabbaths I had lost and misspent" (124). After she has been ransomed and reunited with her family, she sees that the old stability and comfort she had is gone forever. She notes that she "used to sleep quietly without workings in my thoughts, whole nights together, but now it is other ways with me" (166). She relives both the horrors of the captivity and God's saving love for her. Above all, "I have seen the extrem vanity of this World: One hour I have been in health, and wealth, wanting nothing. But the next hour in sickness and wounds, and death, having nothing but sorrow and affliction" (166). At one time, she had almost wished for affliction as a mark that she was special before the Lord, just as Job was singled out to be tested. Now that the affliction has come, and she has endured, she sees, "when God calls a Person to anything, and through never so many difficulties, yet he is fully able to carry them through and make them see, and say they have been gainers thereby" (167).

As powerful as Rowlandson's framing of her experience is, and as much as her written version of the eleven weeks in captivity gives her a public voice as a Puritan, there is yet another voice in the narrative, one that is probably easiest for most of us—secularized women and men of the late twentieth century—to relate to. Rowlandson's resourcefulness and openness to seeing the Indians as humans are at least as impressive as her ability to quote Bible verses. She sews and knits for them, receiving pay in return. For all the times when she is mistreated, deprived of food and shelter, there are at least as many when she is offered food and other kindnesses; sometimes she has a place to stay and not everyone else does. After an absence of three weeks, her master asks whether she has bathed. When she says she has not, he gets the water himself, gives her a mirror, and then asks one of his wives to feed her: "So she gave me a mess of Beans and meat, and a little Ground-nut Cake. I was wonderfully revived with this favour shewed me" (150). Rowlandson sees God as having brought her through. The task would have been a lot more difficult without the qualities Rowlandson brought to the experience and allowed to flower. She says she is writing "for the benefit of the afflicted"; while her story works as a testimonial to God's grace, it is certainly at least as powerful as a record of what an individual woman can do in adverse circumstances. What seems to us to be her real voice as a woman comes through her unself-conscious retelling of her own part in her struggle for deliverance.

And yet I cannot discount the power of Rowlandson's conscious framework for the story. She would not have been satisfied with a retelling that emphasized simply her own accomplishments—that is a result of my feminist reading of her story. I never get the sense, as I do in reading the poetry of Rowlandson's contemporary, Anne Bradstreet, that Rowlandson is conscious of a double voice in her work, the one public and acceptable, a suitable expression of a Puritan woman daring to speak; the other, a more private and individualized voice, insisting that she too has a right to be heard on her own terms. The faithful Puritan and the gritty, ingenious woman exist side-by-side, each ignoring the other.

There is no reason for me to deny the authenticity of her convictions. They also seem to have only positive results: being able to appeal to an unquestioning and unquestioned authority works for her. The need Sennett says we have for autonomous authority has been satisfied for her. It gives her the determination to survive; it may also predispose her to treat the Indians in humane ways, thus lessening our perception of them as the Other.

This same unshakable faith gave my parents the rationale for sending away my siblings and me. It was a rationale I accepted until I was well into my thirties. I believed my parents loved me; it was just that they loved God more. The first time I overtly questioned their actions was after my husband and I adopted a six-year-old boy. He was so young and needed so much. How could a child of this age, even one who had spent its entire life with the same parents, function on its own?

My husband's rationale for leaving the marriage relied on the same kind of thinking that can shape any event into a reflection of some larger purpose. For much of the time before I left, he succeeded in making me feel that there was something wrong with me because I couldn't "understand" and "accept" why he was doing what he was doing. The lessons of my childhood were still with me. Authority that comes from the outside in this way demands submission. There can be no dialogue, no mediator. As my husband said repeatedly, one has the choice of either accepting or rejecting the will of God; if accepted, it must be carried out unquestioningly.

What would a more balanced, organic expression of authority look like? Could Rowlandson have written a narrative that both acknowledged her belief in God and her own impressive contributions? Is there a way to be in the world that carries with it a certain lightness, one in which the world does not need to be defined exclusively in one's own terms? Can one then still retain one's integrity as an individual and allow others to do the same? The answers have never come easily to me, and, when they've been there, have often been contradictory.

When I was in sixth grade, I wrote a short essay called "The Auto-biography of a Piece of Chalk." One of my brothers found it a few years ago and sent it to me. The essay is the story of a beautiful piece of dark-green chalk, the largest and most beautiful piece of chalk in the box. It is elected president of all the pieces of chalk. Because it is so beautiful, it is often selected when a human needs something to write with. It allows itself to be used, even though being pressed against the blackboard is very painful. When it has been worn way down, in an attempt to escape the pain, it works its way to the bottom of the box, where, covered with dust from other pieces of chalk, it hides success-fully. The essay ends with the chalk remaining in this way to manage its existence.

Earlier this year, when I had been gone for one week from my husband, I dreamed there was a knock on the door in the middle of the night. Without looking through the peephole in the door, I opened it up. A small man with a knife in his hand strode in, announcing that we should get ready for sex. He was on top of me with the knife at my throat before I realized I didn't have to do what he was asking me to. I was a Brunhilde sort of woman—tall, solid and muscular—and pushed the man off my body, picked him up, carried him through the front door, threw him off the porch, and went back in, locking the door be-hind me.

Throughout the experience of my divorce, I have continued to re-turn to the relationship between authority and voice. I don't think one can have a voice without authority. Authority in voice is what gives one the confidence to speak; it's also why others listen. The authority itself can come only from one's own sense of self. One of the earliest and most enduring concerns of our most recent feminist movement has been to give women a voice. We feminists have learned how com-plicated that question can be as we have seen that there is no single voice for women, that we must acknowledge our own positioning and that of others. What I have learned about my voice in the last few months complicates and confuses what had been my understanding of its sources.

I see now that, when I was married, most of what I did that mat-tered was built on what I believed to be the security of my relationship with my husband—regardless of how self-contained I and others thought I was. Who I was, and therefore my voice, came from that

CATHERINE E. LAMB

connection. With the basis for that connection gone, for now, only the emptiness remains. It is a shortness of breath, and sometimes a tightening of my stomach, that occurs in the gaps: at the start of a day that is relatively unstructured, before I sit down to eat, when I have finished eating, or when I start up the stairs to go to bed. My marriage at its best and its worst taught me at the most profound level about what it means to be human and to be in a relationship. It transcended, as it should have, any particular label. At the same time, I can see now that I made that connection into something I assumed would be permanent. It had a reality outside myself that I never seriously questioned.

When I was first forced to admit that my marriage might end, I dreamed I had to leave a house and walk across a narrow ledge. Then I had to climb up a steep hill covered with smooth dirt, lacking hand holds of any kind. I was terrified but able to climb to the top. When I got there, I saw there was another path I could have used, one with rocks to step on. But that was not my path.

The poetry of Emily Dickinson, with which I ended the semester in my American Literature class, suggests that an honest exploration of voice and authority is a lifetime process, in which contradictions may never be resolved. The question of voice for Dickinson is much more problematical than it is for Rowlandson. Dickinson saw herself unequivocally as a writer and devoted her life to developing herself as a poet. Rowlandson would probably never have written anything at all for a larger public had it not been for the experience which set her apart, convincing her that she had something to say that would benefit others. The language on which she relies for authority is the received language of the Bible, imposed on her experience. The basis for her claim of authority would have been part of why her "Narrative" became popular so quickly. Dickinson's authority is one she nurtured and claimed for herself. Because her vehicle was lyric poetry, usually unconnected to a particular event, she had a freedom of interpretation that Rowlandson never allowed herself. Perhaps most profoundly, there is the authority that comes from Dickinson's use of language. Her irony and wit, her alteration of syntax, quixotic use of words, and unconventional punctuation—all heighten the possibility for transformation that is present in so many of her poems.

If Dickinson's voice is far more original than Rowlandson's, it also makes her much less accessible, as we see in the literary critic Thomas Higginson's initial, skeptical response to the poems she sent him (Sewall 2:538–50). The fragility of Dickinson's sense of her authority may be reflected in her decision to publish only a handful of the seventeen hundred poems she wrote during her lifetime. Critics, especially feminists, have discussed at length how one is to reconcile Dickinson's highly original voice with the existence of a group of poems—most but not all written in the first part of her career—in which the speaker, a woman, is so clearly subservient to a male figure, either an actual man (as in the "Master" poems) or God. The images and metaphors are straightforward in the relationship they portray. The speaker is a "little Hound" (186), a Daisy following the Sun (106, 232), a River to his Sea (162), a statue which he carves (603), a "small Hearth " for "His fire" (638). The speaker's authority, like Rowlandson's, comes only from its relationship to a male presence.

When the female voice is exploring questions of creativity, the expressive life force is often male, most notably in "My Life had stood—a Loaded Gun—" (754). She is the gun, who "speaks" for the Owner. Their enigmatic relationship is summarized in the last stanza:

Though I than He—may longer live
He longer must—than I—
For I have but the power to kill,
Without—the power to die—

Critics have had a range of responses. One idea is that, as in the other poems, the masculine self is in control (Dobson); another that it has been transformed (Gilbert); another that the speaker is being ironically critical of herself (Weisbuch). And Baym wants us to recognize the tension between giving in and fighting back in this and other poems.

Rich and Bennett are as straightforward as anyone in dealing with the "problem" of the male creative persona: in a culture which dissociates women and creativity, why wouldn't a poet who is a woman choose a masculine voice to embody her creative self? (What greater authority than the Bible could Rowlandson have chosen as a frame for her story?) Both Rich and Bennett see a poem like "My Life had stood" as embodying Dickinson's *acceptance* of herself as a poet, making possible the exuberance in poems such as "Title divine—is mine!" (1072). Whether or not Dickinson's emergence as a poet is connected to her rejection by a suitor in late 1861 (Sewall 2:492–3), the voice is clearly there.

Like Rowlandson, Dickinson possesses a deep desire to shape the experiences she writes about into something beyond themselves—a reflection of their common Puritan heritage. Rowlandson is a descendent of Job; but for Dickinson, life lived in its ordinariness is enough of a teacher. It is a selection of poems on this theme which I'd like to use to illustrate Dickinson's mature voice. The speaker in 875, stretched between the heavens and the earth, has no assurances about what lies in the future:

> I stepped from Plank to Plank
> A slow and cautious way
> The Stars about my Head I felt
> About my Feet the Sea.
>
> I knew not but the next
> Would be my final inch—
> This gave me that precarious Gait
> Some call Experience.

There is little comfort in life lived this way; there are no Bible verses to immediately make sense of what is going on. The speaker is forced to live as fully in the moment as she can bear, with no promise of reward for having done so. In another poem, 1142, also written in the mid-1860s, the shape of the life is closer to something Rowlandson might recognize. There is a goal that can be reached. Here the metaphor is building rather than walking:

> The Props assist the House
> Until the House is built
> And then the Props withdraw
> And adequate, erect,
> The House support itself
> And cease to recollect
> The Auger and the Carpenter—
> Just such a retrospect
> Hath the perfected life—
> A past of Plank and Nail
> And slowness—then the Scaffolds drop
> Affirming it a Soul.

There are many poems that attest to the way in which the building gets done, to what it is that can account for a transformation as abrupt and cataclysmic as scaffolds dropping. As for Rowlandson in her "Narrative," the necessary agent is pain and suffering: "A *Wounded* Deer—leaps highest— / I've heard the Hunter tell—" and later in the same poem, "The *Smitten* Rock that gushes! / The *trampled* steel that springs!"

(165). In another poem (546), the connection between pain and being able to move on is even more intense because the image is more personal:

> To fill a Gap
> Insert the Thing that caused it—
> Block it up
> With Other—and 'twill yawn the more—
> You cannot solder an Abyss
> With Air.

Filling the gap with the "Thing that caused it" is like facing into the wind, embracing what it is that has created this gaping hole. Writing about the experience this way makes it sound noble, a realization of what it truly means to live existentially. Sometimes, Dickinson even sounds like she could be Rowlandson: "There is a strength in proving that it can be borne / Although it tear—" (501). On the other hand, a poem like 650 conveys quite directly the particular terror of filling the gap with the thing that caused it:

> Pain—has an Element of Blank—
> It cannot recollect
> When it begun—or if there were
> A time when it was not—
>
> It has no Future—but itself—
> Its Infinite contain
> Its Past—enlightened to perceive
> New Periods—of Pain.

When one is trying to fill the gap, there is no guarantee that it will ever be filled or how one will feel when the pain is over. There is nowhere to go to escape from its intensity. The limitlessness of this feeling can also, paradoxically, be constricting, as in 1099: "My Cocoon tightens—Colors tease— / I'm feeling for the Air— / A dim capacity for Wings / Demeans the Dress I wear—."

If one engages in this experience, what can happen is, quite literally, poetry on the level of Emily Dickinson's. A naked accepting of pain means that the usual defenses are down because they are of no use. It does not matter what I have written, how well I teach, or how strong I might seem to other people. There is only the experience of the pain at that moment. Ego has no voice at all. The fragility of one's being makes possible a receptivity towards other people and the natural world. Boundaries are now permeable; there can at least be moments of no separation. There is no need to appeal to something outside one's self because there is nothing there. The only authority that matters derives from one's receptivity to the reality of lived experience: "To hear an Oriole sing / may be a common thing— / Or only a divine" (526). An image like this makes concrete another poem: "Between the form of Life and Life / The difference is as big / As Liquor at the Lip between / And Liquor in the Jug" (1101).

A week before my divorce became final, I dreamed about a woman who had to die. She knew it and could accept it. My sister and I were to kill her. My sister shot her first, in the chin just below the lip. Then I shot her, right between the eyes. The shots left neither bruises nor blood. The woman said she wanted to lie down and went over to a couch. I asked her whether she wanted us to hold her, and she said yes. She died quickly and peacefully.

Six months after I saw the white bird flying straight down, I know and usually can accept that I am not on this journey with the purity and clarity of that bird's flight. While I believe in a life force pervading the universe that I am willing to call "God," I know that any voice I have does not derive its authority in some direct fashion from this being—as Mary Rowlandson, my father, and my ex-husband would claim. That I have a voice seems clear even though the self-denying piece of green chalk is still a part of me. The voice of the woman in my dream, who was strong enough to throw the small man off her porch, appeals to me, but only as something to call on in an extreme. With the necessary death of the old self, the lightness and openness I see in Dickinson's poetry, which carries with it a sense of indeterminacy, seems closer to what may be my new self.

Any voice I have and authority it may carry are not Sennett's autonomous authority. I want the organic alternative I described earlier— an authority that exists only in the context of a particular situation, in relation to someone else. I have seen its expression most clearly in my friends and family and their response to me in these past months. Their acceptance of my pain has been key to my being able to transform it. They have brought with them who they are, and together we have made something different from what any of us would be on our own. Having a voice hardly seems an issue anymore because I see that I have been exercising it throughout this process. Recently, after I had settled into my new home, I had a house blessing and picnic and invited everyone who had made a difference in some way, along with their families. Sixty people were there—from two six-month-old baby boys to two seventy-seven-year-old women. I shall always carry with me the image of all those people eating on the lawn, all in some way connected to me and I to them.

WORKS CITED

Baym, Nina. "God, Father, and Lover in Emily Dickinson's Poetry." *Puritan Influences in America.* Ed. Emory Elliott. Urbana: U of Illinois P, 1979. 193–209.

Bennett, Paula. *My Life a Loaded Gun: Female Creativity and Feminist Poetics.* Boston: Beacon, 1986.

Dickinson, Emily. *The Complete Poems of Emily Dickinson.* Ed. Thomas H. Johnson. Boston: Little, Brown, 1960.

Dobson, Joanne A. "'Oh, Susie, it is dangerous': Emily Dickinson and the Archetype of the Masculine." Juhasz 80–97.

Gilbert, Sandra M. "The Wayward Nun beneath the Hill: Emily Dickinson and the Mysteries of Womanhood." Juhasz 22–44.

Juhasz, Suzanne, ed. *Feminist Critics Read Emily Dickinson.* Bloomington: Indiana UP, 1983.

Rich, Adrienne. "Vesuvius at Home: The Power of Emily Dickinson." *On Lies, Secrets, and Silence.* New York: Norton, 1979. 157–83.

Rowlandson, Mary. "Narrative of the Captivity of Mrs. Mary Rowlandson, 1682." *Narratives of the Indian Wars.* Ed. Charles H. Lincoln. New York: Charles Scribner's Sons, 1913. 109–67.

Sennett, Richard. *Authority.* New York: Vintage, 1980.

Sewall, Richard B. *The Life of Emily Dickinson.* 2 vols. New York: Farrar, Straus, and Giroux, 1974.

Weisbuch, Robert. *Emily Dickinson's Poetry.* Chicago: U of Chicago P, 1975.

CATHERINE E. LAMB

Being an I-Witness—My Life as a Lesbian Teacher

Barbara DiBernard

When I began writing this essay I was "out" as a lesbian in my department, the English Department at the University of Nebraska-Lincoln, although still not out to most of my students—and it had taken ten years to get to that place. As lesbians and gay men know, coming out is not a one-time activity, but an ongoing process. I have left this essay as I wrote it in 1990, with a short Afterword to bring it up to date.

A couple of years ago when someone would ask me if I was out at my job, I would say, "I think so." I had signed a letter along with the other lesbian and gay professors in my department asking our colleagues to include lesbian and gay literature in the reading list of a new course we were designing. When the English Graduate Student Association and the Teaching Committee put together a panel on "Sexism, Racism, and Homophobia in the Classroom," they asked me to speak on homophobia. A colleague who runs a first-year Foundations course asked me for speakers who could address gay and lesbian issues for his students. Once a colleague's wife talked with me about her lesbian daughter. Obviously lots of folks "knew."

Yet I still felt that people could easily ignore that aspect of my identity if they wanted to, and increasingly that felt uncomfortable for me. I felt very lonely as a lesbian teacher and an academic. I could talk to many colleagues about literature, about teaching, and about our profession, but I felt there was no one except one gay male colleague with whom I could talk about being a lesbian academic. I thought often about whether I should come out in class, I worried about putting on my vita my talk to the Gay and Lesbian Student Association at a nearby college, I wondered how my colleagues and family would react to my first article on lesbian studies, but I shared none of these worries with heterosexual colleagues. Eventually I realized I was also suppressing a great deal of anger that I "had to" expend so much time and energy on these concerns. What I felt from my colleagues was what Suzanne Pharr has described as "an acceptance drawn from the politics of tolerance and compassion, not equality" (28). While people knew I was a lesbian and I experienced no overt discrimination, my life as a lesbian teacher remained largely invisible. But my inner discomfort had become so acute, a beginning gut knowledge of what "Silence = Death" means had become so strong, that in the last months I have begun being out to my colleagues more insistently. In doing so, I have asked them to acknowledge my experience as a *lesbian* academic.

Two years ago the student senate denied funding to a lesbian and gay student group and was upheld by the university administration. While this controversy went on, hateful and ignorant homophobic letters to the editor were the rule for weeks. I was surprised as I became increasingly depressed and angry, as I think of myself as quite resilient and having lots of resources. After all, I'm comfortable with my lesbian identity, I have a strong support network, I have job security. Part of my anger and depression was, I think, at how unaware and uninvolved even my most liberal colleagues were. Often when I mentioned the specifics of the case, otherwise aware colleagues had no idea what I was talking about, although the issue had been reported on the front page and the editorial page of the student newspaper almost daily. Therefore, I decided to talk about how I experienced this as a lesbian whenever I could. I wanted my colleagues to know that this mattered to me, that it was painful to me. I wanted them to know too that lesbian and gay students were suffering. I didn't want my pain to be invisible because it involved my lesbian self.

When I spoke on homophobia at the English Graduate Student Association's panel on "Sexism, Racism, and Homophobia in the Classroom," I publicly identified myself as a lesbian for the first time in the department. I spoke not only of the homophobia expressed by our students in the classroom, but also of the homophobia that teachers bring into the classroom, as evidenced by the near-invisibility of lesbian and gay writers *treated as* lesbians and gays in our curriculum. I felt that it was important to be out unequivocally, so that no one in the department could pretend that she or he does not have a lesbian colleague, so that when issues came up I could address them publicly out of the context of my own experience.

Since my Chair was at the session at which I came out, I felt I could, without any preamble, use my annual review with him as a time to discuss homophobia on campus, particularly the silencing and harassment which my lesbian students experience and share with me. I told him of the lesbian student who received three obscene phone calls the day she came out in class; of the lesbian student who heard no mention of homosexuality in her sociology course; of the lesbian student who sat through a class in Abnormal Psychology in which other students pronounced lesbians and gay men "sick," "sinful," and "perverted," with no intervention from the instructor.

I hope that in telling my stories as a lesbian teacher and academic and in relating my lesbian students' stories I perform a function similar to what Margaret Atwood claims for the writer:

> *Come with me*, the writer is saying to the reader. *There is a story I have to tell you, there is something you need to know.* The writer is both an eye-witness and an I-witness, the one to whom personal experience happens and the one who makes experience personal for others. (348)

But telling is not enough; there must also be hearing, and beyond that, action. Although it has felt good and powerful to be out with my colleagues, to be an "I-witness" for myself and for my students, the atmosphere at the University of Nebraska seems at best a kind of liberal tolerance and at worst overt homophobia. While we have a non-discrimination policy which includes sexual orientation, no administrator on my campus has initiated a policy or action to make this a better environment for lesbians and gay men.[1] A group of concerned students, faculty, and staff who constituted themselves into a Homophobia Awareness Committee had to wait for over a year to be officially appointed as a committee, in spite of repeated requests to a vice-chancellor.

When I have told members of my own department about the homophobia experienced by lesbian and gay students and faculty here, I have felt them rush into defensiveness which I feel gets in the way of their hearing the stories and therefore taking responsibility and moving from a place of acceptance to one of active alliance. Several colleagues have "cautioned" me against finding homophobia everywhere, telling me that not every criticism of a gay or lesbian person is an example of homophobia, that some of us deserve criticism. What I experience during these times is a dismissal of my experience and that of my students, and a profound sense of not being heard.

My being out has caused me little or no overt discrimination. What has pained me, however, is a kind of liberal tolerance which amounts to support for the status quo. Even some of my most supportive colleagues, for example, have told me that they are frightened to use lesbian or gay material in class, either because they don't know how to deal with it themselves, or they fear hostile student reactions.

While my coming out to my colleagues has been a long and evolving process, my coming out to my students is even more problematic. I have been reading and teaching Audre Lorde for years. Her message that we must break silence about those things which we need to say has affected me profoundly. I believe, as she does, that breaking silence brings strength and connection. I regularly assign *The Cancer Journals* and read Lorde's words aloud to my students:

> I was going to die, if not sooner then later, whether or not I had ever spoken myself. My silences had not protected me. Your silence will not protect you. But for every real word spoken, for every attempt I had ever made to speak those truths for which I am still seeking, I had made contact with other women while we examined the words to fit a world in which we all believed, bridging our differences. . . .
>
> What are the words you do not yet have? What do you need to say? What are the tyrannies you swallow day by day and attempt to make your own, until you will sicken and die of them, still in silence? Perhaps for some of you here today, I am the face of one of your fears. Because I am woman, because I am black, because I am lesbian, because I am myself, a black woman warrior poet doing my work, come to ask you, are you doing yours? (20–21)

When I first read those words of Lorde's, I vowed to try to live and do my work so that I could answer her question affirmatively. I redefined my work as encompassing not just my career as a professor of English and Women's Studies at the University of Nebraska, but as empowering women through women's literature, always inclusive of lesbians. As part of this re-definition, I began to do more community work, writing articles about women authors, including Lorde, for the local feminist newspaper; facilitating reading groups through the YWCA; giving talks on women authors for community women; giving readings of lesbian literature to groups on and off campus.

Nonetheless, I felt hypocritical. Even after I had begun to be very open about my lesbianism to my colleagues and in the community, in my classes I was silent on this central aspect of my identity. I tried to imagine the scenario of coming out in class. I fantasized making an announcement, but became angry and resentful that I would have to make such an announcement when heterosexuals did not. Since there

BARBARA DIBERNARD

seemed no equivalent of coming out for anyone else I felt unfairly burdened. But at bottom I was scared, and unhappy about the distance between my beliefs and my practices.

Now I see that, just like coming out to my colleagues, coming out to my students is not one act but many. Through the years I have brought my lesbian self and concerns into the classroom in a variety of ways. I never had a problem identifying myself as a lesbian to lesbian students. The community in Lincoln is quite small, and I regularly meet my students at lesbian events. When they are in my classes, most of them are out about their lesbianism in their journals, as I am in my responses. Also, in conference in my office I am open in talking about my own experiences as a lesbian.

My lesbian students have helped me to bring lesbian material into the classroom more overtly, through the example of their own courage. I remember one occasion not long after my own coming out, when I was still quite nervous about even using the "L-word" in class. When I was cueing up a tape of May Sarton reading I had a real struggle with myself over whether to include the introduction of the tape, in which she was identified as a lesbian. The struggle was actually physical, with me rewinding and fast-forwarding as I wrestled within myself. I was treating Sarton's lesbianism as I did my own. I knew students would like her as an author—then, if they found out later that she was a lesbian, I reasoned, they would still like her because she was the "same person." However, I was afraid that if the students knew first, they would dismiss her before they read her. Other lesbians and gays will probably recognize this scenario. But then, I pictured Jennifer's face, Jennifer sitting in our feminist circle, Jennifer who had come out to her classmates a couple weeks earlier, and I knew I had to include this part of the tape. Now, years later, as I write this, it seems quite trivial, hard to believe it was such a struggle. But it was, and I acknowledge it as part of my process as a lesbian teacher.

This semester, in a course in which I did not come out, it was another young lesbian woman, out to me but not to the class, whose courage helped me decide to use a video about Project 10, a support system for lesbian and gay students in the Los Angeles school system. I was nervous because a few students had already attacked material in the class as immoral, anti-Christian, and pornographic. Alice had spoken to me of the pain and isolation she felt as a lesbian in high school, of her suicide attempts, of her dream of someday being a counselor for lesbian and gay teenagers, of the high school teacher who "saved her life" by being supportive and helping her find a counselor. With Alice's face before me and her words in my ears, I decided to show a film in which lesbian and gay teenagers speak of the harassment they experience in school, and in which the mother of a gay son who committed suicide states tearfully that while before "my beliefs shaped my reality, now reality shapes my beliefs."[2]

In recent years I have used lesbian literature regularly in my classes, and I would like to think I have helped some students become aware of, educated about, and more open to lesbians and their experiences. Students at Nebraska include a large number of people from very conservative backgrounds who think they have never met a lesbian or gay person. When I teach lesbian material, I get a fair number of journal responses which say that lesbianism is "sick," "perverted," and "immoral." I always respond in writing to these comments, and in a non-confrontive way supply stories, statistics, information, and questions that ask the student to open up to new ways of thinking. Although I'm not out to these students, I use my experiences as a lesbian to give them information that I hope will help them break through culturally reinforced stereotypes. Often this will include stories of people I know or references to other reading material.

To a student who wrote in his response to *The Cancer Journals* that homosexuality was "unnatural," that people who "chose" it were sinners, I wrote:

> Many homosexuals feel that their sexual orientation is not a choice. It seems that throughout history, in different times and cultures, about 10% of the population is consistently homosexual. So it seems to some to be a natural phenomenon.
>
> I'm glad that although you disapprove of Lorde's lifestyle, you could still read and appreciate *The Cancer Journals* and listen to what she was saying about her own experience. As I said in class the other day, the last part of the book is very important to me too, where she explicitly links the personal and the political. Most of us would like to believe that those in charge have all our best interests in mind, yet it seems that profit is put above people most of the time.

Another student wrote in her journal that she didn't condemn lesbians, but they made her uncomfortable. She added that she "just didn't understand" lesbianism, or why some women would try to be men. To her I responded:

> I appreciated your openness here and in class about how hard it is to be open-minded about lesbianism when it's a new

topic for you. My belief is that literature gets us as far into other people's experience who are different from us as it's possible to get. Therefore, I use literature from all kinds of different women in this course. We don't exactly know why some women are lesbian; it seems as if throughout history about 10% of women have been. It just seems to be. Lesbians don't think they are men, or try to be men. They are women who love women. I appreciate your willingness to try to be accepting. Many people stay where they were when they first enter college, and never change their minds about anything. I find I'm always coming up against my own limitations, trying to get past them.

As I type these responses now, they seem overly careful. They may strike some of you as not challenging the students enough. The truth is I *am* careful when I encounter such resistance. I try to respond within the student's own framework. Very occasionally I get some feedback which lets me know I am sometimes successful. This summer I received a letter from a student who had a course with me three years ago. She wrote: "Although I was *extremely* homophobic at the time I took this class, those things you said and wrote in my journals somehow sunk in. I guess the actual thanks goes for your attempts to open my mind, even in the face of my hostility. Learning to accept 'those people' has come to enrich my life."

I use in-class exercises to enable us to discuss the students' feelings about lesbians and gays in a non-threatening way, but which also, hopefully, reveal hatred or fear of lesbians and gays as based on lack of information, personal experience, or thoughtfulness. For example, on the day we discussed "The Two" from Gloria Naylor's *Women of Brewster Place*, I asked the students to do a five-minute anonymous free-write responding to the question, "How would Lorraine and Theresa be treated in your hometown, the neighborhood you grew up in, your dorm, your sorority, or the neighborhood in which you now live?"[3] After we were done writing, I had one student collect the responses, shuffle them, and hand them out again randomly. Then I asked students to volunteer to read aloud the ones they had. There were many powerful, real-life stories of teachers "run out" of small towns, women forced to leave sororities, women shunned on dorm floors, as well as lesbian couples accepted as nurturing "aunts" in a neighborhood. I think the fact that, contrary to what they claimed, many students had knowledge of harassment against lesbians made a strong impression.

In another case when we were reading love poems by Amy Lowell to Ada Russell, I asked the students to address in small groups the question of whether, if they were editors of an anthology of "100 Great Love Poems," they would include these poems and, if so, whether they would include information which indicated that they were written by a woman for a woman. When they received the exercise in class, many students reacted in shock, saying they hadn't realized that these poems were written by a lesbian to her lover (even though the introduction in our anthology, which I had asked them to read, stated this clearly). Most students said that this information was necessary and should be included in any anthology, yet during the discussion at least half the students denied that these were lesbian love poems. Several had elaborate readings of the poems which turned the speaker into a male addressing a female lover (although when questioned they could give no support from the poems except that in one of the poems the speaker has "come home from work" and the lover has been home sewing). Two Catholic students read Lowell's poem "Madonna of the Evening Flowers" as a tribute to the Blessed Virgin Mary (although they could not explain why Mary was in the speaker's garden telling her that the peonies needed spraying). And one student declared that he simply "forgot" that this was a women's literature course and assumed that the author of the poems was male. I hope this exercise helped students see how easy it is to erase lesbians. Several weeks later, when some students were complaining that Audre Lorde didn't have to repeat over and over again that she was a lesbian in *The Cancer Journals*—that they "got it" the first time—I reminded them of what had happened during our discussion of Lowell.

Still, I had not, in all this time, come out in class. Why? I was, by this time, tenured, with a reputation as a good teacher (I had, in fact, received a Distinguished Teaching Award). When I thought about it, it seemed I had little to risk. But I was afraid of the responses of my students. I didn't want to "lose them," I said to myself and to friends. As I have said, I work with many students with little exposure to "out" lesbians or to lesbian issues. Even when I'm "in the closet," my use of lesbian literature is too much for some of them. One student in a sophomore level Twentieth-Century Women Writers class wrote on her evaluation: "Awareness of the feminist movement was what stuck in my mind, however I thought the course was heavily biased toward lesbian women writers. I didn't like having that pushed at me all the time." A student in another section of the same course wrote: "I do not think it is appropriate for anyone to read about lesbians and their habits. . . . I realize this is the 90s but there are some of us who still value decency, purity, chastity, and Christianity. . . . As far as [the teacher's] choice of materials and her own personal convictions, I am violently opposed. Her hero is Audre Lorde—big time lesbian. I find that a problem."

Yet I don't think that it is really fear of these students or fear of "losing them" that has kept me from coming out in these classes. I think it's something deeper. I want my students to like me, and I'm afraid that they won't if they know I'm a lesbian. This is internalized homophobia, but in spite of being able to name it and analyze it, I haven't routed it yet. Suzanne Pharr points out that when a lesbian passes as heterosexual by hiding her lesbianism she demonstrates a belief that others' acceptance of her is conditional—she believes they would reject her if they knew she was a lesbian. This, then, is the dynamic I set up with my students. As Pharr states, in this situation the lesbian can never truly believe in others' approval (73). What has resulted for me has been the increasing gut discomfort I described earlier.

In the spring of 1990 I taught Audre Lorde's *Zami* in a senior-graduate level Twentieth-Century Women Novelists course. I knew that not many students would have previously read anything by a lesbian in which the author makes the personal and political implications of her lesbianism one of the most important aspects of her book. From past experience I also knew that the responses to this book would be powerful, that most students would respond to Lorde's honesty and the poetry of her writing with strong emotion. Therefore, I decided to use a round-robin technique in class that night, a technique I use sparingly but have found very effective with emotional or controversial material. I had a student distribute a number to each person in the class. My only instructions were that we talk in turn, that when each person had the floor she could talk as long as she wanted, signaling when she was done by calling the next number, and that no one could interrupt for any reason—we would hold all comments and questions until the end, after everyone had a chance to speak.

I had manipulated things somewhat by grabbing a number somewhere in the middle of the pile, as I did not want to be either first or last. The first student, a heterosexual student I knew well from a previous class and was out to, startled me—she panicked and could not speak. But another student quickly traded numbers with her and, without comment, read the beginning of the very sensuous Prologue of *Zami*:

> I have always wanted to be both man and woman, to incorporate the strongest parts of my mother and father within /into me—to share valleys and mountains upon my body the way the earth does in hills and peaks.

I would like to enter a woman the way any man can, and to be entered—to leave and be left—to be hot and hard and soft all at the same time in the cause of our loving. I would like to drive forward and at other times to rest or be driven. When I sit and play in the waters of my bath I love to feel the deep inside parts of me, sliding and folded and tender and deep. Other times I like to fantasize the core of it, my pearl, a protruding part of me, hard and sensitive and vulnerable in a different way. (7)

It was a breathtaking beginning. As the responses continued, I thought that maybe I would come out. A number of women said they had been uncomfortable reading the book when they found out that Lorde was a lesbian, but that they came to appreciate her directness. "I found out that lesbians are people too and their relationships are just like anyone else's" was repeated two or three times. This is a beginning, but I hoped for a much more complex response. I want students to know that it's not the same—that because a lesbian can't hold her lover's hand as she walks down the street, because a lesbian's family might disinherit her because her lover is a woman, because a lesbian is afraid her classmates will likely taunt and harass her when they find out—being a lesbian in the twentieth-century U.S. is different than being a heterosexual. I wanted them to know much more too, about how being a lesbian is "nothing so simple and dismissible as the fact that two women might go to bed together. It was a sense of desiring oneself; above all, of choosing oneself; it was also a primary intensity between women . . ." (Rich, 200). But when I thought of coming out, I got so nervous that I couldn't hear what anyone else was saying; I knew that if I kept thinking about it that I literally would not even be able to speak when my turn came. So I steadfastly did not think about it.

"Number 21." The student's voice rang out clearly. It was my turn.

"*Zami* is important to me because of what it says about connection among women. It begins and ends with connection, and throughout Lorde acknowledges that she has become who she is because of the love and support of other women. This book is also important to me because I am a lesbian." My heart was beating loudly and my voice shook as I said this. I gazed out into the class, but did not focus my eyes to meet those of the students sitting in a circle around me.

"Number 22," I said, calling on the next student.

I did not hear the next student's response to *Zami*. My heart was still pounding and my hands were shaking as I tried to continue to take notes casually, as I had been doing throughout the exercise. I had just come out in class for the first time.

My first response was one of elation. Students responded warmly and supportively. After class, two lesbian students came up and said, "Thank you." A heterosexual graduate student said, "I wrote this in my journal, but I also wanted to tell you that I think you are brave and I really appreciated what you did." A heterosexual undergraduate with whom I've worked before but hadn't been out to handed me a note in pencil on a half-sheet of notebook paper—"Dear Barbara, You are wonderful. I want to grow up to be just like you." Another lesbian student gave me a "Lesbian of the Year" card from *Lesbian Connection*.

Disappointingly for me, however, there seemed to be no real follow-up. In the round-robin that night in class, before we got to me, several students had responded to *Zami* by saying that they didn't know any lesbians, but they hoped someday a lesbian friend would trust them enough to come out to them. I was hoping, I guess, to be that person for some of them. I was hoping that heterosexuals who had questions or needed information might ask me for it. But after that night and a couple journal entries which came in the next week, there seemed to be no further ripples from what was, for me, a very momentous event.

Still, as I write this, I know that there were ripples—some which I experienced, some which I did not. I remember, for example, sharing personal experience in my responses to the journal entries on *Zami*. Perhaps I have begun to be an "I-witness" for some of my heterosexual students. I was heartened when, on the last night of class, at a party at my house, one student performed "Church Lady," a parody of a talk show hosted by an evangelical type. In calling various people in the class to task for feminist doings (leaving their children and husbands home alone to come talk about women's literature, for example), she called me to task for my lesbianism. Her skit was very funny, and I felt good that my identity as a lesbian was so much a part of the class for her that she could joke about it. Another student, who runs a film theater, gave me a poster from the popular lesbian film "Desert Hearts."

Still, of my three classes that semester, all women's literature classes, I came out only in this one. The others felt too risky; I was afraid. My coming out is a process, never finished, always evolving. In my work as a lesbian teacher I will continue to fight my own fears of others' judgment and rejection of me, remembering Audre Lorde's words: "[T]hat visibility which makes us most vulnerable is that which also is the source of our greatest strength" (*Cancer Journals*, 22).

Afterword: It has been four years since I first wrote this essay. I came out as a lesbian to a sophomore-level class for the first time the semester after I wrote it, in circumstances much like those detailed here, while we were discussing *Zami*. The very next semester, I came out to all my classes in a letter at the beginning of the semester. Initially, being out from the start was a real liberation for me; in addition, I felt that having my lesbianism as a given affected the classes positively in ways I couldn't begin to know about during the semester. However, in the years since, when I've been out to every class I've taught the first week of classes, my being out has complicated things far more than I anticipated. Unexpectedly, when we got to the Amy Lowell poems and my editing exercise, I felt more constrained than before. I began to worry that anything I said would be taken as "special pleading," that the students would perceive me as teaching this literature for personal reasons only. In subsequent semesters, these feelings have abated a bit, but I find the whole process of being out with my students much more complex than I originally expected it to be.

Regardless, I know that writing this essay was a crucial part of my finally being able to be fully out in the classroom—a tribute to the power of writing and of visibility.

[1]In 1994, this is no longer the case, although examples are still few.

[2]Information about the video "Who's Afraid of Project 10?" can be obtained from the founder and director of the project, Virginia Uribe, Fairfax High School, 7850 Melrose Avenue, Los Angeles, CA 90046. I recommend it highly for use with high school and college classes or with teachers and counselors.

[3]My colleague and running partner George Wolf devised this imaginative and successful exercise. We refined it on many runs together.

WORKS CITED

Atwood, Margaret. "An End to Audience?" *Second Words: Selected Critical Prose*. Boston: Beacon P, 1982. 334–57.
Lorde, Audre. *The Cancer Journals*. San Francisco: Spinsters Ink, 1980.
_____. *Zami: A New Spelling of My Name*. Trumansburg, NY: The Crossing P, 1982.
Pharr, Suzanne. *Homophobia: A Weapon of Sexism*. Inverness, California: Chardon P, 1988.
Rich, Adrienne. "It Is the Lesbian in Us. . . ." *On Lies, Secrets, and Silence: Selected Prose, 1966-1978*. NY: Norton, 1979. 199–202.

BARBARA DIBERNARD

MOTHER/DAUGHTER DIALOG(IC)S
IN, AROUND AND ABOUT AMY TAN'S *THE JOY LUCK CLUB*

BONNIE BRAENDLIN

The word in living conversation is directly, blatantly, oriented toward a future answer-word: it provokes an answer, anticipates it and structures itself in the answer's direction.

Mikhail Bakhtin

For woman to produce a narrative that challenges present hierarchies and creates a space for their remaking . . . "patriarchal" language itself must be given a new dimension, must be brought back to earth and made playful.

Patricia Yaeger

I n the 1970s I became, almost simultaneously, a feminist teacher/critic and the mother of a daughter. While analyzing novels emerging from the Women's Liberation Movement, where daughters struggle to free themselves from enslaving ideologies of wife/motherhood, I tended to identify with the daughters and to deplore the maternal machinations of fictional mothers, often characterized as little more than co-opted wives in cahoots with domineering fathers to coerce rebellious daughters into traditional wife/mother roles. As a mother of a daughter in an era when feminism was demanding a place for women in male-dominated culture, I often felt the conflicts among my perceived duty to socialize her toward survival and success in a masculine world, my determination not to replicate my own mother, and my desire to be my own woman and to let my daughter be hers. And just as often my daughter seemed caught between her need for parental direction and her desire for independence.

Excerpt from *All About Baby*: BABY is a (fill in the blank) girl; Nicole (Nikki) Lucile Braendlin, born on the 24th day of August, 1972, at 4:22 A.M. o'clock. Breast fed every four hours; begins taking vitamins at two weeks, spits most of the liquid out. At three months begins eating vegetables, spits her first bite of sweet potatoes right into Mommy's face. Hates her first bath; cries angrily. By fourteen weeks she likes her bath (never does warm up to vegetables). At one year she begins to walk and to talk; by eighteen months she eats grapes, salami, noodles and pancakes.

Antagonisms between mothers and daughters in U.S. history and literature became particularly acute during and after the 1970s, when the women's movement—advocating equality in a man's world—defined subjectivity in masculinist terms that privileged independence, self-sufficiency, and autonomy at the expense of traditional "feminine" relational values of nurturing and caring. Because these values had been embodied in an ideology of motherhood defined and dominated for years by patriarchal males, daughters of the liberation movement viewed them as outdated restrictions foisted upon them by their retrograde mothers. Defining themselves in ways formerly allowed only to men, "liberated" daughters wanted to usurp the traditional son's position, to move out of the home and into the workplace, to climb the ladder of success.

At age three Nikki tells everyone that she saw her daddy's "peanut and teckafuls" and that when she grows up, she wants to be a daddy and have "a peanut as big as da sky!"

Conflicts between mothers of one generation and daughters of another are inscribed in numerous texts of the liberation era, for instance Rita Mae Brown's *Rubyfruit Jungle*, Alice Walker's *Meridian*, Lisa Alther's *Kinflicks*, Margaret Atwood's *Lady Oracle*, and Maxine Hong Kingston's *The Woman Warrior*, all published in the early to mid-seventies. In *Kinflicks*, independence for the daughter necessitates both divorce and rejection of her own child, and her mother's abrogation of maternal control. The novel represents maternal self-sacrifice as a fatal blood disease, implying that mothers must die in order for daughters to live. Hong Kingston's fictionalized autobiography also portrays the mother-daughter relationship as antagonistic and obstructive to female development, but she at least spares the mother, and at the end her "Song for a Barbarian Reed Pipe" unites autonomy, nurturing, and artistry, albeit in a fantasy of utopian female solidarity.

In fifth grade Nikki begins to dress up for school, exchanging her grungy blue jeans and tee shirts for a short black knit skirt with a black and white polka dotted blouse. Just before she leaves the house she clamps on black curly-que earrings. "Mom, why are you crying?" she asks me in astonishment. "Just one tear, Nik, to celebrate your maturation!" I joke. Despite my determination to raise a liberated daughter, I have just seen her join the line of women—grandmothers, mothers, aunts, cousins, daughters—who have postured through time before endless mirrors, heads cocked to one side, hands adjusting earrings. Birds banding themselves.

In the eras following the women's liberation movement, we daughters of the seventies have become disillusioned with and conscious of our own co-option in masculinist ideologies and our efforts to replicate our fathers at the expense of maternal values; we've begun to identify with the mothers we had formerly rejected, thus complicating what formerly seemed to be a simple daughter versus mother conflict. Women can now, if they wish, be nurturing without being servile and can encourage men to care about others, protect and nourish relationships. In both fictional and critical texts, moreover, we are moving from antagonistic dialectic arguments—which were often (among critics and between mothers and daughters) really monovocal power plays—to more polyvocal, more dialogic, forms of spoken and written communication.

Dialogism, according to Mikhail Bakhtin, is the constant interaction among meanings expressed in spoken or written communication, insuring that no word, ideology, or discourse is privileged or remains privileged, even when it is supported by some kind of authority. In life, the development of individual subjectivity (personhood or self) occurs in the context of one's social and cultural languages (discourses); during the development process, when adolescents and young adults are encouraged—or coerced—into internalizing the discourses of their elders, conflicts arise because the new generation also resists becoming the old. But while individuation is the process by which a society indoctrinates its young into its value systems, it also creates a space for defiance of tradition and of choice among other, competing ideologies. Resistance to and re-evaluation of old values, coupled with new choices, introduce new voices into society; thus as the young grow up into adulthood, becoming modified versions of their parents, they promote and insure sociocultural change (if not, necessarily, progress). In the novel, Bakhtin suggests, the interaction among discourses appears as dialogues among characters, between an author and the characters, between readers and texts, and among various ideologies that permeate a work, linking text and contexts. Literary characters may be read as representing various subject positions, beliefs and behavior patterns that shift and change as the characters act and react within their fictional milieu. And we as readers interpret literature in the context of our own lives; who we are—our cultural, social, political, and psychological selves—guides our reading. Those selves, of course, change over time, modifying the way we read.

As my daughter grows up, I am changing as a mother, becoming less concerned about guiding her development and more willing to appreciate her as a fellow adult, a young woman who struggles to make her own decisions, to become the person she wants to be, while retaining something of her parents' values and mores. She, I can tell, vacillates between resistance to becoming like me and a desire to emulate those qualities in me she admires. And my reading of literature continues to be guided by my own experiences as a daughter/mother and also by my study of contemporary feminist theory. Increasingly, feminist authors, theorists and critics—as we wrestle with issues of gender, race, and class, of history, ideologies, and aesthetics—are calling into question binary oppositions such as culture/nature, male/female, and mother/daughter. Cultural feminist theorists are redefining these putatively "natural" oppositions as socially constructed and thus dependent upon consensus for their continued existence and also open to modifications. Not only have I changed as a reader and critic since the 1970s, but women-authored novels have changed as well, reflecting the increased diversity of American culture and the literary scene, as formerly marginalized and silenced women and ethnic groups voice their perspectives. Published in 1989, Amy Tan's *The Joy Luck Club* both imitates and revises works like *Kinflicks* and *The Woman Warrior*, which antedate it by some fifteen years. Tan's novel depicts the socialization of young women as a dialogical process in which the mother/daughter opposition becomes more complicated, with mothers and daughters still antagonistic, but also more accepting of the similarities between generations. Instead of one daughter confronting one mother, Tan creates four mothers (three living and one deceased) and four daughters—contemporary young women caught in the marriage/motherhood discourse of western bourgeois capitalism. In conflict with their mothers, who embody marital/maternal ideologies of old China, the daughters express their desire for individuality and independence,

BONNIE BRAENDLIN

often entailing divorces from marriages that entrap them in "other-defined" roles. While their mothers object to these separations and appear to coerce their daughters into remaining in marital "enslavement," their own stories of their early lives in China reveal a female desire for self-definition and resistance that transcends generations, closing generational gaps. And, unlike earlier novels where the daughters' stories predominated, even to the extent of eclipsing the mothers' autobiographies, *The Joy Luck Club* foregrounds the mothers as characters and narrators who tell their own stories.

It's our voices, I think, that link us together—grandmother, mother, daughter. I resemble my father—blue eyes, premature gray hair—while Nikki has her father's baby face and slender ankles. But when my mother complains about the cold or coaxes our cat onto her lap, I hear myself in her vocal inflections. And several times recently, when I've called her college dorm, Nikki tells me, with a mixture of pain and pleasure in her tone, "Everyone says I sound just like you!"

The mother-daughter dialog(ic)s of Tan's novel inscribe various discourses, both traditional (for example, patriarchal ownership of women, the sacredness of motherhood) and resistant (as in the desire for independence and selfhood). These are not exclusively expressed by either the mothers or the daughters; although communication between the two is hindered by differences in language and social orientation, both mothers and daughters share inherited beliefs about wife/mother roles that empower and disempower women. Both are in conflict over simultaneous desires to comply with and to resist society's demands and definitions of women. And although the mothers feel compelled to persuade their daughters to accept prescribed marital and maternal duties, they too resist total compliance with demands made by these roles. Some readers of *The Joy Luck Club* complain that its ending, with daughters reunited with one another and with the spirit of the dead mother, is too easy, too simplistic, too utopian in light of the continued conflictual relationships between "real" mothers and daughters. As a feminist mother in the nineties, I read the ending of the novel, where Jing-Mei Woo holds her long-lost Chinese sisters in an embrace, as a resurrection and vindication of their dead mother, who longed to reunite her daughters, and as a rewriting of earlier novels where lone daughters repudiated their mothers' desires. Like *Kinflicks*, Tan's novel kills off a mother, but then replicates her in her daughter, creating a matrilinear genealogy of resemblances less utopian than that in *The Woman Warrior*. It can also be argued that closure in Tan's novel applies an Eastern philosophy of "both/and" to a Western predicament of either (daughter)/or (mother).

What I want to do in the remainder of this essay is to change the format to reflect the multiplicities of mother/daughter relationships and feminist readings of them in literature. As a feminist critic I object to the authoritarian word of the "fathers," the master scholars who appropriate knowledge, possess it, and (often reluctantly) give it over to their chosen initiates. Thus, instead of insisting upon a position as a mother who replicates the fathers by preaching the authoritative interpretation of a novel, I want to open my text to multiple voices and invite you as readers to interact with them, to participate in a dialog(ic) that "concerns the relations among persons articulating their ideas in response to one another, discovering their mutual affinities and oppositions, their provocations to reply, their desires to hear more, or their wishes to change the subject" (Bialostosky 789).

What follows is a scenario I have created as a dramatized pastiche of *The Joy Luck Club*. Imagine the table around which three of Tan's mothers and one daughter gather to play mah jong and to socialize the daughter into the mother role. Just as Tan increases the number of voices and hence complicates the socialization process by interpolating the stories of other mothers, grandmothers, and daughters, so I wish to complicate (but also illuminate) the issue of mother/daughter relations by gathering together around the table several women for a discussion, mixing in postmodern fashion textual figures and "real" people. I as moderator work to unify the group and focus the discussion, in much the same way as a mother might attempt to orchestrate a dining-table conversation (like Mrs. Ramsay in Virginia Woolf's *To the Lighthouse*, for example) or as a novelist, according to Bakhtin, tries to orchestrate the "Tower of Babel mixing of languages," the "heteroglot voices among which [her] own voice must also sound" (278) in her text.

By illuminating subtleties in the mother/daughter binary opposition, this polyvocal conversation suggests ways in which mothers and daughters may exchange and sometimes change their (and our) ideological positions and thus encourage a better understanding of one another's views. This dialog(ic) inescapably reinscribes but also defies the opposition—socially and textually constructed in the liberation era—through interchange of ideas and identities among women who both adhere to and resist traditional roles, who agree and disagree, exchanging roles and positions so "that [binary] oppositions are only apparent, that the alleged polarities inhabit each other" (Hekman 47). In the women's discussion, differences may not be resolved, but emerging similarities among the women call into question the divisive mother/daughter dichotomy that plagues intergenerational relationships.

My scenario opens Tan's text to a contextual dialogue that resists the closure of any one interpretation; in the end, there will be no resolution to the discussion or to the generational conflict. But I hope that through the exchanges and in the gaps and interstices between them, meanings will be made and interpretation enhanced by the participants, including you as reader. Here you may participate in the dialogue as one does in any conversation where speakers anticipate answers and exchange ideas, constructing meaning in the process; you are invited not to be "a person who passively understands but . . . one who actively answers and reacts," offering either "resistance or support," but in either case "enriching the discourse" (Bahktin 280–81).

Mother/Daughter Dialog(ics)
A Scenario in One Act with a Beginning, a Middle, but No End

I/Moderator: We are pleased to welcome you all, especially those of you who are mothers and daughters, to our discussion. Our topic is "Contemporary Mother/Daughter Relations" and we will begin with **Jing-Mei Woo**, a daughter from *The Joy Luck Club (JLC)*, relating a conversation with her dead mother's friends who want to send her to China to find her half-sisters, the daughters of her mother's first marriage, and tell them about her mother.

Jing-Mei Woo: "'What will I say? What can I tell them about my mother? I don't know anything. She was my mother.'
The aunties are looking at me as if I had become crazy right before their eyes.
'Not know your own mother?' cries Auntie An-mei with disbelief. 'How can you say? Your mother is in your bones!'
. . . 'Imagine, a daughter not knowing her own mother!'"(*JLC* 31).

The noted psychoanalyst and linguist **Julia Kristeva** smiles: "As the addressee of every demand, the mother occupies the place of alterity. Her replete body, the receptacle and guarantor of demands, takes the place of all narcissistic, hence imaginary, effects and gratification . . ." (*Revolution* 47).

Luce Irigaray, a fellow French psychoanalytic theorist, looks angry: "With your milk, Mother, I swallowed ice. And here I am now, my insides frozen. . . . You flowed into me, and that hot liquid became poison, paralyzing me. . . . I want out of this prison. . . . You take care of me, you keep watch over me. You want me always in your sight in order to protect me. You fear that something will happen to me. . . . But what could happen that would be worse than the fact of my lying supine day and night? Already full-grown and still in the cradle. Still dependent upon someone who carries me, who nurses me . . ." (60–61).

"Wait at minute," I plead, "Are you arguing with Kristeva or venting your spleen? Could we please keep the discussion on track?"

But **Irigaray**, still fuming, interrupts: ". . . If you turn your face from me, giving yourself to me only in an already inanimate form, abandoning me to competent men to undo my/your paralysis, I'll turn to my father. I'll leave you for someone who seems more alive than you. For someone who doesn't prepare anything for me to eat. For someone who leaves me empty of him, mouth gaping on his truth. I'll follow him with my eyes, I'll listen to what he says, I'll try to walk behind him. He leaves the house. I follow in his steps. Farewell, Mother, I shall never become your likeness. . . . I'll leave us. I'll go into another home. I'll live my life, my story" (62–63).

Kristeva shrugs her shoulders and raises her eyebrows: ". . . the daughter is handed the keys to the symbolic order when she identifies with the father: only there is she recognized not in herself but against her rival, the vaginal, *jouissante* mother. Thus, at the price of censuring herself as a woman, she will be able to bring to triumph her henceforth sublimated sadistic attacks on the mother whom she has repressed and with whom she will never cease to fight, either (as a heterosexual) by identifying with her, or (as a homosexual) by pursuing her as erotic object" (*About Chinese Women* 30).

Jane Gallop, famous for *The Daughter's Seduction*, says: "To speak 'the same language' is to speak the *langue maternelle*, the mother tongue, taught the daughter by her mother. Irigaray does not want to 'reproduce the same history,' and 'reproduce' is the mother's domain. . . . The obligation to reproduce—the daughter's obligation to reproduce the mother, the mother's story—is a more difficult obstacle than even the Father's Law, an obstacle that necessarily intrudes even into the lovely, liberated space of women among themselves" (113).

Joan Delacourt, the protagonist of Margaret Atwood's *Lady Oracle*, reports citing a familiar figure in her London living room: "It was her astral body, I thought, . . . I pictured my mother floating over the Atlantic Ocean, her rubber band getting thinner and thinner the farther it was stretched; she'd better be careful or she'd break that thing and then she'd be with me forever, lurking around in the parlor like a diaphanous dustball. . . . What did she want from me? Why couldn't she leave me alone?" (137).

The **narrator of Sue Miller's *The Good Mother*** ruminates: "My relations with my mother were strained—it was clear that she blamed me for having lost custody of Molly. . . . It seemed astonishing and sad to me that all the affectionate and difficult hierarchy, the complexity of my mothers' family, should have been reduced, finally, to these diminished and fragile connections. Except, of course, for the claim of personality it would exert in different ways on each of us forever" (459).

Ann Ferguson, an expert on mothering, interjects: "Contemporary motherhood creates an ambivalent relationship between mother and child that is extreme. Children are no longer apprentices to parents nor may their adult lives be much like those of their parents, so it is hard for mothers to see their children as products reproducing their interests and skills. From the child's point of view, parents become increasingly outmoded authorities . . ." (172).

The **narrator of *The Joy Luck Club*** smiles as she relates an incident from the novel:
"'Do not ride your bicycle around the corner,' the mother had told the daughter when she was seven.

'Why not!' protested the girl.

'Because then I cannot see you and you will fall down and cry and I will not hear you.'

'How do you know I'll fall?' whined the girl.

'It is in a book, *The Twenty-Six Malignant Gates*, all the bad things that can happen to you outside the protection of this house.'

'I don't believe you. Let me see the book.'

'It is written in Chinese. You cannot understand it. That is why you must listen to me.'

'What are they, then?' the girl demanded. 'Tell me the twenty-six bad things.'

But the mother sat knitting in silence.

'What twenty-six!' shouted the girl.

The mother still did not answer her.

'You can't tell me because you don't know! You don't know anything!' And the girl ran outside, jumped on her bicycle, and in her hurry to get away, she fell before she even reached the corner" (*JLC* 87).

Delighted to hear a family story, **I** begin to reminisce about a conversation I had with my mother when my daughter was younger.

"If Nikki really wants to shave her legs, maybe you should let her."

"MOM. How can you say that, she's only *eleven*."

"Well, how old were you when you started shaving? Around twelve or thirteen. Anyway, girls grow up faster nowadays."

"She also wants to have her ears pierced. And she wants *me* to have *mine* done, too. Now what do you think about *that*?"

"You always were a baby about pain."

Jing-Mei Woo speaks about her mother: "I used to dismiss her criticisms as just more of her Chinese superstitions, beliefs that conveniently fit the circumstances. In my twenties, while taking Introduction to Psychology, I tried to tell her why she shouldn't criticize so much, why it didn't lead to a healthy learning environment.

'There's a school of thought,' I said, 'that parents shouldn't criticize children. They should encourage instead. You know, people rise to other people's expectations. And when you criticize, it just means you're expecting failure.'

'That's the trouble,' my mother said. 'You never rise. Lazy to get up. Lazy to rise to expectations'" (*JLC* 20).

"But," **I** say to my group, "haven't things changed in the last decades? Aren't mothers beginning to have a voice in literature, to have 'selves' independent of their mothering, to become reunited with their children?"

"Yes," says **Maya Angelou,** remembering when her son left for university: "My reaction was in direct contrast with his excitement. I was going to be alone, also, for the first time. I was in my mother's house at his birth, and we had been together ever since. . . . [H]e had always been the powerful axle of my life. . . .

"I closed the door and held my breath. Waiting for the wave of emotion to surge over me, knock me down, take my breath away. Nothing happened. I didn't feel bereft or desolate. I didn't feel lonely or abandoned.

"I sat down, still waiting. The first thought that came to me, perfectly formed and promising, was 'At last, I'll be able to eat the whole breast of a roast chicken by myself'" (272).

Marianne Hirsch, author of *The Mother/Daughter Plot*, adds: "[In the Demeter/Persephone myth] [l]oss is presented as inevitable, part of the natural sequence of growth, but, since time is cyclical, mother-daughter reunion forms a natural part of the cycle. In ancient times, the mysteries at Eleusis celebrated this mother-daughter connection as the union of light and darkness, life and death, death and rebirth. The hymn [to Demeter] itself, however, grants legitimacy to the mother's feelings of bereavement, anger, and wild desire, even as it insists on the inevitability and the necessity of separation.

. . . The 'Hymn to Demeter' thus both inscribes the story of mother and daughter within patriarchal reality and allows it to mark a feminine difference" (*Plot* 5–6).

Adrienne Rich, poet and scholar, says: "The loss of the daughter to the mother, the mother to the daughter, is the essential female tragedy. We acknowledge Lear (father-daughter split), Hamlet (son and mother), and Oedipus (son and mother) as great embodiments of the human tragedy; but there is no presently enduring recognition of mother-daughter passion and rapture" (237).

An-Mei Hsu, a mother from *The Joy Luck Club*, laments: "Yesterday my daughter said to me, 'My marriage is falling apart.'

"And now all she can do is watch it fall. She lies down on a psychiatrist couch, squeezing tears out about this shame. And, I think, she will lie there until there is nothing more to fall, nothing left to cry about, everything dry.

"She cried, 'No choice! No choice!' She doesn't know. If she doesn't speak, she is making a choice. If she doesn't try, she can lose her chance forever.

"I know this, because I was raised the Chinese way: I was taught to desire nothing, to swallow other people's misery, to eat my own bitterness.

"And even though I taught my daughter the opposite, still she came out the same way! Maybe it is because she was born to me and she was born a girl. And I was born to my mother and I was born a girl. All of us are like stairs, one step after another, going up and down, but all going the same way" (*JLC* 241).

Nancy Chodorow and Susan Contratto, who have exposed the ideology of "perfect motherhood" as "fantasy," chorus: "The assumption that women have the right to mother, as well as not to mother, and the recognition that mothering, though it may be conflictual and oppressive, is also emotionally central and gratifying in some women's lives, has created a level of tension and ambivalence in recent writing that was missing in the earlier discussion" (55).

Nan Bauer Maglin informs us that "[i]n the literature of matrilineage, five interconnecting themes appear and reappear:
1. the recognition by the daughter that her voice is not entirely her own;
2. the importance of trying to really see one's mother in spite of or beyond the blindness and skewed vision that growing up together causes;
3. the amazement and humility about the strength of our mothers;
4. the need to recite one's matrilineage, to find a ritual to both get back there and preserve it;
5. and still, the anger and despair about the pain and the silence borne and handed on from mother and daughter" (258).

Amy Tan talks about her mother's reaction to *The Joy Luck Club*: "When she read the stories, the ones set in China, she laughed. She didn't see that they were anything at all like her life. There was one story in particular, 'The Moon Lady,' that has nothing to do with her life. . . . But she got to the end of the story and she said, 'I feel like I was that little girl. That story is about me.' . . . That made me feel really wonderful. . . . I thought, My god. She got exactly my whole feeling about the story" ("Interview" 106).

This Christmas **Nikki** left early to join her swim team in practice for upcoming meets. "I don't think I'll be home again until next Thanksgiving," she tells me at the last minute, hoping to forestall any arguments. Later I hear her tell her grandmother, "Mom's unhappy that I'm not coming home this summer, but I have to work in Baltimore." "Well," says my mother, gleefully, I think, "What goes around, comes around. Now she knows how I felt when she left home for a year in Europe. She's finding out what it means to be a mother!"

Irigarary looks at me: "You look at yourself in the mirror. And already you see your own mother there. And soon your daughter, a mother. Between the two, what are you? What space is yours alone? In what frame must you contain yourself? And how to let your face show through, beyond all the masks?" (63).

Marianne Hirsch says, "Desperately trying to untangle herself from within her mother and her mother from within herself, Irigaray comes to acknowledge and to accept the interpenetration that characterizes female identity" ("Review" 210).

Rich smiles, saying, "[Mothers and daughters share] a knowledge that is subliminal, subversive, pre-verbal: the knowledge flowing between two alike bodies, one of which has spent nine months inside the other" (220).

I smile back: "I can just hear my daughter groan, 'Oh, *gross!*' But perhaps that view of mothers and daughters can help us appreciate the ending to *The Joy Luck Club*, where Jing-Mei Woo meets her dead mother's older daughters in China and . . . "

"Yes," **Jing-Mei** interrupts, "although we don't speak, I know we all see it: Together we look like our mother. Her same eyes, her same mouth, open in surprise to see, at last, her long-cherished wish" (332).

"We are," says **Rich**, "none of us 'either' mothers or daughters; to our amazement, confusion, and greater complexity, we are both" (253).

And so mothers and daughters converse textually and contextually, rehearsing our grievances, expressing our frustrations, lamenting/ celebrating differences and denying/affirming similarities. There is no end to the dialogue; it continues in our social and literary texts, weaving itself around, about and in our lives, as we desire, resist, accommodate, defy, and change our discourses and ideologies of mother/daughterhood.

WORKS CITED

Angelou, Maya. *The Heart of a Woman*. 1981. New York: Bantam, 1982.
Atwood, Margaret. *Lady Oracle*. New York: Simon and Schuster, 1976.
Bakhtin, Mikhail. "Discourse in the Novel." *The Dialogic Imagination: Four Essays by M. M. Bakhtin*. Ed. Michael Holquist. Trans. Caryl Emerson and Michael Holquist. Austin: U of Texas P, 1981. 259–422.

Bialostosky, Don H. "Dialogics as an Art of Discourse in Literary Criticism." *PMLA* 101 (1986): 788–97.

Chodorow, Nancy and Susan Contratto. "The Fantasy of the Perfect Mother." *Rethinking the Family: Some Feminist Questions*. Ed. Barrie Thorne with Marilyn Yalom. New York and London: Longman, 1982. 54–75.

Ferguson, Ann. "On Conceiving Motherhood and Sexuality: A Feminist Materialist Approach." *Mothering: Essays in Feminist Theory*. Ed. Joyce Trebilcot. Totowa, New Jersey: Rowman & Allanheld, 1983.

Gallop, Jane. *The Daughter's Seduction: Feminism and Psychoanalysis*. Ithaca, New York: Cornell UP, 1982.

Hekman, Susan. "Reconstituting the Subject: Feminism, Modernism, and Postmodernism." *Hypatia* 6 (Summer 1991): 44–63.

Hirsch, Marianne. *The Mother/Daughter Plot: Narrative, Psychoanalysis, Feminism*. Bloomington and Indianapolis: Indiana UP, 1989.

_____. "Review Essay: Mothers and Daughters." *Signs* 7 (1981): 200–22.

Irigaray, Luce. "And the One Doesn't Stir without the Other." Trans. Helene Vivienne Wenzel. *Signs* 7 (1981): 60–67.

Kristeva, Julia. *About Chinese Women*. 1974. Trans. Anita Barrows. New York: Marion Boyars, 1986.

_____. *Revolution in Poetic Language*. Trans. Margaret Waller. New York: Columbia UP, 1984.

Maglin, Nan Bauer. "'Don't never forget the bridge that you crossed over on': The Literature of Matrilineage." *The Lost Tradition: Mothers and Daughters in Literature*. Ed. Cathy N. Davidson and E. M. Broner. New York: Ungar, 1980.

Miller, Sue. *The Good Mother*. New York: Dell, 1986.

Rich, Adrienne. *Of Woman Born: Motherhood as Experience and Institution*. New York: Norton, 1976.

Tan, Amy. "An Interview with Amy Tan: Fiction—'The Beast that Roams.'" *Writing on the Edge* 1 (Spring 1990): 97–111.

_____ *The Joy Luck Club*. New York: Ivy Books, 1989.

Yaeger, Patricia. *Honey-Mad Women: Emancipatory Strategies in Women's Writing*. New York: Columbia UP, 1988.

OFFSHORE WOMEN
A PERSONAL LOG

NANCY PAGH

P ro Log: This project began with my interest in sea logs and with
my desire to find a larger context for the logbooks my mother
kept as my family boated in our cabin cruiser through the San
Juan Islands of Washington State and up the Sunshine Coast of British
Columbia in the 1960s, 70s, and 80s. My father had begun the logbook
and my mother began to correct his spelling and add a few details to
his entries. Before long they were sharing the responsibility of writing,
and after the first year she seems to have appropriated the space and
kept the log herself. It occurred to me that my mother had taken a form
of travel writing that was traditionally the exclusive domain of the male
conqueror—the explorer, the naval officer—and put it to her own use.
Or at least, she had made that form compromise for her; she would list
weather conditions, record departure times, and note the presence of
other vessels, but she would also describe ice cream bars that weren't
as good as those she'd had as a child, and she would wonder in the text
what her baby daughter was doing at grandma's house while she was
boating with her husband.

My curiosity about convergences and divergences in the experiences of boat travellers along the Pacific coast led me backward and
forward through time. I read the writings of explorers, naturalists, scientists, artists, fishermen, and vacationers. As I worked, it became clear
that I could not pretend to be objective about this project; after all, *I* was
the baby daughter left at home, and later was the subject of many of
my mother's entries as I boated with my parents. I could only read the
works of writers who traveled the Northwest as someone who had
been there, someone with ideas about how boating ought to be done.
And I read of expeditions as a woman—as someone traditionally not
wanted on the voyage. I found myself yearning to find a female role
model in this genre, and my search for her became my focus.

What follows are excerpts from my personal reading voyage. I
structured the work as log entries for several reasons. First, the form
granted me the opportunity to insert and assert myself alongside early
explorers and among the all-male expeditions—in the spaces where

women have seemed not to exist. This form made it possible for me to locate each entry within the particular time and space of a specific text, and to interrupt it with my own desires and to slide quickly from one idea to another, from one voyage to another. Finally, the log form allowed me to be reflective in a way that is discouraged in formal scholarship. Because I focus on gender issues, it was appropriate to choose a format in which I could explore my own voice and my own experiences.

---

11 March 1940, Monterey
We had planned to sail about ten o'clock on March 11, but so many people came to see us off and the leave-taking was so pleasant that it was afternoon before we could think of going. The moment or hour of leave-taking is one of the pleasantest times in human experience, for it has in it a warm sadness without loss. People who don't ordinarily like you very well are overcome with affection at leave-taking. We said good-bye again and again and still could not bring ourselves to cast off the lines and start the engines. It would be good to live in a perpetual state of leave-taking, never to go nor to stay, but to remain suspended in that golden emotion of love and longing; to be missed without being gone; to be loved without satiety. How beautiful one is and how desirable; for in a few moments one will have ceased to exist. Wives and fiancées were there, melting and open. How beautiful they were too; and against the hull of the boat the beer cans from the fiesta of yesterday tapped lightly like little bells, and the sea-gulls flew around and around but did not land. There was no room for them. . . .   (Steinbeck & Ricketts 27–28)

John Steinbeck and Ed Ricketts chartered a seventy-six foot sardine boat and sailed to the Sea of Cortez to collect marine invertebrates. I read eagerly, hungry to understand what happens on a sea "expedition." I can chase Sally Lightfoot crabs across the shore, steal a lemon pie and devour it under the bedclothes in my bunk at night, buy drinks for the locals at a cantina, come to understand the development of navigation, philosophize about "man" and the coming war, wage a battle with an outboard motor, and—perhaps best of all—laugh with the community of men aboard the *Western Flyer* and get all their jokes. I am one of them; or at least, as I read, I can pretend I am one of them. Caught up in their excitement, I am glad to leave the "melting and open" women at the quay. There is no room for them on this voyage.

And yet I am a woman. When, in my mind, I see the *Western Flyer* nose past the breakwater, something splits inside of me. I know that my imagination is invited to come aboard, to sail with the men—and I am eager to go with them, to be one of them. But a part of me remains at the pier with the empty beer cans, the crying gulls, and the women who shade their eyes with their hands and watch the ship slip away. I wonder, was this leave-taking as pleasant for the women as it was for their fiances and husbands? Were these women "melting" with love? With the foreknowledge of loneliness? Perhaps with a longing to go somewhere too, with the desire to be the center of attention, the one who decides when to cast off the lines?

I am a woman. And the older I get the more I come to realize how important it is to read other women's stories, to see into their lives, and to embrace my connections to them. After reading books such as Carolyn Heilbrun's *Writing A Woman's Life*, I've grown to acknowledge that women need the nourishment that the knowledge of other women's lives brings. I accept that only by understanding who other women were—the roles that they played, the choices that they made—can I define myself. Without stories about other women, women live in isolation and are without the insight or the power to name and define ourselves.

But I also love the salt water. Since I was a small girl I have delighted in its textures, its scents, its movements, its colors, its sounds, its invitation. When I am driving in a car with my father and we pass a stretch of smooth water on a brilliant day, an expression of near agony comes over his face and he says "look at that water"—which means "we should be out there." I suppose it is what the poets called "sea fever." My point is this: who could say I feel that ache one iota less than my father does?

Why is it that as a reader of sea-travel writing I seem to have to split myself? Part of my imagination is called to sea with the men, and part values the company of women and therefore feels obligated to stay on dry land with them.

Summer 1975, B.C. Fishing Grounds

Not all women were left at the quay, of course. There are the paying passengers. But I believe that what I long to find are women who had a role significant to the purpose of a voyage. Women who had a job to do, a space to fill, responsibilities which must be met for the voyage to be a success, a more permanent relationship with the vessel and the sea.

Searching for women who work aboard, I find Edith Iglauer's *Fishing with John*—the implication of the title being that she fishes alongside him. In 1975, late in her life, journalist Iglauer is on assignment with John aboard his commercial troller in British Columbia, falls in love with him and his "way of life," and stays. They try to share the space aboard the *Morekelp* together, and Iglauer undergoes a sea change—it is even reflected in her face:

> John suddenly swooped from his perch on the steering seat seized the square mirror from its slot behind the sink, and held it up to my face. "Look at yourself!" he exclaimed. "Look at yourself in the mirror and tell me whether you think this fishing life with me agrees with you or not."
>
> I looked from his beaming face into the mirror and saw, as if for the first time, the sunburned face, brown eyes, white hair, and freckles of a woman I was familiar with, all right, but the glowing look was new. I turned back with astonishment to John, who was still holding the mirror up to my face. "Is that really me?" I said, and covered my face with my hands. He took my hands away and looked at me.
>
> "I guess I've come to stay," I said. (187)

John allows her into his space despite his awareness of the superstition that, in his words, "the worst thing of all . . . was a woman on a fishing boat" (128). But there is always an undercurrent of tension because of her awareness that this boat is *John's* space; she says, "I was afraid of being a nuisance by getting in the way" (32). "What? Where?" she cries again and again as John barks instructions (36–37), until at last she admits:

> "Nothing that has to be done on this boat comes naturally to me," I said unhappily. "I don't think I can do any of the things you really need."
>
> "Like what?"
>
> "Oh, cleaning fish, or making up gear or jumping off the boat and tying it up to docks when you bring it in, and I'm not very good at steering. I don't understand compasses and charts, and I can't do *anything* mechanical."
>
> "You'll learn. You'll learn," he said. He leaned over and took one of my hands in both of his. "All my fishing life, I've dreamed of having someone like you with mental protein

between the ears as a permanent partner on my boat. I've fished alone most of my life, so I don't need help there." (37–38)

Iglauer is not simply a paying passenger, but clearly, it is always *John's* boat, not theirs, and the partner John has always dreamed of is one who will support him without interfering with his role as the one who actually fishes. Iglauer is wanted and valued on the voyage and she has a role: "By silent agreement, I gradually took over all the traditional female household chores—especially cooking and laundry. It was what I knew how to do, and I wanted to be useful" (89). As I read, I am encouraged to find a woman who had a job to do aboard, who earned her keep; yet Iglauer isn't the role model I've yearned to find. This was a woman who had borne and raised two children, survived on her own in New York City, and made a name for herself as a journalist travelling through Europe, the Northwest Territories and the eastern Arctic—yet throughout *Fishing with John* she writes of herself as an incompetent; everything that John does easily and gracefully is extra hard for her because she is slight and female: "We walked up the beach in single file, past an old fish boat on its side above the high-tide mark, and over some logs that John stepped across easily but that I had to scramble up and down" (146). Because *Fishing with John* serves as a eulogy to the now-deceased John, I suspect that Iglauer paints her physical struggles with a heavy brush, a rhetorical device to make John appear more masculine in contrast to herself. Clearly, John is meant to be the focus of the book; Iglauer concludes: "When John died . . . [I] could not continue alone in the fishing life. There are women who do, but I had been an observer, not a participant; it was fishing with John that I loved so much" (305).

It is an important distinction that she makes; Iglauer is not left on the quay, but she is offshore to be with her lover, not for the experience itself.

August 19, 1933, near Karlukwees Village

Amy and Francis Barrow, a middle-aged couple, cruise aboard the *Toketie* with their two black spaniels, Rinnie and Nanette. Beth Hill collected Francis' logs, arranged them and added historical material, and published them as *Upcoast Summers*. Amy is a find: an offshore woman, a participant, a partner.

In the photographs she is robust, great, smiling, her arm often flung around the slightly hunched and narrower figure of Francis. Together they cruise up and down the Inside Passage between the wars, searching for petroglyphs and pictograms (now preserved at the B.C. Provincial Archives and the National Museum in Ottawa). But their journeys were not so much scientific expeditions as they were simply a way of life in the summertime, poking into bays and inlets, helping the locals with their activities and listening to their "yarns."

Amy seems to be a full partner on the Barrow cruises, functioning not simply in the capacity of Francis' helper. Francis portrays her activities which contribute to the scientific nature of their work. In July 1938, he records: "In the morning Amy and I johnsoned [i.e. motored, the *Toketie* had a Johnson outboard motor used on the dinghy] round to our old anchorage to get water and disturbed a big old 'coon digging clams on the sand flat. Amy found a slate knife" (8). One month later he writes "Amy found another boulder on which were other petroglyphs" (98). During an earlier cruise, "near the entrance to Blind Bay Amy noticed a pictograph about 13 feet above high water on a rock bluff. This, I feel sure, has not been recorded, so we stopped and took photos and made a sketch" (24). In 1936:

> I took a large photo of the pictograph Amy found. She went off fishing while I was busy with the camera, and returned to say she had found two more pictographs a little further on. I could get ashore at each spot and set up the tripod, and old *Toketie* never moved, tied up to a piece of kelp. (99)

The logs imply that Amy often discovered the finds, and Francis sketched or photographed them. However, Amy seems quite capable of sketching, too: "We spent the day reading, letter writing, and Amy made a sketch of me while I was making coloured sketches of pictographs" (95).

Amy surely pulled her weight when it came to providing their food. In 1935 "after lunch we ran back to the picto and I made *Toketie* fast alongside the bluff and took photos and sketched while Amy fished" (46). Barrow notes "Amy went off in the morning and caught a snapper" (79). Her abilities to catch their food and contribute to their scientific work do not seem mutually exclusive: "Amy washed clothes, went off and caught a rock-cod which we had for lunch, and it was very good, and found a bracelet on the beach. I had a lazy morning, the only work I did being to solder McIntosh's gas can" (125).

Besides finding artifacts and fishing, Amy manages the traditionally "female" chore of cooking, doing a rather super job given the limited facilities aboard a small boat: "Amy cooked roast lamb, carrots and

potatoes, and a trifle: some feed" (90). Both share the chore of launder-
ing clothes, to some extent: "We did a 40-piece wash. When I say 'we,'
I did 4 out of 40. The sun is very hot today & the clothes will not take
long to dry on the cod line" (121). Amy even contributes to their trans-
portation: "Amy took me for a row before supper" (33–34). Judging
from the photographs of the Barrows, it is possible that Francis' frailty
may have encouraged Amy to take on many of the traditionally male
duties aboard their boat, but she seems to have tackled the responsibilities with zest, and earned her moments of leisure aboard the *Toketie*:
"Amy found it so hot that she lay on her bunk reading, her only clothing being a pair of spectacles" (74).

The only duty which seems to be Francis' alone is that of engine
repair: "On the way the engine suddenly stopped. It took me some
time to discover the trouble, which I found to be a broken spring on the
timer" (76). This entry makes me pause a moment and wonder—did
Francis always run the *Toketie*? Is the person who can repair a boat
more of an owner than one who cannot? Did Amy feel that the *Toketie*
was as much hers as it was his?

The images of Amy that I can see here encourage me. Reading
Upcoast Summers, I find that my imagination does not have to split
apart—I have a role model. Still, I wonder what Amy thought, how the
logs might be different if she were the writer.

1924, Inside Passage

I am surprised to discover that the first "real" account of North-
western cruising comes from a woman: Kathrene Pinkerton. In his
foreword to *Three's a Crew*, Charles Lillard points out that "unknown to
most, she's . . . the first woman to write about coastal cruising" (10).
Lillard adds that "Today, *Three's a Crew* remains our first cruiser's-eye
view" (12). In the context of this project, it can also be my first glimpse
at more than images of an offshore woman—I can see cruising through
her perspective.

Kathrene Pinkerton is very well aware that her perspective aboard
the *Yakima* and later the *Triton* is different from that of her husband,
Robert. She comments frequently on the roles their sexes cause them to
play: Robert's "fine male horror" at the "small mountain of articles"
she proposed to stow aboard (16), her "female martyrdom" in some
situations (103), her encounter with "that attitude which was to become known in our family as "taking care of mother"" (251), and
Robert's "male viewpoint" (302) and propensity to become "skipperish"
(i.e. ordering others about): "'You can't take your eyes off [the com-
pass] for a minute,' Robert said in his most skipperish manner. 'It's a

lot more important to know where we are than to have apple pie for dinner'" (88).

Of course, Robert is right: providing nourishment is a significant role, but while cruising, the ability to navigate *is* more important, and in *Three's a Crew* we see a woman comfortable in both roles: "I could handle the boat in rough weather" (58). She is also able—with a bit of luck—to fix a motor (260).

Kathrene and Robert cruised from Seattle to Alaska, first only in the summers with their daughter Bobs, then later year-round as they lived aboard. They were both able to live offshore because they were freelance writers. Pinkerton's account of their travels is filled with references to their vessel as a "home afloat," and she remarks to Robert that they seem to have "learned how to live at home while [they] travel" aboard their boat (164). It is important to her that "the Pinks," as their friends knew them, remained a family at sea, and had familial routines:

> This changing life had made the wheelhouse a gathering place. When under way, it was our social center. We hadn't seen so much of Bobs since she had gone to school. She and I joined the skipper as soon as below deck tasks were finished in the morning. . . . The nearness of the bridge to the galley allowed the cook to keep track of events above deck. . . . [T]ravel and [the] routine of living could go on simultaneously. I was always popping up, armed with a basting spoon or a fork, to salute a whale or a passing tug. (34)

It is also important to her to "engage in coastwise neighboring" (300) something like the Barrows did—although the Pinks tended to socialize mostly with other boaters and often travelled in convoy with friends.

Pinkerton writes about a split in her own imaginings and desires, a split between wanting to stay at sea and return to land: "We departed at once for our season of real fall cruising. As we dropped anchor in our first small harbor in Puget Sound, I had an odd dislocated feeling. Perhaps it was a fall nostalgia for the land" (223). She follows these thoughts with a bout of rationalization that changes her mind: "I was at home in what was practically an apartment. I was surrounded by my own things. I was fully occupied and very comfortable. And we had not swung at anchor more than a day before the strangeness of a fall home at sea left me completely" (223). She comes to attribute her dislocated feeling to her femaleness, as she confides to Robert and a fisherman: "'It must have been an atavistic female instinct,' I said. 'The first autumn chill makes a woman think of leaving water for the land, even when there's no rhyme or reason to it'" (223).

Still, her needs for the company of other women and for the land itself are themes which thread their way persistently throughout *Three's a Crew*. Pinkerton makes a point of saying that conversations with other women "ranged through women's topics—marriage, children, families and, inevitably, recipes" (176), and she never presents these exchanges as trivial—not even when she meets a native woman with whom she cannot speak at all: "We squatted there together, plaiting, smoking and stopping occasionally to eat a roasted clam. Talk was not necessary to establish a feeling of friendship and understanding" (173).

Because Pinkerton herself seems to plait together boating and family, but to consciously miss the strand of the land, it is not surprising that she is "fascinated" with the "women in the float houses of that hybrid country of land and sea" (156). Usually the wives of handloggers, these women lived in floating shacks which rose and fell with the tides along inaccessible beaches. Pinkerton is careful to note that "all revealed a yearning for contact with earth. Window boxes, pots of growing things around the float, did not satisfy. Women and hens—they must put their feet on land. Kinship with the earth is femaleness and as insistent as the male instinct for boats" (156). She extends her philosphy to the patterns she notices within her own family:

> I had noticed the difference in our own cruising. The skipper considered land a place for action and spent his quiet hours in his home afloat. He read on the afterdeck. I invariably took my book ashore. He marveled at Bobs' and my elaborate preparations for an afternoon on land and would hand down to the dinghy all our impedimenta—towels, books, sewing, paints, notebooks and pencils—with the remark that girls made a lot of trouble for themselves. If he joined us later for exploring, it was from a desire to see the country and not because his feet, like mine, demanded the feel of earth. Every so often I had to smell the perfume of crushed sweet fern and to walk in open places. (156)

I had hoped to find in Kathrene Pinkerton a woman who loved the salt water, who felt capable and comfortable there. Reading, at last, through a woman offshore, I find that those angles do not complete her. What I eventually come to respect here is that she found a way to explore both sides of herself—the salt water self, the land self. Eventually,

she chose the land. The Pinks sold their boat after seven years of cruising.
1936, Sunshine Coast

They called her "Capi," Muriel Wylie Blanchet, captain of her twenty-five foot cruiser the *Caprice*. Left a widow in 1927, she cruised with her five small children up the Sunshine Coast throughout the subsequent stretch of summers. In *The Curve of Time*, Blanchet is highly aware of the European sailors who have gone before her, and she points out: "We were not exactly trying to follow Vancouver's route—we already knew practically all the places he had been to. But we had a copy of his diary on board and we were filling in the few gaps in our knowledge" (53).

She quotes frequently from Vancouver and his ship's naturalist, Archibald Menzies, and makes connections between their experiences and observations and her own:

> They took shelter and anchored at night in the same coves as we did. They did most of their exploring in their small boats. Except for trying to make friends with the Indians, many of whom had not seen white men before, they lived the same kind of life that we did, and were concerned with the same kind of problems. (34)

Or at least, some of the same kinds of problems. Captain Vancouver did not have to wash clothes and prepare food for five children, nor to deal with a child's concussion away from medical help. The nightmares he had were probably not hers—of rescuing her children—and though he too was responsible for the lives of his crew in a faraway place, he had a surgeon, carpenters, and other specialists to support him. Blanchet was entirely on her own when it came to fixing the engine and navigating rapids, and she had maternal worries:

> A swift tide thrummed its way through the massed kelp, and the eddies sucked and swirled over some hidden reef. If our boat sank in the night, it might be a couple of months before we were missed.
>
> "That little white boat with the woman and children," somebody would suddenly think. "I haven't seen it around this fall." But by this time the little crabs would be playing in and out our ribs . . . and we wouldn't be able to tell anyone that we were lying down there below. (101)

Blanchet notes that "Vancouver's whole outlook on these beautiful inlets was coloured by this desire to find a seaway to the other side of the mountains" (20). She is aware that as captain of the *Caprice*, her outlook is different: "What did it matter to anyone where we went? We ourselves usually had some idea where we intended to go. But we seldom stuck to our original intentions—we were always being lured off to other channels" (128–29).

Bobs plays an important role in Pinkerton's book; likewise, the children are one important element of *The Curve of Time*. Like Pinkerton, Blanchet also takes great care with the picture when she shows us her relationship with other women. It is rare for Blanchet to have the company of other women on these cruises; in this scene she imagines them around her:

> It was harder to imagine the women. Perhaps they were shyer. I could only catch glimpses of them; they would never let me get very close. But later, on a sunny knoll on a bluff beyond the village, I surprised a group of the old ones. They were sitting there teasing wool with their crooked old fingers, their grey heads bent as they worked and gossiped—warming their old bones in the last hours of the sun. Then a squirrel scolded above my head; I started, and it was all spoiled. On the knoll where they had sat I picked up a carved affair—on examination, a crude spindle. The village lay below me, already in the shadows. Beyond, to the west, quiet islands lay in the path of the sun. All around me, perhaps, the old women held their breath until this strange woman had gone. (78)

Pinkerton discusses gender issues openly, but Blanchet does not. Pinkerton's language as she describes nature—in this case the Yucluetaw Rapids—is unabashedly steeped in sexuality:

> A great tree trunk came lunging down, and a whirlpool seized it, stood it on end, waltzed it around and sucked it from sight. A quarter of a mile beyond, the tree was spewed out and tossed into a fresh welter of turbulence and confusion.
>
> Rivers and cataracts have settled and regular movement. Here the tide snarled and surged and doubled its might in savage thrusts as it crowded through the narrow channel. And when the great tidal push increased in power, the roar intensified. The whole surface of the channel would lift suddenly. Then I understood why the Yucluetaws had been known to put a large steamship on its beam ends and hold it there, help-

less in the rapid's grasp.

We sat tense and thrilled as the spring flood built to a climactic burst of power. I was conscious of a tremendous inner excitement while I watched. Occasionally someone would call my attention to a newly forming whirlpool or a mounting boil. I didn't speak. I was exalted. Only a few great symphonies have moved me more. In the end, I was very weak and very tired. (83–84)

Here, clearly, Pinkerton identifies the movements of the rapids through the channel with her own sense of female sexuality. It is interesting to compare her passage with Blanchet's description of crossing the rapids at the entrance to Princess Louisa Inlet; although it seems less contrived, her description is undeniably sexual as well:

The entrance is a little tricky to get through at low tide unless you know it, but there is plenty of water. From water level, the points on one side and the coves on the other fold into each other, hiding the narrow passage. It is not until you are rushed through the gap on a rising tide that the full surprise of the existence and beauty of this little hidden inlet suddenly bursts on you. It is always an effort to control the boat as you hold her on the high ridge of the straight run of water down the middle. Then, as you race past the last points, the ridge shatters into a turmoil of a dozen different currents and confusions. Your boat dashes towards the rocky cliff beyond the shallow cove on your right; and the cliff, equally delighted, or so it seems, rushes towards your boat. You wrestle with the wheel of your straining boat, and finally manage to drag the two apart . . . and you are out of danger in a backwater. (22)

I did not find similar passages in the works of any of the male writers. What fascinates me is that Pinkerton describes the rapids through a metaphor of female sexuality; Blanchet writes from a male perspective—navigating an entrance, finding the hidden surprise of an inlet, feeling the sides of the cliff rush toward you, a turmoil, shattering, and straining, then dragging apart. I do not know why these two perspectives are so alike yet written from diffent angles, except that it seems clear to me as a reader that Blanchet is much more a captain than is Pinkerton, and she identifies closely with her boat. At another point in her narrative Blanchet remarks: "Perhaps it was because I was on someone else's boat and not my own, but I have never felt so insignificant [as I did there]" (114). Pinkerton identifies with nature itself, with the scenery which they move *through*.

Am I inventing the connections I see between Pinkerton's writing and Blanchet's? They seem so clear to me, and I want them to exist— even if these things may not be what I thought I would find written by offshore women. Blanchet, too, I am surprised to find, comes back to the land. "Four months of each summer were spent in our small boat up the long and indented coast of British Columbia," she writes, "but the focal point of our lives was Little House in the middle of the forest" (208). It cannot all be just my imagination. Capi Blanchet uses a feminine metaphor when she returns to the land; she calls this chapter "The Gathering In."

25 July 1978, Lumber Camp Bay

My memory, my entry. A few moments in a quiet place. It was hot—one of the hottest days ever out in the boat. Because of the heat, my father had rigged a patch of shade in the back of the boat by draping material over two oars he had propped up. I was down in the cabin, in the darkness, reading, and I could hear the voices of my father and sister carry over the water as they swam near the boat. My father was laughing; my sister was panting and giggling, calling out for him to wait, slow down. I closed my book and came up into the bright sunlight, thinking I might swim too. I remember evergreens extended out from the shore, the smooth surface of water, light green, pale with the reflection of oyster shells. I remember my mother sitting in the shade, between those oars, with a book open in her lap. But I saw that she was not reading, and was crying, and I could not imagine why. "Why are you crying?" I asked. She did not reply for a moment. Then, perhaps deciding it did not matter that I was too young to understand, she answered: "Because I'm so happy."

I was partly embarrassed over her show of emotion, partly confused. It seemed too girlish, inappropriate for the boating environment; I thought my father would not approve of this crying if he knew. I have never forgotten the moment, and return to it again and again in my mind, trying to make sense of it.

In her essay "Somebody Must Say These Things: An Essay For My Mother," Melody Graulich showed me that:

> women often cannot understand the significance of their own experience until they see it mirrored in literature . . . our best reading, like psychoanalysis, leads to an examined life. It leads also to an acknowledgment of our connections to other women

and to an awareness of how those connections shape our insights and conclusions. (2)

Laura Beatrice Berton's autobiography *I Married the Klondike*—like most of the logbooks and cruising narratives I have been captivated by—may not be Canonical Literature, but it offered me a mirror and helped me understand my most significant memory from cruising with my family.

Not unlike my mom, Laura Berton was put into a boat by her husband and was pretty much left to make the best of it with her children as the family travelled through the wilderness. In Berton's case the family passed down the Yukon River; like my mom and many "cruising moms," Berton was in charge of cooking, washing, and sharing the responsibility of the children's safety. Her role aboard fits the pattern of many other wives aboard boats; Berton's husband chose the vessel, the route, and the schedule, as well as controlling the craft. Like my mother, at times Berton was apprehensive, even frightened (perhaps she even moaned "Oh God" as my mother would do in rough water). But at other times she was comfortable in the wild environment:

> The children were tucked together into the prow of the boat. I sat amidships. In the stern, paddle in hand, watching the river, was Frank. I began to experience a sense of excitement and adventure, and the feeling of foreboding that had been strong within me at Whitehorse now passed. (175)

It is her conclusion to this memory that gives me a new context for the afternoon that my mother sat in the back of our boat, crying because she was "so happy." Berton writes about the end of the trip, when the family disembarked from the boat and returned ashore to their home:

> A feeling, half of relief, half of elation, not unmixed with a certain sadness, came over me as we entered the house. I was beginning to realize that these two weeks had been among the happiest of my life. All this took place almost thirty years ago, but the memory of those lazy days drifting with the current through that silent, wild country, with my children young and my husband in his prime, has never left me, and remains as vivid and as sharp as if it all happened a week ago. Wishing is futile, I know, but I would give a great deal to be able to do it all again. (190)

Seeing back into the history of Laura Berton through her narrative, I gain a new understanding of my mother's tears. I am no longer uncomfortable with her "inappropriate" or "feminine" behavior on board. I think now that my mother cried because she recognized and appreciated what Laura Berton saw only in retrospect: that there would be a time when her husband could not be strong, when her children would not be young and dependent upon her, when her role would change even though the wilderness that surrounded her might remain unchanged.

What did she write about that day? What did my mother log for that breakthrough, my most important memory? Turning through the musty smelling pages, suddenly valuing her words more than those of any explorer, I search for that day. And find it.

Tuesday   7/25/78
Sun shining on our window at 6:30.
    Sure would be nice to stay another day but it's too hot
. . . . we've got to move just to cool off. Kids got towed in
the dinghy. There's a boat in Nifty Bay that looks like he's
going to stay there for the summer—an anchor and three lines
ashore. Boats in Neat Bay also. We anchored in Lumber Camp
Bay. It's so hot! Swam a lot. Daddy fixed up a sunshade with
the oars and the back-drop.

My mother did appropriate that logbook and make a space for her own perspective. But there were limits; she did not say all the things that were—that must have been—important to her on those voyages. She gave my family an outline. The rest is for our imaginations to fill in. Her aim in writing, I think, she shared with Pinkerton and Blanchet. "This is neither a story nor a log; it is just an account," (7) begins Blanchet in her foreword, inviting us to lay aside our expectations and accept her own way of discoursing. Pinkerton, too, abandoned the expected forms of writing to describe her cruising experiences. Her husband "jeered" at her for keeping what she called her "personal log," but later admitted the value of her work (150).

I have had to lay aside my expectations, too. I have been surprised to find that the core of this project moved away from my search for a female role model who is as sea-fevered as the next man. I think I have been searching for a stereotype—Captain Ahab in a skirt. Thank god I never found her. In the end, what I have come to admire most about these offshore women is their ability to love and master sea travel while they maintain relationships and guard tender connections to the land.

Berton, Laura Beatrice. *I Married the Klondike*. Toronto: McClelland & Stewart, 1972 (orig. publ. 1954).

Blanchet, M. Wylie. *The Curve of Time*. Sidney, B.C.: Gray's, 1980 (orig. publ. 1961).

Graulich, Melody. "Somebody Must Say These Things: An Essay for My Mother." *Women's Studies Quarterly* 13 (Fall/Winter 1985): 2–8.

Heilbrun, Carolyn. *Writing a Woman's Life*. New York: Ballantine, 1989.

Hill, Beth (ed.). *Upcoast Summers*. Ganges, B.C.: Horsdal & Schubart, 1985.

Iglauer, Edith. *Fishing with John*. Madeira Park, B.C.: Harbour, 1988.

Lillard, Charles. "Foreword: What the Pinks Saw." Kathrene Pinkerton, *Three's a Crew*. Ganges, B. C.: Horsdal & Schubart, 1991.

Pinkerton, Kathrene. *Three's a Crew*. Ganges, B.C.: Horsdal & Schubart, 1991 (orig. publ. 1940).

Steinbeck, John, and Edward F. Ricketts. *The Log from the Sea of Cortez*. New York: Viking, 1962 (orig. publ. 1941).

Metamorphosis
Mutations of a Hungarian Continental Drifter into an American Woman

Olga Klekner

America

The gold of her promise
has never been mined

Her borders of justice
not clearly defined

Her crops of abundance
the fruit and the grain

Have not fed the hungry
nor eased that deep pain

Her proud declarations
are leaves on the wind

Her southern exposure
black death did befriend

Discover this country
dead centuries cry

Erect noble tablets
where none can decry

"She kills her bright future
and rapes for a sou

Than entraps her children
with legends untrue"

I beg you

Discover this country.

—*Maya Angelou* (Poems 78)

L oud, wild geese are passing over my house, and landing on the thirsty golf course stretched across the street. Primal instinct compels robins to chase one another. Summer has finally arrived: The migrating birds are nesting.

Birds, coming home, seem to be in transit, in a permanent in-between situation, never leaving, and never arriving. They bring to mind never-forgotten noises and sounds, tastes and smells nestled in the protected part of my memory. It used to sadden me when I remembered these things, when a startlingly alive morsel of past experiences suddenly escaped from my sealed yesterdays. It was a survival method, to seal the past, when even the present was painful and offered only broken wings to fly with.

Unlike the birds in their endless, tireless efforts to ease back and forth between two homes, I stay on my adopted soil and visit my past only briefly. I am afraid to disturb the once delicate but now solid new roots I have forced into the American soil.

Maya, I am starting to discover your pulsing America.

A little more than twenty years ago began the journey of a Hungarian girl who finally became an American woman, whose invited and uninvited ghosts and angels melded with her like daybreak melds with loyal skies. Writing, in a way, always involves some self-examination, and this essay offered a much welcomed chance to confront those unwelcome ghosts that are slowly corroding inside me. Writing is a confession also, and confessions are known to clean the soul.

I was born in 1952, behind the "Iron Curtain" in socialist Hungary. At that time, only a short seven years after the country's liberation from Germany's much hated Nazi terror, Hungary went through a profound change in governmental practices. This new government, based on Marxist ideology, promised a more equal, better tomorrow for the poor, who by history's magical touch, almost overnight had gained tremendous political power. Under a microscope, weakness can be found in most ideologies, and the actual execution of the Marxist ideology showed monstrous flaws without any enlargement. It created an incredibly austere political apparatus from ill-prepared citizens, some who were survivors of the underground movement.

As a child, I was fascinated with stories of underground heroism during the siege of Budapest. The taste of World War II was still in the veins of the country long after peace survived fears. Soviet authors flooded Hungarian bookshelves. I was insatiable in my appetite for reading. As I read, I became the hero or the heroine, determined to wipe evil off the surface of the earth. I was becoming larger than life, able to influence nations. One time, I will never forget, I *became* Lenin. In a composition class we were assigned to write an essay about our chosen idol. My twelve-year-old enthusiastic mind chose the legendary man who looked us square in the eyes from banners, buildings, office walls, calendars and bookshelves. I *was* Lenin, who loved freedom and hated imperialism. Lenin, who loved children and spent many happy hours among them. Lenin, whose unquestionable wisdom and foresight made it possible to rid his country of the brutal rule of the czar. I credited Lenin for freeing Hungary from the Nazis—after all, without him there would not have been a Soviet Union to save the world from fascism. As socialist eagerness dictated, Lenin had become Hungary's adopted father, strangely giving him almost real life among us. This was, of course, the Hungarian government's grateful political gesture toward the Soviet Union, which stationed thousands of soldiers on our soil to protect our nation from the "evil of the West."

My early school experiences were underlined with literature born out of postwar ideology. Growing up in the sixties and seventies was a great experience. I was a fairly normal teenager, except that I was wild about poetry, which I started writing at around eight years of age. I loved what we called "beat" music; I lived for reading and argued world politics. I accepted the socialist idealism presented to us through a controlled media and controlled school system. Propaganda about the West was alive and well. Capitalist exploitation was characterized as the core of Western democracy. I cannot recall many positive opinions being voiced about the United States. Along with "primitive sexual immorality," the darker side of wealth was always emphasized: the poor, the neglected, the homeless, the exploited, and especially the ghettos.

When black people living in America, if one could call that living, stared back at me from magazines, they never showed carefree smiles, or if they did, they still seemed to be flustered and high on God-knows-what kind of strange chemical substances to help them cope with their bleak lives. I used to think about the "ghetto people" living among "real" Americans but not allowed to be part of white society. Blacks, I concluded, were prisoners of a continent that punished them for being helpless victims of destiny. I had read in magazines and also learned in school that America, with her capitalism, was rotting and falling down, and only communism could save her from complete disaster. Little did I know back in the sixties that America and its "rotting capitalism" would survive the fall of the Berlin wall, witness the folding of socialism in Europe, and eventually offer to bail out the "greatest socialist superpower" in the world, the Soviet Union. Little did I know that one day I would be living in the country whose people I feared most, the American people. Little did I know that one day I would fall in love with millions of these people, white and black alike, and consider them to be the greatest, best-hearted, best-willed people on earth. Little did I know that one day I would thank God for giving me the gift of sharing my life, my dreams, my fears and my joys with these beautiful, truly free-spirited people of the United States of America.

Maya, you are the first American Poet who taught me to slash my soul and bleed to be free.

I believed that I was free in Hungary. I was firmly guided by a determined school system that taught Hungarian classics and required readings from the Russian giants of literature as well as world-class masterpieces, to become a socially conscious young woman. By the time I finished high school I had studied the Russian language for seven years, French for four, read most of Shakespeare and fallen in love with Homer and Dante. Hemingway offered a chance to peek into the American personality. Tolstoy's *War and Peace* became my Bible , wherein I read and reread Pierre's reawakened love for Natasha:

> Often in afterlife Pierre recalled this period of blissful insanity. All the views he formed of men and circumstances at this time remained true for him always. He not only did not renounce them subsequently, but when he was in doubt or inwardly at variance, he referred to the views he had held at this time of his madness and they always proved correct. . . .
> Pierre's insanity consisted in not waiting, as he used to do, to discover personal attributes which he termed "good qualities" in people before loving them; his heart was now overflowing with love, and by loving people without cause he discovered indubitable causes for loving them. (1248)

Since becoming part of the project for *Private Voices, Public Lives,* I have had many quiet moments of reflection wondering if these early readings shaped my life. But the question should really be "how" not "if," for I believe they did, with surprising power. The core of my personality may have come from generations of genes, but I also give substantial credit to books for shaping me into a young Hungarian ideologist dreamer. Reading makes one knowledgeable, and the right kind of knowledge has the power to beautify the soul.

With my ripe idealistic agenda neatly serving me as a comfortable "body halo," I pursued my interest in writing poetry and becoming a journalist. Then one afternoon, a chance meeting with a young man searching for his roots in Hungary turned my life upside down and soon afterward forced me to make the most difficult decision of my life.

When I met my future husband in 1971, I was a robust, life-loving, nineteen-year-old student on summer vacation, working hard under an extremely fashionable beehive hairdo to have men notice me. I was rather successful in that attempt: I finally got someone to buy me a coke on the beach. He was so handsome that I was slow to recognize a slight accent. Then he told me. He was from the United States. My blood froze in mid-August. I was sitting across from a real capitalist, who was probably on drugs, had nude pictures of women pasted on his walls, and was looking for sex only. For the next hour I gave the lecture of my life on the subject of proper "within the iron curtain" morality and my disgust for Americans in general. I had been an easy target for all the political propaganda I had been taught; I earnestly believed in it.

That young man who listened to my heartfelt but angry speech was, nevertheless, most impressed. A year later we got engaged and in the summer of 1973 I married the most decent human being I have ever met in my entire life. In the fall of that year I left behind everything else that was precious to me: Hungary and my entire family.

I arrived in the U.S. on October 27, 1973, with a vocabulary of "hello," "thank you," and "I love you," thus beginning my journey as a woman who would forever be a guest, in symbolic transit between two great continents. Thus, a twenty-one-year-old young woman, full of passion and naive idealism, made a decision that the forty-two-year-old woman I am today must live with for the rest of her life.

In the next five years, following the initial culture shock which left me despondent, I refused to learn English. I was frustrated that what I read with my eyes was so incredibly different when it was pronounced. The small amount of energy I had, I spent hating the language. I know now that when we do not understand a language, we judge it and respond to it by the simple sound waves it creates. To me, English sounded cocky, like a badly written ballad. I had no desire to sing it. I had no desire to read it.

I survived by using "kitchen English." I spent long hours watching old, romantic movies. Unintentionally, I became a quick learner. I started reading magazines, and if I could not understand a word, I guessed its meaning from a sentence's intended purpose. But I still wrote exclusively in Hungarian. I published my Hungarian poetry and articles in several newspapers. Under the pseudonym "Szivarvany," which means "Rainbow" in Hungarian, I published about fifty of my poems in 1979. In 1980 I was invited to join the Canadian-Hungarian Author's Association. A year later some of my poems were selected to be published by the Ontario Ministry of Culture and Recreation in an anthology titled *Living Free*. That something was seriously missing from my life, I only vaguely understood. I was lost in a culture I thought I left years ago but found again as I sat perched on the brim of the American melting pot. As I look back now, I clearly see that I only needed to leave a nest of ethnicity to learn finally to fly free. I could not understand back in the early eighties that for me, access to this freedom meant learning to love the English language.

In 1980, I was offered a job as Director of Advertising for an office equipment dealership. I knew nothing about advertising, but the owner, with his second-generation Hungarian eyes, must have seen unusual imagination and presence in me. Some wit—and ninety credit hours of European university classes—seemed to pave my way to ten years of job security. My first year in advertising was fantastic, the second was good, and from the third on it became merely routine. My colleagues, customers and clients were "charmed" by my accent. To myself, I sounded like a continuity of broken images.

In 1984, in a desperate search to express myself non-ethnically, but still within an art-form, I enrolled to study art at Henry Ford Community College in Dearborn, Michigan. I quietly and bitterly said "good bye" to a career in literature, knowing absolutely positively that I would never be able to write a sentence in English that could ever stand a chance of competing with my writings in Hungarian. I had never taken an English class prior to my enrollment, and I did not dare take one now, promising myself that drawing, photography and pottery were creative without the need for words to express their meaning. I had certainly picked up enough knowledge of English through my work to "get by" in my classes, but I found that just getting by was uncomfortable in a college setting. Often I felt the crimson of embarrassment melt on my face as I struggled in class to talk about my works, which nevertheless often ended up in student exhibits. With all my relative success, I still knew that something was missing. Expressing myself in clay was not the same as offering my exploded soul to the "gods of poetry."

It took me quite a while—until the spring of 1991—to make a decision to change course. I took aptitude tests and career exploration classes. I found out that a smart choice of career for me was in either writing or counseling. I was in shock. I knew for a fact that I could never write creatively in English. The other choice was psychology, so in the summer of '91 I officially enrolled in HFCC's program in psychology. At that time, the only English novels I ventured into reading were romances. I liked them for simple reasons: they were easy to read and even easier to forget. There was no literary quality to them. Then one hot summer morning in '91 I found myself sitting in a required English composition class. I was scared to death. My professor required reading books by authors I had never heard of. I was introduced to *The*

Golden Bowl by Frederick Manfred, a simple saga of the dust bowl era, a story as much about surviving the land's capriciousness as about finding a primordial mission, one's place in the land. I was not prepared for the English words' attack on my Hungarian nonchalance:

> And the wind came. Clear at first, it rolled and lifted, blustered hard and blustered soft. The wind raked the land. The sun parched it. The wheat, corn, pasture, and hay land became yellow, then brown, then black. The land hardened, fissured, broke into lumps, into powder. The once-clear wind became bronze wind that shadowed the land as it beat upon it. (6)

I don't know if there is such a thing as love at first sight, but the moment I started reading *The Golden Bowl* I was touched by the endless magic of this magnificent language and now I am forever lost in its breathless wonder and exciting possibilities. Manfred's powerful words described the Bad Lands I have never known yet have felt, I have never seen yet have heard of; land that could slowly rust into infertility under the people of Hungary too. I remembered rich, ripe fields from my childhood's travels as well as stunted, dried-out corn fields. Abundance has always been a hard-earned gift and forever in transit. Yet some invisible umbilical cords keep farmers faithful to dustscape and to memories of hope and prosperity. Manfred's zesty, rhythmic, and exuberant sentences kept me intense and angry about something unjust that hovers above the wind-raped land like sea gulls circling above the exquisite depth of the ocean that holds secrets and surprises. I don't know what could have possibly forced someone to say that a picture is worth a thousand words. To me, one word is worth at least a thousand pictures. One can whisper "meadow," and every color of the spectrum will be painted on my mind's canvas: blades of grass gracefully bending under warm winds, curious clouds gathering above green patches to gossip about worn edges and cutting embraces.

One needs to be possessed by unyielding intensity to be a poet, and Manfred is a poet who is blessed with an inner vision that reflects past, present and future on raw, vibrating landscapes that taste like rhythms on fire:

> East of the house gate, where a washout, or gully, turned with the highway, the roots of a tree-stump hung octopus-like from the gully's upper fringe. The skull of a cow, a broken box-wagon, an old bedspring, and other metal scrap littered the floor of the gully. (12)

I am grateful for *The Golden Bowl*; I am grateful for Frederick Manfred whose poetry in prose awakened the seed of interest in me towards the English language and its magic. I fell in love with poetry and its poets, whose hearts inherit bursting words and generations of fertile soil, images in greens and purple.

Maya, spirits of thousands of poets are nesting in your heart.

After I discovered Manfred, I started reading American poetry with unprecedented appetite. Among others, I enjoyed the poems of Louis Simpson, Sandburg, Frost and Whitman. In my second semester at HFCC, I enrolled in a creative writing class. After our first assignment's reading, I was devastated. The talent in my classroom floored me. I felt inferior. I was envious. How lucky the others were, being capable of bringing to the surface words that they had learned as they studied and questioned the world as children! I didn't want to embarrass myself in front of the class reading my simply stated epistle. After class, I hurried to see my professor and told him I was planning to drop the class. He delivered my second shock that day. He liked my writing. He didn't let me quit. From that point on my confidence grew in direct proportion to the volumes I wrote. At the end of the semester I was shocked again to have found myself winning second prize at the school's annual creative writing contest. A sestina I wrote was choreographed by Diane Mancinelli, Director of HFCC's Full Circle Dance Company, for one of the school's spring dance concert numbers. A year later I won first prize in the creative writing contest, and I was eligible to participate in a state-wide competition. I will never forget the call that came one afternoon. A woman who could barely hold back her excitement told me that I received first prize (out of twenty-nine colleges) in the state-wide creative writing contest.

Maya, I learned how to dance with my tears and laughter that afternoon.

By that time I was a regular, paid columnist for our "underground style" student paper. I was on a journalism scholarship for three semesters, writing almost exclusively about what I believed was the most serious problem in this country: racial prejudice. I was always approached by students and teachers with their opinions. One professor sent some of my columns to the White House, while another cursed me for being inflammatory. One day I decided to join the schools' African-American club. To my surprise, I was the first white person to ever become a member. When the president, who was paralyzed and in a wheel chair due to multiple bullet wounds, found out about my interest, he came to see me in the news room. In his whispering voice, carefully searching my face, he asked me, "why?"

I wanted so much to tell him. But I only said that I believed the first human being emerged from the beautiful continent of Africa. We all possess a tiny particle of the first womb that insured the breathtaking birth of humanity. That first womb was a black woman's womb. In a very real way, I feel I am part of him and his hyphenated world as much as he is part of me and my world. And the world is simply "us."

What I did not tell him at that time—for the realization had not crystallized in me yet—was that a gentle black woman had the most tremendous influence on my life. Rosa Parks, America's own Mother Theresa, was solely responsible for my continuing to live in the United States. Her marvelous pride and integrity planted a seed of resistance in oppressed people and started a movement that slowly lifted the blindness of ignorance from most of white America. With my young Socialist "true equal rights" belief, I could have never lived in the country that the United States was before the Civil Rights Movement graciously uplifted her and offered her a chance to reflect dignified humanity.

Yet in my studies, I was never exposed to African-American writers. It was not until 1993 that I discovered black poetry and fiction. With the rest of the world, I watched wide-eyed as gentle explosions of words were broadcast into the awakened universe on January 20, 1993, when Maya Angelou rendered with unprecedented resonance, a magnificent poem on the occasion of William Jefferson Clinton's inauguration.

A Rock, A River, A Tree
Hosts to species long since departed,
Marked the mastodon,
The dinosaur, who left dried tokens
Of their sojourn here
On our planet floor,
any broad alarm of their hastening doom
Is lost in the gloom of dust and ages.
(*On the Pulse of Morning*, 1)

Maya Angelou offered a myriad of the most compelling sensory experiences I could ever hope to be a part of. From her dignified soul flowed Biblical passages from an unwritten Gospel of primal religion, whose Spirit has never left mankind alone and thus has witnessed the human struggle to shape the history of a sacred land. And sacred land

---

lives all around us; it cries for rain in Manfred's Bad Lands, nurtures seeds of plenty on Ukraine's friendly fields, bathes in diamonds and dust in South Africa.

Maya, on that January day, I cried long and hard and felt very American when I was listening to you.

I am eternally grateful for my youthful decision to move to the United States, not because of material possessions, but rather because it gives me a forum to freely explore so many avenues of learning. Every day offers a chance to fall in love with something new or something old.

Maya, there is something positive and wonderful about being a part of this universe, a part of hyphenated America.

To view the American way of life from up close allows us to see flaws as well as gems. Clearly, Maya Angelou's magnificence lies in the gift of being able to help others to see both. In Hungary, I never thought I would become one of the foster children of America, who, in our hyphenatedness, would join African-Americans.

I wonder if that old socialist government would have let Hungarians see and hear Maya Angelou reading her poem on that January day. After all, nothing was supposed to be positive about America, and yet here was a black woman giving an uplifting message to the rest of *her* hyphenated Americans:

You, the Turk, the Arab, the Swede,
The German, the Eskimo, the Scot,
The Italian, the Hungarian, the Pole,
You, the Ashanti, the Yoruba, the Kru, brought
Sold, stolen, arriving on a nightmare
Praying for a dream.
Here, root yourselves beside me.
I am that Tree planted by the River,
Which will not be moved.
I, the Rock, I, the River, I, the Tree
I am yours—your passages have been paid.
Lift up your faces, you have a piercing need
For this bright morning dawning for you.
History, despite its wrenching pain,

Cannot be unlived, but if faced
With courage, need not be lived again.
(*On the Pulse of Morning*, 6-7)

History was in the making in those unforgettable moments when I discovered Maya Angelou. The next day the paper brought the full printed version of her spoken words and I lost myself in her message. Soon I scanned book stores looking for her works. I purchased *I Know Why the Caged Bird Sings*, the rest of her five-volume autobiography, her poems, everything. Each page taught me the saga of pain, of oppression, of pride, of beauty and the constant shadow of mistrust for white America, the America that never apologized to her African children for centuries of mistreatment and was slow to embrace their beauty, their grace, their wonder, their worth, their exquisite warmth.

Maya Angelou taught me lessons I will never forget. She painted pictures that will never hang in a forgotten corner of my mind. I learned how to close a door behind me and never look back, how to create a healing home within, how to radiate pride even in defeat. Once again, she reminded me, everything started in Africa. Even the shame of America.

I can't even begin to understand what it must mean to have pasts rooted into mortification or how it feels to have been found guilty of innocence. But when I heard Maya Angelou reciting her poem, something started to dawn on me that I could not fully realize, yet it unconsciously vibrated in all my molecules. It was freeing me from those who hate for the sake of hate: those who hate accents, who hate colors, who hate religions, and hate every disposition that has a different tone from theirs.

Here on the pulse of this new day
You may have the grace to look up and out
And into your sister's eyes,
And into your brother's face,
Your country,
And say simply
Very simply
With hope—
Good morning.
(*On the Pulse of the Morning*, 10)

Maya, these words can set caged birds free.

I used to think that I would never be free again. A Hungarian-American, although I lived in the freest country in the world, was a hyphenated American, and this hyphenation kept me in a political coma, pulling my identity in two directions, never allowing me to break free from this strange one-hundred-eighty-degree gravity. The hyphen, in its brokenness, suggested a brokenness in me.

Thanks to reading the words of Frederick Manfred, to hearing and reading the words of Maya Angelou and other great teachers, I have since discovered I no longer feel like a prisoner. In a sense, I have become the hyphen, the controlling force. I was raised by literature to become a woman, and by reading American authors on America's ancient, sacred fields I became an American woman. At last, I found the land that called for my maturity as it claimed me for its own. I am pulling closer to a golden past while I bath in sunshine streaming from the bursting buds of explosive new growth. Golda Meir once said, "those who do not know how to weep with their whole heart don't know how to laugh either."

Maya, I am laughing with all my freed soul and all my restless heart, as I tell you, as I tell our America, simply, ever so simply: "Good morning."

WORKS CITED

Angelou, Maya. *Maya Angelou: Poems*. New York: Bantam Books, 1986. 78–79.
_____. *On the Pulse of Morning*. New York: Random House, 1993.
Manfred, Frederick. *The Golden Bowl*. Albuquerque: U of New Mexico P, 1976.
Tolstoy, Leo. *War and Peace*. Inner Sanctum Edition. New York: Simon and Schuster, 1942.

Trapped—Then Released—by a *Gift from the Sea*

Lois Hassan

For some women, the hectic world of work, marriage, and motherhood, coupled with the problems of coping with the middle age leaves little time for relaxation and personal growth. As a college English professor, wife of a busy businessman, and mother of two teenagers, I was never able to find a few precious moments for such luxuries. Experiencing this confining feeling slowly surround me, I felt my inner self drifting farther and farther from my being as I met the constant demands of others. Fortunately, before I was completely subject to a total robotic state, I realized that the key to my freedom, literally, sat before me. It was like a secret treasure box overlooked day by day as I went through my normal routine.

Frazzled by my fast-paced lifestyle which lacked an opportunity for rest, I found what I believed to be an escape and solution to my need for peace. Shortly after turning forty, in the process of raising my teenagers, having a full-time career, and trying to plan for retirement, I decided I needed a place to escape from the chaotic daily pressures. I decided to search for a "cottage." Certainly, it would need to be one only a short, convenient distance from home, so I could use it as a weekend and summer retreat until I could eventually retire and make it my permanent home. Never did I anticipate that it would be here that I would discover much more than just a hideaway from the engaged world around me.

At first glance, this humble habitat was a far cry from the "dream cottage," I had imagined. It was in Fair Haven, Michigan, the perfect location, a little more than an hour away from my home in Livonia. It had a dock directly on Bouvier Bay. It was a small home that had been sorely neglected by a previous owner. However, the moment I walked in, I knew I wanted to someday spend my retirement there looking out the large windows at the breathtaking western sunset. I knew that with a labor of love, I could transform my dream into a reality.

My new interest in the bay view prompted one of my dearest friends to remember me with a very precious gift, Anne Morrow Lindbergh's *Gift from the Sea*. Receiving it, I knew I had the perfect rest-ing place for it. Yes, it would sit on the coffee table at the cottage—a definite addition to the motif.

At first, there was little time to relax, but as the cottage became more organized, I began to treat myself to small visits with Lindbergh, reading a little passage at a time while enjoying the bay view. When I first began, I considered my visits pleasure reading, but soon I realized that they were truly therapeutic, and before I knew it, I became akin to Lindbergh, her sentiments, and her life struggles. It was Anne Morrow Lindbergh who brought hope for my tired spirit, offering me a refreshing look at myself by unlocking the magic from the shells. Her simple explanation of the beauty locked in the shells helped me to discover that my life resembled the lives of others who were experiencing the same distresses and frustrations. She helped me understand that my own cries for rediscovering myself could be considered "normal," and I, like others, could learn from the sea how to release myself from the constraints and find beauty.

My trips to the cottage were enhanced by reading Lindbergh's *Gift from the Sea*, helping me to realize that I felt much the same as Lindbergh: "At first, the tired body takes over completely.... And then ... the mind wakes, comes to life again. Not in a city sense—no—but beach-wise"(10). I, like my new found counterpart, began to enjoy life again, to feel free like the waves that follow no special pattern but roll like a free spirit blowing in the wind. For the first time in a long time, I began to seize the day and relish in its treasures. During my weekend and summer visits to the cottage, my family and I had no set mission, no set time limit, no set pattern. There was no need for impatience. As Lindbergh explained:

> To dig for treasures shows not only impatience and greed, but lack of faith. Patience, patience, patience, is what the sea teaches. Patience and faith. One should lie empty, open, choiceless as a beach—waiting for a gift from the sea. (11)

And this was my quest, a search for myself.

From the *Gift from the Sea*, I have learned many lessons. From my trips to the cottage, I have solved many problems and dealt successfully with many trials. I have tried to incorporate Lindbergh's wisdom into my daily life, and yes, when the stress of the everyday fast-paced world causes me to lose my own self, I find peace by remembering my cottage visits with Anne Morrow Lindbergh and the three precious shells that helped me to understand myself: Oyster Bed, Moon Shell, and Channelled Whelk.

Oyster Bed

The term "shell" is often used in our daily speech. We refer to an introverted person as a person hidden in his "shell." The outer coverings of a turtle, lobster, crab, and snail are referred to as "shells." The important covering housing a new life is also called a "shell"—such as an egg shell. A covering for an explosive is called a "shell"—a cannon shell, a shotgun shell, and a bullet shell. The term "shell" is used in cooking to refer to a pastry shell or a pie shell. In science, nucleons of approximately the same energy are labeled as "shells." In fashion design, the outer covering to which an inner lining is attached is a "shell." The term "shell" can also be used as a verb. To "shell" nuts, peas, and even corn can mean to release the fruit from its covering. The word "shell" can be used in slang, as to "shell out" money. Here, it can mean to empty out. As beach jargon, to "shell" along the beach means to look for and gather shells. However, it was not until I began moving closer and closer to midlife that I began to realize how my own body "shell" was changing overnight, and my youth was beginning to slowly drain away as I undertook my journey into the "Silent Passage" Gail Sheehy describes as menopause.

Even though I did not consider myself a "beauty," I had still felt as though I was "young." The signs of aging—greying and wrinkling—had not affected me up to this point. Also, time had never been a problem, as I was naturally energetic, and I felt I could always make time for whatever I wanted to do. Completing goals was never a problem either. I always had places to go and things to do. But one day, overnight it seems, I became old. My body began to change, and I was a young person caught in what seemed to be a weary "shell" of a body with no way to escape. Each and every ache was magnified 1000 times, and a somewhat average body began to double in size even though my eating habits had not changed. Even my fashions changed to compensate for my new shape. I tried to camouflage my new appearance with long shirts and baggy sweaters rather than the short shirts and waisted dresses I was used to. Looking back, I believe the only person I was trying to hide myself from was myself. I did not like this change, but I could do nothing about it. Time for "The Change" had come, and I finally came to realize that I was aging. Standing before the mirror, I actually believed that I could see the wrinkles form and the dark circles expand. I became depressed as my outer shell began to go through a silent metamorphosis. According to Gail Sheehy:

> With menopause there is no choice. It happens to teach-

ers and discount store clerks and dental hygienists. . . . It happens to Navy pilots and gray-haired graduate students and former Olympic athletes. It happens to women of color, to women in the home, to women of glamour like Jackie O. It happens even in Hollywood. Raquel and Farrah and Ann-Margaret, too, must deal with menopause. (5–6)

Like many others faced with the same dilemma, I began questioning the chain of events, and with the help of Anne Morrow Lindbergh's look at the oyster shell, I found the comfort and hope necessary to accept this change:

> [The oyster shell] is humble and awkward and ugly. It is slate-colored and symmetrical. Its form is not primarily beautiful but functional. I make fun of its knobbiness. Sometimes I resent its burdens and excrescences. But its tireless adaptability and tenacity draw my astonished admiration and sometimes even my tears. And it is comfortable in its familiarity, its homeliness, like old garden gloves which have molded themselves perfectly to the shape of the hand. (77)

As Lindbergh explained, my goal in life, like that of the oyster shell, should be "tireless adaptability" (77). And this is not my goal alone. Sheehy's words helped me to realize that forty-three million women right now are in perimenopause (first signs of menopause), menopause, and past menopause (8). These women face this same path with no opportunity to retreat, and the only way to survive is to view this change as it should be viewed—as a positive stage in growth. As Sheehy reveals, "In truth, menopause is a bridge to the vital and liberated period in a woman's life" (6).

Reflecting on Lindbergh's thoughts, I can see now that:

> Perhaps middle age is, or should be, a period of shedding shells; the shells of ambition, the shells of material accumulation and possessions, the shell of ego. Perhaps one can shed at this stage in life as one sheds in beach-living; one's pride, one's false ambition, one's mask, one's armor. Was that armor not put on to protect one from the competitive world? If one ceases to compete, does one need armor? Perhaps one can at last in middle age, if not earlier, be completely oneself. And what a liberation that would be! (79)

For myself, shedding of ambition meant not to volunteer for every committee. It meant that I should not spread myself so thin that I could not be a valuable contributor. I knew my energy was limited, and for the first time in my life, I would need to learn how to say "No" without feeling guilty. Sheehy confirmed this as normal: "many women do experience waves of fatigue and bouts of the blues" (6).

I experienced another type of shedding, too. After striving for years to provide my family with a nice home and the necessities in life, I began to eliminate some of the treasures that I realized I had no use for. It was time, I realized, to pass on baby clothes and baby toys. It was time to eliminate extras such as extra towels and extra pots and pans and bowls that had not been used for years. For the first time, rather than accumulate things, I began to eliminate things.

As far as shedding my ego, I feel that aging forces women to be "humble." I know for the first time what I can accomplish, what I can hope for, and what I will look like is out of my control. I have "good days" and "bad days."

As far as embarking on new adventures, the mid-forties seems late to undertake new quests or try to be the best, smartest, and most beautiful. I know now that "time" is in control. Now, I realize the meaning of "The mind is willing, but the body can't go," and I know I must accept my fate and find a new way to feel fulfilled. So what was to replace my need to succeed, physically, emotionally, and economically? Lindbergh pointed out that:

> We, Americans, with our terrific emphasis on youth, action, and material success, certainly tend to belittle the afternoon of life and even pretend it never comes. We push the clock back and try to prolong the morning, overreaching and overstraining ourselves in the unnatural effort. We do not succeed, of course. (80)

I, too, did not want to accept my new fate. I felt it could happen to everyone but me. My strong desire to resist the changes made it almost impossible for me to accept; however, with Lindbergh's help, I found this was normal. We will do anything rather than face the need to shed the shell of youth and accept the chance "to fulfill the neglected side of one's self" (82).

> But in middle age, because of the false assumption that it is a period of decline, one interprets these life-signs, paradoxically, as signs of approaching death. Instead of facing them,

one runs away; one escapes—into depressions, nervous break-downs, drink, love affairs, or frantic, thoughtless, fruitless overwork.(82)

I now realize that no matter what I do, I cannot turn back the clock, and I, like Lindbergh suggested when meditating on the oyster bed, need to look at this period of my life as a "second flowering, second growth, even an adolescence" (81). Now I was being given a chance to develop "for growth of mind, heart, and talent; free at last for spiritual growth" (82). Concerning youth, I realized with Lindbergh's help, "beautiful as it was, it was still a closed world one had to outgrow" (82). And so with Lindbergh's vision, I began to look forward to my new challenges. The first, although I have resisted it wholeheartedly, I have begun to see as a chance to develop a new beauty through new opportunities, an inner strength.

Channelled Whelk

Once I realized that "menopause was the youth of my second adult-hood" (Sheehy 10), my new questions were "How do I make the best of this?" and "What process should I use to bring out the best in me?" Again, Lindbergh came to the rescue with her reflections on the Chan-nelled Whelk. She taught me that like the channelled whelk, whose basic necessity of growth was "simplicity," my goal to grow could only be accomplished if I looked at my untidy, complicated world and tried to "simplify" my lifestyle. Lindbergh pointed out as she meditated on the channelled whelk that those who occupied the shell had died, and a little hermit crab was now living in it. It was now bare but still beau-tiful.

> Small, only the size of my thumb, its architecture is per-fect, down to the finest detail. Its shape, swelling like a pear in the center, winds in a gentle spiral pointed apex. Its color, dull gold, is whitened by a wash of salt from the sea. Each whorl, each faint knob, each criss-cross vein in its egg-shell texture, is clearly defined as on the day of creation. (16)

I felt relief when Lindbergh confessed that her own shell was "not like this. How untidy it has become," she continued. "Its shape is hardly recognizable any more. Surely, it had a shape once. It has a shape still in my mind. What is the shape of my life?"(16).

I, too, questioned, "What is the shape of my life?" If I was to accept my destiny, I knew I first had to answer this question. As a wife, a mother, a career woman, who tried to pull forty-eight hours out of a twenty-four hour-day, I knew I could not continue this pace. As Lindbergh stated, "I want to give and take from my children and husband, to share with my friends and community, to carry out my obligations to man and this world as a woman, as an artist, as a citizen" (17). How relieved I was to find that finally someone actually was faced with the same dilemma as I, and that she too had the same ultimate goal as I—to be at peace with the self.

I think this was why I found refuge at the cottage. It was a change— a chance to move away from the hectic, complicated world to a very simple, uncomplicated world. At this point in my life, I felt lost. "How could I find my way back," I contemplated. Again Lindbergh aided me to understand that "simplification" was necessary. At the cottage, there is little to clean and little to wash because clothing here is a necessity, not a fashion statement. Food is simple too—no time-consuming dinners—so life there is a simple one. So it is here that I began to find my inner self. I found that my quest for simplicity meant more time, time for me. For once, I had time to begin my search for self and my acceptance of my new stage in life.

Lindbergh explained that to achieve the goal of simplicity, I must cut out distractions. So I began to look at my life at the cottage in order to analyze what made it so different from my home in the city. Cottage life was more focused on self than others, while city life was focused on others more than self. And although it may seem selfish to concentrate on one's self, it is an essential "refueling" process if one is to continue to help others. Lindbergh helped me to perceive that women fill voids in their lives with endless distractions—until the well is empty. My own fragility helped to change my life. I had to learn to say *"no."* This demanded the art of shedding, and the place I began that process was at the cottage. Here I have fewer things to buy and to care for and fewer tasks to complete. So when I returned to the city after my first week's summer vacation at the cottage and just before the fall semester began, I decided to renew myself one day a week, usually Wednesday, by trying to have a stress free day even though I am in the city. On Wednesdays, there is a cottage menu, a simple soup, sandwich, or even a carry-in dinner. On Wednesdays, there is a cottage clean-up, no need to vacuum or dust; skipping one day does not hurt. On that day, I look forward to thirty minutes for me to fill with a walk, a bath, a book, or even a sketch. My midweek respite helps me to successfully fulfill my obligations.

I also followed this practice after considering Lindbergh's belief that today in America, more than anywhere else in the world, we have the luxury to choose between the simple and complicated life—and for the most part, we who could choose simplicity, choose complication only because we do not realize the advantages to simplicity. After finding the simple life at the cottage, I felt more and more drawn to striving for a simple life at home in the city as well.

Once I had realized the value of quiet time and the necessity for a healthy mind, body, and a renewed spirit, I found myself watching out for others. I found myself approaching my friends, both men and women, whom I saw falling prey to their endless sense of duty, with a word of caution. I felt the need to warn them before they too suffered both physically and emotionally as I had.

Moon Shell

"Eternally, woman spills herself away in driblets to the thirsty, seldom being allowed the time, the quiet, the peace, to let the pitcher fill up to the brim" (Lindbergh 39). Like other women, I was a victim of what Lindbergh referred to as "Zerrissenheit," a German word meaning "torn-to-pieces-hood"(50). I knew, if I continued in this mode, I could not survive. As I glanced through Lindbergh's discussion of the moon shell, I realized that this year, more than ever before, I felt that I had lost myself. I wondered who I was. Yes, I was wife, mother, professor, and committee member, cancer volunteer, chauffeur, housekeeper, accountant, secretary, and so many other positions, I forgot what it was like to be me. I wanted to be myself again. It was the moon shell that helped me find myself. I will be forever grateful.

The moon shell is a snail shell, round, full, and glossy as a horse chestnut (comfortable and compact). Lindbergh describes it as a moon "solitary in the sky, full and round, replete with power," or "an island, set in ever-widening circles of waves, alone, self-contained, serene," wherein the "past and the future are cut off; only the present remains. Existence in the present gives island living an extreme vividness and purity" (34).

Everyone is an island. As Lindbergh suggests, this basic state of solitude is not something we have any choice about. "It is, as the poet Rilke says,'not something that one can take or leave. We are solitary'" (qtd. in Lindbergh 35).

It is by being alone that one first becomes aware of one's self. It is in quiet solitude that I found myself again, and I realized that in reality, I was never lost. I was merely hidden beneath the untidy distractions in my life. There was no time for me. I, like Lindbergh, needed time to "refuel." Lindbergh reminded me that "Except for the child, woman's creation is so often invisible, especially today"(40). Being alone for a few hours at the cottage on Saturdays provided me with the opportunity to think without interference, to work without pressure, to dream without limits. It was a luxury I had never encountered in my city life. Lindbergh advised that "It is a difficult lesson to learn today—to leave one's friends and family and deliberately practice the art of solitude for an hour or a day or a week" (36). At first, to prefer solitude to other activity results in guilt. Lindbergh's insights helped me to relieve myself from guilt. She explained that if women were convinced that a day off or an hour of solitude was a reasonable ambition, they would find a way to attain it. Being alone allows a person, man or woman, to delve into areas that there is not time to delve into during a busy day. Lindbergh suggested:

> The artist knows he must be alone to create; the writer, to work out his thoughts; the musician, to compose; the saint, to pray. But women need solitude in order to find again the true essence of themselves; that firm stand which will be the indispensable center of a whole web of human relationships. (44–45)

And so I began to put other things on hold as I made my quest for solitude a priority rather than a luxury. From each solitary moment, as brief as it may have seemed, came immeasurable rewards. It was as if I had been dipped into the fountain of youth, and after immersion, I longed for another opportunity to be submerged again and again because I felt myself so renewed—so much more like myself.

It was by reading *Gift from the Sea* that I recognized that this challenge was not mine alone, but a challenge to all women. Lindbergh stated:

> Woman must be the pioneer in this turning inward for strength. In a sense she has always been the pioneer. Less able, until the last generation, to escape into outward activities, the very limitations of her life forced her to look inward. And from looking inward she gained an inner strength which man in his outward active life did not as often find. (51)

It was with sadness that I left the cottage after that first summer vacation. Even though I knew I could return on the weekends throughout the school year, I wanted to savor the memory of my discovery, so I brought a small moon shell home to the city. It rests on my desk, and when I gaze upon it, I can hear Lindbergh's words of wisdom:

> You will say to me "solitude." You will remind me that I must try to be alone for part of each year, even a week or a few days; and for part of each day, even for an hour or a few minutes in order to keep my core, my center, my island-quality. You will remind me that unless I keep the island-quality intact somewhere within me, I will have little to give my husband, my children, my friends or the world at large. You will remind me that woman must be still as the axis of a wheel in the midst of her activities; that she must be the pioneer in achieving this stillness, not only for [my] own salvation, but for the salvation of family life, of society, perhaps even of our civilization. (52–53)

My walk with Anne Morrow Lindbergh on the beach can be likened to my walk through life. Her book pointed out the need to see the real beauty in the beach and in life, and the necessity to be patient, patient, patient. *Gift from the Sea* served as my guide. From the oyster shell, I learned that acceptance of changes can bring a new hope and excitement for things to come. From the channelled whelk, I learned the need for simplicity and the way to accomplish it, and from the moon shell, I learned the need and means to build inner strength by undertaking a quest for solitude.

I thank my dear friend for giving me the book that revealed a way to break out of a slowly closing shell that was cutting off my vitality, my desire, and my future. Without her timely present, Anne Morrow Lindbergh's *Gift from the Sea*, I probably would not be as sensitive to the beauty of the sea and, even more importantly, the beauty of my own life.

WORKS CITED

Lindbergh, Anne Morrow. *Gift from the Sea*. New York: Pantheon Books, 1991.
Sheehy, Gail. *The Silent Passage: Menopause*. New York: Pocket Books, 1993.

Speaking Across Boundaries and Sharing the Loss of a Child[1]

Melody Graulich

All sorrows can be borne if you put them into a story or tell a story about them.—Isak Dinesen

I. Just a Different Kind of the Same Thing

In Susan Glaspell's feminist classic, "A Jury of Her Peers" (1917), Mrs. Hale tries to imagine the isolation and silence of Minnie Wright's life by wondering "how it would seem . . . never to have children around?" (377). Minnie is not there to answer, but Mrs. Peters is: "I know what stillness is. . . . When we homesteaded in Dakota, and my first baby died—after he was two years old—and me with no other then—" (378). Later Mrs. Hale sums up this moment: "We live close together, and we live far apart. We all go through the same things—it's all just a different kind of the same thing! If it weren't—why do you and I *understand*?" (378).

This essay is about women who know stillness and loss and from that knowledge reach out to understand other women. It is about going through different kinds of the same thing. And about the consolation of knowing that other women can understand, despite often living far apart.

II. How Is the Truth To Be Said?

In 1988 I wrote a poem called "Grieving For Something Stillborn." The poem was about a love affair that never came about. The title was, I thought, purely metaphoric.

"Both of your fallopian tubes are blocked," the doctor told me in January, 1989, after the tests, after the fertility drugs, after months of trying to get pregnant. "Unless you have major surgery, you will never have a baby. If you have surgery, if it is successful, if we don't find anything else wrong, if we can provoke you to ovulate, then you might have a fifty percent chance of getting pregnant in two years—if the tubes don't re-scar."

The next several months of my journal are filled with my despair and grief. Numb, I struggled to find the "right" tone, the right voice, to write about what I called "the worst thing that has ever happened to me." Lines like that led me to question every thing I wrote, every phrasing: "I can't be melodramatic. And that's not simply pride. I don't want to be false about this" (January 30, 1989). Some entries are defensive, filled with bitter humor.

> Last week I wrote Bill, a brief letter about my . . . I can't find a word for it. Barrenness is too ironic, too defensive; infertility too sterile. . . It is too easy for me to joke. "Problem" has lost its humor. Maybe naming it would be claiming it. What is most comfortable is too long, "my inability to have a baby." Is there an acronym? MINTHAB. INFERT. I did refine it from "inability to get pregnant," that not being the point. Ah. I've got it. My block. That story I wrote once, "Building Blocks and Bridges." My block. I like it. (Feb. 22, 1989)

Sometimes I did melodramatize: "I am a quiet, empty place" (February 25, 1989). In other entries I tried to find a way to accept feelings I had spent my life controlling:

> And I would have been a good mother. Thinking that, I almost censored it. You're being self-pitying, yelled one of my voices, and I started to cry. But I can't censor all my self-pity, or I can't grieve at all. I don't think I'll be a mother, and I do feel sorry for myself, and I want a baby, and I feel the loss. And sorrow. (March 1, 1989)

And in others I howled my outrage at the doctors at the University of Virginia student health center who in 1973 had refused to renew my prescription for birth control pills, telling me that an IUD would be much safer. And so they inserted a Dalkon Shield. After surviving a whole year crippled with cramps, I returned to Student Health:

> And [Dr.] Van Slyke, I go in there crying and saying I hurt, I hurt, and I don't know what's wrong with me, and I'm bleeding, but I know something's wrong, something's wrong. And he looks at me, all pus-y from infection, and he says, "Don't you wash before you come in here?" and stomps out

of the room. And tears come into my eyes and the nurse puts her hand on my arm and says, "I'm sorry. He shouldn't have said that. It's okay."

And he yanks it out, and I gasp and yelp. And I'm still afraid because he's pinched my ovary and said it's twice its normal size and there might be a cyst. But in a few days I'm better, and I can stop clutching my stomach all the time, and I stop bleeding so much, and I don't double up in bed. And though I can't stand the thought of his touching me again and though I know he doesn't give a fuck whether I'm okay or not, I go back. And maybe I don't see him, maybe by then I've learned to go when I know he's not there or to ask the nurse if I can see one of the residents. But they look at me and they feel around and they say my ovary is okay. They say I'm okay. But I'm not. I'm scarred. I'm scarred by a stupid plastic spider that my body tried to reject for a year before I got "help." And I'm scarred by being abused and mistreated and made to feel dirty and disgusting. By being treated roughly and pinched and prodded. . . .

I don't want to think about this anymore. It hurts me. (March 15, 1989)

Looking back, I can see that I trusted my angry voice a lot more than my "hurt" voice. I questioned my very ability to know what was in my heart. "Maybe you are not being honest with yourself about your unbaby. Or maybe you are finding out something important about your heart and what's in it" (March 3, 1989).

My journal represents my effort to find a voice I could trust to write about a loss. I never found it.

Looking inward only further depressed me, and so I looked to others. I have spent my life trying to find what's in the hearts of characters in literature, hearts that can tell me things about my own. Trying to understand how to mourn for my "unbaby," for a child who had never been, I remembered a poem by Gwendolyn Brooks called "The Mother":

Abortions will not let you forget.
You remember the children you got that you did not get,
The damp small pulps with a little or with no hair,
The singers and workers that never handled the air.
You will never neglect or beat

Them, or silence or buy with a sweet.
You will never wind up the sucking-thumb
Or scuttle off ghosts that come.
You will never leave them, controlling your luscious sigh,
Return for a snack of them, with gobbling mother-eye.

I have heard in the voices of the wind the voices of my dim
          killed children
I have contracted. I have eased
My dim dears at the breasts they could never suck.
I have said, "Sweets, if I sinned, if I seized
Your luck
And your lives from your unfinished reach,
If I stole your births and your names,
Your straight baby tears and your games,
Your stilted or lovely loves, your tumults, your marriages,
          aches, and your deaths.

If I poisoned the beginnings of your breaths,
Believe that even in my deliberateness I was not deliberate.
Though why should I whine,
Whine that the crime was other than mine?—
Since anyhow you are dead.
Or rather, or instead,
You were never made.

But that too, I am afraid,
Is faulty: oh what shall I say, how is the truth to be said?
You were never born, you had body, you died.
It is just that you never giggled or planned or cried.

Believe me, I loved you all.
Believe me, I knew you, though faintly, and I loved, I loved you
All. (1945)

Like Brooks, I felt as if I were tangled in "faulty" thinking, whining, struggling to discover "how is the truth to be said?" And of course she gave me some answers. Her poem expressed and paradoxically fed the hunger I felt; it now had words: "You will never leave them, controlling your luscious sigh,/Return for a snack of them, with gobbling mother-eye." Like her, I wanted to make absences into presences; she gives the children lives so as to more fully grieve their loss. The poem is not about guilt but about regret. I felt a similar kind of bitter regret for accepting the Dalkon Shield, a choice with consequences, something I had done, to myself and my unborn children.

Of course I thought about the differences between me and "The Mother." Brooks's speaker faced a far more complex emotional decision than I confronted, whether to have an abortion; she "knew" her children, "though faintly." Although the poem has no obvious racial signifiers and Brooks gives no causes for her mother's decision, Brooks commonly writes about African-American women like herself, often from poor families, women who could not afford another child, women for whom abortion was perhaps less an option than a necessity. A middle-class white kid, I used my resources at a prestigious university to delay childbirth until I had established my career; ironically, my privilege did me in. The historical context in which Brooks wrote about female experience is best conveyed by what the speaker does not have to state: in 1945 abortion was illegal. While my experience—and the daily experience of workers at women's health clinics—certainly suggests that women's bodies are still at risk, I write at a time when women are speaking with unprecedented freedom about what used to be called "deeply private matters." While we both mourned the loss of children who had not come into being, these differences helped determine the different choices and lives we had to live with.

Yet across those boundaries, and as I write now, Brooks helped me recognize and express my own feelings, a fundamental truth of feminist criticism: one cannot fully claim one's own experience without seeing it—or variations of it—explored in literature. Reading other women writers, I realized that though we were going through different kinds of loss, some much worse than others, I was not alone in struggling to find a voice to express my grief.[2] Like Brooks, women who write about lost children often listen for "the voices" of the "children" or of other women before writing. The theme crosses racial, class, ethnic, even historical boundaries, suggesting that such a loss—and the fear of it—is one of the most fundamental female experiences. Listening to the echoes reverberate across the gulfs between us, I felt immeasurable consolation. Extending my sorrow from my own life to the lives of other women, whose circumstances were often so much more desperate and entrapped than my own, freed me to learn how to feel it. Contrary to the image of the isolated artist, over the years I have learned that I write better in relationship, as I try to understand others: as a literary critic, I write *with* others, in connection with them. If I can't find my voice alone, I can find it together. As I write this essay. . .

III. Entering into Her Feelings Considerable

In 1849, Harriet Beecher Stowe wrote the following passage in a letter to her husband:

> At last it is over, and our dear little one is gone from us. He is now among the blessed. My Charley—my beautiful, loving gladsome baby, so loving, so sweet, so full of life and hope and strength—now lies shrouded, pale and cold in the room below. . . . He has been my pride and joy. Many a heartache has he cured for me. Many an anxious night have I held him to my bosom and felt the sorrow and loneliness pass out of me with the touch of his little warm hands. Yet I have just seen him in his death agony, looked on his imploring face when I could not help nor soothe nor do one thing, not one, to mitigate his cruel suffering, do nothing but pray in my anguish that he might die soon. I write as though there were no sorrow like my sorrow. . . . (qtd. in Boydston, Kelley, and Margolis 76–77)

Stowe records a common occurrence in nineteenth-century women's lives, the loss of a child. "Women had, on the average, seven live births in the course of their lives; a third or a half would not survive to the age of five" (Ehrenreich, 185). Women responded to these losses with a host of artistic forms to remember the dead: mourning pictures; hair wreathes and jewelry; consolation poetry; memorial quilts; photographs of the dead in their coffins. These often formulaic popular arts were so widely known that Twain could satirize them in his portrayal of Emmeline Grangerford in *The Adventures of Huckleberry Finn*, who draws pictures of dead birds with titles like "I Shall Never Hear Thy Sweet Chirrup More Alas."

Mockery and accusations of sentimentality and ghoulishness have been common responses to these popular art forms: acquaintances commonly respond to the hair wreath on my wall—made by a nineteenth-century woman from the hair of departed loved ones—with an "Ugh, you're kidding."[3] Although the mourning arts are generally seen as a mawkish nineteenth-century women's tradition, dismissed by elite culture, they continue to offer modes of self-expression for ordinary women (and men) and women writers into the twentieth century, as do quilting and other traditions.[4] Women often use this intensely private art form to cross from the private to the public. Mourning literature has provided women with a way to reach out to other women and to recognize commonality. As the impoverished childless poet of Mary Wilkins Freeman's "A Poetess" (1891) says when writing a consolation poem about the dead child of a middle-class woman, "I guess I can enter into her feelin's considerable" (187).

Indeed women have consistently extended the boundaries of mourning literature to recognize how women go through "different kinds of the same thing." When I began to think about how women were using the conventions of mourning literature to explore different kinds of losses, I was amazed at how often variations of the "lost child" theme recur in women's literature. The loss of a child—through death, abduction, miscarriage, adoption, abortion—is one of the most widespread themes in women's literature and art, continuing into the twentieth century in works by white middle-class authors like Charlotte Perkins Gilman, Mary Austin, and Jessamyn West; working class authors like Edith Kelley, Meridel LeSueur, and Harriet Arnow; American Indian writers like Beth Brant and Leslie Silko; African-American writers like Brooks, Alice Walker, and Toni Morrison; and Asian-American writers like Sui Sin Far, Maxine Hong Kingston, and Amy Tan. As I read these and other works, I was reminded that a literary tradition is a mighty comforting thing.

One day as I read "The Mother" with a class as an example of a mourning poem, I found myself unexpectedly telling my mostly-twenty-year-old students about the many women of my generation I know who are struggling to get pregnant and about my own infertility; feeling like Cassandra, I predicted that women would adapt mourning conventions to a new kind of loss, babies never conceived. (I did not offer to share my journal with them.) I recognize that many women of my generation did not have the resources or desire to delay childbearing; I also recognize the dangers of embodying my infertility in my "unbaby," the dangers of overlooking the fact that watching a child die or be taken from you is *not* really the same thing as mourning a child that never was. Yet the mourning tradition is a welcoming one. It is filled with texts where women reach across various boundaries to offer understanding to other women.

Asked what led her to write *Uncle Tom's Cabin* (1852), Stowe replied that the "book had its root in the awful scenes and bitter sorrow of that summer" when she lost her child:

> It was at his dying bed and at his grave that I learned what a poor slave mother may feel when her child is torn away from her. In those depths of sorrow which seemed to me immeasurable . . . I felt that I could never be consoled for it

unless this crushing of my own heart might enable me to work out some great good to others. (qtd. in Boydston, Kelley, and Margolis 178)

Stowe described herself as having "spent many a night weeping, the [new] baby sleeping beside me as I thought of the slave mothers whose babes were torn from them." These lines provide a context for the last line of her letter, "I write *as though* there were no sorrow like my sorrow" (my emphasis). Stowe well knew that her "sorrow" was widely felt, by many other women, and she used her own experience and the available convention of mourning literature to imagine the loss of slave mothers, to cross the boundary from the personal to the political in writing *Uncle Tom's Cabin*, with its repeated passages of babies being torn from mother's arms.

Of course, losing a child to a "natural" occurrence, death, is very different from losing a child to an human-created institution, slavery or boarding schools, from being denied one's fundamental right to one's child. We cannot speak across boundaries by denying their existence. Solaced by her Christianity, Stowe did not have to feel the same anger she gave to her character Cassie, whose "master" silences her "curses" and makes her "as submissive as he desired" by threatening to "sell both the children, where you shall never see them again"; tired of her, he keeps his promise (Vol. 2, 207). Nor would Stowe be forced to kill her own child rather than allow it to be sold like an animal. Yet Stowe and other mourners provide a model for imagining, for entering, the feelings of the "other"; they are examples of the feminist approach described by Peggy McIntosh where "the Other stops being considered something lesser to be dissected, deplored, devalued or corrected. The Other becomes, as it were, organically connected to one's self. Realities, like people, seem plural but unified" (19). Stowe knew mother love, worry, anguish, helplessness, sorrow, loss, grief, emotions she recognized as human, belonging to slave women as well as white women; caught up in our debates about essentialism, it is difficult for us to remember just how radical that belief was in 1850. But in creating Cassie, Stowe also recognized differences; she saw the inevitability of a black woman's rage and accepted, without judgment, her sexual negotiations and her decision to kill her child; Cassie is a remarkable creation from a woman so caught up in middle-class domestic ideology.

African-American women writers certainly did not need a white woman to show them the horrors of slavery, yet as Elizabeth Ammons has demonstrated, their work often has "strong affinities with *Uncle Tom's Cabin*" ("Stowe's Dream of the Mother Savior" 177). A few years after the publication of *Uncle Tom's Cabin*, Francis Harper wrote two poems in response to the novel, "Eliza Harris" and "Eva's Farewell," as well as "The Slave Mother" (1854), a poem which echoes with "shrieks" of loss.

> Heard you that shriek? It rose
> So wildly on the air,
> It seemed as if a burden'd heart
> Was breaking in despair. . . .
>
> She is a mother, pale with fear,
> Her boy clings to her side,
> And in her kirtle vainly tries
> His trembling form to hide.
>
> He is not hers, although she bore
> For him a mother's pains;
> He is not hers, although her blood
> Is coursing through his veins.
>
> He is not hers, for cruel hands
> May rudely tear apart
> The only wreath of household love
> That binds her breaking heart. . . .
>
> They tear him from her circling arms,
> Her last and fond embrace.
> Oh! never more may her sad eyes
> Gaze on his mournful face.
> No marvel, then, these bitter shrieks
> Disturb the listening air;
> She is a mother, and her heart
> Is breaking in despair.
> (quoted in Ammons, "Profile of Frances Ellen Watkins Harper" 65)

Like Stowe, Harper saw herself as a political activist; like Stowe, she recognized that the repeated line, "She is a mother," could speak across racial boundaries and engage the emotions of a white audience familiar with mourning literature; white women who had experienced Stowe's feeling of helplessness at being unable to protect their children from pain could be encouraged to mourn the black woman's helplessness to avert an even more painful and bitter loss.

Cassie, of course, ultimately rejects submissiveness and helplessness and refuses to allow her third child to be sold away from her. Stowe illustrates the tragic parameters in which she can act: "What better than death could I give him, poor child," Cassie asks (Vol. 2, 210). Until I began to think more deeply on the lost child theme, I had always been surprised at Stowe's apparent confidence that her audience would extend their empathy and understanding to Cassie's decision that because she loved her baby so much she could not allow him to "live to grow up" in the world of slavery. Even Toni Morrison, whose Sethe in *Beloved* (1987) commits the same desperate act, imagines Sethe's black community as judging her action. Yet many women from diverse backgrounds have felt Cassie's and Sethe's desperation; the theme of killing a child or allowing a beloved child to die crosses racial boundaries but is rooted in powerlessness and poverty. In 1909, Mary Wilkins Freeman wrote an eerie story which seems to anticipate today's custody fights, "Old Woman Magoun," where an elderly grandmother seeks to protect her granddaughter from sexual abuse; she allows the child to eat deadly wild nightshade berries rather than turn her over to the father. In 1912, Chinese-American writer Sui Sin Far published *Mrs. Spring Fragrance*, which contained the story "The Wisdom of the New," in which an isolated Chinese immigrant woman, Pau Lin, caught in a culture clash, fearing she has lost her increasingly Americanized husband, kills her young child rather than lose him to an American school. Variations on the theme abound. Thinking about her abortions, Brooks's "The Mother" speaks to her "killed children" and questions, "why should I whine/Whine that the crime was other than mine?" Many working class writers describe women unable to feed and care for children in the midst of poverty. In Tillie Olsen's *Yonnondio* (1974, but written in the 1930s), for instance, Anna accepts a miscarriage gratefully for she cannot adequately care for the children she has.[5] These women struggle painfully with their love for their children and their own feelings of guilt and responsibility over their ability to give life, as we can see in Edith Summers Kelley's *Weeds* (1923):

> As Judith sat by the bedside of the sick child that she had begrudged the life before it was born, her heart failed her at the thought that the little one might die. . . .
> And yet at the same moment that she yearned over the sick child, another set of thoughts, strange and sinister, came . . . thoughts that had come to her at other times and before which she had quailed, as, in the darkness of a wakeful night, one quails before thoughts of approaching death.

Of what use after all that this baby should live? She would live only to endure, to be patient, to work, to suffer; and at last, when she had gone through all these things, to die without ever having lived and without knowing that she had lived. Judith had seen grow up in the families of the neighbors and among her own kin dozens of just such little girls . . . [to pass] quickly from that into . . . the . . . burdens of too frequent maternity. . . .

Sitting by the sick child through the long vigils . . . the mother dwelt upon these thoughts. . . . And following them out to the end they brought her relentlessly to the conclusion that it would be better that the child should die. . . . No, she could not have her baby die. She must not die. . . . The mother shrank and quailed, feeling her burden greater than she could bear. (quoted in Olsen 104)

Like Cassie, Old Woman Magoun, and Pau Lin, Judith bears her burdens alone, struggling to answer "of what use" is her daughter's life—and her own.

It is difficult, impossible, for me to imagine living with Judith's burdens as she mourns her child's stunted life. Yet I recognize her desperation by the loss she is willing to consider. Reading Kelley, I think again of Stowe's line, "I write as though there were no sorrow like my sorrow" and of her feeling that consolation for her sorrow could only come about through attempting to understand and articulate the even greater sorrows of others. I think about my grandmother, isolated, battered and poor, whose toddler died of an accident while she was caring for him; I try to imagine the stories she never told. I think about how self-discovery and self-expression often begin with establishing a relationship between your own experience and someone else's, with looking out, not in. I think about writing as braiding.

IV. Braided Stories: A Place of Power

Like Judith, Leslie Silko's Ayah feels a pain greater than she can bear, a pain she carries in her belly like a child. She imagines singing a lullaby to her lost children, kidnapped by a white legal system and sent to boarding school, denied of their family, their traditions, and their identities "for their own good."

It was worse than if they had died: to lose the children and to know that somewhere, in a place called Colorado, in a place full of sick and dying strangers, her children were without her. There had been babies that died soon after they were born, and one that died before he could walk. She had carried them herself, up to the boulders and great pieces of the cliff that long ago crashed down from Long Mesa; she laid them in the crevices of sandstone and buried them in fine brown sand with round quartz pebbles that washed down the hills in the rain. She had endured it because they had been with her. But she could not bear this pain. She did not sleep for a long time after they took her children. . . . She carried the pain in her belly and it was fed by everything she saw: the blue sky of their last day together and the dust and pebbles they played with; the swing in the elm tree and the broomstick horse choked life from her. The pain filled her stomach and there was no room for food or for her lungs to fill with air. (46)

Ayah's grief echoes throughout American Indian literature, which is filled with stories of lost children. One of the most poignant mourning stories is by Mohawk writer Beth Brant. Brant tells what she calls "A Long Story" to draw parallels between the "legal kidnapping" of Indian children and of contemporary children of parents deemed "unfit" by the courts or social services. By braiding together the two stories, Brant erases the boundary between the injustices of the past and the present: when the government disapproves of a woman's behavior or wants to eradicate her way of living, it takes her children. She also braids together the strands of her own history and identity.

"A Long Story" alternates two stories, labeled only "1890. . . ." and "1978. . . ." The 1890 story is narrated by an unnamed American Indian woman, called "Annie" by the whites; I will call her by her children's name for her, "Nisten ha," mother. She remembers how her two children, She Sees Deer and Walking Fox, were taken from her:

[I see] my son and daughter being lifted onto the train. My daughter wearing the dark blue, heavy dress. All of the girls dressed alike. Her hair covered by a strange basket tied under her chin. Never have I seen such eyes! They burn into my head even now. My son. His hair cut. Dressed as a white man, his arms and legs covered by cloth that made him sweat. His face, wet with tears. So many children crying, screaming. . . . The women, standing as if in prayer, our hands lifted, reaching. The dust sifting down on our palms. Our palms making motions at the sky. Our fingers closing like the claws of the bear. I see this now. The hair of my son is held in my hands. I rub the strands, the heavy braids coming alive as the fire flares and casts a bright light on the black hair. They slip from my fingers and lie coiled and tangled on the ground. I see this. My husband picks up the braids, wraps them in a cloth; takes the pieces of our son away. . . . I see this. (78)

Throughout the story Brant focuses on identity, language and self-expression. The children turn into strangers called Martha and Daniel, who are "learning civilized ways" and who send her a letter written "in their hateful language" (80). Nisten ha's brother, who "understands their meanings, . . . pretends to be like those who hate us . . . [and] gets more and more like the child-stealers," reads her the letter. But she rejects her brother's assimilation and tears up the letter, burying "the names Martha and Daniel" (81). Changing from the "dead woman" who had "stopped talking," having "used [her] sound screaming their names," she talks to the children because she can hear them crying and "howl[s] at the sky every night" (77, 80). Her brother says that she is "crazy" and "bring[s] shame to [the] clan," that she "should accept the fate." But she knows that evil and witchery are abroad and continues to howl her challenges: "Why do they want our babies? . . . They want our power. They take our children to remove the inside of them. Our power" (84). In Nisten ha's dreams she hears the screams of wounded people and watches the earth soaking up blood. "What is left?" she asks? "I am a crazy woman. That is what they call me." As the story ends she still hears the children "crying for [her], though the sound grows fainter" (84).

Although Nisten ha and Mary, the narrator of the 1978 sections, live in very different worlds, Brant constructs her story, which is actually quite brief, around concrete parallels between the two women's stories. Mary also has dreams. Her story begins, "I am awakened by the dream. In the dream, my daughter is dead. Her father is returning her body to me in pieces. He keeps her heart. I thought I screamed . . . Patricia!" (78) She too sees her daughter taken away, her "face looking out the back window of his car. Her mouth forming the word over and over . . . Mommy Mama" (79). She too receives a letter, apparently dictated by the father, which she tears up; like Nisten Ha, she knows her daughter will be taught to hate her. Facing silence, she too "howls" her grief. She too is the victim of language used against her:

The word . . . *lesbian*. Lesbian. The word that makes them panic, makes them afraid, makes them destroy children. The word that dares them. Lesbian. *I am one.* Even for Patricia, even for her, *I will not cease to be!* (85)

Both Mary and Nisten ha reclaim the language, express their pain in strong, rebellious voices and remain true to who they are, but there is one crucial difference in their lives. Early in the story Mary raises the central question of all mourning literature: "How is it possible to feel such pain and live?" (79). Like other mourning stories, "A Long Story" pays tribute to the consolations of sharing pain with another woman, but it focuses on a specific kind of relationship, a lesbian bond. While Nisten ha is unsupported by her husband and brother, and no women friends are mentioned, Mary has a lover, Ellen, whose "mouth is medicine" (83). The two of them "share" the "heartbreak" by making love. Their "hair braids together on the pillow . . . [and they] move to [their] place of power" (82). While Nisten ha defiantly accepts that she is alone and "crazy," Mary's place of power sustains her and helps her to accept life; instead of Nisten ha's vision of the earth soaking up spilled blood, Mary "feel[s] the blood pumping outward to [her] veins, carrying nourishment and life" (85). Ellen's profession elliptically suggests the role women play in the lives of children and each other: she is a nurse. Recognizing the importance of braiding women's lives and stories, "A Long Story" is a healing story.

V. I Thought She Was Talking about Herself

In 1899 Mary Austin wrote a story about how the act of mourning a child brings together a group of women across both racial and religious boundaries. "The Castro Baby" describes a "bazar" held in a small western town, Maverick, to raise money for a protestant church. When a traveling photographer offers a free set of photos "as a prize for the handsomest baby," "Maverick . . . had a baby show," the voting "paid for at the rate of five votes for two bits" (*Western Trails*, 224). Balloting is brisk, with the "plumpest" baby of a respected man in the community well in the lead when Mrs. Castro, a poor Mexican woman from an outlying district, arrives with her "pitifully quiet" baby with its "wasted little face" dressed in its "best frock" (225–66). The doctor cannot understand why she's walked in the "blazing sun just to show off her kid, when it won't live a week at the outside, and she knows it" (226). But as the narrator says ironically, "feminine instinct comprehends even that which is beyond the wisdom of doctors," and even the childless young beauty, Miss McCracken, recognizes that Mrs. Castro thinks her baby is beautiful and wants a picture of it. The women of the town flock to Mrs. Castro to admire her baby. The woman in the lead, the unnamed wife of the mine owner, has a particular reason for reaching out to Mrs. Castro. She has recently lost her own child, and until Mrs. Castro's arrival, has sat watching "the mothers of children" in the baby show, "and her heart was very bitter" (225). Her comment that the baby is very pretty causes a "thin smile" to break across Mrs. Castro's face and lifts her own bitterness: "And the fairer woman smiled back understandingly, as she lifted the child with a thrill of aching remembrance at its feather weight." All of the women want to hold the baby, but when Mrs. Castro gives it to the mine owner's wife, "they understood that also" (226). By the day's end, Mary Carmen Mercedes Castro has won the prize and been photographed. The story concludes a few days later when the whole town turns out for "the burial of the Castro baby" (227).

The kind of story that is often labeled "slight" or "sentimental," despite its ironic tone, "The Castro Baby" chronicles a moment of understanding in the face of difference, a recurring theme in Austin's work. It expresses a woman's need for other women to acknowledge her as a good mother, to support her, to understand her loss. Read psychologically in the context of Austin's life, it is a deflected plea for women to reach across other kinds of boundaries to offer compassion and understanding—to herself and to her friend.

During the 1890s two young women who would become celebrated writers became friends as each struggled with a decision about "giving up" her child. The author of "The Yellow Wallpaper," Charlotte Perkins Gilman had just made the decision to send her young daughter Katherine to live with her father. Like her new friend, Mary Austin had also gone through a difficult childbirth and postpartum depression, with poor medical care, and when she met Gilman, she had begun to acknowledge that her daughter Ruth was severely retarded. Years later in her autobiography, Austin recounted how she defended Gilman against charges that she was an "unnatural mother": "I don't know what else . . . could have been done about the little girl. Charlotte had no way of making a living except by lecturing, to which she could not drag the girl about . . . . I was for her, and for the freedom from convention that left her the right to care for her child in what seemed the best way to her" (*Earth Horizon* 293). In defending Charlotte, she also defended herself, for almost everyone, including Austin's own mother, had blamed her for her child's problems. Ultimately, with the encouragement of a young woman doctor who began to practice in the region and perhaps thinking of Gilman's right to care for her child in the best way, Austin made the difficult decision to institutionalize Ruth. In the autobiographies the two women wrote many years after their friendship began, their pain at "losing" their children still remains fresh. Describing the difficult decision to send her child to live with her former husband, Gilman concludes "this seemed the right thing to do":

> No one suffered from it but myself. This, however, was entirely overlooked in the furious condemnation which followed. I had "given up my child."

> To hear what was said and read what was printed one would think I had handed over a baby in a basket. In the years that followed she divided her time fairly equally between us, but in companionship with her beloved father she grew up to be the artist that she is, with advantages I could never have given her. I lived without her, temporarily, but why did they think I liked it? She was all I had. (163)

After describing her attempts to smile cheerfully as her daughter departs on the train, Gilman says:

> That was thirty years ago. I have to stop typing and cry as I tell about it. There were years, years, when I could never see a mother and child together without crying, or even a picture of them. . . .
> What were those pious condemners thinking of? (163–64)

Writing about herself in the third person, Austin also focuses on misunderstanding, on pain and loss suffered alone:

> It was not long after that she put Ruth in a private institution in Santa Clara where the difference between herself and other children, which was beginning to trouble her, would not be felt, where it would not be known. Here the inability of other people to bear her cross would not be taxed; where one could say if questioned, "We have lost her"; . . . where the pain could be borne alone, as it was for another twenty years. It is a relief to speak of it now, of the cruelty, the weight, the oppression of its reality, the loss of tenderness, of consideration, the needless blight and pain. (*Earth Horizon* 295)

Both women describe wounds which never healed, or even scarred; they remain fresh years later. Austin's friendship with Gilman and their mutual support for each others' decisions must have greatly comforted both women. It certainly helped Austin to define the role of the woman artist: "to help other women to speak out what they think, unashamed" (*A Woman of Genius* 290). Austin beautifully captures the ways women express such support and understanding in another story, "Frustrate." Talking with a new friend who seems to understand just how she feels, the narrator says, "I suppose the writer woman must have seen how it was with me, but I thought at first she was talking about herself" (*Western Trails* 234).

Of course the writer woman *was* talking about herself; she recognizes the narrator's feelings and conflicts because she has gone through a different kind of the same thing. The narrator recognizes herself and her feelings in the writer's stories because, despite their real differences, their experiences overlap. The writer woman helps her to find a voice. Austin implies the universality of this kind of encounter by leaving both women unnamed. These are the moments I've tried to write about in this essay.

V. Filling the Silence

Her love for the children she "did not get" makes Brooks's speaker "the mother," but I believe that she has heard not only the voices of her "dim killed children," but also the voices of living children; her "gobbling mother-eye" recognizes the details of mother love. Perhaps her understanding of that love makes the absences in her life all the more painful. The Mother crossed one of the most significant boundaries between women: she became a mother. I look back at my journal entries critically for if I thought I knew loss and vulnerability then, I know them in an entirely different way now, since I became a mother.

Five years ago I left the (male) gynecologist who had told me my tubes were blocked, who didn't return my phone calls, who never tried to explore the particularities of my case, who kept saying, "Let's just wait and see what happens." I began to see Dr. Susan Tredwell, who said, sympathetically, "It's so difficult to do an internal exam on you because you're so scarred. But it doesn't look so hopeless to me. I'm more of an interventionist; let's see what we can do." She called some specialists for advice and substantially upped my dosage of Chlomid. A few months later I settled my class action suit against Robbins, the makers of the Dalkon Shield, for $750. I had a weak case anyway, my medical records "routinely" destroyed by Student Health at UVA. But I was glad to settle: I was pregnant. Four years ago I gave birth to my son Corey, a child Dr. Tredwell referred to as "the miracle baby." Like

Brooks's speaker, whose tender details of children's lives reveal her to be a mother, I had a child whose voice filled the silence.

Perhaps one miracle is all we're entitled to: I have been unable to conceive another child. But I am no longer mourning for myself. I now face a new challenge of reaching across boundaries as I try to imagine and share with the daughter I am about to adopt her South Korean birth mother's love for her and sense of loss, as I think about the circumstances in her life that forced her to this decision. There are some things I already know. I know that I need to listen, as undefensively as possible, to those who will think of me as one of the child-stealers. I know that my happiness grows out of her sorrow. I know that though I will probably never meet her or even know her name, our shared daughter will forever connect our lives. This essay is my beginning effort to reach out of myself to understand.

---

[1] Melody Graulich would like to thank the New Hampshire Council for the Humanities for a grant which helped her complete this essay.

[2] At the time I was thinking about my infertility and this essay, I did not know any literary explorations of infertility, one of the reasons I stretched across boundaries to look for women writing about similar kinds of experiences. While I've been writing the essay, two nonfictional books have been published where women talk about their infertility, *Dear Barbara, Dear Lynne: The True Story of Two Women in Search of Motherhood*, by Barbara Shulgold and Lynne Sipiora, and *Family Bonds*, by Elizabeth Bertholet. The few literary treatments I've discovered are generally not consoling. In Virginia Sorensen's *On This Star* (1946), for instance, the young Mormon heroine sees what she thinks of as her "sterility" as a punishment from God for having sex before marriage.

[3] For a sharply critical contemporary analysis of the mourning arts which seems to echo Twain's, see Douglas, *The Feminization of American Culture*, especially the chapter entitled "The Domestication of Death." For a much more sympathetic study of how the popular culture forms of the mourning arts influenced a major poet, see St. Armand, *Emily Dickinson and Her Culture*, especially the chapter called "Dark Parade." For an excellent recent study of mourning in popular culture which includes many primary texts, see Simonds and Rothman, *Centuries of Solace*.

[4] Although the artistic traditions associated with mourning are generally created by women rather than men, I hope it is obvious that men also struggle to express their grief. African-American male writers have written especially eloquently about loss. In James Baldwin's "Sonny's Blues," the narrator reconnects with his brother after the death of his daughter. Several works by Charles Chesnutt explore the loss of a child, notably his fine novel *The Marrow of Tradition*, which climaxes as two half sisters, one "white," one "black," provide a particularly ironic example of sharing the loss of a child.

A fine treatment of how a man and his wife grieved together over the loss of their children can be found in Johnsen, "'Our Children Who Are in Heaven': Consolation Themes in A Nineteenth-Century Connecticut Journal." Indeed, as one would expect, women writers often suggest that while women and men grieve differently, they can reach across these boundaries to share sorrow. See, for instance, Jessamyn West's wonderful story, "The Vase." For an interesting contrast, read one of the most famous poems about mourning a dead child written by a man, Robert Frost's "Home Burial," where the bereaved husband and wife are totally unable to console each other.

MELODY GRAULICH

[5] While women could speak and write openly about the death of a living child, until recently miscarriage and infertility have been seen as embarrassing private matters, increasing the sense of isolation of women suffering from them. One example poignantly illustrates this point. The western writer Mary Hallock Foote published some twelve novels and several collections of short stories during a long and successful career, but none of them explore the kind of moving and personal matters she wrote about in her letters to her friend Helena De Kay Gilder, letters which she said contained "the cries one woman utters to another." "There is no one but a *woman* who can listen properly to this kind of talk," she wrote in 1884.

> I have been ill again, a bad miscarriage from which I am very slow, I think, in recovering. This is my third week, and I can only crawl about from bed to chair . . . . You know this time I had all the regular pains of childbirth, prolonged because there was no life to help itself out. And you know how sad it was to lie there and suffer and know it was all for nothing—all to end in loss instead of gain. I was an awful baby about it, and cried like one. (1884)

There is plenty of material for a whole essay on the often oblique treatment of miscarriage in women's literature. For moving contemporary examples, see Simonds and Rothman, *Century of Solace*, especially a poem by Barbara Crooker called "The Lost Children" (245).

Works Cited

Ammons, Elizabeth. "A Profile of Frances Ellen Watkins Harper." *Legacy: A Journal of Nineteenth-Century Women Writers* 2 (Fall 1985): 61–66.

_____. "Stowe's Dream of the Mother Savior: *Uncle Tom's Cabin* and American Women Writers Before the 1920's." *New Essays on Uncle Tom's Cabin*. Ed. Eric J. Sundquist. New York: Cambridge UP, 1986: 155–95.

Austin, Mary. *A Woman of Genius*. Old Westbury, N.Y.: Feminist P, 1985.

_____. *Earth Horizon*. Albuquerque: U of New Mexico P, 1991.

_____. *Western Trails: A Collection of Stories by Mary Austin*. Ed. Melody Graulich. Reno and Las Vegas: U of Nevada P, 1987.

Bertholet, Elizabeth. *Family Bonds*. Cambridge: Harvard UP, 1993.

Boydston, Jeanne, Mary Kelley, and Anne Margolis. *The Limits of Sisterhood: The Beecher Sisters on Women's Rights and Woman's Sphere*. Chapel Hill: U of North Carolina P, 1988.

Brant, Beth. *Mohawk Trail*. Ithaca, N.Y.: Firebrand Books, 1985.

Brooks, Gwendolyn. "The Mother." *The Norton Anthology of Women's Literature*. Ed. Sandra M. Gilbert and Susan Gubar. New York: W. W. Norton & Company, 1985.

Douglas, Ann. *The Feminization of American Culture*. New York: Avon Books, 1977.

Ehrenreich, Barbara and Deirdre English. *For Her Own Good: 150 Years of the Experts' Advice to Women*. Garden City, N.Y.: Doubleday Books, 1979.

Foote, Mary Hallock. Letters to Helena De Kay Gilder. Stanford University Library Collection.

Freeman, Mary Wilkins. *Selected Stories of Mary Wilkins Freeman*. Ed. Marjorie Pryse. New York: W. W. Norton & Company, 1983.

Gilman, Charlotte Perkins. *The Living of Charlotte Perkins Gilman: An Autobiography*. New York: Harper and Row, 1975.

Glaspell, Susan. "A Jury of Her Peers." *American Voices, American Women*. Ed. Lee R. Edwards and Arlyn Diamond. New York: Avon Books, 1973.

Johnsen, Norma. "'Our Children Who Are in Heaven': Consolation Themes in A Nineteenth-Century Connecticut Journal." *The Connecticut Historical Society* 51 (Spring 1986): 77–101.

McIntosh, Peggy. "Interactive Phases of Curricular Re-Vision." Delivered at the Claremont Colleges conference, "Traditions and Transitions: Women's Studies and a Balanced Curriculum," February 18–19, 1983.

Olsen, Tillie. *Mother to Daughter, Daughter to Mother*. Old Westbury, N.Y.: The Feminist P, 1984.

Shulgold, Barbara and Lynne Sipiora. *Dear Barbara, Dear Lynne: The True Story of Two Women in Search of Motherhood*. Reading, MA.: Addison-Wesley Publishing, 1992.

Silko, Leslie. "Lullaby." *Storyteller*. New York: Seaver Books, 1981. 43–51.

Simonds, Wendy and Barbara Katz Rothman. *Centuries of Solace: Expressions of Maternal Grief in Popular Literature*. Philadelphia: Temple UP, 1992.

St. Armand, Barton Levi. *Emily Dickinson and Her Culture: The Soul's Society*. New York: Cambridge UP, 1984.

Stowe, Harriet. *Uncle Tom's Cabin*. Columbus, Ohio: Charles E. Merrill Publishing, 1969.

TRAILING WEST

SUSAN NARAMORE MAHER

Every increment of consciousness, every step forward is a *travesía*, a crossing. I am again an alien in new territory. And again and again. But if I escape conscious awareness, escape "knowing," I won't be moving. Knowledge makes me more aware, it makes me more conscious. "Knowing" is painful because after "it" happens I can't stay in the same place and be comfortable. I am no longer the same person I was before. (Gloria Anzaldua *Borderlands/La Frontera* 48)

I n 1992, my first year as a tenure-track assistant professor at the University of Nebraska at Omaha, I attended a welcome party sponsored by a joint faculty-administration women's group. Formed to encourage professional mentoring among university women, this group took upon itself to introduce new faculty to experienced women, women who had negotiated the exacting topography to tenure and beyond. At this meeting, I was introduced as a "trailing spouse," a term, I then discovered, defining the spouse who follows along after his or her partner finds a teaching position. I had never trailed before, professionally. Through graduate school, first in Columbia, South Carolina, and then in Madison, Wisconsin, my partner and I had worked together to assure each other's success—until, of course, he finished his doctorate first and signed a contract to begin teaching geology in Nebraska. My decision to "trail" rather than commute has shifted my scholarly interests in serendipitous ways. Like the great Platte River Road itself, whose vestige wagon ruts braid across Nebraska, my personal and professional journeys have meandered, veered, and crisscrossed unpredictable terrain. At first I was a reluctant migrant, an accidental tourist. But I quickly learned to embrace the surprises along the trail. Adaptability, suppleness, bending to the conditions of Nebraska life, enabled me to shake the rigid mantle of graduate school and grasp the fluid art of improvisation. Moving taught me "knowing." Though introduced professionally as a "trailing" woman, I have come to redefine that label on my own terms.

I left Madison with an unfinished dissertation that explored three centuries of the English novel. I made the move alone, five months pregnant with my first child and accompanied only by my cat because my husband, Harmon, was pursuing field work in the North Atlantic island of Svalbard. I'm afraid I did not attend too much to the land I drove through. I was spent. Coping with the interstate summer traffic across the undulant hills of Iowa, enduring heated, buckling roads without benefit of air conditioning, sapped my concentration, and feeling the strains of pregnancy, I was not thrilled to be moving to Omaha, Nebraska. I was an inveterate northeasterner, born in Summit, New Jersey, and an anglophile to boot. To me, Nebraska in 1983 seemed a backwater. Dismissing it as a dead end destination, I envisioned a short interval on the Great Plains followed by a more promising, adventurous life. The siren song of coastal cities called to me, and I did not yet hear the splendor of rustling western grasses.

But I've always tended good survival instincts. I decided that one way to accept my lot in life was to start reading the literature of Nebraska writers. If I learned their reading of the land, I reasoned, perhaps I could come to respect it, too. As a neophyte Nebraskan with a bookish bent, I naturally sought my compass points in print. For the first time in years, I read indiscriminately, locust-like and voracious, without rhyme or reason, without a professional agenda, without the need to write a paper or excel on a test. Approaching regional writers in this way loosened me from an obeisance to my graduate training, weaned me from an over-reliance on scholarly literature, allowed me free-play, and brought back to me the joy in reading that Wisconsin, with its endless competitive hurdles, had repressed. In the backwater, I became less provincial.

I started with Willa Cather because she was the only Nebraska writer I recognized. Her astute delineation of human character, her lyrical passages, and allowance for both tragic and comic impulses in her texts astonished me. Why hadn't we read more of her in graduate school? Clearly she was brilliant, yet she did not fit comfortably into the "Wasteland" paradigm Americanists privileged in the seventies. Selecting Cather forced me both to question the canon I had absorbed as a student and to critique the category "regional literature." Too many significant writers have faced a lonely burial in "regional" ground.

I next skipped to contemporary collections, like Ron Hansen's short stories in *Nebraska*, fell back a few decades to Mari Sandoz's *Old Jules*, crossed genres—poetry, life-writing, fiction, essay—and eagerly time traveled through unconnected decades. At first, to use a stock-schlock western term, I moseyed around only in Nebraska, a tenderfoot easterner. Then I expanded my literary geography, gathering in western writers in general, from old stalwarts like Mayne Reid and Owen Wister to western revisionists like Tom McGuane, Marilynne Robinson, and Wallace Stegner. I would focus on a particular state for a time, say California, and then savor such disparate writers as Scott O'Dell, Joan Didion, and Jack London. When William Least Heat Moon explored the weighty minutiae of the Flint Hills of Kansas, I secured myself for the ride. I joined Edward Abbey in the desert. I trailed along with Lillian Schlissel's pioneer women's diaries, seeing parallels in my own changing story, as I felt increasing isolation in my home, caring for infants, hundreds of miles from my nearest relations, in my own urban homesteading experience.

In my imagination, I was "in process," like women along the Oregon trail, adjusting to a mixed bag of delight and disappointment. Mowing the front slope of our home (built circa 1908), more or less benchpressing the machine up and down the incline, I would think of those earlier trailing Euro-American women and their challenges, much more poignant and difficult than mine. Marilynne Robinson has honored these women in her essay "My Western Roots," noting "how beautiful human society seems to me, especially in those attenuated forms so characteristic of the West—isolated towns and single houses which sometimes offer only the merest, barest amenities: light, warmth, supper, familiarity" (171). These stoical women cast long shadows, putting my own struggles with cloth diapers, home renovation, and (for our first years in Nebraska), a single salary—my husband's, occasionally augmented by my part-time teaching—into comic perspective. Tales of the settlement West allowed me to keep my humor and perfect a stiff-upper-lip posture. Seldom was heard a discouraging word from my lips.

Reading settlement literature also increased my understanding of the land and its allure. Once my quadrilateral Nebraska yard had been part of a larger deciduous forest, alive with burr oak, hawthorne, and cottonwood trees, flanking the Missouri River. Now Omaha, like many "New West" cities, is a jigsaw puzzle of sub-developments, mini- and maxi-malls, recreated "green spaces," and industrial/business zones. Settlers displaced native people, forcing an irrevocable revision of space and culture. Literature records shifting responses to the land. Before settlement, especially in the years between 1830 and 1840, prairie travelers submitted their journals and diaries for publication. It has always fascinated me that littoral people, like Captain Frederick Marryat in his *A Diary in America,* could best appreciate the unplowed prairie. The grasses, played upon by wind, would bow and break, much like sea waves. After the Civil War, my region of the country was appraised, an endeavor recorded in Ferdinand Vandeveer Hayden's 1867 Geological Survey of Nebraska. The land became a thing to use. Then immigrants from war-torn, class-bound Europe and from more crowded parts of America began arriving in droves on the Great Plains.

Historical recreations like Laura Ingalls Wilder's family saga, the Little House series, chronicle the joys and terrors settlers faced: *Little House on the Prairie* celebrates the openness of the terrain where no road, "not even the faintest trace of wheels or of a rider's passing, could be seen anywhere" (26). The plains are as uninscribed as the "great empty sky," bearing no palimpsests of Euro-Americans' technology. But the land isn't "empty." Forced to look down, Laura learns to appreciate its multifarious life. Wilder's prairie harbors many wonders and protects its native peoples. Recently, Kathleen Norris has commented on the land's ability to command our vision. Looking down, for me, was not natural; summers in the Adirondacks and marriage to a geologist who privileged sublime relief trained my eyes upward. But as Norris explains, the "so-called emptiness of the Plains is full of . . . miraculous 'little things.' The way native grasses spring back from a drought, greening before your eyes; the way a snowy owl sits on a fencepost, or a golden eagle hunts, wings outstretched over grassland that seems to go on forever" (10). Not everyone accepts such miracles. In Wilder's book, the settlers, hoping to secure proprietorship of the vast Kansas Indian territory, fear much of what they desire. Reading as many pioneer narratives as I could find, I came to appreciate this paradoxical relationship to the land. Despite venerating the Edenic, settlers squared off the land into controlled, uniform parcels, loving yet destroying the subtlety of the plains. They could not preserve the miracles.

I hitched up to the Western Literature Association in 1987 and followed behind the members who had already discussed the tension between "virgin" lands and utilitarian impulses. I discovered a new and inspiring connection in this salient feature of western texts: attitudes toward land reflect attitudes toward women, and ideologies of dominion necessarily corrupt personal quests. Through my western literary travels, I laid a stronger claim to the rich veins of feminism and environmentalism.

Recognizing this obvious parallel between the control of females and of nature came at a time when I re-entered the academic world as an Assistant Professor in 1992. A hired hand in the English department, and designated Women's Studies faculty—indeed I was *the* professor of women in literature, a daunting prospect with so many centuries, so little time—I was given carte blanche to create courses in my designated area. I had no doubts about my first imprint on department curriculum: "Women Writers of the American West." The reading I had accomplished as a trailing spouse enabled me to reshape my career as an academic. Without that time to lie fallow, I would have been pigeon-holed as a "Brit Lit" specialist with a concentration in Victorian literature. Instead, I broke away from the Old World and planted myself squarely in the West. My own western migration had transformed me in significant ways, and like the voices in the literature I read with my students, I was forced to confront how place shapes destiny in both desirable and painful ways.

Historian Peggy Pascoe has defined the West as a "cultural crossroads," a place demanding a complex synthesis of narratives if one is to make sense of its history and literature (40). Her metaphor of crossroads helped structure my course. I wanted my students to value intricacy and contradiction; I wanted them to see we still participate in the aftermath of settlement. Juxtaposition of older and newer texts, crossing borders of time, genre, and experience, allowed us to challenge entrenched family and national myths of westering. There are many Wests. The land itself bears witness to millennia of human habitation, its soil horizons preserving evidence of encampments, burials, battles, and farming. Flyways, animal trails, Indian footpaths, trading routes, and wagon roads shadow the superhighways that now span the West. I can never drive Interstate 80 without connecting it to the intercalations of human history—of human stories. Intercalation is a word my geologist husband provided me: he used it scientifically to denote strata; I picked up on the word, and it became a metaphorical bonanza for my inner landscapes. My students and I would attempt, through sixteen weeks and fourteen texts, our own literary digging in an effort to unearth and relate women's stories—including our own— about this vast, transfiguring West.

The first time through, I selected a safer chronological organization. The summer before teaching this course, my family and I had journeyed to western Nebraska. Leaving our campground north of Ogallala, we drove west toward Scottsbluff. The highway rose evenly until we were up on a solid plateau, an apron of sediments deposited from the Rocky Mountain uplift. We were traversing the famous Gang Plank. This route allowed secure passage through the Rocky Mountains for pioneers, surveyors, and railroaders. I desired such solid crossing for my students, so we steadily journeyed decade by decade. We began with first and second generation settlement women and then broke camp to contemporary Anglo revisionists, Marilynne Robinson and Molly Gloss, and non-Anglo "border" writers Leslie Marmon Silko, Louise Erdrich, Gloria Anzaldua, Sandra Cisneros, and Maxine Hong Kingston. But despite the linearity of time's arrow, our writers kept cycling back to integral questions. How does uprooting, the experience of displacement, alter a woman's psyche? How do women preserve culture and community within a larger context of change and isolation? In what ways do women, like the land, resist or yield to men's shaping? Helen Hunt Jackson's Ramona suffered a legacy of loss that reverberates through a century of women's writing about the West. Enduring cultural and familial collapse, Ramona emerges with strengthened "heroic fiber" reserved for those who "had trial of cruel mocking, wandered about, being destitute, afflicted, tormented, wandered in deserts and in mountains, and in dens and caves of the earth" (Jackson 342). *Ramona* became our textual epicenter, and when we ended with *Housekeeping*, we continued to feel the seismic echoes.

Our earlier texts—*Ramona, Land of Little Rain, Letters of a Woman Homesteader, Old Jules, Free Land*, and *Pale Horse, Pale Rider*—bridged regions and diverse ideologies. Anglo women writers are not monocultural; they are as various as the prairie grasses that find refuge in protected pockets of my city. Intrepid Elinore Pruitt Stewart waxes lyrically about homesteading:

> To me, homesteading is the solution of all poverty's problems, but I realize that temperament has much to do with success in any undertaking, and persons afraid of coyotes and work and loneliness had better let ranching alone. At the same time, any woman who can stand her own company, can see the beauty of the sunset, loves growing things, and is willing to put in as much time at careful labor as she does over the washtub, will certainly succeed; will have independence, plenty to eat all the time, and a home of her own in the end. (215)

But Mary Austin's ecological tour of the Mojave desert laments settlement's encroachment on "this long brown land" that "lays such a hold on the affections" (11). And Mary Beaton, in *Free Land*, stares vacantly at the land, "[her] very mind . . . sick from the heat and the wind" (282). Another Mary, Jules Sandoz's wife, physically and emotionally contracts from the harsh treatment of land and husband: "Mary had three anaemic, undernourished children very close together, without a doctor. She lost her teeth; her clear skin became leathery from field work; her eyes paled and sun-squinted; her hands knotted, the veins of her arms like slack clothesline" (215). Katherine Anne Porter's Texas threatens to bury its settlers, but mainly her people are to blame. They have dragged west the cultural baggage of the decaying South; they have faced change with a mix of *ennui*, delusion, and irresolution. Memory either defeats or delivers them. When Miranda flees the living death of Texas, taking a reporting job in Denver, she begins life anew with Adam. But Adam dies and Miranda awakens from a near-fatal bout with influenza numb and alone. Retreating farther west has not offered her salvation. Women writers with direct links to settlement days present different truths, spanning the tragic, the comic, and all stops in between. Their writings defy any streamlined literary history of the region that posits a dichotomous Old West/New West.

My students delighted in these earlier writers' shrewd psychology, careful artistry, and political uneasiness. A century before, half a century before, women had spoken out against genocide, environmental damage, and familial violence. Even a settlement advocate like Pruitt Stewart speaks eloquently of the land's spiritual qualities. "When you get among such grandeur," she writes, "you get to feel how little you are and how foolish is human endeavor, except that which reunites us with the mighty force called God" (30). Why, one could almost imagine joining Mary Austin for a bowl of sprouts at a trendy little art colony cafe! The American West has nurtured critical spirits for many generations. Ecofeminism, resistance to monoculture, and ambivalence toward development are not our inventions. By traveling back, by tracing the intellectual and spiritual paths of these writers, we understood ourselves better. Moving is knowing, Anzaldua emphasizes. But that moving, we decided, may be in all directions, toward the past, out of our experience, or inward to our memories. "Only looking back," Louise Erdrich's Nanapush explains in *Tracks*, "is there a pattern" (33).

Over the last twenty years of my life, I have moved around quite a bit. Hopping from college to college—Albany, New York, to Columbia, South Carolina; to Madison, Wisconsin; to Omaha, Nebraska—my husband and I pursued our degrees, never putting down deep roots because we always expected to move on. As a suburban child anyway, a product of tract housing, shopping malls, and the auto culture, I adapted to rootlessness. But as I grew older, I began to regret my obscure origins. I had no strong sense of place, so I found myself increasingly absorbed by writers who insisted upon the primacy of place. I also tracked down western women whose sense of place the dominant culture assailed. The Diaspora of Native Americans so poignantly recreated in *Tracks*, the cost of assimilation so painfully presented in *Ceremony*, the erosion of identity captured in *Woman Hollering Creek* and *China Men* powerfully rounded out the settlement stories I chose for my students. The West is not simply a place of rebirth, a romantic haven for the lost, the eccentric, the lonely, or the ambitious. It is also a place of death. Silko's Tayo returns from World War II a sick man; the drought-plagued earth is also suffering. In his own room, Tayo awakens "feeling that there was no place left for him; he would find no peace in that house where the silence and the emptiness echoed the loss" (32). To lose connection to family, to land, and to the stories that tie humans to place is to lose all. Contemporary women writers from the West struggle hard against the flattening of cultural homogeneity, the denial of origins. Threatening absorption hangs over much of their writing.

The writing of stories, then, is as much an act of survival as it is a blessed act of creation. Nanapush, in *Tracks*, tells his granddaughter, Lulu, "I shouldn't have been caused to live so long, shown so much of death, had to squeeze so many stories in the corners of my brain. They're all attached, and once I start there is no end to telling because they're all hooked from one side to the other, mouth to tail" (46). Nanapush persuasively suggests the necessary synergy between self and tale. We exist because of our stories. We understand because of our stories. We find peace or damnation because of our stories. Too often, as we successful ones chase promotions, kudos, tenure, or publication, we cut ties ruthlessly from stories that helped shape us. I would face the same pressure of erasure if I were working my way up in business like my older sister Kris or hoping to escape rural farm life like some of my students. An unspoken coercion encourages us to keep wiping the slate clean. In *China Men*, Maxine Hong Kingston catalogs the changes that repudiate identity:

> You say with the few words and the silences: No stories. No past. No China.
> You only look and talk Chinese. There are no photographs of you in Chinese clothes nor against Chinese landscapes. Did you cut your pigtail to show your support of the Republic? Or have you always been American? Do you mean to give us a chance at being real Americans by forgetting the Chinese past? (14)

The daughter of such confusion, Hong Kingston must write out and interweave the family stories, cultural myths, official and unofficial histories to remake, albeit imperfectly and unresolvedly, her immigrant father's life. From loss she seeks integrity.

The strong message from contemporary western regional writers is resist, resist, resist. Tayo finds healing from relearning his people's myths and his family's stories. Nanapush passes along his streaming stories to Lulu to keep the family from unraveling. Only storytelling, Gloria Anzaldua insists, can give us "a validation vision" (87). My students and I swapped many stories in the course of sixteen weeks, and I gave them the option to submit a personal family history rather than the traditional research paper. Life-writing, in the forms of diaries, letters, memoirs, autobiographies, biographies, and genre-bending narratives like *Borderlands/La Frontera*, remains a vital pattern in American Western literature. I wanted my students to have a go at it, to seek themselves in their own private West. Even a fiction writer like Molly Gloss owes gratitude to the many westering women before her who put pen to paper: "I am greatly indebted to many published and unpublished diaries, letters and journals of women who settled the West," she writes in her acknowledgement to *Jump-Off Creek*. "I hope their strong, honest voices can be heard in this work." I wanted my students, as well as myself, to develop such strong, honest voices, aloud and on paper. One of my students commented, "We need to become like Felice in Cisneros's *Woman Hollering Creek*. She drives a pickup and says what she wants. When she drives over the *arroyo*, she doesn't think 'pain or rage' like Cleofílas. She hoots and hollers." Gloria Anzaldua also speaks of the need to articulate as an antidote to abyssal states. We must protect our "wild tongues": "Wild tongues can't be tamed, they can only be cut out" (54). By semester's end, our readings were no longer objects of study. They had become part of our own intersubjective realities, part of our created community of voices, part of our own journeys.

If trailing conflates the contradictory notions of following and breaking anew, then I contain within me that tension. If I had not "trailed" my husband, I would never have received the gift that Nebraska has become for me. The best gifts enter unexpectedly. I moved to Nebraska diffidently, but now I remain here by choice. Though Omaha, Nebraska, is by no means Lemmon, South Dakota, I find myself returning to Kathleen Norris's apologia of her western existence. She helps explain my own desire to dodge those faster, deadlier tracks of late-century American life. Living in the desert "is a way of surrendering to reduced circumstances in a manner that enhances the whole person. It is a radical way of knowing exactly who, what, and where you are, in defiance of those powerful forces in society—alcohol, drugs, television, shopping malls, motels—that aim to make us forget" (23). Paradoxically, following another person released me from my own timidity. Following helped situate me. Meeting the West with curiosity rather than contention enabled me to awaken, not forget. I attend better to voices now, whether without or within.

I came of age in Nebraska, as a woman, a mother, and a professional. Here I have blazed my own trails, some of them exhilarating, some of them painful. I grow as a teacher and a parent, but I have parted ways with my husband. Despite Roy Rogers and Dale Evans's pleasant sing-song farewell, trails aren't always happy. Not all lead to fairy-tale endings. I try to keep the words of Sandra Cisneros's narrator of *"Bien Pretty"* in mind:

> One way or another. Even if it's only the lyrics to a stupid pop hit. We're going to right the world and live. I mean live our lives the way lives were meant to be lived. With the throat and wrists. With rage and desire, and joy and grief, and love till it hurts, maybe. But goddamn, girl. Live. (163)

Nebraska brought me a confluence of the everyday, the mythic, the mundanely professional, and the eternal. Here I'll learn to live my life the way it was meant to be lived.

Olivia Frey ponders the way our reflective selves touch upon our everyday selves; how "thinking, learning, studying, making mundane decisions like what color to paint the house or what to cook for dinner" plays against or with "making more significant decisions" (509–10). Painting my old house all week (dear friends organized a house-painting party reminiscent of barn-raisings), I prepared not only the surfaces of eaves and shingles but also the outline of this narrative. I mulled over shaping, supporting, contextualizing. In a direct and satisfying manner, replenishing my house led to the finishing of this essay. I hope to sell this house in a year's time. I need a study for my writing and reading, my children need room to grow, and the memories born of this house need airing, distance, and reexamination. Though I've finished the work on both house and essay this week, such closure anticipates new entrances. As I have done over and over again the last year, I return to Gloria Anzaldua: "To survive the Borderlands/you must live *sin fronteras*/ be a crossroads" (195).

Works Cited

Anzaldua, Gloria. *Borderlands/La Frontera*. San Francisco: Aunt Lute, 1987.

Austin, Mary. *The Land of Little Rain*. Illus. E. Boyd Smith. Albuquerque: U of New Mexico P, 1974.

Erdrich, Louise. *Tracks*. New York: Harper & Row, 1988.

Frey, Olivia. "Beyond Literary Darwinism: Women's Voices and Critical Discourse." *College English* 52.5 (1990): 507–26.

Gloss, Molly. *The Jump-Off Creek*. Boston: Houghton Mifflin, 1989.

Hong Kingston, Maxine. *China Men*. New York: Vintage, 1989.

Jackson, Helen Hunt. *Ramona*. New York: Signet, 1988.

Lane, Rose Wilder. *Free Land*. Lincoln: U Of Nebraska P, 1984.

Norris, Kathleen. *Dakota: A Spiritual Geography*. New York: Ticknor and Fields, 1993.

Pascoe, Peggy. "Western Women at the Cultural Crossroads." *Trails: Toward a New Western History*. Ed. Patricia Nelson Limerick, et al. Lawrence: U of Kansas P, 1991. 40–58.

Robinson, Marilynne. "My Western Roots." *Old West-New West*. Ed. Barbara Howard Meldrum. Moscow: U of Idaho P, 1993. 165–72.

Sandoz, Mari. *Old Jules*. Lincoln: U of Nebraska P, 1985.

Silko, Leslie Marmon. *Ceremony*. New York: Penguin, 1986.

Stewart, Elinore Pruitt. *Letters of a Woman Homesteader*. Illus. N.C. Wyeth. Boston: Houghton Mifflin, 1988.

Wilder, Laura Ingalls. *Little House on the Prairie*. Illus. Garth Williams. New York: Harper Trophy, 1981.

Dakota: A Spiritual Geography, Revisited

Michele Potter

During the summer of 1993, I went to visit hallowed ground, hoping to hear the spirits of my ancestors. I was reading Kathleen Norris's *Dakota: A Spiritual Geography* as I was at a crossroads. I had recently finished three years' worth of teaching and done the course work for a master's in creative writing. Now I'd have to reinvent myself all over again. Who would I become? Was I anybody yet? My mother's fiftieth high school reunion was occasion for a large family gathering, and I knew being back in South Dakota would reorient me.

As I packed little boys' underwear and toothbrushes, made peanut butter sandwiches and searched for extra pillows for the long drive, I found I had turned into my mother. How many years had it been since I'd watched her pack the station wagon for the yearly pilgrimage back to South Dakota, after we left for Oregon when I was sixteen?

Dakota was my spiritual and literary guidebook. It was here I found another human being who had eaten from the same oatmeal bowl. I was finally reading the truth about where I come from, including both the open-heartedness and closed-mindedness of small Dakota towns. One chapter is even entitled: "Can you tell the truth in a small town?" I long to holler, "No! Not if you plan on living there." Norris thinks you can, depending on how much faith you have.

I had other reasons for wanting to go to South Dakota. I wanted to use *Dakota* as the central text in a paper for an annual Western Literature conference I attend, and I was finishing a novel partly based in Dakota. In it the two main characters—a white woman and a Native American from opposite sides of the river in South Dakota—return to home ground. I knew the trip would help my writing and my life, one and the same, really. Focusing on one helps set the other right because you're leaving it alone for a moment. It's like looking at Orion in order to see Pleiades. If you look straight at the seven tiny stars, you cannot see them. If you look nearby at something else, there they are all right there in your peripheral vision. Seeing where I came from, I hoped, would help me see where I was. And if nothing else, there would be plenty of characters to write about. As Norris puts it, it's a place of "good telling stories."

But I was afraid to write what I knew, and about whom I knew. I felt like the woman Norris knows who says "I'd like to write about my relatives but I'm no good at disguising things." Reading *Dakota* was funny. I've long had a theory that verbal humor is mostly just truthtelling—we get the truth when we no longer expect it. Norris's humor is a poet's quiet humor, the kind that makes you smile.

Reading *Dakota* became a way of measuring my own feelings and thoughts against the author's, like taking the measure of the day in Fahrenheit and Celsius. *Dakota* is expansive, freeing (as in "the truth shall set you free"). I come from a long line of people who are compulsive about not lying, but who will also go a long way not to have to tell the truth. But Norris's truth shed light on my own history—to the many layers of who I am and where I come from.

Where I come from is like this: My mother's family, at least, were among the earliest Scandinavian immigrants to flock to farm towns on the flattest part of the prairie in northeastern South Dakota. The work ethic is strong. My mother, aunts, and grandmother, didn't argue with their husbands, from what I could hear, nor did they drink or smoke. I wondered if they ate. I never saw them sit. Even at family dinners, they hovered. They waited. They cooked, urging everyone to eat and afterward, they cleaned up and started in again. Food was one kind of religion. But the credo was conformity. Doing anything out of the ordinary was considered an affront.

Sometimes everyone ate pheasant. The men stomped the fields on weekends in the late fall, scaring the birds up from the fields, and we'd dine on pheasant and mashed potatoes with gravy, occasionally chomping down on a piece of gunshot. And then the following image: Being in church on Sundays, the Lutheran holy light shining through stained glass windows on iridescent pheasant hats with their emerald, blood-red, and dusky brown feathers. There were bandeau and pillboxes, but it seemed to me, they were all wearing the same hat.

But I was not the same. I felt different. Actually, I wanted to be an Indian. This was more concept than reality, of course, since I didn't know any Indians. Yet I remember, as a small child, telling this to adults. As I grew older, I became a member of the Wannabe tribe (you have to move out of state to become one): I wanted elders, I wanted tobacco ties, I wanted dances and songs. I wanted not to be a nice white girl from the flattest dullest part of South Dakota prairie. I didn't want to be white bread anymore. I didn't want to be perky and enthusiastic. I wanted to be passionate, powerful. I didn't appreciate what my own heritage had given me, nor did I see that waiting or serving or seeing to someone else's need first might be an essential part of life.

The central message for me in *Dakota* then, is interspersed among the weather reports (philosophy), gossip (holy stories), and geography (knowing one's place), and it is about acceptance. Reading *Dakota* helped me appreciate who I am by knowing where I come from. Norris would call it conversion. She writes:

> Conversion means starting with who we are, not who we wish we were. It means knowing where we come from. It means taking to heart the words of Native American writer Andy Smith, who writes in *Ms.*, "a true medicine woman would . . . advise a white woman to look into her own culture and find what is liberating in it" (131).

By reading *Dakota*, and going there, I found myself on terra firma again. The place steadied me. "Home is where when you go there, they have to take you in," writes Robert Frost in "Death of a Hired Man." I found the steadiness satisfying—like a boat anchor when you don't know where you're going. It gave me a chance to rid myself of some of the extraneous "me's" I had added along the way in hopes of becoming "somebody" (meaning, of course, somebody else). It took me back to who I was—to ground zero, I want to say. But as Norris points out, parts of Dakota are so impoverished that many people welcome using the state as a prime site for locating nuclear waste and weapons silos.

For herself, Norris would say that Dakota has been "a crucible," molding her into who she is. She writes that "as it turns out, the Plains have been essential not only for my growth as a writer, they have formed me spiritually. I would even say they have made me a human being" (11).

But how, I still wondered, could someone like her live there, someone who had lived a "cultured life" in New York City? Wouldn't it be limiting to someone who had seen and done so much? Norris, however, refuses to see its limits. She tells a story about the time her husband once settled a barroom dispute by calling up a distant library for facts, a notion so bizarre as to become part of local legend. Norris herself escapes through books and travel and the monastery and her own thoughts. She is not spending her life on a tractor.

Norris doesn't even seem to recognize the limits of *when* she's living. For example, she differentiates little between saints and the everyday people she finds in Lemmon. When I later met her at the literature conference, she spoke of "Big Tess" and "Little Tess"—in reference to the saints Theresa who have been gone for several centuries. I accused her of speaking as if they currently resided there.

But Norris's ability to live with paradox is the sanest possible reaction to living in a place of great extremes. She appears to find herself in relationships simultaneously with fourth-century saints, monks, and Dakota farmers—all with equal ease. She stretches the boundaries. For refuge she chooses among solitude, counter-cultural values, books, friends, the monastery.

After a friend referred to the western Dakotas as the "Cappadocia of North America," Norris wrote:

> I was handed an essential connection between the spirituality of the landscape I inhabit and that of the fourth-century monastics who set up shop in Cappadocia and the deserts of Egypt. Like those monks, I made a counter-cultural choice to live in what the rest of the world considers a barren waste. Like them, I had to stay in this place, like a scarecrow in a field, and hope for the brains to see its beauty. (3)

Norris's lives, like mine, appear to be delineated by place. Perhaps that stimulates the imagination. She grew up in Hawaii, spent summers in Dakota, moved to New York City for several years to work after college, and then returned to Dakota about twenty years ago. I have been away now longer than she has been there. I've lived in several western states and Germany, and now, for the last five years, in New Jersey.

I've had to be imaginative about living in the most densely populated state in the country when I grew up in one of the scarcest. I try to see why I'm here. Perhaps it's retribution for being an Aspen ski instructor and swearing that the one thing I'd never be was a New Jersey housewife with two kids. Instead I have three. I see, by living here, more fully who I am: a middle-class, mostly nice girl from South Dakota beginning the final half of my life in the last gasp of the twentieth century. From living so many places I see who I am: a Westerner.

Norris writes: "I hope I know a blessing when I see one." Perhaps living here is one for me. New Jersey has given me an intellectual life, a chance to articulate my past. Perhaps the intense domesticity and lack of rootedness was responsible for that, too: I poured myself into writing, teaching, reading, as well as mothering. I so longed for escape that I did not notice where I was: I found myself nursing a third child while stirring the soup after coming home from classes and teaching during graduate school. I wanted to write and read about other places and other lives like the life I'd had. My focus became the West. I wanted to resurrect the joy western places had given me. But I knew inside that you can't live in the past, and that an academic life is not a balanced one. I tucked my baby inside the front of my parka in late fall, and in spring my boys threw sticks in the Rockaway River. Words don't suffice to pass on messages to kids. I taught them to listen to cardinals and talk to them, to feel the slip of ice under their skates in winter, to get sweaty and grovel in summer. Children need what we all need—to know where the river comes from and where the garbage goes. They need to know their bioregion, as Gary Snyder puts it, and they need to stay put and pay attention long enough to hear the spirits of the earth (Snyder 37). You might say they need to know their own geography.

Norris points out that the word "geography" comes from two Greek words meaning earth and writing. I can't tell you the names of the plains and moraines, like a cartographer, nor do I recall last month's rainfall, like any good Dakota farmer, but I keep writing about the places I've been. And what I keep trying to fathom is this: How can we connect with each place? Call me a geographer then.

When I first picked up *Dakota*, I was attracted by both its cover and its title. The book jacket reveals a vast prairie, but ninety percent of the space is sky. This is what dominates Dakota: space, weather. And the subtitle *A Spiritual Geography* is apt. Places *are* both spiritual and physical—geography is both inner and outer. Dakota has been, for thousands of years to its native people, both a physical and spiritual home. If interaction with place molds our identity, Dakota reorients me as to "who in the world" I think I am.

Norris quotes Ortega y Gasset in the dedication to *Dakota*: "Tell me the landscape in which you live, and I will tell you who you are," while Gretel Ehrlich, in *The Solace of Open Spaces*, chooses to quote Joseph Brodsky: "geography added to history equals destiny."

When I left Dakota, the "who" that I was died. Certainly my childhood ended. It was a closure to my first life, the death of a way of life that included an extended, close-knit clan, where a cousin or grandmother could and would stay the night or indefinitely, on the couch or tucked in with you; at their house, you did the same. My father spoke of "in-law casserole" which we invariably seemed to have on Monday nights, when the stores in Aberdeen stayed open late and my mother's relatives came to town. Even now, one of my brothers will talk—perhaps sentimentally—about how we never should have left, but I'm more of the mind that you can't go home again. My older brother went back to live for a spell, taking his bride with him, but they are no longer married.

Dakota reveals a growing-up in Hawaii, a life in New York City, and the author's return, with husband, to the Dakota of her childhood summers to claim the inheritance of her grandmother—an inheritance that becomes spiritual as well as material. Why else would a New York poet, married to another one, well on into sane adulthood, leave an environment that fosters intellectual growth and creativity? And forsake it for a place, I would say, of extreme conformity? As Norris points out, of the four or five best-known North Dakota writers, only one still lives in-state.

But to live *well* in the Dakotas—or anywhere—requires creativity. Norris claims that the Dakotas have given her "her stories." If you believe, as I do, that the history Brodsky is talking about is your *own* history, then certainly Norris would seem to be a case in point: Geography (the Dakota plains) and history (her own stories) have provided her with her destiny.

You might say that Norris and I have eaten from the same bowl of oatmeal, but perhaps a bowl of jello is more appropriate. Norris states that in 1925, when about half of American homes had electricity, the figure for eastern North Dakota was thirty-eight percent; for the western part of the state, it was about three percent. This begins to explain certain social and cultural differences based on geography, such as why jello remained elusive at many church suppers, especially for farm women, until around the 1950s (Norris 137).

Norris's town, Lemmon, is what I would call a "biggish" town of 1500 in the northwest; while I am from the northeast. The "real" (bioregional) division between us would probably be determined by the Missouri River. But they divvied the territory up the wrong way, into North and South Dakota, a differentiation that no outsider can make anyway. Norris therefore, simply calls it "Dakota." I'm from East River, the side with more jello, and Norris is West River—which some eastern Dakotans like to think of as the wrong side of the tracks (of course there aren't many tracks—they have been abandoned to the prairie—thus isolating small towns even further).

On the trip to my mother's reunion, I saw that appearances in small towns had not changed much. And the land, of course, was still so flat you could stand on a Schlitz can and see forever. It is a place "where time stands still as it does in the liturgy," as Norris puts it. Langford looked about the same as it had before, in 1987 which was its 100th anniversary—the same as it looked on its 75th when, dressed as a pioneer girl, I rode a float for my grandfather's meat market. I remember my relatives, many of which have passed on. Main Street looked the same each time. We still have the facades of old buildings, but less and less goes on behind them, and there are fewer cars on Main Street.

The truth is: I have never lived in Langford, this little town I write about, which nevertheless holds my cultural identity because my relatives still live there. Nearby Aberdeen, where I grew up, is now the third-largest town in South Dakota—having gone from 15,000 when I lived there to 25,000 now. Aberdeen is modernized, changed. Langford has lost about seventy-five percent of its population since my mother lived there—down to, optimistically, 250.

There are a couple of pickups in front of "Swedes Corner"—the bar that used to be my grandparents' meat market—and one in front of the Post Office. Though I had not lived here, it seemed like everyone else in my family did—my father's family lived in the next town over, and their farms were in between. As a child, I spent Christmases, birthdays, holidays and weekends either in Langford or on my cousins' farm, which is now owned by someone else. The house stands abandoned; the barn, like many others in that part of the country, has fallen over.

The landscape, otherwise, looks the same: there are railroad tracks (unused), and the grain elevators, castles of the prairie, rise over every town. The land offers neither a loop nor a swoop. The once-rich black earth is cut up into rectangles, forming a kind of midwestern gridlock from which there is no escape. The highest points on the landscape besides the grain elevators are church steeples and water towers. (Sociologists like to point out that a culture is defined by whatever is highest—when I hike a nearby park in New Jersey I can see the tops of New York's Twin Trade Towers).

In Langford, as in many small Dakota towns, a gas station, the "rec" hall, the senior citizen's center, and a couple of churches remain. They are lucky: the school, consolidated over time from country schoolhouses and other small-town schools, also remains. One grocery store is still open.

On Sunday I drove out with my cousins to Highlanda Church, small and white amidst the fields. Here, my grandfather had been confirmed. I went across the road to the cemetery and I found the graves of my grandparents and my great-grandparents. I had no flowers; instead I took photographs and hurried across to the church, the incessant wind blowing my dress against my legs as I watched people park on the grass in front of the church, slam car doors, get their bulletins and find a place to sit (not a problem).

The minister appeared monkish in her dark robe. Yet she is sturdy and attractive—a fresh-faced, young blonde who seems to have both feet planted firmly on the ground. She offered what I would call farmers' prayers. In a land of feast-or-famine, this had been a flood year. She helped us to pray for crops, for families, for ourselves. We have all lost so much, I remember thinking, and it is only love and luck sometimes that keeps us going. We pray to withstand the weather. Like a windbreak, we are either dumb enough or brave enough to huddle here together, like a series of trees planted against a wind which has nothing to stop it within a hundred miles.

The woman's husband, also a minister, is preaching on the other side of town at the Swedish Lutheran Church. They are new blood—outsiders. I wonder how long they will stay. Norris writes of the small-town tendency to do things as they have always been done, until someone tries to find a better way. "No good deed goes unpunished" she notes, and newcomers are both welcomed and feared. But it was this woman, I have been told, who helped both my aunt and uncle when they were dying. She accompanied them on that terrifying and hopeful pilgrimage to the Mayo Clinic that so many midwesterners make when they fall ill. It is the only place they trust within hundreds of miles, but then, midwesterners are undaunted by distance.

A classmate of my mother's sat in the pew behind me, beside her husband. It is hard, in these parts, *not* to be recognized. Though my mother isn't with me, the woman knows who I am: "You're Margaret's girl. Your mother and my husband got the prize for youngest-looking at the reunion."

I smiled at her husband. "Well, what's the trick?" I asked.

"A good wife," she answered for him.

I tried, during the service, to accept what it is I'm supposed to be a part of. I want to fit in but can't. The words to the liturgy were permanently installed in my brain during childhood, but I found myself hitting a lot of wrong notes. They have changed the music. Looking out the window, I saw lilac bushes blowing in the wind; I saw Holsteins across the way, grazing on the pasture past the cemetery. I thought about the bones of my ancestors now beginning to pile up here. I thought about never having seen virgin prairie.

Norris writes: "We who live in Western Dakota look forward to the day when we will rest in some forlorn prairie cemetery with relatives and friends around us, the land and the weather forcing us to live in light of that reality: we belong to the land" (67). I, too, plan to be buried here some day. Where else do I belong?

My cousin exemplified Dakota generosity and Christian kindness by helping me drive back to New Jersey with three small boys. We went by way of Sisseton, South Dakota, stopping at the Tekawitha Arts

Center, hoping to show my children a culture older than our own. The kids said the Indian music "all sounded the same" but "they liked it anyway." We went by the lake area of northeastern South Dakota, where we hoped to swim, but there was too much rain and too many mosquitoes. We went to the Buffalo Lake restaurant where Indians and whites both go, where real live buffalo still roam. The kids and I stretched our necks for buffalo but saw none.

Later, back in New Jersey, my eight-year-old finished a story for his third-grade class about his love for South Dakota. And why shouldn't he love it? He had forgotten crying in frustration over mosquito bites and boredom. He remembered the generational weight of his family: the indulgence of his grandmother, aunts, and cousins. He had found friends and freedom: he was allowed to bike around town, buy his own candy at the store, and visit his cousin's farm. He wrote: "I want to grow up to be a farmer. I want to move to South Dakota and buy a Mo-ped and live forever."

Back to my novel after the trip, the white heroine returns to her small home town to save her family farm, she drives a tractor, and she grows up. Personally I have no wish to be a farmer, drive a tractor, move back to Dakota, and only occasionally do I entertain a fleeting wish to grow up.

And from my New Jersey distance, I wonder if what I have heard is right: we should take the less-populated parts of the prairie and turn them all back into grassland, let buffalo roam again, in spite of the chagrin of people whose culture is struggling to survive. I think of other mad projects: somebody's proposal to install a herd of bronze buffalo that will turn in the wind. Then there's the juxtaposition of Mt. Rushmore, the famous presidential faces in what was known as "Paha Sapa," holy ground. My six-year-old tells me of a hilarious cartoon in which a jet flies up Washington's nose. Then there's Crazy Horse monument, dreamed up by a Polish artist. Enough of the mountain has been dynamited away that you can almost see the outline of Crazy Horse, the man who could not be tamed.

I harbor a secret longing to be not a farmer but a wanderer, a hunter-gatherer. I long for tribe, for roots—and I see that in Dakota I have that. There I can see the benefits of peacemaking through cake-baking. What other things am I too blind to see?

My cousins have sent me a video of *Dances with Wolves*, but it's too sad to watch. I love the buffalo scene, worthy of Cecil B. De Mille. But the days of the buffalo hunt are over and so are the homesteading days and so, I am told, are the sixties. You can't make it with an acre and a cow or even stomp off somewhere with a backpack—at least in eastern South Dakota. All the land is spoken for, owned, domesticated, and you don't just go tromping off across someone's pasture unless you're carrying a gun and looking for pheasant.

After a New Jersey pow wow one of my boys said, "Those aren't real Indians, Mommy—they're all dead." And I pray—to Wakan Tanka, Jesus, Buddha and the Goddess within and anyone else who will listen—that he is wrong. Because we need them. Another time, I had to be reminded: "Mommy, you can't be an Indian. Your mother wasn't an Indian."

The only South Dakota Indian I ever really listened to was one I paid $25 to hear—at the Sheraton in New York. His name was Wallace Black Elk. I wanted to touch him—at least to shake his hand as he had touched my spirit. Was it what he said or the way he said it? Was it the prayers or the smoke? Was it first the spirit, or the words? He reminded us that it is the earth trying to save us, not the other way around. He helped me feel the respect for all life forms, the four-leggeds, and the two-leggeds and all creatures. "Mitakuye oyasin," he said. Repeat it like a mantra: "We are all one people."

But in South Dakota, the Indians are invisible. We don't see them. As Norris puts it: "The two cultures live alone together" (105). Mary Crow Dog, in her autobiographical work, *Lakota Woman*, expresses the belief that South Dakota is the most racist state in the country. "The life of an Indian is not held in great value in the state of South Dakota," she writes (25). But if the poverty at Pine Ridge is worse and more damning than anywhere else in the country, as an article in *The New York Times* reveals, it nevertheless exists also in white culture. Many white farmers, too, have lost their land, and their way of life. They, too, are invisible. And, of course, the loss is not merely financial. This way of life—as I knew it growing up—will be relegated to Garrison Keillor country.

I hope that Billy Graham's words—that "you can't be a Buddhist and a Christian" are wrong. I hope that Gandhi, who said, "I am a Buddhist, I am a Muslim, I am a Christian," is right. And I suspect that Norris's conversion is really integration, coming from the Benedictine Monastery nearby, the church down the road in a town called Faith, and from the land itself. She embraces forsaken ground, accepting her inheritance in its fullest sense. I call this integration. Norris's example of an Indian woman who believes in the cross *and* carries the pipe makes perfect sense, as long as you don't get too logical about it.

In the end, then, Norris's book is perhaps not a celebration of life in the Dakotas, nor is it an elegy. It is about accepting who you are. South Dakota friends report that Norris seems to have a "love/hate relationship" with the state. After all, they say, lots of people there are *content*. And that is the problem.

At the literature conference, my paper on *Dakota* was a sort of novelty, perhaps. Nearly everyone responded: "I've never met anyone from there before." And it's good to know that South Dakota writers, at least, *do* still live in-state, even if, as was pointed out, most North Dakota writers live elsewhere. South Dakota writers Linda Hasselstrom, Dan O'Brien and Kathleen Norris were keynote speakers, all powerful, place-oriented writers. Dakota has forged their identities. At least South Dakota is on the map literarily.

I can't tell the people of the Dakotas (I am now an "outsider") that they should resist casinos, Citicorp, and nuclear waste disposal sites. What would they do for money? How would a Jersey housewife sell counter-cultural values—solitude and self-reliance (à la Thoreau)—in this very domesticated territory? Norris has likened the process to seeking a desert within a desert. She describes solitude as a way of

> surrendering to reduced circumstances in a manner that enhances the whole person. It is a radical way of knowing exactly who, what, and where you are, in defiance of those powerful forces in society—alcohol, drugs, television, shopping malls, motels—that aim to make us forget. (23)

Another thing about South Dakota that keeps it from being overrun: the weather. A popular saying is that "at least it keeps the riffraff out." Parts of the Dakotas are now again so sparsely populated that they fit the definition of frontier once more. In one of Norris's interspersed weather reports she recalls this canticle, or psalm:

> Cold and chill, bless the Lord
> Dew and rain, bless the Lord
> Frost and chill, bless the Lord
> Ice and snow, bless the Lord
> Nights and days, bless the Lord
> 　　　　Light and darkness, bless the Lord.

But it doesn't say anything about the wind. If that's God's blessing, you wish so many times He would bestow it on somebody else. At my novel's end, back in South Dakota, the wind is still blowing. And if you listen, there is a message.

There is no mixed blessing like a Dakota storm. It's impossible not to feel passionate over a summer thunderstorm. Afterward, you feel your very soul has been washed clean. I've heard said that the spirit can now be explained by science—it's just a million neurons firing at once. In such a storm, then, there must be a billion electrons firing at once. It is an incomparable, beautiful violence. Norris calls it an "experience of the holy."

Appropriately, then, Norris ends with one of the many "weather reports" that are interspersed throughout the book, and of course, they report more than the temperature. *Dakota* gets the last word.

> Weather Report: December 7
> 3:00 A.M.
> Unable to sleep, I've been reading the words of a modern monk: "You have only to let the place happen to you . . . the loneliness, the silence, the poverty, the futility, indeed the silliness of your life." (220)

And her book ends this way:

> Listening to the voice of the sky, I wonder: how do we tell our tales, how can we hope to record them? I'd like to believe that deep in our bones the country people of Dakota, like poets, like monks, are, as Jean Cocteau once said of poetry, "useless but indispensable." (41)

WORKS CITED

Crow Dog, Mary, with Richard Erdoes. *Lakota Woman*. New York: Grove Weidenfeld, 1990.
Ehrlich, Gretel. *The Solace of Open Spaces*. New York: Viking, 1985.
Norris, Kathleen. *Dakota: A Spiritual Geography*. New York: Houghton Mifflin, 1993.
Snyder, Gary. *The Practice of the Wild*. San Francisco: North Point Press, 1990.
Thoreau, Henry David. *Walden*. 1854. New York: Harper and Row, 1965.

III

TEACHING AND WRITING THE SELF

Growing Up with Doctor Spock
An Auto-Biography[1]

Lynn Z. Bloom

Trust yourself. You know more than you think you do. Don't take too seriously all that the neighbors say. Don't be overawed by what the experts say. Don't be afraid to trust your own common sense. —beginning of *Baby and Child Care*

I wrote the biography of Doctor Spock in the same way I have lived my marriage—under the threat of opprobrium and exile. Both have been intense commitments, intimately intertwined. Both have been worth the risks, in their infinite possibilities for excitement, growth, pleasure—and pain.

I have always ignored advice I didn't want to hear. "Sacrifice," urged my mother and grandmother in rare concord during grandma's annual summer visit to our family in New Hampshire. "When you get married you'll have to sacrifice what you want for your husband and children," they said, imparting Lessons in Life along with practical instruction. On this hot sticky day, they were piecing together strips and scraps from grandma's vintage fur to make a coat for me to wear to first grade, and teaching me to sew. The fashionable garment during the year World War II broke out was the teddy bear coat that resembled neither bear nor coat but wadded chenille. "Sacrifice. Practice now for what you'll have to do when the time comes." "I hate that word," I shouted, "and I won't wear the fur coat, either."

My forearms protruded from my corduroy jacket, chapped and red in the deepening autumn chill. "Wear the coat," my mother urged. I didn't argue. I seldom argued, having already learned its futility. But I flung off the furry bundle as soon as I fled the house and left it on the front step. "Wear the coat." The week before Thanksgiving my mother took me, shivering, to Boston on the train and with largesse rarely permitted by my father's faculty salary let me pick out any coat I wanted in Jordan Marsh. The blue British tweed with deep velveteen lapels and matching bonnet cost ninety dollars. I savored its elegance with delight for the next three years, until my forearms again protruded. My brother, too young to protest, got the fur coat; he looked like a thatched hut.

To major in English was inevitable; the call of stories had been a siren song ever since childhood. My mother fed us a wholesome diet of library books, with slender spines and thick paper and elegant illustrations, fresh from the library every week. My father's nightly stories were dessert, high calorie adventures of a boy and a girl whose misjudgments kept them on the knife edge of disaster until—just before lights out—the Churl-Churls, a band of gruff, sententious little men, came to the rescue. To delight readers with words, my own and others', was the most exciting life I could imagine. "You can do it," was my father's refrain, from the emergence of my first work, "The Foney Book of Jokes," cartoons I had cut from *The Saturday Evening Post*, with my original captions, through my editorship of the high school paper. "You're a good writer," he'd beam when I won school essay contests. I lost only once, by writing—at his insistence—"Why I Am Proud to Be an American" in the style he taught his chemical engineering students.

"Why do you want to go to graduate school?" asked my senior honors advisor when I went to see him, encouraged by the faculty's award for academic distinction. "I love literature and writing. I want to teach in a college." This denizen of Michigan's English department that had never hired a tenure-track woman faculty member peered at me over his glasses, looking me up and down, from head to foot. Finally he said, "You're not deformed, are you?" "No." I blushed. "What difference does that make?"

"Well, then," this scholar replied—he had married one of his students, very beautiful and a foot taller than he—"you'll probably get married and have children." "I hope so," I barely whispered. "Then you'd better sacrifice graduate school. Every child a man has is an incentive for him to work harder, but every child a woman bears is a millstone around her neck. Why don't you go into high school teaching, so you'll have something to fall back on? The only successful women college professors," he offered the conventional wisdom, "are unfit for marriage. That puts them on the same plane as men. There's . . ." and he named a distinguished scholar, "crippled, can hardly walk. And that hunchback. . . ." He paused, "And of course"—he identified a critic I'd been reading with admiration, "so fat she's out of the running. Piano legs. You'd better get a PHT—Putting Hubby Through—instead of a Ph.D."

His specialty was George Eliot, on whom I had labored over an honors thesis. Although I usually wrote with ease, working on that paper was like stuttering. I wanted to express feminist ideas for which no sources, no language existed, as the anemic result sadly demonstrated. It would take another twenty years for the concepts and language to emerge that would enable "The Morality of George Eliot" to become appropriately fleshed out. My advisor began drawing on his pipe.

"Thank you," I said, and fled to the Graduate Office to apply for the M.A. program. The next week I was admitted. A semester later I approached the doctoral advisor. "Let me in." But he barely glanced at me as he barked, "Your grades aren't good enough." "What do you mean? I had straight A's last semester, and a 3.89 undergraduate average. The catalog says you can get in with a 3.5." "What the catalog *means*," he replied, "is that men can get in with a 3.0. Women need a 4. Your record is not acceptable. You have no right to take a man's seat in the doctoral program."

There was no way to appeal this decision; I could say nothing. So I accepted a TA-ship in the doctoral program at Ohio State, and reapplied to Michigan. In an eloquent page I said I lusted after scholarly research, *exclusively* scholarly research. I didn't tell the admissions committee that I so loved to read that bread wrappers would do in a pinch, that teaching was so much fun I would do it for free, and that I really wanted to be a creative writer. I had won *Mademoiselle* College Board prizes for both fiction and creative nonfiction, but there was no way to earn a doctorate in it. I especially didn't tell them that I was getting married and of course expected to have children and that Michigan was the only school my fiancé and I were applying to. Why apply anywhere else when we wanted to go only there?

Martin and I had become engaged just before he went overseas for a year's graduate study in social work. We visited both families. "Convert!" urged the good Jewish mother to the shiksa fiancée. "No," Martin answered in my defense. "Break it off!" hissed my parents, their lukewarm Christianity boiling in Martin's mild presence. Treating him like water, they spoke only to me. "And take off your ring!" commanded my mother, glaring at Martin's talismanic gift. My rebuttal blazed on my finger.

We'd marry the next summer in England, we promised, rather than endure a boycott at home, and travel around Europe for the entire summer. As Martin sailed for Southampton, I headed for the vast Midwest, a year of disjunctive correspondence, tense talks with both sets of parents, poverty (I wangled a credit card to buy Christmas presents for these very tormentors)—and an alien academic world. In the gracious rhythm of the academic semester to which I had been accustomed, there was a time for reading widely, a time for writing reflective papers, even a time for sleeping. The quarter system's frenetic tempo threatened all that. Graduate courses met every single weekday; having from Michigan snobbery taken the hardest and most arcane courses that Ohio State offered, I endured up to ten hours of preparation each night, in addition to grading the weekly set of themes from my sixty freshman students. Moreover, following the only advice the new TAs had been given as we were headed toward our first class, "Have the students write something every day so you can be sure they've done their assignments," I felt obliged to read and respond to all sixty daily exercises, as well.

A particular killer course was the two-quarter seminar in literary biography, with a twelve-page, single-spaced reading list—four extra pages between quarters—and weekly papers to be researched from primary sources. Half of its students not only dropped the course after the first quarter, but left graduate school. One re-enlisted to fight in the Korean War, another returned to disc jockeying, the others simply vanished. Five nights a week I haunted the library stacks until closing time; as we were laboring over a particularly difficult assignment, another overworked student taught me all the four-letter words I'd missed in childhood; I had to type through the night before each paper was due.

Nevertheless, I loved that course. Everything about it was new. The questions the course asked, "What is the truth, the meaning of a life?" "How do you know?" were fundamental, powerful, generative. But in 1957 they were asked by philosophers, and by individual biographers, not by critics. Except for book reviews, there was hardly any criticism on either biography or autobiography—we had to work in primary sources, the biographies and autobiographies themselves, and in the biographers' source materials—letters, diaries, documents, manuscripts. Everything we investigated was original, and the possibilities were endless. Everything we discussed leapt or ignored the boundaries—between literature and history, philosophy and psychology, fact and fiction, bellettristic writing and criticism. The literary landscape, grim and drab from critical strip mining, with deep pits around the Major Literary Figures, became instantly reconfigured as a glimmering Garden of Eden, with a myriad of possible new avenues of access to familiar literary figures.

Where do Sam Johnson's theories of biography come from? How are they manifested in *The Lives of the Poets*? How do they influence Boswell's *Life of Johnson*? In what ways is Johnson—or anyone—a self-created artifact? An artifact of Hawkins, Thrale, Boswell, and later biographers? In what ways does Lytton Strachey overturn the earlier conventions of biographical writing? What does he borrow from fiction—and is it the fiction of Mr. Bennet or Mrs. Woolf that most strongly influences him? Examine two, three, four biographies of the same subject. Compare any or all of these with the subject's autobiography. What is the truth of those lives? What does Woolf's *Orlando*, with its insouciant, elegant blending of genders and genres, reveal about the theory and practice of biography?

Such questions electrified my world and it has remained incandescent ever since. "What is the truth of a life? How do you know?" have become the questions of a lifetime of research and eventually, of teaching, too. Because they were the wrong questions to ask in a New Critical age, they also became, in the short run, the basis of a scholarly commitment to marginality. I didn't mind; I didn't have a clue about how to publish anything anyway, despite the professors' comments that overran the margins of my graduate papers, "Publish this." "Try this journal." And sometimes simply, "Yes." Perhaps these questions impressed me so profoundly because of the running obligato of analogous questions in my personal life: Who am I? What do I know? Where do I belong? What will I become? How will I best spend this life?

The answers varied, depending on how my teaching had gone that day, what I'd discovered in the stacks, whether I'd had enough sleep. The day's mail particularly affected the answers. "Convert!" "Come home!" "Marry me!" "Take off your ring!" "Bill overdue. Remit at once!" I had spent what money I had on a one-way ticket to Southampton. "Honor your parents!" "Do what you love"—my own voice—surfaced all too seldom.

By the end of the year at Ohio State I had completed the doctoral residency requirement and language exams—my version of "something to fall back on." My former Michigan roommate drove me back to New Hampshire to help with a week of sewing before I left for England. My parents made one message excruciatingly clear. "If you marry Martin, you will be the victim of prejudice for your whole life. People are violently anti-Semitic. You'll be ostracized." I said nothing; what could have convinced them?

As I proceeded to pack, they proceeded to prove their claim. "If you marry Martin, we will have nothing to do with you, or your husband, or any children you might have." My private voice sent a different message, clear and distinct: "It's their life or mine. Sorry I have to choose." But again I said nothing. Although I remember sobbing from the shock, it couldn't have lasted long because the picture my father took of my mother and me at the train station that day shows us smiling, relaxed, arm in arm. We might have been setting out for a day of shopping in Boston.

Well, dear reader, Michigan let me back in and gave me a TAship that they let me keep even after they realized I was married. Five years later, they awarded me a Ph.D. It would make a better story if I could add, "against incredible odds," but in truth—given Michigan's stringent admission standards for women—I encountered no difficulty in leaping the requisite hurdles on schedule: coursework, prelims, topic approval, dissertation defense. In fact, after several futile attempts to convince me to write a critical dissertation on Milton, or Cowper, or Landor, or Arnold, my advisors' favorites, they even let me write the dissertation I passionately wanted to do, *How Literary Biographers Use Their Subjects' Works: A Study of Biographical Method, 1865-1962*—so far out of the New Critical mainstream as to be virtually invisible. But I was pregnant while I wrote the first four chapters, and therefore lost to the profession anyway.

My dissertation research yielded amazing discoveries, had anyone in addition to myself cared to look. Nearly every biographer of Herbert, Swift, Dickens, and Shaw throughout the entire century of biographies that I studied read these authors' poetry, nonfiction, novels, and plays as "personal equations," straight or thinly veiled autobiography. These biographers showed little understanding of the creative process and the way real writers work, who inevitably transform the facts of a life to the necessities of the art. "Gulliver's travels were Swift's travels," asserted Carl Van Doren, "Among the Houyhnhnms [in Book IV] Gulliver was almost undisguisedly Swift" (307, 191), a view echoed by biographers Phyllis Greenacre (60) and the team of Mario Rossi and Joseph Hone, "Swift remains always the true protagonist of his tale" (319). Likewise, Dickens's biographers claimed that the more vivid and intense his novels were, the more closely they resembled his life. Characters whose initials were D.C. and C.D., such as David Copperfield and Charles Darnay, were scrutinized for particular resemblances to the author. For instance, Edgar Johnson's work, well-received and reissued in 1977, found both David Copperfield and Pip in *Great Expectations* "deeply revealing" of "the wounds that were still unhealed after a quarter of a century" (678; see also 982–83). How wrong the critical biographers were, I thought. And how arrogant of me, an unpublished beginner, to challenge established scholars, those emperors of ice cream with brilliant reputations. Did my new doctorate entitle me to do that?

I wrote the last chapter of my dissertation in Cleveland, where we'd moved when Bard was ten days old for Martin's first job as a new Ph.D., in gerontological research. For 50 cents an hour, the grandmotherly babysitter I'd hired for three mornings a week would talk to Bard when he was awake, in standard English, I insisted, no baby talk, and erase typos on the dissertation carbon copies during the rare moments when he was asleep.

By the time I finished my dissertation, I knew I'd have to write a biography to understand biographical method as an author, rather than as a critic, thereby anticipating by two decades the theory of Robert Scholes's *Textual Power*—create a text to respond to a text, and to understand it. What kinds of connections would *I* make between the subject's works and the life? How can one be understood in isolation from the other? Perhaps something in the genre itself led inevitably to the general misrepresentation of the creative process. More likely, I had concluded, though I didn't dare to say so in the dissertation, it was the biographers' obtuseness. They didn't understand how creative writers wrote because they themselves didn't write creatively. The experience of writing a biography would either make me more tolerant of what my predecessors had done, or even more critical, but at least I'd understand better how biographers worked and why they made the choices they did. Then, if the conclusions of my dissertation were corroborated, I could publish them with confidence. If not, I'd have spared myself the public embarrassment of being wrong.

But whom to write about? For two years I pondered this, in the interstices between editing two textbooks, teaching half-time, and having another baby. My first choice was George Herbert. I loved his poetry. The existing biographies were skimpy and out of date. His life had been relatively uneventful and uncontroversial, so I could count on finishing the book in two or three years, rather than the decade or more that a biography of a writer with a larger body of work, a mass of supporting documents, and a morass of controversy would require. How much of my own life did I want to devote to re-creating another's, anyway? However, to write on Herbert I would have to go to England to do the research—impossible, with two young children at home, and no research support.

By then I knew that I wanted my first biography to be the first one written about whomever I would choose, derived as far as possible from primary sources. I wanted to write on a person whose life and work were of considerable significance to a great many people. I realized, as Mark Schorer has observed, that "A prominent man is in many ways a mythological man," and I knew would have to penetrate what-

---

ever myths, public and private, had adhered to my subject. Although prudence dictated waiting to write the life until the person who had lived it was safely dead, the advantages of having firsthand access to the subject, the milieu, and the family and friends dictated for me a living subject. Besides, it would be a lot more enjoyable to work with real people than in a library. Nevertheless, Mary McCarthy, my next possibility, was out of the question for a different reason. Even if she'd been willing to cooperate with a biographer—and, as an autobiographer, why would she willingly relinquish authorial control?—she was writing at such a pace that a biography would be forever in flux. Over tea, I asked a good friend from Michigan who had dropped out of the doctoral program for a life that my honors advisor could have scripted, "Helen, if you were writing a biography, who would you write about?" Hugging her own toddler to her pregnant stomach, she replied without hesitation, "Doctor Spock."

Benjamin Spock lived about a mile from us in Cleveland Heights; in line at the supermarket or browsing in the library I was forever hearing gossip about him and his wife, Jane. We even used the same TV repair shop. He taught in the pediatrics and psychiatry programs at Case Western Reserve, the same university that had hired me two years earlier as a half-time Assistant Professor of English. "What a great idea!" I told Helen, thinking of my own tattered copy of *Baby and Child Care*. There were no biographies of Dr. Spock, whose book, selling steadily at a million copies a year since 1946, had made him grandfather to a generation of America's children. At sixty-four, his life was established and predictable, I thought, not likely to veer off in some unexpected direction that would require a major expansion of the necessary research. What fun it would be to write a biography of the man whose writings influenced not only millions of parents, but an entire culture. At 8:00 the next morning I called Helen, "Are you really going to write that biography?" "No, I'll never get to it with two babies." "Do you mind if I do it?" "Go right ahead!"

At 9:00 I called Dr. Spock himself and got right to the point. "I've recently finished my Michigan doctoral dissertation on literary biography—looking at the kinds of connections biographers make between authors' lives and their writing. Now I'd like to write a real biography—of you." In the long silence that followed, I hoped that Spock could hear Bard chattering in the background. Finally the pediatrician said, slowly, "We-l-l-l, I'd thought of writing it myself." There was another excruciating pause, and then he said, "But I'm so busy I'll never get around to it for years. Why don't you come over and we'll talk about it."

Fortunately for my research, Spock was as innocent of celebrity protocol as I was. After an hour's conversation I floated into the October sunshine, buoyed by the verbal agreement that we honored without ever again debating or even discussing it during the subsequent six-year process. Spock was planning to retire in the following May (1967), and was eager for someone to put in order a lifetime accumulation of primary sources—a treasure trove of professional papers, manuscripts and early editions of his books, editorial and parental commentary on *Baby and Child Care* (some ten thousand letters), royalty statements, tax returns, newspaper clippings beginning with his undergraduate days at Yale, his Olympic gold medal (Yale crew, 1929), and family photographs that would have made Cecil Beaton envious. He would let me have exclusive access to everything—no strings. He would meet with me weekly for interviews, and I could interview his wife weekly at their house. He would write letters of introduction to anyone I needed to see, even—as it turned out—enemies. I could follow him around the hospital, attend his classes, and sit in on his one-on-one pediatric practicum with a second-year medical student—he'd lend me a white coat so I'd blend in. He could read my completed manuscript and supply corrections for errors of fact, but the interpretation would be my own. I'd get whatever royalties there were—and of course, I would change the world with my first book, just as Dr. Spock had done with his.

And, I realized in a second wave of elation, with this book I would write myself back into the family that had evicted me. My parents would be so proud. After one letter to me in London before my wedding ("Break it off. There's still time.") my father had never written or called me, my mother's occasional letters were addressed only to me, despite my careful signature, "Love, Lynn and Martin"—sometimes with the comma omitted. Nevertheless, after the children were born they had visited us twice—one day for each baby.

In fact, Dr. Spock trusted me more than I trusted myself. It never occurred to him to ask whether I'd ever written a biography (I hadn't), or had a publisher (I didn't), or how likely it was that this Heights Housewife, as we part-timers were called, would complete such an extensive research project in a reasonable time—if at all. Indeed, how could I, who as a new mother had switched from reading novels to short stories to be sure of finishing something, have been able to make such a guarantee? The trusting Spock never even looked at my writing to see whether my dissertation style, perforce formal and bristling with footnotes, would be compatible with his friendly advice to parents and teenagers. It wasn't, at the outset. But in time I learned from analyzing the style of this Strunk and White of baby book authors, to write with clarity and precision—as if a child's life depended on it, to translate technical language into nonspecialized terms, to break up long sentences and paragraphs to please the ear and the eye. Spock composed aloud, and from him I learned to listen to the words, the music, the sounds of silence.

Martin, Helen, and her husband, a professional writer and editor, were as excited as I about the prospective biography. When with pride and pleasure I announced the impending project to my department chairman he reacted as if I had become pregnant for a third time. "Why," asked this Academic Eminence, "do you want to write about"—long pause—"that man?" Weren't the reasons self-evident? As I began to explain, he cut me off. "Perhaps," he said kindly, "you don't understand the rules of the game. To write about a popular figure is professional suicide." "Even one whose book sells a million copies a year?" "*Especially* a best-selling, author, particularly one who's alive. No one can do serious scholarship on such a popular figure. Why don't you," he advised, "write a series of biographical articles about authors of quality literature? After you've placed them in professional journals—if anyone is publishing biographical articles these days—you can afford to throw away your reputation by writing about a popular writer." I thanked him and began the research that in fact contributed to my being fired two years later, along with all the other part-time and therefore by definition non-serious, non-professional faculty.

Although only one subversive among the full-time faculty ever discussed my work-in-progress, the word was out. When Spock retired his life took a dramatic left turn into antiwar politics; as his protests against the Vietnam War escalated amidst increasing publicity, he came under FBI surveillance—and so did I. A student informer followed me as I followed Spock, notebook and tape recorder in hand, to cocktail parties, ice dancing lessons at the skating rink, the Child Rearing research playgroup, and peace rallies—where my own children came along for the stroller ride. For different reasons, militant feminists also regarded my project with skepticism. "How can you write about that privileged white male chauvinist oppressor?" they'd hiss, and turn away in scorn when I'd coo, "He's a very nice man." For seven years our phone was tapped; the eavesdroppers would have heard an occasional muffled query from my mother, "How are things going?," but never a word from my father.

Thus *Doctor Spock: Biography of a Conservative Radical* itself came of age in the real world, increasingly fascinating and in continual flux. Very little that I had learned in graduate school about research methods—all library-based—was germane, for very little of my material was in libraries. Of necessity I became a guerilla researcher, continually improvising my research methodology beyond the boundaries of conventional literary scholarship. Although I knew what I needed to find out—one gap led to another as the subject itself continually expanded—I had to locate the source and context of each bit of information and then figure out how to get it, and to corroborate it. My sources ranged from a plethora of doctors, peace activists, and politicians to lawyers, editors, publishers, parents of "Spock babies" (including Margaret Mead and Gregory Bateson), and the very babies themselves—among them my own children—how did they fare under Spock's advice? (Just fine, Martin and I concluded, finding that Spock's mixture of consistent firmness and love was producing, as he predicted, healthy children of good will and good cheer.) I discovered, on my own, what experienced journalists have doubtless long known—how to look nonchalant while eavesdropping, sifting through wastebaskets, or reading handwriting upside-down on the desks of people one is interviewing. I hired Spock's former secretary, herself home with an infant, to transcribe my interview tapes—and fill in the blanks—names, dates, contexts.

Given my subject I could scarcely say to Bard and Laird, "Go away, don't bother me, I'm busy writing about Doctor Spock." I learned to work in short batches of time snatched from carpools, nursery school schedules, housework, and entertaining a host of friends and international visitors. I wrote in our booklined bedroom that doubled as a study, often with the children and their friends and their toys literally underfoot. Martin's job kept him out of the house, alas, during most of their waking hours, except on weekends when the boys followed him like Lorenz's ducklings. So preoccupied was I with the research, notes scribbled on the edges of recipe cards and grocery lists, that every night when we'd tumble into bed Martin would clear the air, "Move over, Ben!"

For two summer vacations we combed the Northeast in quest of corroborative information about Spock's childhood and college years (all spent in New Haven), his work in New York and Pittsburgh, and his sailing vacations in New England, upstate New York, and Maryland. Martin took the boys to beaches, playgrounds, museums, while I interviewed Spock's publishers, medical and peace activist associates in their offices, homes, hospitals, and behind the scenes at protest meetings and during the trial of the "Boston Five"—Spock included—in 1968 for conspiracy to encourage draft resistance. Visits with Spock's sisters were almost as much fun as the interviews with Ben himself. I interviewed Sally in her swimming pool in Providence, and our entire family descended on Marjorie's oceanside organic farm in East Sullivan, Maine, where she grew all her own food and food for her prizeworthy goats and chickens. "You'll never have a sick chicken if you feed it earthworms," she said, and showed us the dirt-filled troughs where she raised the worms, too. Although my ethnographic methodology would have been congenial to anthropologists, had I known any, I was becoming more and more estranged from my nominal colleagues, academic researchers in English.

As the mosaic pieces that were to become the man emerged, the myth of Spock the Superman, the Superdoctor, receded. His family closet held as many skeletons as my own—and perhaps any American family's, despite the fifties myth of the upstanding, hardworking father, the devoted homemaker mother, flanked by two cherubic children and a photogenic dog. The Spocks had the dog, all right, and two handsome sons not immunized by their father's status and their mother's patrician background from either physical problems or the psychological traumas of coming of age in the turbulent sixties.

Because of his openness and his determined, democratic indifference to status, I know that Spock would have received whoever initially volunteered to write his biography with the same cordiality he showed to me. That I got there first became our mutual good fortune, for in the course my research I learned a great deal that a more sensation-hunting biographer would have leapt to publish. For instance, early in my research I became aware of reasons for the escalating tensions between Ben and Jane that ultimately led them to divorce after forty-nine years of marriage, three years after the publication of *Doctor Spock*.

My personal ethics superseded the demands of comprehensive scholarship as I chose to respect the privacy of these deeply reticent people. Even in this day of talk show confessions I do not regret that choice. Indeed, I turned down the first publisher's offer because he wanted, he said, dripping cigar ashes on my precious manuscript, "an exposé of the good doctor." By chance, I met another publisher, a vice-president of Bobbs-Merrill, while returning home in flight from the first. At the end of the plane ride he emerged from my manuscript, beaming, "I love every word of it. Don't change a thing." I signed the contract as soon as he could get it typed. My good reasons for a public emphasis still remain appropriate: "I decided to focus on those aspects of [Spock's] life for which he is best known and in which popular interest has been the greatest—those related to *Baby and Child Care* and to his involvement in the peace movement. Except for his childhood"—

to which I devoted considerable space—"his public life has been far more significant, unusual, interesting—and controversial—than has his personal, private life" (xxi).

Nevertheless, many of the decisions we make as biographers are dictated as much by analogy with our own lives as by the demands of scholarship; we come to understand our subjects as we come to understand our own families, ourselves. Spock's family could have been my own, its public veneer of reticent dignity masking a convoluted interweaving of complex and difficult relationships. My parents were continually reinventing their history to conform to the same fifties' myth that dictated the Spocks' annual Christmas letters. Martin and I collaborated with this by erecting a wallpaper-thin facade of friendliness during the brief tense visits that began during the Spock research, for I wanted my parents to know and love their grandchildren and I wanted the children to love them. For my sake, Martin acquiesced, despite the festering anti-Semitism threatening to contaminate each visit: "Of course we never see the Lavines [a colleague] socially. You can't get too close. They might want to marry. . . ." Although my father never uttered a syllable about our marriage or my work, he revised the Churl-Churl stories to include the children on his lap.

Yet the only letter my father ever wrote to me after my marriage was to acknowledge my gift of *Doctor Spock*. "What a clever book," he wrote. "How subtly you cut Dr. Spock down to size with your penetrating satire. Congratulations on your marvelous hatchet-job." To say this was to profoundly misread my entire life as well as my book; like Cordelia in *King Lear*, I could say nothing.

None of the numerous reviewers read *Doctor Spock* that way nor, to my knowledge, has anyone else. The book's modest sales, despite uniformly favorable reviews around the country, including a full front page in the *Washington Post Book Review*, barely paid back the publisher's advance. In the year that *Doctor Spock* was published Richard Nixon, then President, paid no income taxes. I, on the contrary, as a consequence of federal wiretapping, was hauled into tax court to defend a deduction of $1500 in expenses incurred in writing the biography—standard IRS harassment, I later learned, for antiwar protestors and their fellow travelers. It cost the entire amount to hire a tax accountant to demonstrate in court what should have been obvious from my five books in print—that I was indeed a professional author.

Although *Doctor Spock* has not changed the world at large, growing up with Doctor Spock profoundly changed my own world. As I wrote Spock's life I wrote my own independence. I developed a language, a voice, a research methodology, an ethical stance that have enabled me to re-enter and remain in the profession on my own terms. Did I ever publish my dissertation findings? Not on your life. The easy answer is that most of the biographies I had studied in my dissertation were being supplanted by new models, updated in content and more sophisticated in both theory and methodology—which I have explored in various articles on biographical method ("Reunion," 1990; 1991). I'd have had to rewrite the entire work, but without the excitement and discovery that I experienced the first time around. Ho-hum. And I'd have had to write in new language, for the uppity shrillness of the *scholar nouveau* required tempering by simplicity, gentleness, good humor. Spock's style.

The more complicated answer is that in the process of becoming a biographer I had become a colleague, not a critic, of other biographers. As I wrote, in search of a shape and a center of gravity in this deceptive genre (Roland Barthes has called biography "a novel that dare not speak its name"), I discovered what some of the biographers in my study had known all along—that biography has not only a human face, but a human heart. I learned to understand metaphor not as a trope but as a rendering of the truth that is at the deep heart's core of both imaginative literature and biography. I learned to trust hunches, intuitive connections, insights—reinforced, always, by double-checked facts. Aha! Edgar Johnson, I now realized, was right in interpreting Pip in *Great Expectations* as an analogue of Dickens, who transformed his own "youthful humiliations and griefs" into sources of shame that had "emblematic significance" for his hero (982–83). Spock was right in claiming that "I, myself, am the model for the first child in *Baby and Child Care*." Aha! This understanding has transformed, utterly, my critical writing about autobiography—("Escaping Voices," 1990)—and it has finally enabled me to write autobiographically, as well (1992). I know more now, and I claim less.

As the subjects that contributed to my exile—biography, autobiography, and personal writing—have moved gradually from the margin to the mainstream, I have tried to convey to my own students what my own very sophisticated education never hinted at—the inventive nature of research that has a heart and soul; the virtues of improvisation necessary to satisfy, as Einstein says, "a holy curiosity." Each semester I now require all my students to experience a microcosmic version of what I encountered in writing *Doctor Spock*, by writing at least one short paper in a genre they are studying; textual terror is invariably transformed to textual power (forthcoming, 1995).

My personal and professional lives remain as inseparable as ever. What I have learned during the process of writing *Doctor Spock* has enabled me, on most occasions, to transcend the volcanic substratum of family history. My mother began addressing letters to both Martin and me as soon as my father died; as she ages with vigor and vitality, she is a person I usually like to know.

Three years after my father died we celebrate Thanksgiving in my mother's new house, airy and arty, whose construction he had forbidden throughout their forty years in Durham, "If we owned a house we'd be stuck in this town. We'd never be free to move." Over pumpkin pie my mother offers reconciliation, "Jews aren't nearly as offensive now as they used to be. They're not nearly so orthodox." Martin and our sons, on break from graduate work at MIT for this special occasion, watch me in silence as my mother continues. I leave the table, go upstairs and brush my teeth, but there is no escaping her penetrating voice. So I return, and for the first time since I refused to wear the fur coat, I shout. "Think about what you're saying, how that attitude has hurt us all these years."

"Don't raise your voice to me, young lady," she snaps, and we leave the table. But when our sons are out of earshot she turns to me, furious, "Now that the boys know how you feel they'll never want to see me again." "Mother," I reply, "they've grown up knowing how I feel." After a long pause she asks, "They have?"

"Yes," I say, "Yes." For my family, like my students and my research, are worth the risks of commitment. And so we negotiate this truce, this life, with fear and pity, hope and love.

---

[1] First published in *a/b:Autobiography 8* (Fall 1993): 271–85. Reprinted by permission.

WORKS CITED

Bloom, Lynn Z. "Auto/Bio/History: Modern Midwifery." *Autobiography and Questions of Gender*. Ed. Shirley Neuman. London: Frank Cass, 1991. 12–24.

_____. *Doctor Spock: Biography of a Conservative Radical*. New York: Bobbs-Merrill, 1972.

_____. "Escaping Voices: Women's South Pacific Internment Diaries and Memoirs." *Troops versus Tropes: War and Literature*. Ed. Evelyn Hinz. Winnipeg: U of Manitoba, 1990. 101–12.

_____. "How Literary Biographers Use Their Subjects' Works: A Study of Biographical Method, 1865–1962." Diss. U of Michigan, 1963.

_____. "Reunion and Reinterpretation: Group Biography in Progress." *Biography* 13.3 (1990): 222–34.

_____. "Teaching College English as a Woman." *College English* 54.7 (1992): 818–25.

_____. "Textual Terror, Textual Power." *When Writing Teachers Teach Literature*. Eds. Toby Fulwiler and Art Young. Portsmouth, N.H.: Heinemann Boynton/Cook, forthcoming 1995.

Greenacre, Phyllis. *Swift and Carroll: A Psychoanalytic Study of Two Lives*. New York: International UP, 1955.

Johnson, Edgar. *Charles Dickens: His Tragedy and Triumph*. 2 vols. New York: Simon, 1952. rpt. 1 vol. New York: Viking, 1977.

Rossi, Mario M. and Joseph M. Hone. *Swift: or, The Egotist*. New York: Dutton, 1934.

Scholes, Robert. *Textual Power: Literary Theory and the Teaching of English*. New Haven: Yale UP, 1985.

Spock, Benjamin. *The Pocket Book of Baby and Child Care*. 1946. rpt. New York: Pocket, 1958, 1967.

Van Doren, Carl. *Swift*. New York: Viking, 1930.

FROM IMPERSONATORS TO PERSONS
BREAKING PATTERNS, FINDING VOICES

CHARLOTTE S. MCCLURE

Tell all the Truth but tell it slant
—Emily Dickinson, 1129

[W]omen who moved against the current of
their times ... [have] some condition in their lives
[that] insulated them from society's expectations
and gave them a source of energy, even of destiny, which would not permit them to accept the
conventional female role.—Carolyn G. Heilbrun,
Reinventing Womanhood, 30.

P eople welcome someone else's patterns of thought and behav-.
ior in their lives; patterns make one's life have purpose and
provide a comforting identity as a self and a belongingness to a
common group. Yet throughout the history of human beings' acceptance of structures and ideas, women as well as men have recognized
two voices within themselves: one that accepts without frustration the
pattern of public and private spheres to balance work and love, and
one that wants/needs to break the given pattern and to speak and act
as an individual. These two voices, the outer and the inner, often in
conflict, appear over and over in real and fictional worlds. The first
voice impersonates society's expected role, e.g., a lady, a gentleman, a
domestic "true" woman, a businessman, these roles invented to provide order in human activity. The second voice objects to the pattern,
impelled to break away from impersonating a role to a personal voice
that tells different stories from those commonly heard. My middle-class
experience, both actual and derived from literary study, tells me that
women more than men meet barriers in their desire to break out of the
conventional pattern.

As an early storyteller nicknamed Mother Goose, whose tales were
frequently published in the high school newspaper, I wanted my female character to be the heroic problem-solver or the rescuer of a victim
or the builder of a campsite for shipwrecked people on a remote is-

land. I reveled in talking to whoever would listen about how stories get told. However, as no compelling model of a professional woman writer, either in real life or in fiction, showed me the way at a crucial time for my decision, I succumbed to the social pattern of a traditional woman's life, forsaking my early stint as a journalist to live the nomadic life of an Air Force wife and parent. Those years of living among people in a variety of communities and cultures turned out to be the crucial experience to guide me to find real models of women who, divided between love and their work, discovered ways to reinvent the pattern of womanhood, to learn of the existence of women who express in their own voices the natural capacity of women for public work and private love, for independence and connectedness. Such women's strivings to be whole selves illuminate Jane Tompkins' tentative breaking out of the conventions of literary criticism in her desire to write about her feelings.[1]

After living in Europe for three years and then in the three-culture milieu of New Mexico, I discovered how much I was an impersonator of someone else's idea of the nature and role of woman. My children then in school, my inner voice clamoring to speak out, I enrolled in graduate school, hoping to formalize my real-life experience so that I would know what to do when the empty nest syndrome happened to me. I did not have the language then to explain to myself the transition I was undergoing. Since then, Carolyn Heilbrun's phrase—reinventing womanhood, becoming independent, maintaining one's own selfhood—helps to clarify my state (17). As Myra Jehlen might observe, I was beginning to tell my own story, preparing to act in the public domain instead of staying submerged in domesticity (596). In this state of change, searching for new knowledge, I found several western American women writers whose lives at the turn of the century were so patterned that they were constrained from telling stories in their own voices but who nevertheless wrote against the current of their times. Their achievement inspired me during my twenty-two-year academic career as well as now when I reinvent my love-work situation in retirement.

In their drive for liberation from their conventional lives, Gertrude Atherton, Mary Austin, and Kate Chopin confronted the impact on their desire to write of three social forces: the real-life protective title of lady, a denial of bonding with women and their concerns and achievements, and the pressure to accept the values of the patriarchal mainstream of business and competition. In their own lives, as revealed in recent biographies,[2] these authors had impersonated their society's expectation of them as women. At the same time they struggled to

---

CHARLOTTE S. McCLURE

become woman-identified persons by inventing the independent, self-reliant and loving woman-artist in their fiction. To read their works again in the late twentieth century in light of the rise and fall again of women's effort to speak publicly and feelingly in their own voices, makes me raise a significant question: Were their writing careers and their fictional portraits of independent women mere wishful thinking that women could have their love and work too, or a means of persuasion that this new woman was needed for the evolution of the individual and American society? Having raised a daughter and two sons, I asked myself whether the full development of mothers and daughters with men's support throughout society would enhance the well-being of all individuals, and, ultimately, the health of American families.

I became acquainted with the lives and works of Atherton, Austin, and Chopin, among other women writers of their period, when I began my dissertational search for the figure of an American Eve in the fiction of the turn of the century to match the opportunity of R. W. B. Lewis's American Adam. If Adam, bereft of history, was to overcome in America the restrictions and corruption of Europe, then, I believed, an American Eve would have a similar second chance, especially if she were able to grow and reinvent herself in environments removed from the eastern areas of the United States where the traditional influences on her would be strongest. Such an Eve, I thought, would shed the characteristics of the nineteenth-century True Woman, trading dependence, domesticity, and spiritual devotion for making and maintaining her own self, intellectual, questioning, and independent of man's approval and admiration, yet needing/wanting love. She would seek connectedness rather than the alienation characteristic of the figure of Adam. Atherton, Austin, and Chopin became writers on the verge of the settlement and the western frontier—Chopin in Louisiana and Missouri, the jumping off place to the West; middle-western Austin, the desert devotee in California and the Southwest, seeking a language of land and life beyond the traditional mode; and Atherton, an urban Californian looking East to validate a western-style birth of womanhood.

Delving into their lives and works, I discovered how easily they impersonated the received image of American womanhood embodied in their mothers and how difficult it was to discover their own nature. In their similar stories of women's self-conflict, I recognized my own early impersonation of my mother's ladyhood and my later rebellion against it. They record their conflict in their own autobiographies. Their biographers, who have the advantage of seeing the authors' lives wholly, clarify even more that struggle to identify and present a woman-identified natural woman, who tries to steer her way through the Scylla of love and the Charybdis of work.

In the short space of this essay, I reveal a little of what I learned about myself as I identified with a few of the fictional portraits they present through the three perspectives mentioned above: the author's experience of being a woman as she sees herself;[3] a biographer's version of her; and the loving-working woman character projected in fiction. A brief overview of these authors' early lives when they were impersonators—when they lived according to the way girls/women were supposed to be, until they arrived at a critical point in this supposed-to-be destiny—reveals the similar effects on them of the True Woman ideal and what they had to overcome in order to become their natural selves. Each author's evolution into that natural person can be seen in cameo as she invented portraits of herself and her characters as independent, self-informed, and loving of work and people—at least as far as was possible in their time.

Although Atherton, Austin, and Chopin had western experience and attitudes somewhat in common, outlooks that made them rebel against convention, they spent their formative years in California, Illinois, and Missouri respectively. They were precocious children, affected by their mothers' lives but rebellious against ladylike restrictions. While Chopin's extended family in one household in St. Louis provided a warm, affectionate atmosphere and early opportunity to observe varied human behavior (71), she still felt like "a belle caged by conventions," reports her biographer Emily Toth (97). Throughout her life, Chopin remained very close to her mother, and her multigenerational family living arrangement gave her multiple insights into human behavior and rich resources for writing stories. On the other hand, Atherton and Austin were starved for affection, Atherton's mother being an alcoholic self-centered belle and Austin's being one who preferred her older son to her daughter. These conditions ironically impelled these young women to choose a conventional way to escape from their mothers' conventional fate —in marriages that took them into different but not necessarily fulfilling existences. In marriage, Atherton stayed in California but gained a more stable emotional experience, although both her husband and her mother-in-law restricted her ambition to write. At twenty, college-educated Austin moved with her family to homestead in a parched area of Southern California. Married at twenty-three, Austin began her study of the western desert, which became the basis for her dealing with a dissatisfying marriage and for propelling her into the work of writing. All three bore children, but when they were about thirty, Atherton's and Chopin's marriages ended with the early death of their husbands; neither married again but they, as well as the divorced Austin, were always popular with or attracted to men. I was curious to find out if, as rebels against society's expectations of their role and as mothers of daughters (and sons), they passed on to their children, especially their daughters, their own desire for self-identified work and love. Discovering their characterization in fiction of women as artists and lovers of men, I began to include their best works in my American literature courses.

As a widow who left her child in California to pursue her own work in the public arena of New York, Atherton preferred to be called "Mrs. Atherton" for the rest of her life. That choice gave her a traditional and acceptable role within which she could invent other roles without exciting adverse comment on her behavior as a woman in public. Using the language and social customs of the eastern publishing world in order to achieve symbolic rooms of her own, i.e., to write at any place she chose, Atherton stormed offices of publishers and magazine editors in New York. They and reviewers often rejected her early books because her stories of unconventional women, they said, shocked the reading public, especially Howells's young girl. In her first fictional portraits—a rebellious unattractive woman (*Hermia Suydam* 1889), a December wife with a May husband (*A Question of Time* 1891), and a modern intellectual and beautiful Helena (*A Whirl Asunder* 1895)— Atherton believed that she extended the drab lives of her intended audience of middle-class women with alternative views of female intellect, beauty, and friendship with women as well as of marriage. At this time she could not invent for her redefined woman character any independent work that would be possible in late nineteenth-century America. Yet Atherton fought the rejection of and indifference to her works by male editors and publishers; she cultivated literary people and reviewers in London in the 1890s. There, combining her social skill and attractiveness (her desire for connectedness), she promoted her works to gain British recognition of her novels as well as money to support members of her family in California; this latter action partially overcame her guilt at leaving her daughter in the care of her grandmothers. Atherton, like Charlotte Perkins Gilman, braved public criticism of her apparent abandonment of her daughter by providing a loving surrogate, while she pursued her work. (Atherton's daughter Muriel, after marriage, motherhood, and divorce, became host of Atherton's literary salon in New York and San Francisco.)

In her candid and self-deprecating memoir, *Adventures of a Novelist* (1932), Atherton reminisced the first seventy-five years of her life, fortyfour of them at work making a living and marketing herself. She described herself as "an imp of the perverse," who possessed a "rotten spot" in her brain and dared a life of trial and error that provided sources for her fiction. She acknowledged her brattish behavior, her wanting attention from men, and her sometimes abrasive interaction with people in all walks of life. Skillful (sometimes malicious) at playing off contradictory elements in social and economic situations against each other, Atherton was able to create assertive, beautiful achieving women heroes even though she usually denied that she was a feminist.[4] However, for late twentieth-century feminists she does not provide an attractive role model, observes her biographer, Emily Leider, in *California's Daughter: Gertrude Atherton and her Times;* Leider captures Atherton's dual nature:

> As a younger woman, [Atherton] often justified her displays of temperament, cruelty, and spite as prerogatives of the "savage" West. . . . She took from the American West its tradition of fearlessness, buccaneering individualism, and impermanence and grafted onto it a Henry Jamesian quest for the cosmopolitan. . . . She possessed little of the "negative capability," or ability to submerge the self, common to great artists. Rather, she imagined herself in myriad guises. Atherton could not escape herself, but whether she truly knew herself is another question. (6, 7, 8)

In light of recent research in the psychology of women, e.g., that of Carol Gilligan and Mary Belenky, I think that Atherton unwittingly may have invented a model of multiple roles in which a woman could act out her own perceptions of herself.

Atherton's portraits of possible American women present a stunning variety: Patience Sparhawk, first heroine to be convicted of murder, sentenced to die in the Sing Sing electric chair and rescued at the last minute by her ideal lover; Magdalena Yorba, yearning to write like Henry James but, without his talent, having to settle for domesticity; Helena Belmont, a moralistic American Helen of Troy; Isabel Otis, successful as manager of a chicken ranch but unable to find a leadership role in the building of San Francisco in the early twentieth century; Margarethe Styr, rising from prostitution to star in Wagnerian opera in Munich, preferring immolation as Isolde on stage to real-life passion; Mary Zattiany, an energetic, beautiful woman of fifty-nine, finding power and outlet for her talent not in acting on her own in America but as the wife of a powerful Austrian politician; and Mrs. Eddington, a civic-minded sixty-year-old widow with diminished income in the depression years, who attempts to find jobs for young women in San Francisco. In these varied portraits, Atherton entertained her audience of middle-class women with visions of women's nature and talent that, if taken charge of, would produce exciting, self-fulfilling yet independent lives that offered the choice of work and relationships. My correspondence with Atherton's granddaughter, the late Florence Atherton Dickey of Santa Rosa, California, and the biography of Atherton by Emily Leider reveal how much the author's independence and concern for her family influenced the choices her grandchildren and nieces made in their own lives.[5]

Almost more western than California-born Atherton, Mary Austin set two goals to resolve her conflict between love and work: to shift the center of culture from the Euro-American traditions of the East to the American Indian and Hispanic traditions of the Southwest, and to change her generation's attitudes toward women and women's rights. Mary Austin and I have in common a midwestern upbringing—her Illinois and my Ohio—and a life-expanding existence in the California desert and New Mexico. We both were changed forever. Despite her divorce after twenty-three years of marriage (1914) and the institutionalization of her retarded daughter (1905), Austin publicly kept her married name (without the Mrs., a double rebellion from her early life); and in her writing and speaking she emphasized her self-identified dual nature as "I-Mary" and "Mary-by-herself." "I-Mary" names her confident, outspoken self, while "Mary-by-herself" reflects her conflicted relation with her mother and her feeling herself an outcast from social expectations of womanhood. Naming herself thus in her autobiography *Earth Horizon*, Austin empowered her distinctive voice in nature writing, poetry, prose, and fiction. Discarding her midwest inheritance of small town Methodism and her mother's ideal ladyhood, Austin transformed her close observation of the life of the southwestern desert into precisely crafted prose that, like poetry, had carefully measured cadences and mystical insights. For her first book, *Land of Little Rain* (1903), the desert enabled her to breed language forms that were equal to the task of translating its austere beauty for ordinary readers to understand, e.g., the Walking Woman in *Lost Borders* (1909).

Walking Woman, a desert inhabitant, is one of Austin's earliest portraits of a woman trying to live her own life, a creative working life that could also include a relationship with a man. "Walking Woman had walked off all sense of society-made values, and knowing the best [either in work or in a mate] when the best came to her, [she] was able to take it; for [Walking Woman] the best was the work of sheep herding, the love of a shepherd, and the joy of their child." Walking Woman gave Austin a western image for the feminine self-informed woman that Austin thought herself to be—one who sought her own authentic self, even when choosing a life directed away from responsibilities traditionally assigned to woman, yet wanting/needing a "congenial" intellectual relation with a man.[6] Although as an adolescent Mary Austin never felt free to talk about Henry David Thoreau on a date (*Earth Horizon* 112), she parallels Thoreau's image of walking southwest as a necessary mode of the new Americans finding their own self-identity. I view Austin's effort to make her own conversation with men (113) as an early analysis of a communication gap between women and men that continues today. Walking Woman also became a model for an urban New Woman, Olivia May Lattimore in Austin's novel, *Woman of Genius* (1913); Olivia was portrayed as a satisfied woman and an actress successful in New York, even though she had no model to suggest how a woman might combine work and love. Because Austin's publishers resisted acceptance of Olivia as a model of a new American woman, Austin had to confront them to keep the novel in print (*Earth Horizon* 333).

Among several of Austin's portraits of women—the Basket Woman, the chisera—who attempt to live their own lives, Austin shows her concern to identify human genius in whomever and wherever it can be found. This genius she defined as "the free, untutored play of the racial inheritance and the immediate life of the individual."[7] Women as well as men could claim genius as a component of their nature. She believed that individuals can tap into their genius by reaching into the "deep self" in order to build upon "racial inheritance," which was the sum of the capacities acquired by the ancestors of individuals to which they have access in meeting the exigencies of their immediate lives. In this drawing upon one's heritage, I think of my great-grandmother whose Hugenot family had to escape persecution in France in 1676 by fleeing to Germany and who in 1848 saw the need to flee from another social revolution to America. Austin's definition of genius seems to parallel Heilbrun's notation of a special condition that enables women to move against the current of their time and to speak out in their own voices, to tell their own stories of what they think "unashamed" (*A Woman of Genius* 261, 290).

In this perception of genius in everyone, Austin recalls her recognition of special genius that she found in the indigenous inhabitants of the desert, especially the chisera, the strong, witty and daring woman, and that prophesied the existence of a genuine woman's culture. A "desert rat" myself for several years, I understand the remark of Austin's biographer, Esther Lanigan Stineman, that Austin linked her career-long exploration of the nature of genius to her westernness (132), a liberating experience, and to her consciousness of the nobility of the first indigenous inhabitants of the land (161). Something beautiful and mysterious in the desert landscape makes one's senses dance to impulses of community with people and nature not always felt by urban dwellers. Hence her characterization of desert women provides for her and traditional women a gender inheritance, models of women who "in their 100,000 years of managing a family have developed a genius for personal relationship" (Graulich 389).

Austin had to leave the California desert for New York not only to argue with the publishing industry on the importance of the West but also to put pressure on publishers to help her make a living from her books. Austin often complained about male editors and publishers who determine what should and should not be written about the experiences of women as women (*Earth Horizon* 320). In her autobiography, *Earth Horizon* (1932), her final major work, published in the same year as Atherton's memoir, Austin is preoccupied with how to write her life in her own voice that wants to celebrate the individual as well as the need to belong (368), thus expressing her own dual nature (217). Writing of herself in third person, Austin reveals her need for attention, especially from her mother and other women, and her resentment at her life's contingencies. However, as Stineman observes, *Earth Horizon* accurately reflects her world view, one of desperate longing for independence and community, symbolized by the holistic "earth horizon" (217). A maverick in her view of herself, Austin held her dual nature in creative tension to the end, courageously living her own life and speaking out unashamedly.

Kate Chopin lived on the eastern fringe of the nineteenth-century western expansion. Viewing herself as a western writer, she complained in 1894 about the conventional book learning of members of the Western Association of Writers whose standards kept them out of touch with real life, the larger world. Although she was criticized for her frankness when these remarks were published, smarting from the censure of *The Awakening* six years later, she wrote an article, "Development of the Literary West." In it she praised writers such as Mary Hallock Foote, Ambrose Bierce, Owen Wister, Octave Thanet, Bret Harte, and Hamlin Garland as regional writers who were telling "an intensely interesting story developing in the West" (Toth 381–82). I like to speculate that Chopin sympathized with Foote and women characters who gave up eastern city life to accompany their husbands into pioneer life.

In her ten-year writing career, just as did Atherton and Austin, Chopin endured the same problems of getting publishers and reviewers to take her writing seriously. As a spirited flirtatious woman, feeling caged by the social customs of small-town Cloutierville and of the Philistines of St. Louis, Chopin impersonated the lady's role in society, but as a unique person, she walked around New Orleans smoking a cigar, and she kept the room of her own in St. Louis for her writing. Her great-grandmother educated her, teaching her through storytelling, so that at an early age Chopin learned the contradictions, restrictions, and hypocrisies of society, observations she would try to write about. Her imaginative interest in examining independent women and not-so-happy marriages as well as her friendships with independent intellectual people helped her to find language, sometimes thought extreme, that revealed the sensuous and sexual experience of women and the discontent in man/woman relationships (Toth 151, 155). In her commonplace book she recorded her sensation of giving birth as more physical than spiritual (Toth 128), an experience reflected by Edna Pontellier in *The Awakening*. In this scene, Chopin in part creates an alternative view to spirituality associated with the ideal True Woman, portrayed by Adele Ratignole. Chopin dares to refer to a woman's breast in her unpublished short story, "The Storm" (1898);[8] she boldly shows she saw no shame in woman's or man's sexual desire, only the hypocrisy with which it was conventionally viewed.

Although Kate Chopin felt that she lived in the provinces in St. Louis, she kept in touch with eastern publishers and editors, and her stories, when not rejected, appeared in significant magazines. In the years after her husband's death (1882) and after leaving her lover (1884) in order to find herself as a writer, Chopin wrote three novels, eighty-five short stories, twelve essays, twenty-five poems, and one play, although she never earned enough money to support herself from her writing. Nevertheless, in her fiction she creates, without judgment, voices in a tremendous variety of women that reveal a wide range of female natural attributes and experience: passionate women, reasoning women, divorced women, wives with wandering eyes, leisured and idle women doing good, alcoholic wives, a black woman trying to live when someone else possesses her body, women and men unhappy in marriage. Leaving no autobiography but several diaries and her commonplace book, Chopin reveals her deepest interests and concerns in her fiction. She too had a divided self, yearning for passionate connection and needing deep solitude, somewhat like Edna Pontellier, her most enduring portrait of a natural woman.

Earlier I mused on the legacy of Atherton, Austin, and Chopin: Did they pursue their careers and portray loving and independent women in fiction as a wish that would be and must be fulfilled by women in the future? Or did they need to persuade readers that this new woman was needed for the evolution not only of the individual girl and boy but also of American society? I wonder, Did they pass on to their real daughters their desire to define themselves and to live according to their own natures? Atherton's novels contain only a few mother-daughter plots, e.g., the three generations of women in *Black Oxen* (1923) and *The House of Lee* (1940), whereas her own daughter chose a traditional woman's life and her granddaughter had a short career on the stage. In *Earth Horizon*, Austin sympathetically portrays her mother, whom she perceived as caught in midwestern mores; and, not having a healthy daughter to whom to leave a legacy of liberation from social roles, she created fictional female portraits such as the chisera and Walking Woman and Olivia Lattimore. Enjoying affection-ate relationships with her unconventional storytelling grandmother and her widowed mother, Chopin passed on to her five sons and one daugh-ter Lelia a similar unconventionality and a flair for drama and creativity. That Kate Chopin and her daughter, like their grandmother and great-grandmothers, remained widows for the rest of their lives, attests to their independence and a zest for living fully in their society. I did not know whether I had communicated this desire for self-invention to my own daughter until one day, having achieved success in a civil engi-neering project she had charge of, she said to me: "Thanks, Mom, for insisting that I study and work hard as well as play."

These authors spent their greatest energy revealing the situation of women, their mothers in particular, and women writers in their era. They only indirectly produced a legacy to their real daughters, to their fictional daughters, and to succeeding generations of women aspiring to the full life of love and work. I count them as my literary grand-mothers, who, like real-life grandmothers, search among the following generations for women who show their attributes of courage to live their lives according to their own natures, to exercise their talent, and to tell stories that break the silence about women's desire, ambition, and passion. They passed on their discovery of the complexity of choices of people who perform on their own merit in an increasingly techno-logical and competitive world where the rules for the most part reflect the needs of men. Atherton's early marriage to a mother-coddled boy led her to advise mothers to help their sons to mature so as to become companions of their future wives. Kate Chopin's realistic portraits of discontented as well as happy married couples convey her notion of a society that would benefit from male support of female growth and development throughout their society. These authors' analysis of a potential evolution of society in which women and men can fully mature predicts Carolyn Heilbrun's personal evaluation in 1979:

> What I will suggest is that women, while not denying to themselves the male lessons of achievement that almost all our literature and history can afford, recognize the importance of taking these examples to themselves *as women*, supporting other women, identifying with them, and imagining the achievement of women generally. (32)

Imagine what it is like to be a whole, active self in love and work and retirement, Heilbrun would advise in her own reinvented voice, and let "the old idea of womanhood be damned"(34) on the path toward a possible transformed society.

---

[1] Tompkins, quoted by Olivia Frey, "Beyond Literary Darwinism: Women's Voices and Critical Discourse," *College English* 52 (September 1990): 507.

[2] Emily Wortis Leider, *California's Daughter: Gertrude Atherton and Her Times* (Palo Alto, California: Stanford UP, 1991); Esther Lanigan Stineman, *Mary Austin: Song of a Maverick* (New haven: Yale UP, 1989); Emily Toth, *Kate Chopin* (New York: Morrow, 1990).

[3] Gertrude Atherton, *Adventures of a Novelist* (New York: Liveright, 1932); Mary Austin, *Earth Horizon* (1932; rpt. Albuquerque: U of New Mexico P, 1991).

[4] Atherton's one feminist novel, *Julia France and Her Times* (New York: Macmillan, 1912), deals with the suffrage movement in England.

[5] Gertrude Atherton created for her family the image of both an individual capable of an independent life and one on whom others could depend for financial help in a crisis. She enjoyed her adult grandchildren: Florence Russell, whom she chaperoned in Hollywood in the 1920s when Florence wanted to break into silent films but who later had a successful career in real estate; Dominga, who after an unsuccessful love affair, became a nun; and George, who worked in real estate, becoming independent only after his mother's (Muriel's) death in 1962 but still remaining obedient to his grandmother's wishes (Leider 329–30). Barbara Jacobsen, great-granddaughter of Mrs. Atherton, designed the jacket illustration "The Puzzle" for the Leider biography.

[6] "The Walking Woman," *Lost Borders* (1909) in *Western Trails: A Collection of Short Stories by Mary Austin*, ed. Melody Graulich (Reno: U of Nevada P, 1987); Stineman, pp. 212–13.

[7] Quoted by Stineman, p. 133. In Austin's introduction to *Everyman's Genius* (Indianapolis: Bobbs-Merrill, 1925), she provided a glossary of words on genius: psyche, race, racial inheritance, talent, immediate-self, deep-self, intuition, and supernormal faculty.

[8] Toth, p. 317, states that this description perhaps echoes James Lane Allen's similar reference in his book, *A Summer in Arcady* (1896).

Works Cited

Atherton, Gertrude. *Adventures of a Novelist*. New York: Liveright, 1932.
_____. *Black Oxen*. New York: Boni & Liveright, 1923.
_____. *Hermia Suydam*. New York: Current Literature, 1889.
_____. *The House of Lee*. New York: D. Appleton-Century, 1940.
_____. *Julia France and Her Times*. New York: Macmillan, 1912.

_____. *A Question of Time*. New York: John W. Lovell, 1891.

_____. *A Whirl Asunder*. New York: Frederick A. Stokes, 1895.

Austin, Mary. *Earth Horizon: An Autobiography*. 1932. Albuquerque: U of New Mexico P, 1991.

_____. *The Land of Little Rain*. Boston: Houghton Mifflin, 1903.

_____. *Lost Borders*. New York, London: Harper, 1909.

_____. *A Woman of Genius*. New York: Doubleday, Page, 1912.

Belenky, Mary et al. *Women's Ways of Knowing: The Development of Self, Voice and Mind*. New York: Basic Books, 1986.

Chopin, Kate. *"The Awakening": An Authoritative Text, Contexts, Criticism*. Ed. Margaret Culley. New York: Norton, 1976.

Dickey, Florence Atherton. Letters to Charlotte S. McClure, 1975–1986.

Frey, Olivia. "Beyond Literary Darwinism: Women's Voices and Critical Discourse," *College English* 52 (Sept. 1990): 507–26.

Gilligan, Carol. *In a Different Voice: Psychological Theory and Women's Development*. Cambridge: Harvard UP, 1982.

Graulich, Melody. "Afterword." Mary Austin, *Earth Horizon: An Autobiography*. 1932. Albuquerque: U of New Mexico P, 1991. 373–94.

Heilbrun, Carolyn. *Reinventing Womanhood*. New York: Norton, 1979.

Jehlen, Myra. "Archimedes and the Paradox of Feminist Criticism." *Signs* 6, No. 4 (1984): 596.

Leider, Emily Wortis. *California's Daughter: Gertrude Atherton and Her Times*. Palo Alto, CA: Stanford UP, 1991.

Lewis, R. W. B. *The American Adam: Innocence, Tragedy and Tradition in the Nineteenth Century*. Chicago: U of Chicago P, 1955.

Stineman, Esther Lanigan. *Mary Austin: Song of a Maverick*. New Haven, London: Yale UP, 1989.

Tompkins, Jane. "Me and My Shadow." *New Literary History* 19 (1987): 169–78.

Toth, Emily. *Kate Chopin: The Life of the Author of "The Awakening."* New York: Morrow, 1990.

SEARCH AND RESCUE

BEVERLY CONNER

Give sorrow words; the grief that does not speak
Whispers the o'er-fraught heart and bids it break.
Macbeth. Act IV, Sc. 3, Line 209

I carried my daughter for nine months—a normal pregnancy. Nineteen years later, when the discovery of her body ended a nine-month disappearance, we called it a gestation of grief.

I have never written before about my daughter's death. Pain has silenced me, pain and some sense of propriety that I ought not to be so uncivil as to inflict her murder on the reader (on the student, the colleague, the friend), who might flinch from its violence. That silencing shadow still hovers over the interstices of my personal and professional lives—twin birds that often feed each other but sometimes inflict sharp-beaked damage in ways unique, I believe, to women.

In speaking of Carin, I find the threads that attached us then and bind us now are complex and tangled. Yet perhaps that is the way of all mothers and daughters. Looking back many years before Carin, when *I* was the daughter, my deepest dream was for an education, a dream I was not to come by easily or quickly. No woman in my family had ever been educated past high school. As I neared the end of eighth grade, my parents stated matter-of-factly that I would be taking the "commercial" course in high school—typing, bookkeeping, office practices—rather than the college preparatory course. At thirteen I was still an exceedingly good child. I believed my parents knew best for me, and I was not confrontational in the least. But I lobbied my teacher and my principal, who called my parents in for a conference (less common in those days) in order to persuade them that I needed at least to be prepared for the possibility of college. It was the first and one of the few times that I went against my parents' wishes. We reached a compromise. I would enroll in college prep so long as I also took courses in typing and office practices. In fact, it turned out not to be such a bad idea, as I was later to support myself by my secretarial skills. After all, I was smart, I could type, and by god I could certainly spell. In June of

238

1954, two days after I graduated from high school, the Los Angeles Traffic Court was happy to pay me $221 a month. And with no prospects of going to college, I was glad to get the job.

Today I am amazed that I let my stepmother talk me out of applying for college scholarships. It was not even that difficult for her to do so. She merely pointed out that a scholarship would not cover all my expenses and that she and my father (and certainly not my mother who was barely getting by after the divorce) had no money to offer me. I didn't realize then that even a *declined* scholarship would have reinforced my confidence, certainly more than a stillborn dream. By the time I took my traffic court savings and entered Berkeley two years later, the idea of scholarships had somehow erased itself from my mind. I worked. I took out loans.

For my father's part, Daddy prided himself on being a "regular Joe," as he called it—this despite his voracious reading, his multi-lingual high school education. Here was a man who had turned down a scholarship to Oberlin because all of his older brothers had gone to work for the railroad, as their father before them, and my father believed he had a similar obligation. He was always slightly bemused to find himself years later in the white-collar world of sales.

What *I* really wanted to be was a writer, but who in her right mind would have said *that* in the fifties? So I went to my father and told him I wanted to be an English teacher. He pointed out that teachers made so little money that there was no "return" on the cost invested in their education. Besides, and this was the clincher in those days, "You and Terry are going to get married." I had no rejoinder, even though both my stepmother and my mother were working at minimum wage, part-time jobs. Too big a part of me agreed that marriage and motherhood really were destined to be my main vocation. Later I blamed myself for being so easily swayed. Eventually, I discovered Tillie Olsen's book, *Silences*:

> High aim, and accomplishment toward it, discounted by the prevalent attitude that, as girls will probably marry (attitudes not applied to boys who will probably marry), writing is no more than an attainment of a dowry to be spent later according the needs and circumstances within the true vocation: husband and family. (30)

Even though the wellsprings of scholarship and parental funding evaporated, my determination to find a way burrowed deeper, a channel that continued to trickle for many years. My mother once asked,

"Beverly, are you going to go to school *forever*?" Sometimes it seemed that way to me, too.

And so, after Terry and I married, we both worked and attended Berkeley until he graduated. When he was stationed at Fort Knox, I attended the University of Kentucky. After we settled in the Pacific Northwest, I went to school pregnant. And after a gap of too many years, with two school-age children, I went back to college full-time. My husband cashed in the few stocks we owned in order to come up with the tuition. Finally, in 1978, a month short of my forty-second birthday, with my husband and my son and daughter (teenagers both) looking on, I walked across the stage to receive my Bachelor of Arts degree from the University of Puget Sound (never dreaming that one day years later I would return there to teach). Above the crowd, I heard Carin sing out, "Way to go, Mother!"

Only one of my college teachers recommended that I consider graduate school. I suppose I struck the others as too old, too encumbered with family. Certainly I was the rarity in an undergraduate liberal arts college comprised almost entirely of eighteen- to twenty-two-year-olds.

By that time I was writing short stories and poetry. Truth to tell, I applied to a graduate program in creative writing at another university more from the need to be told I was "good enough" than from any other single reason. An interview, however, with a professor in the graduate English department firmed up my resolve to register. He suggested I enroll as a nonmatriculated student to see how graduate school would "suit me." He all but said the words "older woman," "dilettante." Stung by his dismissive attitude, I marched out of his office and into the registrar's to enroll as a regular student.

Graduate school dragged on as I took courses part-time and commuted an hour each way. I was impressed at how seriously the young men especially took themselves and their writing. They expected to be the next Pynchon, the next Updike. I envied their confidence, their privilege of full-time attendance. What did *I* expect? I didn't even apply for one of the competitive teaching assistantships. I was, after all, a part-time student with children still at home. Without a firm goal in mind, I left graduate school to take a job as an editor for a pension-consulting firm. After about a year and a half, my mind numbed by money managers and small cap stocks, I quit in October of 1982 to work part-time for my husband.

In many ways it was a wonderful autumn that year. To celebrate our twenty-fifth wedding anniversary in November, we took both children to see "The King and I." Early in December, Carin and I together decorated our Christmas tree. We sat up until two in the morning: talking, adjusting the tree's ornaments, admiring our work. I remember appreciating the harmony at the time, the way you do in a house that holds teenagers. There was no way to prepare; there never is. A week later, on December 13, 1982, Carin failed to return home from work. On September 22 of the following year in a damp and deeply wooded forest, mushroom pickers found her remains. She had been dead since the night of her disappearance. Today, her murder still remains unsolved.

Friends have asked how we got through that agonizing period of our life. Only by concocting theories that did our daughter no honor could we hold at bay the certainty of her death: Run off with a former boyfriend? Joined a cult in Eastern Oregon? Or the fantastic: Amnesia? Or the horrific: Kidnapped?

It was every parent's most dreaded nightmare. And though I've tried to write of her over these years, I've always found the narrative voice breaking into fragments, half-thoughts, faced with the impossibility of articulating the whole.

In large part we needed to make it through for the sake of our son, who was a junior in high school at the time. In Marc we found both a reason to keep ourselves from sinking into the morass and a source of comfort. He was elected student body president, was named "Best Male Student of the Year," had the lead in several plays, and was applying to colleges. And when he took the car out on a Saturday night, we tried not to say "Be careful" more than once. Not all children who drive off into the darkness fail to return home.

In a world that had grown suddenly sinister, we took comfort where we found it, and occasionally it found us. I recall how after I had come to teaching, I was blindsided by Anne Tyler's novel, *The Accidental Tourist*. I'd read several of her books and liked her way of taking our everyday foibles and pushing them to the edge of eccentricity (and sometimes beyond) in her characters. Because the book was well-reviewed, I've since wondered how I picked up this novel without knowing the story concerned the unresolved homicide of a twelve-year-old boy. After the initial shock, I remember thinking, "How does she know all that she knows?" marveling that empathy and imagination and intelligence could take Tyler so deeply into grief. I even wondered from what losses of her own she might have spun this story. How does she know, for example, that the tragic and the comic are so closely, so terribly, linked?

In the aftermath of his son's death, when his wife has left him, Macon Leary meticulously practices rituals for protection from a world of random violence, a world grown sinister, as ours had. Depressed, he notices he's losing weight and swings into a manic remedial program that still allows him to hibernate in his bedroom:

> Breakfast: Breakfast was your most important meal. He hooked up the percolator and the electric skillet to the clock radio on his bedroom windowsill. Of course he was asking for food poisoning, letting two raw eggs wait all night at room temperature, but once he'd changed menus there was no problem. You had to be flexible about these matters. He was awakened now by the smell of fresh coffee and hot buttered popcorn, and he could partake of both without getting out of bed. Oh, he was managing fine, just fine. All things considered. (14)

And so were we, all things considered. We exercised aerobically, took vitamins, tried not to smother our son with protectiveness, and cooked dinners we found hard to eat. We knew our health was at risk. We read that our marriage was at risk since many couples do not survive the death of a child. As a family we saw a therapist because, in the end, even the best of rituals offer only the illusion of protection and cannot take us the whole distance we need to go.

When Carin had been missing for about six weeks, I received a call from the chair of the English Department at my alma mater. One of the senior faculty had gone in for emergency surgery. Could I teach two courses in freshman composition?

I had six days to prepare for my first teaching assignment. As you might guess, I stayed one week ahead of the students for the entire semester. But during those unspeakable months of uncertainty when we all but knew our daughter was dead—despite the initial investigation of her disappearance as a "runaway"—the only relief from pain in my waking hours occurred during those fifty-minute classes because teaching was new, scary, and absorbing.

My students were about the same age as Carin. I ran the gamut from deeply needing to teach them to raging inwardly at their being alive when she was lost. And I felt guilty that I forged such connections between them and her when no connections really existed.

Six months before Carin herself was discovered, our car was found—the car that Carin had been driving the night she disappeared. It was a burned-out hulk. All that survived was the coffee mug she had bought for her boss as a Christmas gift, blackened but whole in the back seat. The Search and Rescue organization mounted a systematic search of the forested area near the small town of Shelton, Washington. My husband spent the day with them. He said they covered the area like insects: Nothing was left in their path that wasn't turned over. They brought back bottle caps, hair clips and other trinkets—detritus of the forest floor. But nothing of Carin's, whose body, we would learn eventually, lay a mile and a half outside the area being searched.

To my students that term, I masked my suffering; my evaluations were even quite good. Somehow I compartmentalized; I even taught with enthusiasm. Afternoons, during three-mile runs on the forested back trails of our local park, I railed at the sky. That park is no longer safe for women to run alone in—perhaps it wasn't then, but I didn't care. I only knew that somehow I *would* continue to function, that language offered surcease if not hope. The only way through tragedy is straight ahead. That's not, however, to imply the progression is steady. More like the proverbial ladder: up two rungs, down one, taking any handhold that presents itself for survival. My husband needed me, my son needed me, and I convinced myself those students needed me. And though the temptation occasionally arose, however irrational, to see breakdown as a testimony to my grief, I believed that in some odd way I was honoring my daughter by persevering.

So during those nine months of her disappearance, I returned to graduate school and finished my Master's Degree. In 1986 at the age of fifty, I received a full-time contract as an instructor at the University of Puget Sound. I never expected to be such an old rookie, but it's consistent, I suppose, with the late start. Somehow I think Carin would get a kick out of it all.

Those months of her disappearance also had their share of the bizarre: repeated telephone calls from a former boyfriend of Carin's who was a major suspect. A call from Bates Vocational College to tell us our daughter with the wanderlust had been accepted into their truckdriving school! A call (unrelated to Carin) from Search and Rescue, soliciting donations: (Perkily) "Hi! This is Search and Rescue calling. Don't worry—ha, ha—no one's missing!"

I believe the body may somatize emotional pain, and such was the case in our family. Tyler also suggests this phenomenon. Grieving for his son and deserted by his wife, Macon quite literally stumbles on a device to return himself to the family home of his siblings. He breaks his leg. "He almost wondered whether, by some devious, subconscious means, he had engineered this injury—every elaborate step leading up to it—just so he could settle down safe among the people he'd started out with" (62). Less dramatically, I developed fibroids. A way of replicating in utero what had been ripped from me? My husband, a long-distance runner, developed asthma and a sinus condition that required surgery. A way of weeping without tears? The pain of losing his daughter was no different for my husband than for me, though people tended to ask him, "How is *Bev* doing?" and to say, "This must be hard on Carin's *mom*." As if the father somehow felt less grief or was uniquely equipped as a male to handle bereavement. Though not unkindly meant, it was at one and the same time a discounting of my strength as well as of his suffering.

Life, however, also served up joy to us. Our son went on to win a Mellon Fellowship for graduate study. We gained a wonderful daughter-in-law whom we love dearly. And as I write, Marc has just received his Ph.D. in English Literature from Princeton University. He is living out my early dream. I understand the passion of the Little League father whose son has the potential to exceed him. Marc and I share a love of writing, of literature, and of teaching. Sometimes I marvel at the polarities of his achievement on the one hand and of our loss of future hope in Carin on the other. Sometimes I wonder whether he has tried to excel for two.

Because writing was my first love, I halfway wish I could say that I *wrote* my way through tragedy. It was, however, more the work of standing in front of students and of grading their writing that made the difference. I've sometimes wondered how I might have endured those nine months had I been unemployed, staying home in a house filled with memories of Carin. I remember sifting through her belongings in a room abruptly left in the middle of a messy, sometimes troubled, nineteen-year-old life. I read her short stories, her diary, searched her address book, looking for clues. I cleaned her room, laundered her clothes, keeping alive the illusion that she would come back to these labors of my love for her, knowing such thoughts were delusions as she went on to miss Christmas, then her birthday—a girl who had not yet brought herself even to leave home. But all of these chores were sandwiched in and amongst my teaching duties, which I knew even at the time to be my lifeline.

As I continue to teach adult children of other parents, children who come in waves at the age at which my daughter is forever frozen, I often give them the chance to cull the losses of their own childhoods through writing essays, short stories, and poems, to tell of hopes dashed through injury or accident, of actual deaths that have touched more young lives than I would have dreamed. Together we explore how even the opportunity of choice, no matter how positive, entails a loss of possibilities. Our culture is not especially open to grief in its various forms, grief which changes us for all time. I hope I'm a more understanding teacher for what I have suffered, an expertise I would, of course, gladly relinquish.

Perhaps any work would have had some benefit, but I believe that, in particular, teaching literature and writing helped me deal with events brutal beyond telling. Macon finds he doesn't even *have to speak* the words that his son is dead because friends and relatives fill the gaps for him with their own words of sympathy, their offerings of casseroles and cards. But he is not able to begin the process of his own recovery until he finally speaks these halting words to Miriam:

> "Last year," he said, "I lost . . . I experienced a . . . loss, yes, I lost my. . . . "
>
> She went on looking into his face.
>
> "I lost my son," Macon said. "He was just . . . he went to a hamburger joint and then . . . someone came, a holdup man, and shot him . . . Every day I tell myself it's time to be getting over this . . . I know that people expect it of me. They used to offer their sympathy but now they don't; they don't even mention his name. They think it's time my life moved on . . . This second year . . . I've stopped going to his door. I've sometimes let a whole day pass by without thinking about him. That absence is more terrible than the first, in a way." (189–190).

Macon learns, and we learn with him, that just to say the words can make a difference. Even when life is sliced apart by violence.

My own fiction—my attempts at speaking the words—explored *other* deaths around me: a neighbor's succumbing quickly to cancer, a child's choosing to believe his father dead rather than to face the pain of abandonment. I began writing a series of quirky New Age stories, a way to explore mystery without getting as deathly serious as I sometimes felt, a wry approach to metaphysics. As the artist-narrator in Margaret Atwood's *Cat's Eye* says, "This is the kind of thing we do, to assuage pain" (430).

The paradox, of course, and part of the point of this essay is that whereas my work was a salvation during tragedy, it has also long suffered from the moon's pull of love and family. It continues to do so even today. I imagine colleagues, particularly younger women with children, think my childless home the perfect retreat for the writer in me. But voices of children still haunt my writing hours, and the habits of being alert to the needs of others cause me to hold myself available even when no such needs now exist. Various "angels" hover over computer screens and land not on the heads of pins but on pens too heavily weighted to move across the page. Virginia Woolf and Tillie Olsen write movingly of these deep maternal channels we dig in our psyches and of our opposing need to bury ourselves in the work of writing. Even as I write these words, I'm grateful my husband is off hiking glacial trails in Montana. He supports my writing, encourages me at every turn, but I know this draft came more easily for my having been alone.

In some ways, I suppose I'm half afraid of my own powers of concentration. Writing requires that we leave the physical world around us, and I both love and fear that. Concentrating can be dangerous. For example, there was the bomb scare.

During my leave of absence from grad school, I worked on the ninth floor of the tallest building in Tacoma. I was the newly hired editor and was put behind a folding screen until remodeled office space was available for me. The work was financial material and difficult. I was totally absorbed and had worked half the morning. Eventually, *silence* penetrated my focus (as the silence of children will get a mother's attention). When I peered around my partition, the entire floor was deserted, the office machines stilled. I went icy and ran for the stairwell, thinking it must be a fire and knowing enough not to trust the elevators. As I flew those nine flights to the ground, I saw not one other soul.

It wasn't a fire but a bomb threat that had evacuated the building. The word had been passed quietly to allay panic, and no one had remembered the new hire behind the screen. If we can take ourselves so deeply into the world of the mind that a building can empty without our noticing, small wonder, then, that as women with children we learn to hold such powers of concentration at bay and later find it difficult to resurrect them. No wonder Tillie Olsen calls motherhood "the least understood, the most tormentingly complex experience to wrest the truth" (254). And in an interview, no wonder Anne Tyler speaks with a mother's experience of her own writerly procrastination: "I'd go into my study and think, I really need shoelaces. Then I'd get in my car and drive five miles to get those shoelaces." Of course. Shoelaces are safe; the imagination is dangerous.

During those childraising years, I sometimes "justified" my ambitions by telling myself that achieving my education was necessary because someday I would want to work to help finance the *children's* college educations. In other words, I circumscribed my private vision with a sense of service. This so-called "setting aside of self" has been reinforced in females. In my case, it also stemmed from the impact of some early religious experiences.

During that same thirteenth year that I began my battle toward college, I was also "saved." Actually, I was saved twice, the second time for good measure because one could never be too sure, I figured, about Eternity.

Adolescence is the perfect moment for the conversion experience because at few other times of our lives are we more convinced of our woeful inadequacies. Idealistic, we are also ripe to commit ourselves to *something*. I remember my father's being nonplused by my "testifying" to being saved by grace. "Saved from what?" he asked. "From sin," I intoned. "What sin?" he asked. "I was conceived in sin," I answered, and that seemed to take him aback—mostly, I realize now, from what he thought was my view of his complicity in my conception.

"I am sinful by virtue of my imperfect human nature," I said.

"Well, sure, imperfect—"

"And Christ died for my sins."

"Frankly," my father said at last, "I always figured Jesus could have done a lot more good by sticking around."

Youth for Christ. Christian Endeavor. Mid-week prayer meetings. Crusades in the Hollywood Bowl. I think it no accident that I was saved by a Heavenly Father during the same year that my parents divorced and my earthly father took himself off to an apartment. We began the biweekly visitations common to "broken homes," as they were then known.

As time passed, however, I came to agree more with my father's views than with Billy Graham's. Yet while I set aside my Calvinistic notion of sin and salvation, the allure of service lingered faintly, like leaves whispering after the storm. But sometimes life squares off on us even if we think we're playing by the rules. Anne Tyler knows this. As Joseph Voelker says in *Art and the Accidental in Anne Tyler*, ". . . Tyler has written about people who occupy an accidental world, in which the fault for life's cataclysmic events is finally *unascribable* (italics mine), and the duty of human beings is not to act but to endure, to define the degree of freedom possible within their confinement."

Similarly, like the impulse to be helpful, the hope of human continuance also keeps whispering. After Carin's death, I looked for signs from her, feeling only slightly foolish: in dreams, in eagle sightings, in owl feathers found in unlikely places, and even in rainbows. (How silly, I said to my husband, to think a rainbow is any big deal in a part of the country where it rains all the time. Ah, he said, the wonder is not in the rain but in the sun.) I still look for signs, have been known while walking on a deserted Puget Sound beach to ask her for one. But in the tougher reaches of my heart, I believe that "signs" say more about the seeker than the one who is sought.

Those endless nine months passed. One afternoon the detective assigned to Carin's case called on my husband at work. "The remains of a female have been found," he said. "Did your daughter have extensive dental work?"

"No," said my husband. "She had only one small filling."

Silence filled the air.

"I'm sorry," said the detective. "In that case, I believe we may have found your daughter's remains."

And as dental records shortly confirmed, they had.

Carin's skeleton had been scattered by small animals. We were told we were lucky that for identification purposes her intact skull had been discovered.

Women whose children are stillborn or who decide to give them up at birth for adoption often need to see or touch or even hold those children in order to begin the grieving process. I only knew that my daughter had walked out of our house in her Pizza Hut uniform and I had never seen her again. Unlike a pregnancy, our nine months of waiting had produced not life but bones. I felt impelled to touch her, to hold her, to be reunited with the physical other whom I had conceived and felt kick inside my own body those many years before. It is difficult to explain the intensity of that need for reunion. I wanted to say goodbye to her physicality, to all that remained. I told my husband. I'd never heard of anyone wanting to do such a thing, and I could appreciate how it might strike him as morbid. But he understood and wanted to take this step together. I called the funeral director. He was taken aback. He said he would like to reserve the right to make such a judgment for us. He never called again. We phoned the deputy sheriff who still had her remains in custody and told him what we wanted to do before Carin was released for burial. He said he would arrange it with a different funeral home.

I had one other reason for wanting this reunion. I was absolutely convinced that I would recognize Carin's teeth. All those years of taking her to the dentist. She had fretted over her otherwise perfect front teeth and wanted to have them bonded because of two tiny brown stains some high fever had caused when they were still deep within her baby gums. She and her brother had inherited an enzyme from their father which kept their teeth nearly cavity-free, and I knew where her one filling lay. I knew the shape, the size, the angle of those lovely teeth, and I knew I could forever eliminate that irrational speck of doubt that still brushed me in the night.

Three days later on a brilliant August morning, we were ushered into a small, cool room. In the center was a white cloth-covered table with two chairs drawn up beside it. On the table was an object draped in white linen. The detective and the funeral home employee withdrew, and we uncovered Carin's small, beige skull. There were her perfect little teeth, shockingly large without the soft frame of her flesh.

Time dissolved in those few intimate moments, and we had our reunion with Carin. At the end, I bent and kissed the center of her head. For parents who dealt with blood and snot and diapers, her bones held only tenderness in their surprising smoothness. And in the sense that it was all we had left in the physical realm to say goodbye to, it *was* a healing moment.

At the conclusion of *The Accidental Tourist*, Macon rides off in a taxi, wondering,

> And if dead people aged, wouldn't it be a comfort? To think of Ethan growing up in heaven—fourteen years old now instead of twelve—eased the grief a little . . . The real adventure, he thought, is the flow of time; it's as much adventure as anyone could wish. And if he pictured Ethan still part of that flow—in some other place, however unreachable—he believed he might be able to bear it after all. (342)

Macon's desire for continuance is not far removed from my owl feathers and rainbows—that visceral wish that we and our lost children might go on, somehow together.

Loss and change are inextricably linked. My work has suffered and my work has sustained me. It's a paradox with which I will live, sometimes even joyfully. In this last scene, Macon's search for love and connection ends as his taxi lurches to a stop for Miriam. Tyler's final image is transcendent: the "splash" of sunlight on auto glass, sunlight bright as "spangles," festive as "confetti" (342). In a similar connection, I imagine my daughter cheering the life I continue to live more than a decade past her own. I can hear Carin now: "Way to go, Mother."

WORKS CITED

Atwood, Margaret. *Cat's Eye*. New York: Bantam Books, 1989.
Lamb, Wendy. "An Interview with Anne Tyler." *Iowa Journal of Literary Studies*. U of Iowa, 1981.
Olsen, Tillie. *Silences*. New York: Dell Publishing, 1978.
Tyler, Anne. *The Accidental Tourist*. New York: Berkley Books, 1986.
Voelker, Joseph C. *Art and the Accidental in Anne Tyler*. Columbia: U of Missouri P, 1989.
Woolf, Virginia. *A Room of One's Own*. New York: Harcourt, Brace, Jovanovich, 1929.

DIVERSITY AND THE AMERICAN DREAM

GRACE STEWART

W hen I was about nine, I casually mentioned to my mother while we were doing dishes together that I would like to marry a Chinese man. The color and texture of Chinese people's skin fascinated me. My mother replied, "Then don't expect me to love any child *you* have as much as I would love any child your brother has." The response taught me more about the way bigotry and prejudice is perpetuated and about the way culture is inculcated, than it did about assessing marriageable men. Nevertheless, the admonishment cut deeply enough so that when my son announced he was engaged to a Eurasian woman, I wrestled once again with prejudice. How does one rear a child to be successful in pursuit of the American dream without succumbing to the short-sightedness and weaknesses of that same culture, where relationships as well as race, class, gender, ethnicity, age, and class matter?

Visions of my childhood flooded back to me. I remember riding on a bus to see a Shirley Temple movie, being vocal about my excitement, turning to see a man with a dark face, and asking my mother in a loud voice why his face was such a color. I must have been about three years old. Instead of explaining the delights of diversity in a world where some trees have green leaves, some reddish brown, some purple, and where human beings also come in various shades, my mother shushed me and told me to turn around and sit still.

When I went to grade school and became acquainted with the only black girl there, I was lectured about choosing carefully the friends I kept. Such warnings were not restricted to my friendships with children of color, however. I distinctly remember at a later time bringing home Marian, a Caucasian twelve-year old who was quite heavy. I'm not sure whether her size weighed in the equation of unsuitability, but she committed the crime of crossing her skirted legs with one ankle on her knee. After she left, a discussion ensued about what was and was not ladylike behavior. Marian was not invited back. To this day, I still bristle when I hear or see the word "ladies"—especially if it's on a door to a restroom with a counterpart labeled "Men."

If this all sounds like middle-class absurdity, it may be, but it is also about perpetuating culture. My parents were working class, and their concept of the American dream involved working hard to become middle class, having money, traveling, and having a daughter and a son who were well-bred. We lived with neighbors having similar dreams—two Italian families with daughters who would bedevil me occasionally by speaking pseudo-Italian to exclude me, several WASP neighbors who reported when any of us strayed off set boundaries, and a black family without children, the Rossis.

Mr. Rossi worked on Wall Street (I never knew what he did), but he, too, was pursuing a dream. Although his wife was African-American, Mr. Rossi made it clear that he was from the West Indies and that he wished to be addressed with respect. We were taught to say, "Good evening," or "Good morning, Mr. Rossi," whenever he passed by. "Hi!" simply would not do. My mother was charming and courteous to everyone, but the Rossis were not invited to tea, which took place almost every afternoon as various neighbors and friends dropped by.

My enculturation was complicated by a father who criticized everyone with equal aplomb. The rich were corrupt, the poor were lazy, the Catholics were superstitious, and the Protestants wanted money more than conversions. By the time I was four I recognized the injustice of his accusations. His generalizations were never supported.

Recently I was reminded about the tightropes stretched between the individual and the culture, between generalizations and stereotypes, between teaching and learning, between having values and being valued in a society, between diverse Americans and the American Dream. The impact of race, class, and gender on that dream seemed evident to me in 1993 when I taught composition of the research paper to first-year college students. I had decided to use Lorraine Hansberry's *A Raisin in the Sun* as an example of dramatic structure and to use two video clips of the African dance scene as an example of different dramatic styles of acting and directing. Little did I realize how pertinent would be the issues of documentation and of personal response, especially my own, with a class of predominantly middle-class white students.

Early in the examination of the play, students commented about the poverty of the characters. When asked to support the term "poverty," the students pointed to the fact that Travis, the young son, had to sleep in the living room. Politely querying the class to determine how many slept in separate bedrooms, I recalled that in my family, where relatives—between jobs or just out of the military or newly separated, widowed, or divorced—were always "visiting" for a few months, I slept in the living room, or in the dining room behind a door, or in a not-so-large bedroom with three small beds for my grandmother, my brother, and me. I was not living in poverty—just not in privacy.

When asked for further proof of poverty documented from the text, students pointed to the playwright's description of the set. Hansberry wanted the audience immediately to see the financial struggle of the family and the importance of Walter's handling of money—that he wanted his son Travis to benefit from his "largess," making Walter a "big man" and giving Travis the freedom of an extra fifty cents to flourish. This gesture contrasts sharply with the worn carpet, the cramped quarters, the bathroom shared by other families, and the dim light from one viewless window. Walter was reacting to these conditions in a capitalistic society that determines one's manhood by the amount of ready cash, credit, or capital one has. The students referred to all the clues of financial struggle in order to support their use of the term "poverty."

When we talked about the character of Walter, the students were almost unanimous in believing that Walter was a dreamer, an unrealistic person who wasn't prepared to work hard or persistently to educate himself for better living conditions. I was concerned by this general response. I asked if they understood the conditions in 1959 for a black male, if they knew the background of the decree of Brown vs. the Board of Education, if they understood the difficulty of a black man's attempt to gain employment at that time, let alone employment that led to advancement in status or salary.

These comments prompted several students to research the contrast in the employment and income levels of African-Americans today compared to the fifties. Those who did so quickly categorized African-Americans as poverty-stricken in the fifties and generally better off in the nineties. I feared that my comments had created in their minds another stereotype, and its spectre was once again hovering in class. "What about the Murchisons," I asked? "Let's go to the text. What about Charlie Atkins, who was grossing $100,000 a year?"

Having just read a review of *The Rage of a Privileged Class*, I reminded them that there was more than one socio-economic level suggested in the play and that gender, race, ethnicity, and class could not be separated from the individual and his or her pursuit of the American Dream. One of my students suggested that age could also not be separated because generational differences were another source of conflict. Most of the students did not understand that there have been middle-class black families for decades if not centuries, that this family should not be taken for black families everywhere, and that the drama of this play involved more than just the stereotype of poor blacks in a white world.

This reaction counterpointed another response frequently made to the drama, that the play was about *people*, not about "Negroes." As Ossie Davis commented about a false public reaction, "[The play] was, rather, a walking, talking, living demonstration of our mythic conviction that, underneath, all of us Americans, *color-ain't-got-nothing-to-do-with-it*, are pretty much alike. People are just people, whoever they are; all they want is a chance to be like other people" (Hansberry xiii) and a chance to pursue the American dream. Such a reaction discounts the particular and painful development of blacks living in a ghetto in Southside Chicago in the late fifties, or the development of African-American culture in a patriarchal white power-structure.

The interplay between black heritage and inclusion in the power structure is evident in Beneatha's struggle toward identity and her choice of men if not of mates. Asagai awakens pride in her African heritage. She wears African dress, changes her hair to a natural, and chants and dances to African music. She claims to be fed up with "assimilation," yet she changes her clothing for a date when George Murchison asks her. Although the subjection of women to the whims of fashion and beauty is a general issue (Kilbourne 348–51), when women of color transform their looks to more closely resemble the predominantly white "norm," the conflict is one of heritage versus assimilation.

An incident in class underscored that conflict. A student of color described one of her friends as having "good" hair. Harkening to the research at the basis of Brown vs. the Board of Education (and the issue of black children perceiving "white" to be superior), I quickly responded that we all had "good" hair, regardless of processing or style. Although the student gave me a strange look, the comment slipped by without discussion.

But I was able to focus on the fine line between following current style and becoming submerged "in the dominant, and in this case *oppressive* culture" (Hansberry 81)—a questionable pursuit in a society that measures acceptance by the color of skin—by pointing to Walter's comments about Murchison's "faggoty-looking white shoes" (83) and Beneatha's black stockings, which he claims makes her look "like she got burnt legs or something!" (83). Whereas Ruth can explain the garments as being "the college *style*" (83), Walter is affronted, seeing them as assimilation, as a shameful submission to an oppressive norm.

His perspective is also tinged with a lack of respect for education as a way out of the ghetto. With overtones of Booker T. Washington, Walter claims that college boys are having their heads filled with "culture" but not being taught practical knowledge or how to run the country (85). The issue of education, of language, of culture, and of assimilation was heightened by the class's viewing the two tapes of Walter's transformation to an African chief and his subsequent interaction with the college student, George Murchison. I wanted the students to get a sense of theater, of acting, of direction, and of difference in styles. After viewing the two tapes, each student chose the performance he or she preferred and stated why. The division was clear. Those who chose Danny Glover's performance spoke of the dynamics and the immediacy of his style; those who chose Poitier's performance spoke of the clarity of his presentation, his articulation, and his polish. I admitted I liked Poitier's performance. One or two of the African-American students hesitated and stumbled in their reasons for choosing Danny Glover but eventually proclaimed that Poitier was speaking "white" or standard English, whereas Glover used more of an African-American dialect. The correlation of education (using standard English) and assimilation (thinking and speaking "white") loomed still as an issue of diversity in the classroom as well as in Walter's disdain for George Murchison's education.

Despite Walter's denigration of education, the students saw it as raising possibilities for Beneatha and perceived her as favored. Her mother plans to send her, not Walter, to college. The past welled up within me, and I told the students about my exchange of confidences with a black colleague. I had shared with him the anguish I had harbored for years because my brother had been sent to a university, whereas I was sent to a business school for one year. My parents thought that although I was probably going to get married, I needed a skill I could fall back on in rough times. But I was the honor student, not my brother, who was just an average student.

My colleague shared his resentment that, in his family, the girls were sent to college, not the boys. He explained that the education of black females has been an on-going concern in African-American families, fostered by the need in early days to keep the young women off the streets or out of the domestic scene and thereby to protect them from assault, and fostered by the fact that a black female was not so threatening to white employers as a black male and was therefore much more likely to get employment which warranted the expense of an education. I couldn't help noting for the students' benefit that, generally speaking, women with a college degree earn approximately what men with a high school diploma earn. Despite the fact that, statistically, black women are still below their male counterparts on the employment rung in terms of wages (National Committee on Pay Equity 132), more recent emphasis has been placed on educating the black male to help stabilize his future. As late as 1992 in Detroit, we wrestled with the issue of an academy for African-American males only.

In the play, Hansberry's dialogue highlights the tension surrounding the issue of education and advancement for women and for men. Walter thinks Beneatha ought to be satisfied with being a nurse rather than a doctor. Not only does he denigrate her ambitions and suggest she should instead get married, but he actually admonishes his wife earlier, saying, "That is just what is wrong with the colored woman in this world . . . Don't understand about building their men up and making 'em feel like they somebody" (34). Walter's charge that the black woman is the reason black men do not advance may well raise the hackles on women who fought in the civil rights movement only to be relegated to the kitchen and asked to stand behind their men. As a white feminist, I am extremely sensitive to the claims that feminism is a form of racism. But black feminists have learned they cannot divide themselves in their fight against racism and sexism (Lourde 405). As bell hooks explains, "Feminist thinkers . . . must continually emphasize the importance of sex, race and class as factors which *together* determine the social construction of femaleness (hooks 444). I would add that such social construction is important in their examination of the American Dream as well. In my two-year search for a dissertation advisor in the seventies who would allow me to write on Women and the American Dream, one professor dismissed the topic, saying, "That's rather peripheral, isn't it?" Thirty years later, teaching this play, I found my self proclaiming again that one must take into account the categories of race, class, and ethnicity, as well as gender, when speaking of the American Dream.

But it was the students who reminded me to include generational differences, which they saw in the interaction between Mama and her children. Beneatha's humanist position shocks Mama, causes her to strike her daughter, and dictate the family position, "In my mother's house there is still God" (51). For those who believe in a supreme being, Mama's position is defensible and Beneatha's actions are nothing more than ignorant, childish, and rebellious. To the humanist, Bennie's statement is a challenge to the generations of African-Americans who turned the other cheek and waited for their heavenly reward.

Despite the fact that people are still fighting over the concept of religious freedom, the scene led some students to believe that some of the religious as well as philosophical differences were actually generational differences. That perspective is more evident in the interaction between Lena and her son Walter. While he speaks of risky investment and wanting more than a job chauffeuring a white man, Mama speaks as a survivor of the depression, as a mother who has held her family together, and as a woman who favors small steps toward a solid future rather than large leaps to wealth or ruin.

Although I agreed that generational differences might very well account for some differences, I wasn't so sure the generalization worked here. Those of us who have been reared by folks who lived through the depression know very well its effect on dreams and on the different way family members reacted to it. I can recall my own mother's budgeting Dad's take-home pay and including the notation "$.03 for stamp" because she wanted to write to her mother. Seeing that and knowing that she also put money away for the future, I vowed never to set a budget for myself. I reacted quite differently.

I also recall the properties we drove by, and Dad's pointing out the ones that he had wanted to buy, and what they would be worth today if Mother had gone along with his purchasing them. Security reached in small steps became the primary focus for my mother, while my father wanted to make a killing so that money would not be a problem in the future. Yet when I indicated that I would purchase a Mercedes sports convertible if I had the funds, my dad proclaimed that he would get up out of his grave to spend his last dime if he thought I'd spend my inheritance that way. Something solid, like land, is more secure than a depreciating toy.

Lena Younger, in *A Raisin in the Sun*, also desires a more secure way to spend her husband's hard-earned insurance money. The position she takes highlights both a generational and a gender difference. Mama holds the purse—the $10,000—and realizes she has been holding the power and dominating her son. As bell hooks writes,

> It is necessary for us to remember . . . that we all have the capacity to act in ways that oppress, dominate, wound (whether or not that power is institutionalized). . . . Usually, it is within the family that we witness coercive domination and learn to accept it, whether it be domination of parent over child, or male over female. (hooks 442–43)

But Mama's stance also reflects theories of Carol Gilligan. Mama focuses on love, on the harmony of the household, while Walter strives to build capital, to climb the ladder of material success, and to gain some of that white, patriarchal power. Gilligan generalizes that cognitive development often follows two paths—one pattern experienced primarily by women (where caring and concern are the main focus) and the other by men (where justice and "rights" are primary).

Lena Younger recognizes the power she holds over her son and that she has been the dominant one. She says, "I been doing to you what the rest of the world been doing to you" (106). The difference is that her care and concern are primary. She pleads for her son's understanding, saying, "There ain't nothing worth holding on to, money, dreams, nothing else . . . if it means it's going to destroy my boy" (106). As though bell hooks were writing about this play rather than issues of diversity, she claims (what women are generally taught), "Even though family relations may be, and most often are, informed by acceptance of a politic of domination, they are simultaneously relations of care and connections" (hooks 443). She also preaches, "Love can be and is an important source of empowerment when we struggle to confront issues of sex, race, and class" (hooks 447).

The interaction reminded me of the many ways that care, connection, and love have overcome some of the struggles within my own family. For instance, my husband and I used to pal around with Vic, a black stable-owner. At the time, unbenownst to us, we had purchased a house in a community which secretly excluded blacks, Jews, and Italians. I've always marveled that at the signing of the deed, our white-skinned privilege masked to us the reality of this injunction. We were aware, however, that our friendship with Vic was breaking some of our society's rules. Once when we were at dinner, I walked to the restroom and a man said to me in passing, "Some people don't care who they're with!" I smiled to myself, thinking, "True, that woman with you, for instance!"

My husband and I used to laugh about the neighbors' probable reaction when Vic stopped by to visit us in his truck, full of the manure he was hauling to the city. We didn't laugh, however, the first time a visit from my parents coincided with a visit from Vic. But my parents were complex human beings, and they accepted Vic as our friend, greeting him graciously then and ever after, possibly caring enough about us to overcome their own segregationist philosophy.

Another case of care overcoming conflict stemmed from my reaction when my son announced his engagement to my daughter-in-law. After telling me, he thrust a picture of a very tanned young woman at me (while I was driving the car) and said, "This is Marie." Peering at her, I said, "She looks . . . Phillipine," but I was thinking that, though stunning, she looked like a mixture of African-American and Asian. "She's Korean," he said. Knowing that the Koreans are denigrated by some other Asian groups, I worried over several of the experiences I've had connected with racism and wondered if any children they had would experience the negativism I'd seen. I told my attractive, red-headed son about my mother's reaction to my comment when I was nine, and he replied, "Well, here's your Asian influence."

I cannot explain my subsequent feelings. Worry over the acceptance of any children they might have, worry over what they might look like, and—most supreme—worry over my own reaction became paramount for days. Was I a racist? Had my parents and community won after all? My son had always hated his red hair, which is wavy but not the dry-fly away krinkled type of some red hair. I worried about his having a kinky-haired, reddish-blond African-American baby and hating his own child. I became almost irrational.

I talked with my African-American friends about their reactions: One woman claimed that the African-American community was much more accepting about inter-racial marriage than were whites; another woman said she would be disturbed if her son married a Caucasian; and a wonderful, intelligent, witty professor said, "Honey, as long as their children aren't striped, they'll be okay." Eventually, I realized that what disturbed me most was my own reaction and that what I wanted to feel was joy. Finally, joy came with the love I felt once I met Marie.

As a final example of love conquering conflict I remembered my father, when ill, signing a power-of-attorney that allowed me full control of his worldly goods, knowing that I would place his care as my primary concern, and not being worried about my first buying a Mercedes.

Coming from a different generational and gender perspective from her children and grandchildren, but sharing their dream for a better future, Lena Younger also turns the money over to her son. But these generational and gender differences in the Younger family are minimized by the assault they face from Lindner and the Clybourne Park New Neighbors Orientation Committee, an assault so obvious that I found it difficult to remind the class to consider race, class, gender, and even age and religion as inseparable and as factors that qualify generalizations. The discrimination by Clybourne Park is patently racial.

Despite affirmative action laws and laws against redlining in real estate, the students of the nineties do not find Lindner to be an unrealistic character, although he obviously symbolizes prejudice and bigotry on a larger scale. His actions may be more blatant and crude than the subtle forms of racism today, but he remains a credible character. The fear and subsequent flight of white families from Detroit is an historical fact to our students. The influx of African-Americans to a neighborhood is sometimes still equated with its deterioration, both by blacks and whites.

I was shocked a few months back when my life partner suggested that we should move, should buy a house in a neighborhood that was not "deteriorating." Since my roomy suburban home is fairly new, the landscaping of the neighborhood is without exception immaculate and often elaborate, and a beautiful quarter-million dollar Tudor house had just been added to our subdivision, I was surprised by the suggestion. Surprise turned to dismay when I realized that my Caucasian partner, having lived through the white flight from Detroit, was concerned about the large percentage of African-American neighbors we had acquired. As long as there were only a few people of color among a majority of whites, the neighborhood was upscale; if the percentage shifted, it was deteriorating! I later learned that some white families, a bi-racial family, and a black family had moved with the same reasoning, based on a perception that the resale value of the houses would diminish. Obviously their pursuit of the American dream was a monetary one, not one based on an elimination of oppression or of harmony in a neighborhood. To me and to the students, the character of Lindner remains believable, even realistic, though laws have changed.

Months after using *A Raisin in the Sun* with that class of first-year students and preparing this article, I realize once again that my life has been devoted to blasting stereotypes, educating the prejudiced, and enlightening myself and others to the subtleties of discrimination. I also realize how much I agree with Robert Nemiroff that this play continues its attraction. His introduction to the play ends,

> For at the deepest level it is not a specific situation but the human condition, human aspiration and human relationships—the persistence of dreams, of the bonds and conflicts between men and women, parents and children, old ways and new, and the endless struggle against human oppression, whatever the forms it may take, and for individual fulfillment, recognition, and liberation—that are at the heart of such plays. (Hansberry, xvii-xviii)

In teaching this play, I was taught once again about the way in which one rears children with values that may sometimes conflict with the general or individual pursuit of the American Dream or with one's own upbringing: one rears children with love and by example, and allows them to fly toward their dream in their own way, loving them especially when they falter and loving them more when they develop wings of their own values in a culture that values the eagle rather than the dove.

Works Cited

Cose, Ellis. *The Rage of a Privileged Class*. New York: Harper Collins, 1993.

Gilligan, Carol. *In a Different Voice: Psychological Theory and Women's Development*. Cambridge, Mass.: Harvard UP, 1982.

Hansberry, Lorraine. *A Raisin in the Sun*. New York: Signet, 1988.

hooks, bell. "Feminism: A Transformational Politic." *Race, Class and Gender: An Integrated Study*. 2nd ed. ed. Paula Rothenberg. New York: St. Martin's, 1992.

Kilbourne, Jean. "Beauty and the Beast of Advertising." *Race, Class and Gender: An Integrated Study*. Ed. Paula Rothenberg. 2d ed. New York: St. Martin's, 1992.

Lourde, Audre. "Age, Race, Class, and Sex: Women Redefining Difference." *Race, Class and Gender: An Integrated Study*. 2nd ed. ed. Paula Rothenberg. New York: St. Martin's, 1992.

National Committee on Pay Equity. "The Wage Gap: Myths & Facts." *Race, Class and Gender: An Integrated Study*. 2nd ed. ed. Paula Rothenberg. New York: St. Martin's, 1992.

GRACE STEWART

Women's Literature as Individuation for College Students

Julie Houston

To write is to create the self. To write is to find that I am different from all others, and that I *am* all others. Writing is for me The Journey, The Way, the intake, inspiration of breath/life, being now. It is a walking meditation of my cells, my pen, my breath. And the finished writing is the mirror which I am; what I think, feel, experience, the essence I am. It is an "I" including all time, potentially accessible to all. I am glass shone through by the words of writers who came before. And I, in turn, hold up a true mirror to younger writers so that what they find as life and inspiration in me, they will come to see is the essence of themselves.

To write is to be what one woman wrote of her roshi, her Zen master:

> It is not the extraordinariness of the teacher which perplexes, intrigues, and deepens the student, it is the teacher's utter ordinariness. Because he is just himself he is a mirror for his students. When we are with him we feel our own strengths and shortcomings without any sense of praise or criticism from him. In his presence we see our original face, and the extraordinariness we see is only our own true nature. (Baker 18)

This image of mirrors reflects through the culture of women writers. We use them for the of myriad of reasons anyone weaves imagery. But always a mirror implies a self, someone looking into it to learn who she is, deny who she is, stretch, contract the limitations of identity, answer the essential question of our species: who am I? And it implies another double: looking out of oneself, depending on something else in order to establish a true self image; and yet simultaneously not looking into some *other*, exterior model to see the truth.

Women's literature is a means of self awareness and self expression for both women and men. Women writers of the past sing us half the voice of our human identity; they are our word-mothers. They hold up that rare and brilliant mirror which only art provides because it fingers the strings not only of our intellect, but of our unconscious, our archetypes. Fiction and poetry are the direct transmission of essence, of information, never through a glass darkly, but in sheer glare, truth, actuality.

For women students, reading literature by women creates meaning for their own lives. It announces the integrity of the writer, her own individualization, accomplished and accomplishing itself before us on a page. It lives the process of individualization with us, shows us the way social individuals become different from one another, without excluding commonality. It sweeps us into creating our own answers: of what am I capable? What do I want? What do I experience? Art lays out before us like clouds in sunrise the life-long process: who am I?

Women in our culture have often been taught to deny the answers we find for these questions. And this is particularly so for many of our women students who have been hustled and snake-oiled to deny the validity of their intellects. Reading the writing of women reminds them that they cannot continue to deny their minds without paying an exceptional death tax. The vision of themselves in art gives them power. No wonder some segments of society want to deny women the right to see who they really are. To value yourself is ultimate power.

Each of us has been dreamt by our matriarchs and our word-mothers. Each of us who has mothers, grandmothers, carries a family mythology of words as relentless as DNA, a litany, a recitation, a reason to exist in words. Women are the carriers of history; we name the story of who we were, sing our oral histories with the desperation and savagery of life. Again and again I hear from both women and men that their grandmothers, great-grandmothers and aunts—rarely the men in their heritage—were the singers of this eternal song: repeated phrases inherent to oral legacy, sacred, corrupt words from forgotten ancestral tongues: time capsules which prove lands of origin, ancient accents, moments of long-ago migration.

In my family one repeated phrase was that the family came "at the very end of the sailing ship era." I heard this for years over hot sandwiches and cold salads—enthralled, disdainful and bored as any child. And when all the old matriarchs were dead, and I wrote archives for ship records, there was the exact match of dates for those ancestors: they had sailed from France on a sailing ship when steam already existed.

Think of Alex Haley's fondly repeated anecdotes of hearing his elderly women relatives rock on the porch in Henning, Tennessee, singing the song that defied slavery and dehumanization, and gave him the stories by which to trace from which part of Africa his family had come. These stories promised, "We are, you are"; these stories that give all of us our identity, told in the mythical darkness and heat of sultry summer nights. These are the stories of humanity which defy, dismiss, honor, sanctify, redeem the unutterable. They stand against the worst possible dehumanization; say "We give a gift greater than life: know who you are."

The gift of our matriarchs is who we were, who we came from. It defines a swath of our existence. It is not past; it is the place from which we begin. And the loss evident in those who do not have these stories is obvious: they miss a whole powerful arm of their identity. There is a magic, the understanding of a whole life, a redemption even in cradling only the name of an ancestor. One student told me of an ancestor who was nicknamed "Gaggy" because she was the "bed-wench" of her master, and was gagged to silence her while he raped her (Kemp).

My maternal grandmother gave me more than the past of my identity, the narrative of our communal life. She told me the stories of the *women* who made my blood, gave me the gold flecks in my eyes, bred stubborn fortitude in the walls of my cells. Over those lunches and through those stories she taught me how these women took over their husbands' companies when the men died, how they insisted on education for their children, how they succeeded in a new land, in a new language, in a new social order. She taught me by example: so could I.

I write because of who I am. But I also write because of my grandmother and my mother. My grandmother is my role model; I am her namesake. Emilie Julie Durschang: Professor of Psychology at Fordham, Columbia and Rutgers Universities, proud single mother, proud grandmother. She was proof across the breakfast table that it was possible for a gifted, beautiful, elegant lady to relish a full intellectual life, to demand the world respect her for the life of her mind. I grew up watching her admired and sought out by equals—men as much as women. She presented herself to the world with the tacit statement "Respect me," and I saw that the world did.

From my mother, Belle Louise Schloemer, as well as my grandmother, I heard the narrative in my blood. My mother did not tell me ancestral personal history; she opened for me an eternal history of all species—a history in my mind as wide and timeless as a string of our ancestors two million years ago hunting across the Serengeti Plain, fearing lions. From her I glimpsed a writer's secret: history was not dates but narrative. Out of this my imagination today creates fiction of how the past lives in us all: narrative structures which trace migrations of identities across cultures and centuries. And as a child I also saw through her and other women the life-long anguish they inhabited for not following their careers in the arts. And my mother read to me. And far more importantly, she let me know that the childhood stories I told her must be of value: before I could form letters she wrote down my dictated stories. So that the first time I saw myself in the mirror of the world it was in words, in one woman's personal and eternal narrative, and in the respect of another woman who expected honor for her mind.

For women students, reading women's literature provides further models, provides "I can," provides permission to write. Reading precedes writing; vision precedes doing. It gives students characters who are images of their lives, real women from a female perspective—not women seen only through male eyes.

Reading women's literature gives these students the chance to say "We exist. We have a history (albeit largely written by men), we have a culture, we are different. We have a different experience of life. We think different things are important than have been given us by patriarchal hierarchy. We are unique."

Just as I would not deny the world the male and female characters created by Hemingway and Huxley and Shakespeare, so I would not deny the world the male and female characters created by Morrison and Gordimer and Woolf. Women writing women unveil truths men cannot know about our lives. It is comparable to Toni Morrison's statement that after she had published *The Bluest Eye*, African-Americans came to her and said of white people, "You let them know. . . This was our information" ("Toni Morrison: Writers Talk").

A course I created and taught in 1993 was designed to celebrate the diversity of twentieth-century literature by women. We heard voices across time, cultures, race, age, sexual orientation. Morrison, Woolf, H.D., Sylvia Plath, Maxine Hong Kingston, Isabelle Allende, Adrienne Rich, Nadine Gordimer, and extraordinary nonfiction articles. I agonizingly left out as many exultant songs as I invited in. And even though it was twentieth-century literature, I started the course with the 2,600-year-old words of Sappho, "I say someone in another time will remember us" (*Sappho's Lyre* 81).

And I adopted the belief of the ancient Egyptians, that to say someone's name brought her or him glory in the next life: I listed on the board the names, titles, and dates of European women, abbesses often, who wrote in the Middle Ages; Renaissance aristocrats who wrote; poems and songs from ancient Greece, Egypt, Rome attributed to women, showing women's sensibilities, but now authorless. We celebrated the agony of those women who, born to the wrong culture and the wrong time, were left wordless to the world. We celebrated the extraordinary poetic fragments of Sappho, who in her life published nine volumes of work, considered one of the glories of Greece. And whose power and gift were considered such a threat to patriarchy that apparently Pope Gregory VII held a burning of her books. We celebrated Hypatia, author, mathematician, astronomer, philosopher of Alexandria, who so terrified the church by her brilliance that the patriarchs of Alexandria incited a mob of Christians to pull her from her sedan chair, flay her alive with oyster shells, and burn her body and her books.

There are many results of these courses for our women students: obvious, fear-shattering, life-giving. Reading women writers validates their intellectual and creative selves: offers unachievers a purpose. They glimpse commonality with women they thought once separated from them by puzzling differences. They may get a sense of individual pride. And these authors give reality to students' historic and cultural knowledge. For us, in Bethlehem, Pennsylvania, H.D. is a local poet, increasingly recognized as one of the major poets of the American twentieth century. Possibility itself opens for students to go to the home or burial place of such a writer whose words live for them. As women we are often unaware of our own history to the point of denying our own history. But anyone reading, for example, Morrison's *Beloved,* feels in the cells greater reality of history and slavery than any hundred textbooks.

And touching art opens for these students for the first time—"Is this possible for me?" I lurked through many shelves and the BBC to obtain videotapes of Morrison, Kingston, Plath, and audiotapes of H.D., Vita Sackville-West, Virginia Woolf. I drove several students to Princeton to see Joyce Carol Oates and Morrison. And I saw women students continually stunned by the possibility of what they might do. They were taught every day by a woman writer; could they write too? Could they also read original manuscripts, letters in major libraries—as I did, busing to the Berg Collection every Saturday? They had never considered the sheer possibility of this. It was no longer something done by those far away. I facilitated the entry into a private collection for one of them. And meeting writers and other artists, they listened to conversations, suddenly freed: "Is it possible to think these ideas, say them, say them in public and not be ridiculed?"

This defining of the self included the men in the class, though differently. Many possibilities I've mentioned could awaken any student: possibility does not discriminate. But the men spoke of specific gains: new pride in the work of their female ancestors and the women in their lives, delight and wonder at gaining a kind of secret access into a way of perceiving they had not glimpsed. Through the concrete images of fiction they felt they understood women's communication and experience less abstractly. It encouraged them to see often the commonality of human experience where they thought they were separated by gender. And they batted over many nets the shuttlecock of androgyny and androgynous authorship. What, they debated, in writing and human experience transcends ego and gender-based experience?

The course validated several of the men who had gone into professions formerly held by women. One student, who was a day care teacher, said he began to understand women's anger at being ignored in business settings when he found himself the only male at a day care conference. He regaled the class with anecdotes of speakers whose eyes swept the conference room with a glance, ignoring his bearded, brawny, handsome physique, and announced, "Now ladies . . ." (Lacey).

Women's literature also validates facets of male personality which often have been rejected by patriarchal systems: compassion, sympathy, non-competitiveness—satisfaction in masculine identity—not needing to continually prove masculinity, attention to the importance of individual lives. And this was an unexpected turn-around: the women of the class gaining insight into the men's reactions.

But the essence of women's literature is the mirror. And all that I have said before is the frame, a preliminary, not the image to which we lift our eyes: disturbed, intrigued. For the sight reflected may be reality or illusion—both individual and global.

Let us dismiss the false self-image quickly: the harrowing, narrowing lie which binds feet, cripples minds, blinds wisdom. It is the Barbie Doll image: devaluing women, insulting women, removing all possibility. My students spoke eloquently, anguished, of the fact that in our society most women spend years simply rooting about, trying to find out who we are, believing ourselves to be inadequate because we are so much greater, all-encompassing than the tiny, warped picture held up for us to believe. Society provides men with ready-made, power identities. And then many men must in turn struggle to realize that those wash-and-wear images are for them utterly ill-fitting. So at its best, women's literature questions value systems which denigrate *all* humanity.

Many students are stunned by the validation they receive from fiction just in its image of family. They read, and so they sigh with relief that they are not abhorrent because they did not come from some black-and-white "Leave It To Beaver" rerun family, and neither did anyone else. They see in fact it had been a group delusion. And for another readjustment to correct vision, I asked students to research female ancestors—first in this country, first to vote. Students were stunned—their grandmothers and great grandmothers had not been decorative: they were farmers, land owners, shop keepers, factory workers, some college educated, carriers of their families. They were power.

When I write, I am also a mirror. On September 23, 1925, Virginia Woolf wrote to Vita Sackville-West, "I assure you, if you'll make me up, I'll make you" (Nicolson and Trautmann 219). That was two years before she wove Sackville-West into *Orlando*, a muse-driven book, a personal mirror made art. Women provide for each other this mirror which no one else can—in which we can truly see our essence.

A former student of mine, a poet, said:

> We are telling the mythic story of female individualization: the stages of initiation and beyond, so that we know it's ancient, and centered in women's power, and we are acknowledging this in a culture which devalues the particular strengths of women. Women's literature is true to what we go through. The metaphorical terms of fiction and art help us to understand and delight in our own process. Otherwise we think we are an abhoration, because we stumble through the female process of individualization without a map. (Lyons)

Art shows us that the places we turned were right.

As women, we remain in a culture which is largely not our own, and without a language to express our experience. Language is identity. Simply compare the denial of language and its savaging of identity to Africans brought here as slaves, or punishments for speaking Gallic in Ireland, the attempt by one nation to eradicate another's individuality.

We are writing our mythic identity, recovering female archetypes. And in women's literature courses we find that we have in these authors strong women who have gone before us, word-mothers, and they leap like fire in our brains because *they are who we essentially are.*

That is the mirror.

"Why must I write?" wrote poet H.D. in *Hermetic Definition*.

> You will not care for this
> but She draws the veil aside
> unbinds my eyes
> commands
> write, write or die. (H.D. 7)

As women writers we provide a mirror for each other—the view of who we essentially are. It is a view seen by women, not through the interpretations of men. The mirror rises before us shining: it may be the words of a contemporary writer, artist, friend, older word mother. Whichever, they provide the sensibilities, voice and pattern of mind which are not male. And for men they provide the part of themselves often brutally denied. For all of us art is the journey to establish the home of oneself. And the words of a mother are part of that home.

In words we reflect for each other who we essentially are. We nurture each other with all the intuition and wisdom and ferocity of our ancient mothers: loving, fierce, protective, standing aside and nurturing the personhood of the other. It is the safe reciprocity of fully adult women. And growing in the other's reflection is exponentially more powerful because it is not alone.

We midwife who we are. We midwife the artist of who we are. We trust the process of growing, process of personhood. We learn the message, "Listen to yourself." We have not been taught a language of power about ourselves, of ourselves. Yet here we speak a language of power and truth about each other, to each other, until we own it. In the mirror we let it surface, we know it, we know it intuitively. The mirror becomes profoundly "I can." We believe in each other until we each believe, separate, on our own. And then we see the essence of ourselves is our mirror. The hand that holds the mirror is our own.

For a woman writer the mirror becomes the muse. For men the muse has traditionally been female, external, distant. For women the muse is the hand lifting the mirror to our eyes. In a muse relationship, two people who are creative and open recognize that the self is not limited to ego, but enormous. It allows us to connect to other times, other people, all that has or does or will live. The muse does not say "love some external being." The muse reflects "Love yourself. Discover who you are. Discover that your essence is the world."

Writing—all art—is individuation. In women's literature we find a universal "I," a definition of the self enormous, endless, inclusive. A self which is Self. We find the true subversion of reading—"I matter." We find a ferocious value system of honoring life in all its forms, the earth, the rhythms of the universe, recognizing we are part of nature, not an opposition to it. And we find the beginnings of telling what we have never written: the relationships of women, the relationship of women to the world, without men, without children, as individuals. And for the first time, we—all people—will catch the words, "those unrecorded gestures, those unsaid or half-said words, which form themselves, no more palpably than the shadows of moths on the ceiling when women are alone" (Woolf 84).

JULIE HOUSTON

Virginia Woolf announced our true identity as writers, as poets, as Shakespeare's sister:

> She lives in you and in me, and in many other women who are not here tonight, for they are washing up the dishes and putting the children to bed. But she lives; for great poets do not die; they are continuing presences; they need only the opportunity to walk among us in the flesh. This opportunity, as I think, it is now coming within your power to give her. For my belief is that if we live another century or so—I am talking of the common life which is the real life and not of the little separate lives which we live as individuals—and have five hundred a year each of us and rooms of our own; if we have the habit of freedom and the courage to write exactly what we think; if we escape a little from the common sitting-room and see human beings not always in their relation to each other but in relation to reality; and the sky, too, and the trees or whatever it may be in themselves; if we look past Milton's bogey, for no human being should shut out the view; if we face the fact, for it is a fact, that there is no arm to cling to, but that we go alone and that our relation is to the world of reality and not only to the world of men and women, then the opportunity will come and the dead poet who was Shakespeare's sister will put on the body which she has so often laid down. Drawing her life from the lives of the unknown who were her forerunners, as her brother did before her, she *will* be born (Woolf 113–14).

WORKS CITED

Baker, Richard. Introduction. *Zen Mind, Beginner's Mind*. By Shunryn Suzuki. New York: Weatherhill, 1970.

H.D. *Hermetic Definition*. New York: New Directions, 1972.

Kemp, Wendy. Personal Interview. 21 October 1991.

Lacey, Timothy. Personal Interview. 20 April 1993.

Lyons, Kevra. Personal Interview. 18 October 1993.

Nicolson, Nigel and Joanne Trautmann, eds. *The Letters of Virginia Woolf*. Vol. 3 1923–1928. New York: Harcourt Brace Jovanovich, 1977.

Sappho's Lyre. Trans. Diane Rayor. Los Angeles: U of California P, 1991.

"Toni Morrison: Writers Talk Ideas of Our Time." The Roland Collection of Films on Art. Northbrook, IL.

Woolf, Virginia. *A Room of One's Own*. New York: Harcourt Brace Jovanovich, 1957.

FINDING MY VOICE
CAUGHT BETWEEN A WOOLF AND A CRANE

SANDRA PARKER

I n literature, setting often is relegated to last place. In life, it fares no better, except when a self-conscious, regionally-influenced author, like Toni Morrison, in her Ohio novels tells her readers to exercise rememory of their days as nestlings in such vital environs as "the Bottom," Lorain, or Cincinnati. Each of us exists within such a frame, and perhaps it takes outside commentators to teach that we, too, are merely immigrants shaped by foreign lands.

Since 1970 I have periodically lived as a foreigner in Cambridge, England and have studied the mysterious connections between the places where human beings live and what they write. Delving into East Anglia's literary heritage has taught me uncanonical regional perspectives from such narratives as Charles Kingsley's *Hereward the Wake* and Richard Cobbold's *Margaret Catchpole*. More popular regional authors also instruct me about the significance of place and convey viewpoints about how people are shaped by, and sometimes manage to rise above, their environs. The genesis of my thoughts on this subject comes from a little noted but vital link between region and idea in Virginia Woolf's famous 1929 essay "A Room of One's Own."

The work begins in October with Woolf's female narrator wandering along the Backs, behind King's College Chapel, and sitting on the banks of the River Cam. Her description of this much photographed calendar scene is unique, however, in its terms of elemental and personified imagery: "To the right and left bushes of some sort, golden and crimson, glowed with the colour, even it seemed burnt with the heat, of fire. On the further bank the willows wept in perpetual lamentation, their hair about their shoulders." Between these fiery and lamenting banks, Woolf observes the intrusive and powerful Cam: "The river reflected whatever it chose of sky and bridge and burning tree, and when the graduate had oared his boat through the reflections they closed again, completely, as if he had never been" (5).

This remarkable scene leads her Everywoman speaker to mentally participate in a popular East Anglian men's sport: she goes fishing in the Cam for an idea, but after hooking, retrieving, and laying her fish in the grass, this poetic fisherwoman decides that her catch is undersized and needs to be thrown back into the Cam until it can mature. Before the completion of this humane gesture, a King's College Beadle, called a "curious looking object," makes her move off the grass. He interrupts Woolf's meditation and sends "her little fish into hiding."

At the end of her essay, Woolf circles back to another stream, London's traffic, which she describes in similar terms to the Cam, as each bears away both boats and ideas. She adds that her little fish has matured, despite its precipitous fright, and thus reintroduces the essay's central theme, the paramount significance of the androgynous mind. Woolf's parable of an East Anglian fishstory transcends the more obvious subthemes of misogyny and women's economic dependence; it deftly repudiates the androcentric traditions of sport and education by rendering the River Cam's painterly scenery in terms suggestive of androgynous richness. The setting enables Virginia Woolf to demonstrate her ideal: the fully human, resonant and porous man-womanly or woman-manly mind which transmits emotion without impediment and is "naturally creative, incandescent and undivided" (102). Thus the East Anglian "A Room of One's Own" brilliantly exemplifies the process by which a writer dramatizes how people learn *from* a place, as Woolf's College Backs provide the backdrop of self-satisfied and exclusionary male authority—to which is opposed a foregrounded androgynous mind enabling "complete satisfaction and happiness."

Woolf's clever uses of her environs inspire my admiration and make my mind race. May people like me now be lucky enough to avoid the Beadle and fish at will? Are women free to think, study, earn, avoid misogynistic silencing? What is the next scenario when East Anglia, London, or any other place, will no longer marginalize free spirits?

My own returns from Cambridgeshire to Portage County's Hiram College in Ohio bring these thoughts into focus. Half a century after Virginia Woolf's English struggles, my own American career unfortunately continues to reflect ongoing fears of masculine prohibitions and canonical prescriptions. In 1979 a colleague and I initiated a minor in Gender Studies at our midwestern liberal arts institution. Our program brochure begins: "People experience three basic kinds of relationships: male and male, female and female, male and female; each of these types of interaction requires great human understanding." Provincial suspicion of Gender Studies are hard to dissipate. Many colleagues speculated about its distinction from Women's Studies, or, in any case, whether gender is really a valid, significant, and "useful" academic category.

After a decade and a half, I now see a number of departments accepting gender scholarship, and entry-level faculty arrive with graduate school training and pedagogical expertise in Gender Studies.

The early nineties place such curricular questions into broader national debates about political correctness, multiculturalism, and the canon. The resulting tug of war between traditionalists and curricular evolutionaries, like myself, has perhaps been eased at Hiram College because of our early innovations, pioneering for two decades in multicultural Gender Studies. Nonetheless, a flashpoint occurred during the spring of 1992 when the college's Gender Studies program and related commitment to multiculturalism was virulently attacked in a local newspaper, a confrontation riling conservative Ohio neighbors and galvanizing campus liberals. This led to heavier enrollments in Gender Studies courses but rattled faculty, like myself, who had prematurely believed our subject matter was accepted, "mainstreamed." Somewhat stunned by the attack, I have since recommitted myself to extending multiculturalism's purview at the college. Remembering the college's founder, Alexander Campbell, and his 143-year-old motto, "let there be light," I persist in my belief that each of us must promote the truth.

My truth-telling has led me to a mid-life review of my academic career, which began with my instinctive teaching of women writers in the late 1960s. By the seventies I decided that women's issues could never be understood, except in the context of men's issues. Hence I moved away from pure Women's Studies to Gender Studies. Soon after this, colleagues convinced me to also study a subject I had little prior interest in: middlewestern American regionalism. Graduate school training in nineteenth-century Britain was my chosen area of study, with an emphasis on fiction writers, especially Charles Dickens. But when Hiram College received a National Endowment of the Humanities grant in 1982 for the development of the Regional Studies of the Western Reserve, I joined a faculty study group. Hiram College's Western Reserve Regional Studies program taught me about Ohio's pioneers who came to the West at the beginning of the nineteenth century, settled into the Northwest Territory, and created the state's patchwork identity. For a few fascinating decades, Ohio was America's wild and wooly West; even today it is often called a microcosm of America. Initially I sought out "lost" or overlooked writers, like the influential Englishwoman Jessica Mitford, and such regional figures as Ohio's earliest pioneer writers, Julia L. Dumont and Pamilla W. Ball.

In retrospect, I suppose that Ohio's pioneers were captivating as a contrast to my own undramatic life. Raised in western New York, I came to Ohio in 1965 at the age of twenty-two and set down roots in Buckeye soil. But my traceable family goes back before 958 to Norman England when ancestors, for instance, served as the nucleus of a Pilgrim band on the Mayflower. My most notable precursor was Adrian Scroope, whose actions forced the family's flight from England: he signed the warrant for King Charles I's execution and in 1660 was executed at Charing Cross. "Throope" became the surname for descendants in the New World, Adams who hid their shameful identity and moved West; one was a Forty-niner; another, my great grandfather, Orange Throope, after the Civil War emigrated to Devil's Lake, North Dakota, Sioux Indian country. Was it the secret of their disreputable family background that led these itinerants to never write about their experiences?

Such musings about the Throopes' unpreserved pioneer experiences predisposed my sympathies toward other emigrants, and I worked to discover and harvest Ohio's cache of unexamined prose. Regional concepts crept into my teaching, as well as adding "lost" women authors; currently I am editing the short fiction of Ohio's nineteenth-century women regionalists. Also modern Buckeye authors interest me; what a treasure trove—such Pulitzer Prize Winners as Mary Oliver, Rita Dove, America's new Poet Laureate, and Toni Morrison, recipient of the 1993 Noble Prize in Literature.

Along the way, I also noticed that many male writers have become obscured. For instance, William Dean Howells and Sherwood Anderson are two once lionized literary heroes whose reputations have dimmed. More importantly, I became fascinated by Hart Crane, a poet born in Garrettsville, a village near Hiram College, who spent his youth in the region, especially in Cleveland.

Though professional critics compare Hart Crane to the supreme modernist T. S. Eliot, he is not often spoken of proudly by Hiram locals. If pressed about a prominent regional writer, residents are apt to sing the praises of another poet, Vachel Lindsay, an idiosyncratic Hiram College student and impassioned Disciples of Christ singer of verses who committed suicide by drinking lye. But I wondered why we don't celebrate the great Crane's work? Why hadn't I read Hart Crane's poetry, if only in school anthologies? Was he dishonored by his suicide at sea or another, worse taboo? Might this man's lack of posthumous influence be explained by his poetry's sexual and biographical context?

This inquiry brings together Gender Studies and regionalism; it explains to me why, despite Hart Crane's being Ohio's greatest male writer, his posthumous reputation is not widely touted. Hart Crane was not buried with a stake through his heart at a crossroads or left scribbling on scraps of paper in the sitting room like many women were. Nonetheless, it took Cleveland's Case Western Reserve University fifty-three years to install William McVey's statue of Hart Crane in front of its Freiburger Library in 1985, and Crane's literary reception has been similarly muted within America's literary canon. What liability has caused Crane's regional and national trivialization? From my studies, I have come to believe that it is Crane's life, not his poetry, that offends critics. In short, Hart Crane's liability is not women's "separate sphere," but another gender curse, homosexuality.[1]

Indeed, as we totter toward the twenty-first century America is currently reexamining its estranged canon of writers who are "incorrect," whether because of theme, class, race, genre, gender, or sexual orientation, any of which may prevent sanctuary within the establishment's literary mainstream. Remembering Virginia Woolf's injunction about seeking the androgynous mind which is undivided and incandescent, I finally recognize that it isn't enough to simply "think back through my mothers"; I must try to think back through my brothers, too. My study of Crane's estrangement from our popular canon thus is my exemplum that embodies the drama of straight-laced academia's most recent frontier of critical inquiry.

In 1992 a colleague published *Anthology of Western Reserve Literature* with a cover graced by a stunning regional painting called "Sunday Morning Apples" by a Cleveland artist named William Sommer. Inside the collection was a delightful lyric of the same title written by twenty-two-year-old Hart Crane on Saturday, August 6, 1922. The poem, "Sunday Morning Apples," was published in the summer of 1924 and appeared in Crane's first collection of poetry *White Buildings* (1926). Assuming that the painting inspired the poem, I was attracted to the poem's high energy, challenging imagery, and ecstatic apostrophe to "Bill," to William Sommer. Wondering why I had never before read this lyric, I began researching it, uncovering such accolades as "Sunday Morning Apples" being called a watershed in Hart Crane's career; Paul Sherman labels "Apples" one of the most notable poems on art by an American poet (85). But why has such a masterpiece received so little attention? Why is it so infrequently anthologized?

In order to find out, I began to trace the poem's genesis. Hart Crane wrote to his mother in Cleveland about reading "Sunday Morning Apples," his "poem to Bill Sommer" (*Letters* 195) which he says was created out of "sheer joy" (*Letters* 96). The setting was Paul Rosenfeld's in Brooklyn where Aaron Copeland played background music on the

SANDRA PARKER

piano while Mary Ann Moore and Hart Crane recited poetry to members of the Seven Arts Circle, which included Alfred Steiglitz, Georgia O'Keeffe, Van Wyck Brooks, and Edmund Wilson.

Wanting to discover more about the poem's inspiration, I read further about the friendship that is lauded in "Sunday Morning Apples." This took me to bohemian Cleveland in the 1920s, the era of Hart Crane's and Bill Sommer's friendship, years crucial for Crane's budding literary talents, but often downplayed by biographical critics. I found that a half century of scholarship avoided or distorted the productive aspects of Hart Crane's early homosocial friendships.

Hart Crane's inspirational friend Bill Sommer came to life in the clippings file at the Cleveland Public Library. Born in 1867 to emigrant Germans in Detroit, encouraged by a local sculptor and woodcarver named Gari Melchers, Sommer became an apprentice and lifelong lithographer. Working and studying in Boston, England, Germany, New York City, in 1907 Bill Sommer moved to Cleveland, Ohio. An affable, sensitive, intelligent regional painter whose works are currently owned by the Cleveland Museum of Art, the Metropolitan Museum of Art, the Whitney, and the Smithsonian, Bill Sommer's ongoing local fame is derived from his early advocacy of European modernism within northeast Ohio.

It was 1922, when Hart Crane was twenty-two, that he discovered William Sommer's paintings in Richard Laukhuff's Taylor Arcade bookshop. Laukhuff was a lifelong friend of Sommers who agreed to introduce Hart Crane to the fifty-two-year-old painter who had a reputation as a "godfather to scores of young artists in Cleveland" (Bruner 8). Soon Crane became one of Sommer's followers who on the weekends congregated at his rural Brandywine studio to talk and drink.

Crane's correspondence from this era explodes with his admiration for Sommer as an intellectual mentor and regional free spirit. During 1922 and 1923, before moving permanently to New York City, Hart Crane voluntarily promoted the reticent Sommer's artwork to his eastern intellectual friends, including Sherwood Anderson, William Carlos Williams, and Alfred Steiglitz. In fact, Crane's proselytizing led to sales and the appearance of several paintings in Sibley Watson's *The Dial*.

Bill Sommer, however, was a man who never yearned for an eastern market; he was simply proud to be an innovative Western Reserve regionalist. For decades Cleveland's charismatic "Sage of Brandywine," Sommer helped local artists, such as William Zorach, Abe Warshawsky, Sam Loveman, William Lescaze, Bert Ginther, and Peter Keisogloff, who gathered at Laukhuff's Cleveland bookshop and Cleveland's Kokoon Club, which Sommer had helped to found as a support for avante garde modernists. Sommer encouraged Cleveland artists to experiment with Impressionism, Vorticism, and Cubism. His mentor in nonrealistic representation was Paul Cézanne. Bill Sommer praised the artist's "disinterestedness" and shared Clive Bell's ideas advocated in his influential *Since Cézanne* (1922), which promoted combining color and drawing in a "new synthesis of light and space" (Kramer 28).

Other influences were the German philosopher Friedrich Nietzsche and the Russian P. D. Ouspensky, whose *Tertium Organum* (1949) rejects symbolic representation in art. Sommer's notebooks encapsulate his aesthetics: the artist must become immersed into the form and spirit of a chosen subject; in his words, "the most convincing artists . . . merely reveal the symbol of their innermost experiences." Calling this philosophy "Ding an Sich," Bill Sommer and Hart Crane agreed that Impressionism was "the only satisfactory creative principle to follow" (*Letters* 71). This led to Crane's obsession with "*causes* (metaphysical)," form, subjective unity, and "a solid and clear beauty." In 1925 Hart Crane articulated in "General Aims and Theories" his "Sommerian" philosophy—both men force together divergent realities in order to expose a deeper clarity.

When the poem "Sunday Morning Apples" was published in *White Buildings*, Hart Crane wrote to a New York City friend, Gorham Munson, complaining of the modern world's "inadequate systems of rationality." He insisted that art must force together divergent realities—for example, juxtaposing classical and modern experiences—and thus refocus America's "confused chaos." The poem "Sunday Morning Apples" embodies these critical precepts, drawing, as does his artist mentor, Bill Sommer, upon "chance combinations of related and unrelated detail" (Horton 324). Within the poetic genre, Hart Crane's "practical resources" include classical allusions, such as the poem's references to antiquity: Demeter's procreative love, Jason's golden fleece, and Aphrodite's golden apples. Such resources establish what Crane calls "touchstones of experience" and metaphorical logic in which the world becomes "a springboard, to give the poem *as a whole* an orbit" (Horton 326). Indeed, "Sunday Morning Apples" achieves its goal, a reader's spiritual illumination, as a consequence of the poem's "associational meanings" (327).

But why have critics given such shallow investigation to the poem's gender implications, both in its imagery and narrational voice? That personal voice is the author's extended apostrophe to William Sommer, framing the overarching narrative structure of "Sunday Morning Apples." Its five stanzas or twenty lines of free verse are rendered in complex metaphors and imagery, which Allen Tate's introduction to

White Buildings warns, plunge the reader into an unfamiliar milieu. The poem's referential structure encompasses three seasons—fall, winter, and spring—while its mythopoeic imagery extends through time and place, moving the reader into antiquity and then back into the twentieth century at Sommer's Brandywine farm in Ohio, his own Aix-en-Provence.

Crane teases the reader, also, with allusions, such as Percy Shelley's "West Wind" with its incendiary claims for art. Complex imagery, leaves that "fill the fleece of nature," apples like a "ripe nude with head reared into a realm of swords," and a shadow that cries defiance to snowy winter, are woven into "Sunday Morning Apples" as Crane's "secrets" playfully tossed to the reader. In particular, what does Hart Crane mean in the poem's final, enigmatic, ejaculatory line, "The apples, Bill, the apples!"

Thinking about the fruitful ambiguities of this poem led me to note that both the "apples" and the "Sunday" of the poem's title are simultaneously real and mythic. The apples are far more than merely a form of *malus pumila* which originated some two thousand years ago south of the Caucasus. Golden apples, once significant in Greek myths, also gave knowledge to Eve and precipitated the fall from paradise. In Ohio, Johnny Appleseed's fruit became a distinctive regional tradition. Most immediately, brandywine apples inspired Bill Sommer, whose orchard provided a source of food and income. His notebooks say that apples embody the primal circle; more than an artistic motif, Bill Sommer, like his master Paul Cézanne, taught the value of common objects. He painted numerous still lifes of the fruit. One includes his wife, Martha Obermeyer, paring apples. Another brush and ink with a watercolor wash may be related to Crane's 1922 inspiration for "Sunday Morning Apples"; Sommer's "Portrait of Hart Crane (eating an apple)" is dated circa 1918-1920 by Charles Val Clear, Director of the Akron Art Institute.

I also wondered why Hart Crane's regional poem "Sunday Morning Apples" was actually written on a Saturday. The contextual shift to Sunday places the fruit within a Christian context, god's paradisal day of rest, Christians' day of sacred devotions, and, perhaps more importantly, Brandywine artists' celebrated time for secular gatherings. Like Wallace Stevens's "Sunday Morning" which Harriet Monroe had published in *Poetry* seven years earlier, Crane writes in the unchurched tradition of the famed homosexual poet Walt Whitman, who affirmed the powers of nature by changing perceived notions of paradise. Stevens's poem celebrated Death as "the mother of beauty." Both Stevens and Crane in their respective Sunday Morning poems, draw upon the Demeter-Persephone myth of mother and maiden who inescapably nurture and threaten, making the earth into both a womb and tomb. Crane's opening allusion to Demeter's starved maternal affection embodies the classical world's explanation for seasonal change. However, the poem also encodes images of masculine egotism. Hades is an abducting "husband," and Jason is a thief who steals a fleece, as well as a wife. Similar gender ambiguity is found in Hart Crane's concluding set of classical images, reminding me of the ambiguity of Aphrodite's motives when her golden apples slow Atalanta's usually fleet feet.

Thus, despite Crane's employment of female allusions in "Sunday Morning Apples," I observe that these mythic women are thematically noteworthy for their estrangement. In fact, it is Crane's masculine imagery and erotic allusions that dominate this poem to Bill Sommer. For example, there is phallocentric imagery, such as a "realm of swords" and ecstatic verbs like "bursting" and "straddling." Its playful, homoerotic structure reaches a climax when the narrator's flow of thought is complicated by a glance out of the Brandywine window to Ohio's unmythical landscape where a boy runs with his dog. This ecstatic vision leads to the poem's falling action, a conclusion in which Crane apparently describes Bill Sommer's still life, apples and knife beside a pitcher "ready for explosion."

Obviously "Sunday Morning Apples" is a regional poem about two men who are personally and artistically harmonious. It incarnates their theories regarding the potential of Brandywine's apples, both as literal still life props and spheres that incarnate vast philosophical traditions. Another relevant similarity is the fact that both men were at this time habituated to alcohol. Each rejected Prohibition and justified ecstatic tippling. A biographer notes that Hart Crane and Bill Sommer used alcohol to provide them with the "courage not to deny their artist's vocation" (Unterecker 270). Each defended drunkenness as an intellectually respectable context for inspired indulgence, the door to what Sommer calls in his notebooks "separate art worlds of dreamland." As I read about this early 1920s attitude, I discovered that Sommer's farm was located in a nearby valley which allowed the defiance of Prohibition restrictions because of the ease of producing "brandywine" applejack. Undated notebooks record Sommer's instructions for making not only applejack, but wine, beer, and fermented beverages from mint, orange juice and lemon. Jugs of cider were frequent subjects of his paintings; Sommer, in fact, had a "gargantuan appetite for drink" (Kramer); many weekends were given over to male drinking sprees; over the decades, these "alcoholic and aesthetic benders" eventually destroyed his health.

On the other hand, the twenty-two-year-old Hart Crane's attraction to alcohol dates from only a few months before he wrote "Sunday Morning Apples." During the winter of 1921, Hart Crane became intoxicated from anaesthetic in a dentist's chair. He wrote to an eastern friend that this experience was a "kind of seventh heaven of consciousness and egoistic dance among the seven spheres" which gave him "moments in eternity" and a new artistic self-confidence. Crane adds, "if I could afford wine *every* evening I might do more" (*Letters* 92). Indeed, Crane did not live long enough to become an alcoholic and ruin his health as his friends Bill Sommer and Eugene O'Neill did. Nonetheless, alcohol complicated his life, alienating him from his mother, who was a temperance advocate, and infuriating his rich father.

But Crane's self-serving commitment to "benders" overcame his fear of family disapproval. Crane rationalized by turning to Plato's idea of the poet's "divine madness"; he argued that alcohol provided him with an ecstatic, Dionysian source of energy. [2] In a letter dated March 17, 1926, Crane credits his "sense of affinity with the visionary tradition of poetry." He claimed alcohol gave him a "glimpse into the heart of things," a happiness that connected him with all of life ("General" 316), and opened the windows of his soul, providing true, religious, eccentric vision. Certainly Crane's 1922 "Sunday Morning Apples" embodies this alcohol-driven ecstasy that is metaphorical, as well as literal, when his narrator gazes out a Brandywine window and claims cosmic human connectedness.

The imagery in "Sunday Morning Apples" of windows and thresholds also serves as evidence of another of the poet's parentally disapproved pleasures, homosexuality. In fact, the poem's enjambed imagery and context suggest that Crane was drawing upon Plato's idealization of men's love. The timing of Hart Crane's break from his Ohio family and escape to New York City's bohemian circles reinforces this reading. In December of 1919, Hart Crane first wrote about his homosexuality to his New York friend, Gorham Munson. At that time Crane saw his sexual identity as a "terrible liability." But soon he was back in Ohio, where Cleveland and Akron experiences led the young poet to a more self-accepting image. I learned that by the time Crane returned East in 1923, he believed that his heterosexual friends accepted his sexual orientation with "tolerance and equanimity" (Horton 166). It seems, then, that when "Sunday Morning Apples" was written in 1922 Hart Crane was experimenting with his affection for men and may have been ambivalent about his feelings toward the elder Sommer.

The timing of the poem's genesis reveals the significance of Hart

Crane's elliptical label, "Thinking of Bill — — , etc. — — — —" and description of "Sunday Morning Apples" as a "gay thing" written out of "sheer joy" (*Letters* 96). This may be Hart Crane's homosocial or homosexual joke. "Gay" in the early 1920s was a fashionable label for homosexuality in Greenwich Village and the East Coast intellectual circles within which Crane moved. We know that at this time the young Hart Crane was a raconteur who constantly joked with word play and innuendo. His old friend Sam Loveman, called by biographers the one who "knew him perhaps better than any man," describes the "Gargantuan comedy" of shared Sunday morning Interurban trips from Cleveland to Sommer's studio at Brandywine during which Hart Crane created a "holocaust of laughter because he saw double meanings . . . sexual or phallic undercurrents" in everything. Crane's stream of transforming innuendo (Unterecker 181) and erotic double meanings illuminates his imagery and context in "Sunday Morning Apples," his self-described "gay thing."

After 1922 Hart Crane left Ohio and moved back to New York City; he grew away from his Cleveland friendships. Samuel Loveman once described Bill Sommer's Brandywine homosocial gatherings as an escape from his family obligations to wife and children, calling it the "mess at Brandywine." He believes that Sommer was dissatisfied with Crane's obstreperous boyishness. In Loveman's words, "the first thing Hart did when he met any body and he liked them was to try and seduce them. . . . It occurred to me that this was the reason for the break" (Ingalls 65).

Some critics, like Paul Sherman, read "Sunday Morning Apples" by imposing a heterosexual interpretation that turns William Sommer into a father who impregnates Mother Nature in a Brandywine Eden. Such critics allude to the aging Sommer's genial, heterosexual reputation. Their view builds in Hart Crane's persona only in terms of his alienation from his disapproving millionaire father, C. A. Crane, for whom William Sommer provides a substitute. For example, biographer John Unterecker argues that the mature Bill Sommer was a "surrogate father, counselor, drinking companion, confidant, infallible conversationalist. In Sommer, Hart found an equal, a man of genius whom he could talk to with absolute ease" (203). However, this simplified reading sanitizes Crane's and Sommer's man-to-man bond. I think that the content and context of "Sunday Morning Apples" reveal a more complex, erotically sublimated relationship.

The distortions of this poem's critical reception remind me of a distant afternoon spent in a university library where I happened upon a study of Sappho's poetry which elaborately denied its homoerotic content. Recently I read Joan DeJean's study *Fictions of Sappho* (1992) which synthesizes critics of four centuries who have tried to silence the world's most famous lesbian. Writers like Sappho, Woolf, and Crane whose personal lives have become politicized by conservative literary critics have had their subject matter passionately obliterated. Furthermore, they have suffered the loss of their full audience. I suppose that such homophobic distortions have occurred as a means of protecting a unicultural canon, but it is a dynamic I understand as "The Sappho Effect."

Hart Crane's Brandywine, Ohio, at first glance appears to be a long way from Virginia Woolf's Cambridge Backs, but these disparate settings are linked by strong affinities. Each place is lovingly immortalized by a writer who plumbed its symbolic resonances. Each writer carried the stigma of sexual nonconformity, struggled with imposed gender definitions, and was a visionary who advocated androgyny, true human wholeness.

In my mind, these two writers' treatments of places I also love, and recognize as environments within which one is judged by one's neighbors, have crystallized some painful thoughts. I believe that Hart Crane's undercelebrated status and relative invisibility within the literary canon illustrate America's continuing antagonism toward those whom Woolf labels as having "two sexes in the mind." Virginia Woolf's and Hart Crane's lives illustrate how great, popular writers' posthumous careers suffer from the prejudices of critics, even well-meaning critics. Nonetheless, the fish does come out of hiding; the Beadle is defied. It is, indeed, as the Englishwoman instructs, imagination and memories that reward us; whether poet or audience, the androgynous soul still lives "more than other people" (114).

Since the best pedagogy is truth telling, I conclude that my Gender Studies courses must not yield to narrow, provincial protocol but struggle to incorporate multicultural readings that include sensitive topics like androgyny and homosexuality. Though an early advocate of Gender Studies, I have ironically discovered from the perspectives of local regionalism that there is no repose to be found on the banks of the Cam or the Cuyahoga. The "two-sided mind" Woolf talks about must pledge itself to protecting the environment by preserving a scene that is completed by both the river and the bushes. To fortify myself, I, too, may choose a mental picture and see out my window the artists in Brandywine or a young and spunky Virginia Woolf metaphorically fishing in the Cam.

---

[1] Finally in 1990 a study of Hart Crane's cultural background and major poems has appeared on this theme, but it does not closely examine the poem or homosocial environs of Brandywine. See Thomas E. Yingling *Hart Crane and the Homosexual Text,* Chicago: University of Chicago Press, 1990.

[2] "The Wine Menagerie" in *White Buildings* and "Recitative" have been considered alcoholic companion poems and help prepare readers for his late works "Faustus and Helen" and "The Bridge." "The Wine Managerie" presents alcohol's predatory claws or "wine talons" that transform into flight.

Works Consulted

Anderson, David R. and Haddad, Gladys. *Anthology of Western Reserve Literature.* Kent: Kent State U P, 1992.

Crane, Hart. *The Complete and Selected Letters of Hart Crane.* ed. Brom Weber. New York: Liveright Publishing Corp., 1966.

_____. "General Aims and Theories." *Hart Crane, The Life of an American Poet.* Philip Horton. New York: W. W. Norton & Co., Inc. 1937. 323–28.

Ingalls, Dr. Hunter. "The William Sommer Book." unpublished. Special Collections, Case Western Reserve University Libraries, 1984.

Kramer, Hilton. "An Early Provincial Modernist." *The New York Times,* Section D. June 29, 1980, p. 6, 28.

Martin, Robert. *Homosexual Tradition in American Poetry.* Austin: University of Texas Press, 1979.

Sherman, Paul. *Hart's Bridge.* Urbana; U of Illinois P, 1977.

Sommer, William. "Notebooks." In Special Collections, Case Western Reserve University Libraries, Cleveland, Ohio.

Unterecker, John. *Voyager: A Life of Hart Crane.* New York: Liveright Publishing Corporation, 1969.

Yingling, Thomas E. *Hart Crane and the Homosexual Text.* Chicago: U of Chicago P, 1990.

Literary Criticism with a Human Face
Virginia Woolf and *The Common Reader*

Elsie F. Mayer

I n the1970s several of my colleagues and I were discussing feminist criticism and in particular its break with the New Criticism. When someone challenged the validity of a subjective response to a text over so-called "textual objectivity," he was met with silence. No one, including myself, rose to defend the former. My lack of response, however, was not without consequences, for my silence contradicted my experience with reading literature, driven as it has been from my youth by a personal interaction with texts. Nevertheless, at the time I felt no need to face this contradiction. I had learned as an English major that leisure reading and professional reading differed. A graduate student trained by male mentors, I entered the profession of language and literature an advocate of masculinist criticism. (By masculinist criticism I mean acceptance of the male perspective, experience, and standards of literary criticism as normative.) For a long time my work both as a teacher and scholar reflected my training. With the fervor of a zealot I applied the principles of masculinist criticism inside and outside the classroom. No questions asked.

I have come to realize that my attitude towards masculinist criticism had its roots in my experience as an undergraduate. This experience, I believe, is typical since it resembles that of many of my colleagues who were also undergraduates when the New Criticism dominated English departments. The study of literature was based on the premise that a text held a single meaning. Teachers emphasized the need to search for it. Class periods were devoted to instruction in analytical criticism. There was little difference between examining a literary text and a crayfish. Both were dissected, labeled, and categorized. The scientific method prevailed in literature as it did in zoology. As if excavating an archeological site for treasure, students reconstructed shards of meaning into an abstract whole, always hoping the result conformed to the teacher's expectation, for we never doubted that she/he knew the secret we hoped to discover. When writing about texts, we learned the necessity of mastering the thesis-and-support essay. Unity, coherence, and closure were treated as if absolute standards of good writing.

Our opinion was discredited if not supported with a heavy dose of textual evidence.

When I became a professional, I taught as others had taught me. Like a priestess officiating at a sacred rite, I ensured the privileged position of a single model of literary (read masculinist) criticism. I emphasized analytical criticism. "Think of the text as a specimen under a microscope," I advised students. The thesis-and-support essay, I claimed without reservation, was superior to other forms of writing. In red ink, lest students miss the gravity of their errors, I weeded out traces of subjectivism, banished the first-person pronoun to exile, and commended their use of induction. "Keep your eye on the thesis," I urged them, echoing my past experience as a student. Without equivocation I differentiated between non-professional and professional criticism. One's opinion of a text and the personal voice were acceptable in a private journal (non-professional criticism). In contrast, a literary essay proceeded objectively, its voice impersonal (professional criticism). Although students' essays were often sterile and lacked connective tissue between the text and their lives, I rationalized that such was the nature of academic writing.

Not until I heard the voices of Tillie Olsen and Adrienne Rich did I begin to question the dominance of masculinist criticism. That my past vision was myopic soon became apparent. Had not my practices both as a scholar and teacher contributed to the superiority of masculinist criticism? Had I not as an advocate of masculinist criticism reinforced a hierarchy of rhetorical modes with argument at its pinnacle? Would I not perpetuate hegemonic control over the teaching of literature and composition if I continued to subvert the feminist perspective? That change was necessary became clear to me. Thereafter, my reading of feminist scholarship led me to realize alternatives to masculinist criticism. I was hooked.

A new community of critics whose work rested on an evolving understanding of female epistemology has empowered me to revise both my scholarship and my teaching. As a scholar I have become less dependent on analytical criticism. My understanding of the influence of gender and culture on texts continues to grow. I am learning to recognize the synergistic relationship between a text and the social milieu in which it was created, for no author writes in a vacuum. As a teacher I have loosened my grip on students' relation to texts, allowing them the freedom to connect texts with personal experience. My former advocacy of analytical criticism has been replaced by a new paradigm between reader and text. Closed is the distance between them. Instead, I encourage students to think of texts as living organisms. I am supportive when dialogue between reader and text drives a student's verbal and written response. Especially gratifying has been my learning to appreciate the insights students garner from their reading. This last change has helped me to nod in agreement with Langston Hughes's lines: "As I learned from you, I guess you learned from me—" ("Theme for English B").

The reading of feminist scholarship and criticism has deepened my awareness of the distortions that can result when one relies on a fixed literary position to evaluate a text. An incident will illustrate this point. In the 1980s, I was engaged in a critical study of Anne Morrow Lindbergh's works. At the time I was specifically concerned with Lindbergh's collection of poetry, *Bring Me a Unicorn*, published in 1956. In the course of my research, I read John Ciardi's review of her poetry in *The Saturday Review*. A modernist critic and poetry editor of the magazine, Ciardi condemned Lindbergh's poetry on the grounds that it lacked the qualities of modernist poetry. There followed a debate in the pages of the magazine between Ciardi, whose defense rested exclusively on the modernist tenets advocated by Eliot and Pound, and readers sympathetic to other criteria for judgment. So bitter was the debate that Norman Cousins, the general editor, published a disclaimer in an attempt to distance the view of the magazine from Ciardi's and thus protect the magazine from a possible drop in subscriptions. But the damage to Lindbergh and her readers was irrevocable. Thereafter, she abandoned further publication of her poetry, and readers lost a unique voice in American literature. When the time came to form my own judgment of Lindbergh's poems, I discovered an authentic voice running through them. No posturing, as Ciardi had claimed. She had simply made her experience as a woman the focus of poetry. Though not in the modernist tradition, her poems are carefully crafted and rich in metaphor. Whenever I think about the debate, I become more convinced that had Ciardi placed Lindbergh's poems in a historical context, had he not clung tenaciously to the modernist tenets for judging poetry as if there were no alternatives, had he been less inclined to "rank" them, a different view of her poems would have emerged.

As I continue to revise my professional work (one's work like life itself is always in progress), my reading of Olivia Frey's article, "Beyond Literary Darwinism: Women's Voices and Critical Discourse," has forced me to reflect on the new path I have chosen, for Frey's article is both comforting and troublesome. It is comforting because its presence in *College English* demonstrates the distance feminist criticism has traveled since the latter first entered literary discourse. Yet the article makes me uneasy. The progress towards legitimizing both literary criticism and pedagogical methodology that embody a female epistemology, as Joan Hartman's recent statistical study confirms, is both slow and arduous. Alternatives to masculinist criticism are at best gradually implemented. Women's narratives testify to the fact that publications, by and large, continue to be evaluated by criteria based on masculinist criticism. Frey identifies the underpinnings of this criticism as

> the use of argument as the preferred mode of discussion, the importance of the objective and impersonal, the importance of a finished product without direct reference to the process by which it was accomplished, and the necessity of being thorough in order to establish proof and reach a definitive (read 'objective') conclusion. (509)

Drawing on the research of feminist theorists, chief among them Carol Gilligan, Frey reaffirms the differences between male and female epistemologies—the male rooted in the formal and the abstract, the female in the relational and the narrative. If, indeed, literary criticism is to reflect an awareness of a female epistemology, changes must be made in the dominant position held by masculinist criticism. It is evident that an important breakthrough has already occurred in the once seemingly impenetrable position of masculinist criticism. Witness the success of women scholars and critics who have taken advantage of every crack in the door of the traditional canon to admit works by women writers. I also cite the (re)vision of texts by cultural feminist critics. They have aided not only our understanding of texts heretofore limited to interpretation by masculinist critics but also our understanding of the historical contexts in which they were written. In *Rich and Strange*, for example, Marianne De Koven reads modernist texts from a feminist perspective. The result is a reinterpretation of the texts and a better understanding of Modernism. I am, nevertheless, dismayed at the little progress towards the endorsement of literary criticism that reflects female epistemology. Masculinist criticism continues to stand like a mature individual confident of its importance, literary criticism that embodies female epistemology like a child awaiting adult approval.

Especially troublesome for me is Frey's objection to the "adversary method," which she identifies with masculinist criticism. According to Frey, women critics would benefit from diminishing (or eliminating?) the "adversary method" from literary criticism. This strategy (Is not the "adversary method" a rhetorical strategy of classical argument?) manifests itself in such terms as "misguided argument," "misunderstanding," and "confusion," terms leveled by some critics against their opponents. Frey considers such terms and their modified versions not only mean-spirited but also counterproductive for women critics. For Frey , the "adversary method" amounts to a rhetorical put down and thus is too aggressive for women critics. Presumably, her vision of the ideal is kinder and gentler. Frey would prefer that women critics in contrast to their male counterparts speak in a more benign voice.

Frey's position troubles me because it threatens to raise an argument I thought had long been laid to rest. I have in mind the specious argument associating men with reason and women with feeling. In a recent article, "Cartesian Reason and Gendered Reason," Margaret Atherton reinforces the fallacy of these binary distinctions. There are different kinds of reason, but the capacity to reason is gender neutral. The "adversary method" to which Frey objects is a rhetorical strategy derived from the scientific method aimed at proving or at least advancing a hypothesis. Diminishing its role in literary criticism, I fear, would create a slippery slope for women critics by reviving the debate over women's capacity to reason. Would Frey deny women critics use of the "adversary method"—albeit aggressive—where its use would be effective in achieving a goal? Proof of women critics and scholars using the "adversary method" successfully abounds. I have in mind the work of Annette Kolodny, Elaine Showalter, Sandra Gilbert, and Susan Gubar among others. Their adversarial stance has contributed significantly to acknowledging the contributions of women writers. More recently, I remember cheering Patrocinio Schweickart as I read her essay, "Reading Ourselves: Toward a Feminist Theory of Reading." Assuming an adversarial stance, she challenges the advocates of reader-response theory to address the effects of gender on reading. Indeed, the use of the "adversary method" has helped advance the cause of women in the past and will assuredly be needed in future literary discourse. By including the "adversary method" in the trailings women critics hope to expunge from literary criticism, I fear the loss of precious ore.

Like some of my colleagues committed to changing literary criticism, I have occasionally been torn between masculinist and feminist criticism as if afloat between Scylla and Charybdis. The reason, I believe, is that each methodology by itself imposes constraints. As a reader I approach a text with expectations that it speak to my humanity. I am cerebral; I am also emotional. I am capable of textual analysis, but I also wish to interact personally with a text. I can judge a text; I can withhold judgment of a text and be satisfied enjoying its world. It is evident that masculinist criticism alone, which tends to control texts by analysis, cannot satisfy these expectations; nor can feminist criticism that excludes my arguing from an adversarial position if I deem it necessary. Neither is sufficiently inclusive to encompass the possibilities of reading and interpretation. After reading Frey's article, I found that questions had forced their way into my consciousness begging for answers: Would a plurality of critical paradigms allow me to work efficiently with texts? Would these paradigms open space in which I could move towards a better understanding of a text, its author, and myself? As a teacher I have already experienced the success of paradigms that are inclusive and flexible. Would the same hold true in my work as a critic?

With these nagging questions in mind I turned again to Virginia Woolf, who in the past has guided me through the shoals of uncertainty. Specifically, I picked up her first collection of critical essays, *The Common Reader* (1925), knowing that these essays comprised a challenge to the patriarchal criticism of her day. As I did, the thought struck me that women critics who desire to change the face of literary criticism share a common goal with Woolf. Like them Woolf learned the writing skills necessary for a woman to succeed in a male dominated profession. Readers of Woolf's diaries will recall the discipline and intensity with which she dedicated herself to becoming a professional writer. After her Aunt Caroline Stephen died, leaving her the financial means to pursue a literary career, Woolf studied the conventional rules of journalism. Her goal was to become a literary critic. As an apprentice she experienced the anxiety of meeting publication deadlines; she acquiesced to editors' demands for revision and journalistic tact. From 1904–1915, she contributed her work first to the *Guardian*, thereafter to *Cornhill, The Times*, and the *Times Literary Supplement*. A woman writer under the tutelage of male editors, Woolf observed the conventions of male authorship. As her views increasingly diverged from her editors', however, she became irritated by the constraints of the conventions she was forced to observe. Gradually, as trust in her own insights increased, she departed from the strict observance of them. However, she did not completely abandon them; she simply learned to use them to advance her own views in a voice uniquely her own. She was, in short, an astute strategist.

Encouraged by the similarities between Woolf's early experience as critic and that of women critics today, I was eager to renew my acquaintance with the essays in *The Common Reader*. I first read them as a graduate student under the influence of masculinist criticism. What remains of my earlier reading is the critical view that Woolf's essays illustrate impressionistic criticism. At the time, the latter, because it admitted the critic's personal opinions into criticism, was considered a poor cousin of the New Criticism with its claim to objectivity. Now I shall read them through feminist lens, knowing their author speaks as a feminist on literary and social issues. Indeed, I shall read them as if strolling through a neighborhood, observing a portico here, a garden there. (Imagine it Bloomsbury if you like.)

In the first essay, which serves as an introduction to the volume, Woolf borrows from Samuel Johnson's "Life of Gray," an idea amenable to the critical voice she will demonstrate throughout the essays: "I rejoice to concur with the common reader; for by the common sense of readers, uncorrupted by literary prejudice, after all the refinements of subtlety and dogmatism of learning, must be finally decided all claims to poetical honours" (1). For Woolf, Edwardian criticism was informed by a set of standards so narrow that it favored an exclusive readership. It had become a form of literary discourse that excluded general readers. The naiveté of my earlier reading strikes me like a thunderbolt. What formerly evaded me now appears obvious. Her goal is to free criticism from specialization and position it within a context of general understanding (Johnson's "common sense of readers"). Woolf is committing herself to veer away from Edwardian criticism. Despite the changes in the language of literary criticism since Johnson's and Woolf's day, is my goal not similar to theirs? When I speak of creating a context for literary criticism that includes both masculinist and feminist epistemologies, am I not, in effect, acknowledging a common reader, one who is privileged neither by gender nor by a particular perspective, but rather embraces the perspectives of both genders? Do not the dominant tenets of masculinist criticism echo Johnson's "literary prejudices," to which both Johnson and Woolf objected?

Because I teach a course in the novel, I am naturally drawn to Woolf's essay, "Modern Fiction." Here I note a bold use of argument. In a manner resembling the "adversary method" she clears the ground in order to pitch her tent:

> [I]f we speak of quarreling with Mr. Wells, Mr. Bennett, and Mr. Galsworthy it is partly that by the mere fact of their existence in the flesh their work has a living, breathing, every-day imperfection which bids us to take what liberties with it we choose. . . . [They] have excited so many hopes and disappointed them so persistently that our gratitude largely takes the form of thanking them for having shown us what they might have done but have not done; what we certainly could not do, but as certainly, perhaps, do not wish to do [sic]. (151)

Her thesis: the novelists in question are "materialists" concerned with the societal lives of their characters to the neglect of exploring "life itself." For Woolf "life itself" means the inner (read psychological) life. The failure to explore the characters' inner lives reduces the authors to second rank novelists. If I peel away the Edwardian gentility from Woolf's language, the caustic tone of the attack surfaces—a tone, I observe, as caustic as that found in some masculinist criticism today.

Thereafter, Woolf marshals her evidence to prove her claim. Bennett is "the worst culprit of the three inasmuch as he is the best craftsman" (152). Because his is the greatest talent, he should write to higher standards. But in *The Old Wives Tale* the reader witnesses only exterior reality; the characters' motives are ignored. Neither Galsworthy nor Wells fair better under Woolf's critical eye. Their characters are superficial. She accuses the novelists of erecting barriers that exclude readers from understanding their characters' inner lives. Authoritative assertions, empirical evidence, induction—all common in argument—abound here. Nor is Woolf above ridicule when she wishes to drive home a point. In the midst of presenting her evidence, she pauses to imagine herself dropping a novel, no doubt authored by one of the novelists under attack, and asking the question: "Is it worthwhile? What is the point of it all?" (153). No Edwardian gentility here. Evident is Woolf's use of a heavy mallet of argument when it serves her purpose.

So adept is Woolf at writing argument that she uses it to challenge the patriarchal authority she hopes to dislodge from literary criticism. At my next stop, the essay entitled " Addison," she condemns Macaulay's view of Addison, objecting to the pomposity with which Macaulay rings his authority as critic. Allowing Macaulay his due as an eminent stylist, she nevertheless opposes his view that Addison's portraits rank slightly below Shakespeare's or Cervantes's. She objects to readers relying on past (read patriarchal) critical opinion; instead, from the premise that each generation must weigh the relevance of a writer's oeuvre, she encourages readers to study the original works and draw their own conclusions. Hence, along with Macaulay's reading of Addison, Thackeray's, Johnson's, and Pope's are dismissed. Having deflated past critical opinions of Addison, Woolf guides her readers through his essays. Addison's style, good taste and civility, respect for language, a voice both natural and subtle—these Woolf suggests have relevance for contemporary readers. (I pause to note that Frey would approve of Woolf's gentle nudge here, which has replaced the authoritative shove of the earlier essay.)

So much for my uneasiness over the "adversary method." Woolf assures me of its position in literary criticism. But am I not also questioning the privileged position argument holds in literary criticism? What about the inclusive paradigms I envision? To ease my anxiety, I need evidence of Woolf's break with patriarchal criticism. I am not disappointed, for I am soon to realize that changes exist throughout the essays like confetti scattered on a walkway. In "How It Strikes a Contemporary," an essay concerned with the questionable merit of contemporary writing in contrast to the proven merit of classical works, she enters the battle of the books, weighing both sides of the debate in a voice that strikes me as both reflective and ambivalent. Only in the closing paragraphs does she express hope for her contemporaries. She appears willing to give them more time to prove their worth. Nevertheless, the essay ends without clear resolution. Woolf here admits her uncertainty. Absent is the closure so characteristic of an authoritative voice. In "The Pastons and Chaucer" she frames her reading of Chaucer within an imaginative rendition of the Pastons' lives based on a recent publication of *The Paston Letters*. Individuals become indistinguishable from fictional characters as she narrates events in the lives of generations of Pastons.

By now evidence of Woolf's break with patriarchal criticism rushes at me with every turn. Essays reveal distinct imprints of her personality. The essay "Jane Austen" illustrates this point. The early paragraphs signal a mode of discourse different from conventional discourse. Woolf opens with biographical details from Austen's life, thus setting the stage for a discussion of the author's literary reputation and her novel, *The Watsons*. In addition to textual analysis, Woolf balances conflicting views of Austen, creates fictional scenes of Austen's life as she imagines them, makes observations about Austen's writing habits, and freely comments on her own experience as a novelist. Interspersed throughout the essay are Woolf's critical comments about Austen's achievements and her weaknesses as a novelist. In the end, she speculates about the author's future had she not died at the age of forty-two. In contrast to the exclusiveness of argument, Woolf's essay is eclectic and generous in its display of rhetorical techniques; moreover, the essay is couched in a metaphoric but unobtrusive style. My attention remains riveted on Austen even though I view her through the eyes of a highly creative mind.

In a vivid display of creative criticism, Woolf goes so far as to blur the distinction between fiction and nonfiction. The essay "The Lives of the Obscure," a critique of three memoirs entitled "The Taylors and the Edgeworths," "The Memoirs of Mrs. Pilkington," and "Miss Ormerod," opens with Woolf setting a scene as she might if she were writing fiction. In an old library she requests from the librarian three volumes that have been gathering dust on a shelf. With these few details Woolf establishes the lack of readers' interest in the memoir. Thereafter, she reconstructs the memoirs in the form of a dramatic narrative, intending, I presume, to illustrate how memoirs should be understood. I am soon lulled by her description of eighteenth-century landscapes, the confessions of individual writers, the identification of external forces shaping their lives until in an unexpected moment of self-consciousness, she interrupts the narrative and discloses her manipulation of the text: "It is so difficult to keep . . . strictly to the facts. It is so difficult to refrain from making scenes which, if the past could be recalled, might be found lacking in accuracy" (116). What an unexpected discovery as I wander through this essay. She leaps across the ages and speaks as if an advocate of postmodernism. Without abandoning a critical voice she acknowledges the overlapping of genres. She admits to the blurring of facts by choosing this mode of discourse. Her justification lies in the acknowledgement that absolute recall of the past is unlikely, perhaps impossible. The past is re-created by the circumstances of the present. The only surety is the present.

As a feminist critic I am aware of another achievement here; this essay is a satire of the eighteenth century, especially as its social customs impacted on women's lives. Hedged in by her husband's demands, Mrs. Edgeworth's life is burdensome; any attempt at personal development outside her domestic role is stifled. Laetitia Pilkington, an aspiring young writer influenced by Swift, is forced to sacrifice her talent in order to write for money because she is a woman without other means of income. When she can no longer write, her income dwindles until she ends up in debtors' prison. So much for a woman's promising talent. And Miss Ormerod, although skilled enough to pursue a career as an entomologist, must settle for watching grubs in a tumbler and collecting beetles. Not even her eventual reputation as a renowned entomologist later in life mitigates her tragedy, for we witness the price in unfulfilled human desire such success costs her. Woolf's critique demonstrates the value of the memoir insofar as it reveals the past through its effect on individual lives. But she also seizes the opportunity to attack the suppression of women. Her use of fiction to portray individuals heightens their reality and emphasizes the degree to which women were suppressed in eighteenth-century society. I am reminded of Jane Marcus's observation that Woolf's literary criticism and her social politics were inseparable (10). By embedding her objections to the eighteenth-century treatment of women in the narrative, Woolf keeps an audience she might otherwise have lost had she expressed her opinions bluntly in the abstract. As a whole, the essay demonstrates Woolf's virtuosity as a critic.

At this point I pause, overwhelmed by Woolf's genius at combining argument and personal observations, the former sustained by a thesis and textual evidence, the latter by insight grounded in intelligence. That she refused to embrace argument unequivocally is evident, but neither did she avoid it. Moreover, neither argument nor personal observation impeded her innovation. How perceptive the remarks of Hugh l'Anson Fausset, who reviewed *The Common Reader* in *The Manchester Guardian*: "Brilliance combined with integrity; profound as well as eccentric" (qtd. in Woolf, *Diary*, 3:18, n. 14). Her example ensures me that I need not renounce my training in masculinist criticism and begin at zero. The latter can serve me well if I supply what it lacks, erase its errors, and reduce its excesses. Woolf also empowers me with the freedom to select those paradigms that eventuate the literary criticism I envision.

Coming upon the "Modern Essay," Woolf's review of Ernest Rhys's edition of *Modern English Essays*, I am riveted by her comments about the use of the singular form of the first-person pronoun. Can she help me in my efforts to valorize its use in literary criticism? To begin with, Woolf holds the presence of the writer's personality in high regard. In its ideal form the relation between the essayist and the person is indistinguishable. Max Beerbohm, whose essays for Woolf illustrate the ideal, combines the skills of an eminent essayist and personal integrity. Specifically, Beerbohm's ideas embody the spirit of the age. For Woolf, however, personality must not distract from the idea by calling undue attention to itself. Hence the challenge: "Never to be yourself and yet always—that is the problem" (*Common Reader* 222). Woolf emphasizes the importance of good writing for the essayist. In fact, achievement of the ideal amounts to "a triumph of style." Although her focus is the personal essay and mine literary criticism, Woolf leads me to a discovery I now see as crucial for the next stage of literary criticism. While I want others to respect my right to express my personal relation to a text, I in turn must weigh my experience, sifting the important from the unimportant. I must judge the value of my experience for the reader if I hope to move criticism beyond expressionism. Moreover, I must commit myself to honing my craft. In short, Woolf forces me to see that the drive to valorize the "I" carries with it responsibility. Indeed, wisdom emerges from this passage like a morning mist rising above a pond hidden behind trees.

Sobered by her cautionary advice, I continue in the essay until I come upon a sympathetic Woolf, who acknowledges the dilemma facing the essayist. One who discusses art, music, and literature, must choose between the "I" and the inclusive "we." One must choose between personal insight and consensus, for they are often at odds. If one chooses the former, there is the risk of losing public favor, for readers can grow suspicious of the veracity of the singular form. If one chooses the latter with the hope of retaining public favor, the decline to generalities is inevitable. The essayist's surrender of writing from personal insight, the personal pronoun "I," unfortunately has dire consequences for the essayist and the readers. As the essayist adopts the inclusive "we," her/his insights fall deeper and deeper into the unconscious until to share them even in "a diluted form" becomes "sheer agony." What a price the essayist pays for public acceptance. The essayist's neglect of self-revelation marks a serious loss for readers as well, for the essay then flattens to superficiality. Under these conditions both the essayist and the reader are losers. Woolf's thinking here resonates in my own. The gap between the years is easily bridged. It is convention that keeps me from advancing the boundaries of literary criticism. She reassures me of the need to valorize the singular form of the first-person in criticism. Its presence signals a reading that has been internalized in an effort to expand the notion of what is possible. I leave the essay convinced that the critic who shares the fruits of connecting the self and the text is contributing something of immeasurable value to readers.

Throughout my reading of *The Common Reader* I have been captivated by the provocative nature of Woolf's insights and opinions. (I use provocative here in its etymological sense, i. e., challenging and calling forth.) Woolf has awakened in me an awareness of possibilities lying dormant. When, for example, she charges Wells, Bennett, and Galsworthy with having ignored "life itself" in their novels, she raises the question, "What is 'life itself'?" Although I do not agree with equating the inner life (read psychological life) exclusively with "life itself," her position causes me to reexamine my own views on the subject and to reconsider a novelist's role in the development of the inner life of characters. Nor does Woolf shrink from her position when it is unpopular among other critics. She not only trusted her opinions but had the courage to express them. Her essay "Joseph Conrad" places her in a minority among literary critics, for at the time most critics considered Conrad a novelist of minor stature. Woolf, however, sees in Conrad a master of sea tales and character portrayal. For her Conrad excels in depicting noble human attributes against a foreboding background of nature. His exploration of the inner life of his characters earned him Woolf's approval. Although she acknowledges a decline in his power in the later novels where he replaces nature with society as an adversary, she clings to her view that Conrad's early novels will eventually secure a niche for him among the finest English novelists. As her diary and letters of the period testify, Woolf trusted her views, seeing them through disappointments to publication.

Before leaving Woolf's essays I am eager to identify the underlying principles that may prove helpful for a revision of literary criticism. Two strike me as important: 1) that literary criticism and creativity not be treated as separate genres and 2) that the critical voice be independent. Regarding the first, Woolf favored several paradigms instead of the single paradigm of argument. The eclecticism of the essays in *The Common Reader* is apparent in the presence of narrative, parody, and satire in tandem with exposition. Argument and textual analysis share the page with personal opinion. These are couched in a unique style secure in its use of metaphor and the singular form of the first-person pronoun. In her hands empiricism relinquishes its elite position and assumes an egalitarian one with opinion and insight. With ease the impersonal yields to the personal, objectivity to subjectivity. Nonfiction merges with fiction. Throughout *The Common Reader*, I recognize Woolf empowering the critic to employ those techniques necessary to express her views of a subject. Like an artist holding a palette arrayed with colors, Woolf chooses one technique, then another, whichever will best make a point or clarify a text. In effect, she has given me a glimpse of literary criticism with a human face, a personality, a life beyond masculinist criticism.

John Mepham has made Woolf's innovation throughout her fiction the thesis of his recent study, *Virginia Woolf: A Literary Life*. No two novels, he demonstrates, use identical techniques. Woolf believed there were two forces operating in life—one driving to order, harmony, and unity; the other to disorder and fragmentation. Her experimentation with voice and structure throughout the novels, Mepham argues, is an attempt to convey these forces through the imagination. Noteworthy for women critics is Woolf's innovation in literary criticism, by which she charts a map of new possibilities for critics. Not only her fiction but also her criticism bears the stamp of the creative imagination.

Regarding the second principle, that the critical voice be independent, Woolf understood that a genre, whether it be the novel or literary criticism, changes as societies change. Literary criticism is not a fixed genre; it develops historically in relation to the ideological interests of critics and their readers. This awareness helped her break with her contemporaries in favor of an independent voice. In a letter to E. M. Forster, written two years after the publication of *The Common Reader*, she expresses her disagreement with the popular view of Percy Lubbock's book, *The Craft of Fiction* (1921): "No; Percy Lubbock . . . doesn't 'altogether satisfy' me. But then I don't agree with you that he's a critic of genius. An able and painstaking pedant I should call him; who doesn't know what art is; so though his method of judging novels as works of art interests me, his judgments don't" (*Letters* 3: 437). Nor will she later critique Forster's *Aspects of the Novel* (1927) kindly because of their longstanding friendship. Trusting her own insights as a novelist over Forster's theory, she states that it may be "better than anything I could ever write . . . only it doesn't light up my own particular boggle" (*Letters* 3:439). Woolf's experience as novelist, her keen power of discernment, and the intellectual acumen she acquired through continuous study enabled her to speak in an independent voice. Her criticism moves beyond imitation of the dominant form. She illustrates how a critic can respond to a text intuitively and subjectively without sacrificing credibility if she be allowed to do so. Her example has convinced me that holding fast to one's ideas despite skepticism or fear of failure is necessary to preserving one's professional integrity.

Having concluded my reading of *The Common Reader* (my stroll through Bloomsbury), I am reassured by Woolf's example that at this point in the history of literary criticism the "adversary method" continues to have a role to play, for the struggle to legitimize the changes women critics envision is far from complete. Further, I realize that Woolf anticipated a truth we are only gradually accepting, that the boundaries between genres, like those between genders, are fluid. Refusing to compartmentalize genres, Woolf demonstrates that literary criticism, which traditionalists argue is a form of nonfiction rooted in reason and the abstract, can draw from the creative mind as much as fiction. Woolf's example assures me that the efforts of women critics to redefine the boundaries of literary criticism is worthy of pursuit, for masculinist criticism alone, with its reliance on argument and analysis, neither answers the questions raised in literary discourse today nor reflects readers' experience with texts.

Woolf's literary reputation after the publication of *The Common Reader* was not a straight arrow to success. Given her struggle with mental illness, her personal tragedies, and the rejection of her first novel, *The Voyage Out*, she could have understandably chosen an easier course in life. I sometimes, as the following creative interpretation shows, imagine Woolf weighing her options: returning to journalism, advancing Leonard's career, abandoning writing altogether, or continuing as novelist and literary critic despite the obstacles and disappointments:

> She thinks of pouring tears in jars to display
> on the mantel for speculation by curious

visitors. She hangs instead lace curtains
to catch life's flow—in and out, fans flames
into giants, pens words distilled from fruit,
essences wrung dry, hard pressed.

Woolf's decision to stay the course of her goals as novelist and critic has left women critics a rich legacy on which to build. Her example in *The Common Reader* suggests some alternatives for us as we continue our efforts to liberate literary criticism from the inertia of masculinist criticism and move it closer to a position that acknowledges equality and difference.

WORKS CITED

Atherton, Margaret. *Cartesian Reason and Gendered Reason*. Paper presented at the 1989–90 Center for Twentieth Century Studies. Working Paper No. 6, Fall–Winter 1990–91. Milwaukee: U of Wisconsin-Milwaukee [n. d.].

Frey, Olivia. "Beyond Literary Darwinism: Women's Voices and Critical Discourse." *College English* 52 (1990): 507–26.

Hartman, Joan. "The English Curriculum and Feminist Change: What's Going On?" *Concerns* 23.2 (1993): 41–51.

Marcus, Jane. *Virginia Woolf and the Language of Patriarchy*. Bloomington: Indiana UP, 1987.

Mepham, John. *Virginia Woolf: A Literary Life*. New York: St. Martin's, 1991.

Schweickart, Patrocinio P. "Reading Ourselves: Toward a Feminist Theory of Reading." *Speaking of Gender*. Ed. Elaine Showalter. New York: Routledge, 1989. 17–44.

Woolf, Virginia. *The Common Reader*. New York: Harcourt, 1925.

_____. *The Diary of Virginia Woolf*. Ed. Anne Olivier Bell. Vol. 3. New York: Harcourt, 1980.

_____. *The Letters of Virginia Woolf*. Eds. Nigel Nicolson, Joanne Trautmann. Vol. 3. New York: Harcourt, 1977.

CONTRIBUTOR BIOGRAPHIES

LYNN Z. BLOOM is a Professor of English and Aetna Chair of Writing at The University of Connecticut, Storrs. Her recent books include *Fact and Artifact: Writing Nonfiction* (2nd ed., Blair P, 1994) and the forthcoming *Our Stories, Our Selves: Reading, Researching, Writing Autobiography* (Prentice Hall Studies in Writing and Culture), both written amidst other intense commitments of time, energy, and love: marriage, friendships, teaching, cooking, swimming, traveling—and, hopefully by publication date, grandparenting.

BONNIE BRAENDLIN: I have been a feminist critic for about as long as I've been a mother, and the two roles have intermingled and interacted in my reading, writing, teaching, and child-rearing activities. When my daughter Nikki was born in 1972, I was a left-over-from-the-sixties radical and a soon-to-become-in-the-seventies feminist. As my consciousness began to be raised about gender issues, I found myself trying to raise a daughter during an era when old ideologies were clashing with new, and as a daughter-mother, I felt caught in the middle. I knew I was supposed to initiate my daughter into womanhood, as my culture defined it, and as my own mother—a middle-class, middle-west wife-mother—had (only somewhat successfully) taught me to be. But I also wanted my daughter to be a New Woman, making her own choices and defining herself in new ways.

In my early scholarly writing on the women's liberation novels (*Bildungsromane*), I tended to side with the daughters, paying little attention to the muffled voices of the mothers or the absence thereof in the daughter's maturation stories. Now that I am a mother of a twenty-one-year-old and a grandmother by my older stepdaughter's adoption of two boys, I clearly hear and heed the calls of mother-characters to be recognized and given their voice. My "calling" from now is to call forth the mothers and encourage them to speak.

CAROL S. CHADWICK: Learning to read was one of the most important things that ever happened to me. Once I started, I never stopped. It was magic. I was dazzled with the way that those little black symbols on a page could take a person on fantastic journeys in time and space. They could make a person be someone else with a different life in a different world. I became intrigued to know what conjuring went on between the page and the eye and this fascination led me to what has become my life's work. Today I hold a Ph.D. in Reading; my research was in the linguistics of reading and its cognitive processes.

Born and raised in Detroit, all of my schooling was acquired close to home. In 1964, when I earned my undergraduate degrees in Liberal Arts, English and Chemistry from Wayne State University, there were few career options open to women: nursing, factory or office work, teaching or marriage. Because of my love of reading, teaching seemed a logical choice, so I returned to Wayne State to earn a Michigan permanent secondary teaching certificate and then in 1971, an M.A. in American Literature. All through my teaching career and during a period when I was the director of a private research foundation, I was fascinated with the way the brain worked in perceiving and processing information, especially during the act of reading. In 1976, I received certification in the State of Michigan as a Reading Specialist and the equivalent of an M.A. in Reading. Finally, in 1992, I completed a Ph.D. Since 1972, I have been a full-time instructor of developmental reading and composition at Wayne County Community College in Detroit's inner city.

Today I live alone, although I have lived for extended periods with men, one who died and one from whom I separated. I never had any children but there is usually someone staying with me in some period of transition or another, in my sprawling home in suburban Detroit. My mainstays are my two Siamese cats, Verdi and Pucinni. Strolls through my gardens in summer or blazing fires in the winter are my sources of tranquility. My books and my friends are my treasures. It is doubtful that this paradise would be mine were it not for them.

BEVERLY CONNER teaches creative writing, composition, and literature at The University of Puget Sound in Tacoma, Washington, where she lives with her husband of thirty-seven years. Conner has also served as a faculty writing advisor in The Center for Writing and Learning. Her most recent essay, "Voices from the Writing Center—Storytelling in the Writing Center," appears in *Colors of a Different Horse: Rethinking Creative Writing, Theory and Pedagogy*, edited by Wendy Bishop and Hans Ostrom and published in 1994 by the National Council of Teachers of English.

Conner's alter ego, the fiction writer, works at a word processor in the guest room, imagining it an unheated garret which has a certain cachet in creative circles. She has published poetry and short stories. She expects surprise and hopes for celebration.

BARBARA DiBERNARD was trained as a James Joyce scholar at SUNY-Binghamton and was hired at the University of Nebraska as a "Modern British Fiction" specialist. Tillie Olsen received an honorary degree from Nebraska the year after I began teaching there. In preparation for meeting Olsen, I read *Silences*, and in it found a sentence which would change my life and my teaching forever: "You who teach, read women writers." My education had included very few women writers and it had never occurred to me that I had been missing something. Olsen's words started me on a journey which began with a resolution to make writing by women at least half of the material in any course I taught, and led to a complete change in my teaching and research interests. I now teach women's literature courses and am currently director of the Women's Studies Program at Nebraska.

Reading and teaching Audre Lorde has added another dimension to my teaching and writing. For a time after I "discovered" women writers, I did not write myself. I knew I couldn't continue to write the kinds of articles I had written before, but I did not know any other way to write. Audre Lorde's words about breaking silence helped me find my topics and the courage to write and speak of myself in ways which erased the distinction between public and private.

I am grateful to both of these women, as well as the many other women who have had the insight and courage to break through academic rigidities and write and speak as they needed to.

Currently I am interested in women's autobiographical writings, writing by women with disabilities, lesbian literature, and feminist pedagogy.

ANN FISHER-WIRTH: Though I grew up first all over the world (my father was in the Army) and then in Berkeley, California, I now live in Oxford, Mississippi, having moved here in 1988. I am an Associate Professor of English at the University of Mississippi, where I teach women writers, gender studies, and American literature, especially poetry. In 1989 I published *William Carlos Williams and Autobiography: The Woods of His Own Nature*. I have also published essays on Williams, Louise Glück, Linda Gregg, and Willa Cather. These days I am working on finishing a book, *Parables of Loss: Woman's Body and Desire in the Novels of Willa Cather*. I also write poetry—my first love as a writer—and have published poems in several journals and little magazines.

I am married to Peter Wirth. Between us we have five children, aged ten to twenty.

BETTY S. FLOWERS: There have always been at least two voices within me—the critical voice that writes articles (on Barthelme, Rich, Rosetti and others) and critical books (*Browning and the Modern Tradition* and *Fathers and Daughters* [edited with Lynda Boose]), and the poetic voice (latest poetry book—*Extending the Shade*). It was the poet in me who became interested in reading Jung while writing my dissertation for the University of London. That interest led me to explore "story" as the technology that shapes our view of reality, which in turn led me down many interesting paths, including serving as consultant for the six-part PBS series "Joseph Campbell and the Power of Myth" with Bill Moyers. I edited the accompanying book as well as two other books in collaboration with Moyers: *A World of Ideas* and *Healing and the Mind*. Recently I've taken this interest in story into corporations, for example, helping to write Global Scenarios—the future of the world for the next thirty years—for Shell International in London.

This interest in story has led me to explore radio and TV as storytellers. I host a radio show—"The Next Two Hundred Years"—and am involved in a number of public television projects and forums on the future of technology. These excursions into media and corporate planning as well as my experiences as Associate Dean of Graduate Studies, Director of Plan II (the interdisciplinary honors degree program at the University of Texas, where I am a Professor of English), and co-moderator of Executive Seminars at the Aspen Institute for Humanistic Studies have led me to see the need for institutions to re-examine the stories on which they were founded—and the stories of who they are that sustain them now.

I'm currently working on an edition of Christina Rosetti's poetry and a PBS documentary on American pluralism, and am editing or co-writing four books associated with the power of story: *Predictable Miracles: The Inner Dimensions of Leadership*; *Re-Inventing the Executive*; *Mother Market*; and *Healing Nightmares: the Dreams of Vietnam Veterans*.

MELODY GRAULICH: I grew up next door to and much in the care of my grandmother, Mae Wilkerson, whose second baby, Keith, had died before my mother was born. I remember that his name still brought tears to her eyes thirty years later. My first venture in autobiographical literary criticism, "Somebody Must Say These Things," was about my mother and my grandmother, about daughters telling stories about watching their mothers being battered. I didn't realize until I wrote "Sharing Sorrow" that I was once more in search of my grandmother's story.

LOIS HASSAN: After several years as a "Learning Specialist," a private tutor, and a first grade teacher, I had an opportunity to become a Development Reading Instructor at Henry Ford Community College.

It was here that I found an opportunity to develop my writing skills and open a new vista, "the world of writing." The challenge of teaching writing to college freshmen required a special Masters degree in Written Communication.

While fulfilling my degree requirements, I also began to renew my love of writing. As part of the English Department, I often assist my colleagues in writing proposals, classroom materials, and policy statements.

Writing this essay, "Trapped—Then Released—by a *Gift from the Sea*," allowed me to mingle both my love of writing and my professional work. It is my hope that this candid essay may help others facing the same trials as I by providing insightful answers found in Lindbergh's *Gift from the Sea*.

JULIE HOUSTON: I am a graduate of Beaver College, and hold an M.A. from The Johns Hopkins University Writing Seminars, where my mentor was John Barth. I have published fiction, poetry, and scientific, travel and sports articles since 1972. I traveled six years as a journalist with the Women's Tennis Tour. Presently Associate Professor at Northampton Community College, I am also Director of the Lehigh University Writing Institute, a program I created to bring writers of international importance to an area in which there were no writing programs. I have also traveled, including gaining permission to enter the Lascoux Caves, for a forthcoming novel and scholarly writing concerning the writing relationships of several women authors. My own writing voice is simultaneously my most public and private voice: it is the most intimate, profound way I know to express myself. It is the juncture of being individually me and universally life turning back to observe itself.

OLGA KLEKNER is a bilingual poet and student of psychology at the University of Michigan, Dearborn. She has published her writings in Hungarian in the United States, and a collection of her poems appeared in the Canadian anthology, *Living Free*. In 1974, at the age of twenty-two, she was the youngest recipient of an honorary diploma for poetry of the worldwide Hungarian organization, the *Arpad Academy*.

Only four years ago did she start writing in English. Six months later she won her first recognition and since then she has won several creative writing awards and journalism scholarships. In June, 1994, she was invited to read her essay, "Hypnotized By a Reptile: A Student's Account of How the East Was Won by a Giant's Dusty Roar," at the Dakota History Conference in Sioux Falls, South Dakota. That essay is being considered to appear in an anthology titled *The Lizard Speaks*.

After relentless nagging from her friends and her husband of twenty-one years—a saint, really—she is planning on collecting her English poetry for publication. In public, she is known as a poet. In private, she knows that she can't help it.

CATHERINE E. LAMB: One of the things I like best about the profession of college teaching is that, much of the time, one's life can be a seamless whole. The longer I teach and write and live, the more important it is to me that there be an organic unity between how and what I teach and write, my interactions with others, and my sense of self. The recent experience of my divorce has only intensified these convictions. My interest in alternatives to confrontational arguments has, more than anything, led to my wanting to make these connections. Learning new ways of being in conflict has encouraged me to teach writing differently, also to envision authority in broader ways. I see now that I can expect more in my relationships with students as well as with family and friends.

SUSAN NARAMORE MAHER, Assistant Professor of English, teaches Women's Studies, environmental literature, and composition at the University of Nebraska at Omaha. Her research interests in western American literature and children's literature grew out of her move to Nebraska in 1983 and the births of her two children, Dana Craig (now ten) and Anna-Turi (now six). Her joint affiliations with Women's Studies and Environmental Studies have encouraged her experimentation with personal, familiar essays. She feels most fortunate to teach in a supportive department, to live with two such hearty children, to voice her joys and sorrows to invaluable friends, and to have shared her writing and inner life with a dear, poetic Nebraskan, Al Kammerer.

ELSIE F. MAYER is an independent scholar, lecturer, and poet. She has taught language and literature at Wayne State University and Henry Ford Community College. Long an advocate of establishing the contributions of women writers to American letters, she has lectured and published articles on the subject. Her writing and poetry have appeared in such publications as *America, The Explicator, The CEA Critic, The Keats-Shelley Journal* and *Peninsula Poets*. Subsequent to receiving an NEH grant to study literary biography, she published *My Window on the World* (Archon 1988), the first critical study of the works of Anne Morrow Lindbergh. Believing that over-reliance on empiricism in traditional literary criticism has dehumanized it and alienated students, she has been encouraged by postmodern criticism that legitimizes the reader's personal insights and interests without discrediting empiricism. This approach, because it is holistic, offers hope for the future of literary studies. Empowered by women scholars in their efforts to connect literary criticism and life, she strives for this connection in her own critical voice.

CHARLOTTE S. McCLURE: In a 1960s essay, philosopher Susan K. Langer gave me an image—a web of ideas—to express the way we as human beings imagine our world; we produce images and figments of all sorts that serve as symbols for ideas about ourselves and our world. This "fabric of our own making" results from the self-knowledge and experience, intellectual and affective, that each of us gathers over the span of our lives. Jane Tompkins laments the linear gathering in the literary critical web—from New Criticism to Deconstruction to New Historicism—that emphasizes the intellectual over the affective, the impersonal over the personal, the either/or warp that divides the world. With the image of a fabric, I like to imagine an affective woof that weaves an interaction of the intellectual and the affective that comprise our way of learning about ourselves and the world.

Now, near the turn of the century, retired from the academic world, I look back and marvel at the pioneering fabrics woven by Gertrude Atherton, Mary Austin, and Kate Chopin, among other writers at the beginning of this century. Individuals today, desiring a more complete fabric of living, can count on more social, political, and psychological support than those early writers had, although the weaver cannot afford to be complacent, for the pattern on the basic warp and woof has to be invented over and over. My retirement pattern is one of paying back to the community that supported my years of Loving Work. I am teaching and taking courses in the Senior University of Greater Atlanta; I am working on the memoirs of my husband—the commanding officer of his World War II Fighter Group, who having lost his life thirty-five years ago cannot record his contribution to combat flying—and of a pioneer woman pilot, who flew all kinds of military planes from factory to airbases for the men to fly in combat. I am also working on a national program that promotes educational equity for girls and young women in the classrooms of the public schools. Weaving never ends.

NANCY OWEN NELSON. Compelled by the voices of Western American literary figures, especially writers Frederick Manfred and Wallace Stegner, Nelson changed her academic direction from the study of eighteenth century novelist Tobias Smollett (her Ph.D. dissertation topic at Auburn University) to the study of American fiction. Her research has resulted in her coediting, with Arthur R. Huseboe, *The Selected Letters of*

Frederick Manfred, 1932–1954 and in numerous other articles, reviews and lectures on American culture and literature. The androgyny issues in her essay arose largely as a result of her reading and study of the more intuitive and land-connected writings about the American West. Editing this volume of women's critical essays in personal voice has reinforced Nelson's belief in the importance of the intuitive process in all aspects of her life—personal and public.

NANCY PAGH is a Ph.D. candidate in Interdisciplinary Studies at the University of British Columbia in Vancouver. I am combining the fields of English, geography, history, and women's studies to write a dissertation on women boating the "Inside Passage"—work which has grown from my experiences boating with my family. As a graduate student, I am particularly interested in the potential of wedding personal reflection and introspection with academic discourse. I believe that my struggles to weave together my "personal" and "professional" voices have resulted in my most satisfying and intellectually valuable work as a student—although it has not always been perceived in that light by professors. Too often, students' "real" thoughts and contributions continue to be elided from legitimate classroom discourse, both written and oral. I have published in the genres of criticism (*Mosaic* and *ISLE: Interdisciplinary Studies in Literature and the Environment*), poetry (*Room of One's Own* and *Poetry Northwest*), and children's education (*Alaska Fish & Game*), discovering new combinations of my public and private voices as I go.

SANDRA PARKER: Trained by New Critical scholars during the 1960s, I automatically assumed their masculine stance. As Gloria Steinem once commented, to be told that you write like a man was meant as a compliment. For example, my dissertation on Charles Dickens was judged as successful because I had shown that I could generate third-person discourse in which "I" remained hidden behind the assumed identity of a neutered commentator who weighs, measures, sorts and analyzes. Though as a budding feminist I recognized that this was never a complete identity, the academic mode of discourse was my tool of choice for over a decade; it provided a flattering, safe public role by generating the dishonest corollary that one's personal experiences, emotions, and attitudes were, after all, irrelevant.

But relevance was always what college scholarship was about for me. The more I read women writers, especially their regional letters, diaries, essays and fiction, the more I rethought the means for expressing my critical voice. Never underrating the cleverness of the sophisticated "I" in Virginia Woolf, or undervaluing the naive forth-rightness of frontier settlers, I struggled for a way to respond in kind to their candor. I do not believe that it is easier to write in the female mode or to use the personal voice in discussing literature. Nor do I believe that theoretical feminist scholarship has made this departure neces-sary. Indeed, the personal critical mode is harder to write because, in my case, the shift into this discourse goes against many years of tradi-tional training and secondly, because as Oscar Wilde warns, nothing is so distrusted as the pose of honesty. In the end, the relationship be-tween the personal and public voice has diminished considerably in my writing. Today I practice what I preach—one's autobiographical observations should frame and condition insights, rendering useful perspectives, and in this "mellow" sense, the personal voice becomes the only viable form of literary criticism left open to the mature scholar.

MICHELE POTTER: Born in South Dakota, I live with my husband and kids in New Jersey, but we hope to follow Horace Greeley's advice again soon. They're now packing for a reunion with my husband's relatives in Dakota. We all seem to have the same roots—or at least branches.

My present work is to rewrite my novel. My son reminded me that it took so long to write because I had to take care of all of them. I appreciated that but he forgot to mention that I taught and got my M.A. as well. After that I washed my kitchen floor a lot, trying to wash away domestic guilt. I try to follow something Gary Snyder said: "I for one will keep working for wildness by day." That might mean writing or it might mean walking my kids to the Rockaway River to throw sticks. I sustain myself by reading, writing, and running. I run a mara-thon a year, then rest on my laurels. I'm grateful that my boys (ages three, six, and nine) are at home on skis, bikes and skates. Like me, they become cranky if left indoors too long. I quote my grandmother: "I'm just an outdoor girl."

ANN L. PUTNAM lives in Seattle, Washington, and teaches Creative Writing, Women's Studies and American literature at the University of Puget Sound in Tacoma, Washington, sixty-three miles south. It is on that stretch of road between home and work that she often can be found sitting in rush hour traffic, putting down an idea or turn of phrase on whatever scrap of paper she can grab, which has included from time to time her car registration, paycheck, and jury duty summons. She has published both fiction and scholarly works, and is three-quarters of the way through her first novel. Her three children, one husband, two dogs, and plants too many to count, appear in her fiction from time to time under various assumed names.

ANN ROMINES teaches graduate and undergraduate courses in nine-teenth- and twentieth-century U. S. writing and U. S. women's writing and culture in the Departments of English and Women's Studies at George Washington University. She has published many essays about U. S. women writers and a book, *The Home Plot: Women, Writing and Domestic Ritual* (U Massachusetts P, 1992). Recently, she's grown more and more impatient with the distinctions between the "personal" and the "professional" that her academic apprenticeship taught her to ob-serve. Her current project, a book about gender issues in Laura Ingalls Wilder's Little House series, has brought her back to a favorite writer and a central passion of her childhood. In this project, personal/pro-fessional distinctions are rapidly dissolving, and—as her essay shows—Romines is groping for language that can capture that discon-certing, delicious process of dissolution.

SUSAN J. ROSOWSKI is Adele Hall Professor of English at the Uni-versity of Nebraska-Lincoln. She is a general editor (with James Woodress) of the Cather Scholarly Edition and Editor-in-Chief of *Cather Studies*, both University of Nebraska Press. Her books include *Women and Western American Literature* (coedited with Helen Stauffer; Whitston, 1982), *The Voyage Perilous: Willa Cather's Romanticism* (U of Nebr P, 1986), *Approaches to Teaching Cather's My Ántonia* (ed, MLA, 1989), and *O Pio-neers!* (textual editor with Charles Mignon, U of Nebr P, 1992). In addition, she has published over fifty essays, most on Cather and other women writers. She has served as President of the Western Literature Association and as director of international seminars on Willa Cather, and she is the recipient of the Annis Chaikin Sorensen Award for Dis-tinguished Teaching in the Humanities (1986) and the Great Teacher Award (1981).

Her husband, James Rosowski, is a professor of Botany at the Uni-versity of Nebraska-Lincoln. They have two children, Scott and David, and are for a good part of each summer on the western slopes of the Rockies, where they assemble with extended families.

JO C. SEARLES: Life is good. Childhood was idyllic; marriage and four children, true fulfillment. Lucking into academe for three decades brought the excitement of a new world with its new scholarly language, one I happily adopted and shared with students at Penn State Univer-sity, colleagues around the U. S., and friends in Brazil, Portugal, Greece, and Malaysia.

Yet I never did become reconciled to shrinking either the outside world into a traditional curriculum or my interests into a single academic specialty. Women's writing and women's spirituality have gifted me not only with ways to swirl fresh air into the classroom, but also with the impetus to sing out my own thoughts in my own voice. And now, "moving on" is bringing time, wonderful time, to meditate and write more, give workshops and performances, work with women's ritual, commune with the moon and sun, and play with my calico cat. I'm still working, still learning—and loving every minute.

GRACE STEWART, Ph.D., began her business career in Manhattan as a secretary, progressed in two years to a network TV manager in an advertising agency, increased her responsibility to managing a family, and then began another career in education after earning three degrees at Wayne State University in Detroit. She has written some poetry, several articles, a biographical essay in *Historic Women of Michigan*, and a critical work, *A New Mythos: The Novel of the Artist as Heroine*. She currently directs the Focus on Women Program at Henry Ford Community College and teaches English for the love of it.

INDEX TO AUTHORS, CHARACTERS, SUBJECTS

Bell, Clive, 276
Belmont, Helena, 230
Bergson, Alexandra, 33
Bernikow, Louise, 75
Berton, Laura Bertrice, 138–39
bible stories, 56
Bierce, Ambrose, 233
bildungsroman (female), 33, 35
Billman, Carol, 46
biography, 13, 191, 209–24, 228
birth control, 163–67
Black Stallion series, 29
Blake, William, 72–73
Blanchet, Murial Wylie (Capi), 134–37, 139
Bly, Robert, 70–71
Bohemianism, 14, 15
Bovary, Madame, 32
Bradstreet, Anne, 91
Brandywine (studio/farm), 275, 277, 278
Brant, Beth, 169, 174–76
Braun, Lillian Jackson, 50
British literature, 30–31, 50, 52
Brodsky, Joseph, 198
Brooks, Gwendolyn, 165–67, 169, 179
Brooks, Van Wyck, 275
Brown, Rita Mae, 112
Burden, Jim, 33
Calhoun, Daniel, xvii
Campbell, Alexander, 272
captivity narratives, xxi, 88–91
Cassie, 170–73
Castillejo, Irene de, 59
Castro, Mrs., 176–77
Cather, Willa, 5–6, 11–18, 32–35, 184
Cézanne, Paul, 276, 277
Chaucer, Geoffrey, 31, 291
chauvinism. *See* sexism.
Chessler, Phyllis, 49
child care, 215
childbirth, 11–12, 14, 72
childhood, 72, 82, 86–87, 111–12,

125, 127, 137, 142–44, 173–74, 198–99, 209–10, 247, 250–52, 263–64
childhood in literature, 19–28
childhood reading, 11, 19–28, 29, 41–46, 143, 210
children's literature, 19–28
Chodorow, Nancy, 122
Chomsky, Noam, 50
Chopin, Kate, xxiii, 33, 225–37
Christ, Carol, 78
Christie, Agatha, xxi, 47, 48
Ciardi, John, 285
Cisneros, Sandra, 188, 191, 192
civil rights movement, 149, 255
classics, 47
Clinton, William Jefferson, 149
Cobbold, Richard, 270
Cole, Peggy, 41, 44
Colette, 75
collaboration, 25–27
college life, 29–30, 64–65, 261–69, 283. *See also* graduate school.
coming out, xxi–xxii, 99–110
community, 61
composition, 30
conformity, 12, 15, 199, 225, 226, 227–28
Conrad, Joseph, 294–95
consciousness-raising groups, 35, 55, 65
Contratto, Susan, 122
Copeland, Aaron, 275
Copper, Baba, 84
Cousins, Norman, 285
Crane, C. A., 280
Crane, Hart, xxiv, 270–82
creativity, 33, 94
crones, 83–84
Cross, Amanda. *See* Heilbrun, Carolyn.
Crow Dog, Mary, 203
Dalgliesh, Adam, 50
Daly, Mary, 76
Dante, 144

Hypatia, 265
icons, 21–23, 79, 82–83
Iglauer, Edith, 128
Imgarden, Roman, 50
immigration, 141–52, 195, 273
individuation, 65, 113–14, 261–69
infanticide, 170–72
Ingalls, Laura. *See* Wilder, Laura Ingalls.
Ingalls, "Ma," 21–22
Ingalls, "Pa," 22
Irigaray, Luce, 118, 123
Irons, Glenwood, 52
Iser, Wolfgang, 50
isolation, 127. *See also* privacy.
Italian-Americans, 257
Jackson, Helen Hunt, 188
James, P. D., 49
Jameson, Fredric, 50
Jarrell, Randall, 74
Jehlen, Myra, 226
Johnson, Edgar, 214, 222
Johnson, Samuel, 33, 289
Jong, Erica, 81
jouissance, 118
journal writing, 164–67, 191, 234
journalism, 148–49, 288
Juhasz, Suzanne, 36–37
Jungian theory, 59, 66
Jury, Richard, 50
Keats, John, 33
Keillor, Garrison, 203
Keisogloff, Peter, 275
Kelley, Edith Summers, xxii, 169
Kenny, Susan, 51
Kimball, Christopher, 70
Kingsley, Charles, 270
Kingston, Maxine Hong, 112, 169, 188, 190, 264, 265
Kokoon Club, 275
Kolodny, Annette, 287
Koolish, Lynda, 37
Korean War, 212
Kristeva, Julia, 15, 117, 118
Kronberg, Thea, 33

Kuhn, Maggie, 84
Lamb, Catherine, xxi
langue maternelle, 118
Lane, Rose Wilder, 25–26
Lario, Sarah, 84
Lattimore, Olivia May, 232
Laukhaff, Richard, 275
Leider, Emily, 230, 231
lesbian literature, 99–100, 104, 106; film, 109
lesbianism, xxixxii, 12–15, 74–75, 99–110, 175–76
Lescaze, William, 275
Lessing, Doris, 32
LeSueur, Meridel, 169
letter writing, 13, 15, 168, 170, 175, 191, 267, 274, 275, 276
Lewis, R. W. B., 227
libraries, 42, 44
Lillard, Charles, 131
Lin, Pau, 172
Lindbergh, Anne Morrow, xxii, 153–62, 285
Lindsay, Vachel, 273
Lingard, Lena, 33
literary canon, 46–47, 138, 184, 270–82
Little House series, 19–28, 186
London, Jack, 185
Lorde, Audre, 102, 106, 107
"lost child" theme, xxii, 11–12, 16, 163–82, 238–49
Loveman, Sam, 275, 280
Lowell, Amy, 105–106, 110
Lubbock, Percy, 295
Lynly, Lord, 52
McAllister, Mick, 69
McCarthy, Mary, 216
McClung, Isabelle, 15
McCracken, Miss, 176–77
Macdonald, Barbara, 84
McGuane, Tom, 185
McIntosh, Peggy, 170
McVey, William, 274
Maglin, Nan Bauer, 122

Magoun, Old Woman, 173
Mancinelli, Diane, 148
Manfred, Frederick, xxii, 64–71,
      147, 150
Manfred, Freya, 67
Manly Heart, 68
Mansfield, Katherine, 5–6
Marchino, Lois, 44
Marcus, Jane, 292
Marple, Miss, 47
marriage, 5, 34, 49, 65–66, 72, 209,
      213–14, 228–29, 239–40, 242
Marryat, Captain Frederick, 185
Marsh, Ngaio, 49
masculine behavior, 64, 266, 268
masculinist criticism, xvii–xviii,
      xxiv, 113, 283–97. See also
      argumentative mode of
      criticism.
matriarchy, 60, 262–63
Medusa, 83
Meir, Golda, 152
Melander, Juhl, 67
Melchers, Gari, 275
memoirs, 191, 229
menopause, 84, 155–58
men's movement, 70–71
menstruation, 68
Menzies, Archibald, 134
Mepham, John, 295
migration, 183–93, 194–205, 229,
      231, 272–73
Miller, Nancy K., 26
Miller, Sue, 119
Millet, Kate, 32, 49
Milton, John, 66, 72–73, 214
Milton, John R., 66
mirror imagery, xxi, 81, 123, 155,
      261
miscarriage, 169, 172
misogyny, 65–66. See also sexism.
Mitford, Jessica, 272
modernism, 285, 286
Momaday, Scott, 69
Monaghan, Patricia, 80

Monroe, Harriet, 277
Moore, Marianne, 275
Morrison, Toni, xxii, 169, 172, 264,
      265, 270, 273
mother/daughter relationships,
      xxii, 11, 16–17, 82, 86–87, 111–
      24, 137, 227, 228–29, 235, 238–
      49, 255, 263–64
motherhood. See family relation-
      ships.
mourning, 11–12, 14. See also grief.
mourning literature, 163–82, 238–
      49
Moyers, Bill, 70
multiculturalism, 272. See also
      diversity.
Munson, Gorham, 276, 279
Murchison, George, 254
mutuality, 33
mysteries, 41–53. See also detective
      stories.
Nanapush, 189, 190–91
Nancy Drew series, xxi, 29, 41–53
Native Americans, 66, 69, 88–90,
      173–76, 189–90, 195–96, 202–
      203, 231–32; writers, 169, 173–
      76, 188
Naylor, Gloria, 105
Nebraska writers,
Nemiroff, Robert, 259
New Criticism, 214, 283–84
Nietzsche, Friedrich, 276
Nisten ha, 174–76
Norris, Kathleen, xxiii, 186, 191,
      194–205
Nye, Russel B., 44
Oates, Joyce Carol, 265
Obermeyer, Martha, 277
O'Brien, Dan, 204
O'Brien, Sharon, 13
O'Dell, Scott, 185
Oedipus, 121
O'Keeffe, Georgia, 275
Olds, Sharon, 16
Oliver, Mary, 273